THE Ultimate
SAT Tutorial

By Erik Klass

Klass
tutoring

The SAT Prep Experts

Version 11.1, July 2010
Self-Study Version

About the author:
Erik Klass, owner and founder of KlassTutoring, grew up in Westchester, CA. He studied Mechanical and Manufacturing Engineering at the University of California, Los Angeles, where he holds a Masters in Engineering. He also has a degree in music from Berklee College of Music in Boston, MA. Over the past 15+ years, he has personally tutored hundreds of students for the SAT. This book is the culmination of his work and experience.

Contributing Writer: Antony Voznesensky
Contributor: Jonathan Lotz, Jonathan Gross
Editors: Jeffrey Willis, Antony Voznesenky, and Tamara Black

Thank yous:
To my coeditor, decision-maker, and idea bouncer-offer, Tamara Black: I couldn't have gotten this off the ground without you. To Antony Voznesensky, who put his heart and soul into helping me make this the best tutorial available. To Linda Mark: thank you for holding down the fort and keeping me in line. To my sister, Amy Klass, the most amazing graphic designer in the world. To Kevin Johnson, a jack of all trades and master of *all of them*. To my unofficial and underpaid advisory board: Doug Tsoi, Dave Long, Chris O'Malley, and Kevin Johnson. To all KlassTutoring tutors who have helped build this company into a very small giant. To my family: now you know where I've been the past year or so. And finally and especially to my mom and dad.

KlassTutoring offers full-service, private SAT tutoring. For more information about KlassTutoring, visit our website: www.KlassTutoring.com.

If you have any questions or comments about this tutorial, please email us at:
UltimateSATTutorial@KlassTutoring.com.

To order additional copies of this book, please visit our e-store at:
www.createspace.com/1000244713

Printed by CreateSpace

Printed in the United States of America

TABLE OF CONTENTS

A NOTE FROM THE AUTHOR

Dear Student:

Congratulations! With *The Ultimate SAT Tutorial* as your guide, you are embarking on a journey that should raise your SAT score dramatically and set you on your way to the college of your dreams. You have the advantage of working with the best SAT tutorial available. I know because I have read just about every other tutorial on the market, and unlike many of the techniques found in other tutorials, the KlassTutoring methods taught in *The Ultimate SAT Tutorial* are easy-to-learn, clearly presented, and proven to work.

When I started tutoring over fifteen years ago, I did not have *The Ultimate SAT Tutorial* and was forced to use materials from many other SAT tutoring companies. Frustrated by the ineffective techniques, I had no choice but to begin the book you have now. After literally thousands of hours tutoring hundreds of students, I and the tutors at KlassTutoring have tested and perfected every technique in this tutorial. I know they work because I have been watching them work for years.

But this tutorial does not work magic. You must be prepared to work hard, complete your homework assignments, and diligently study the methods and examples. I can't predict how high your score will go. That is up to you. What I can guarantee is that this tutorial will provide you with the tools and information you need to succeed on nearly every problem on the SAT. With practice and effort, you should walk into the testing room prepared and confident.

Study with discipline and diligence as you set your pace toward the college of your dreams.

Best of luck!

Erik Klass and KlassTutoring

INTRODUCTION

THE ULTIMATE SAT TUTORIAL

This tutorial provides you with the techniques you need to excel on the SAT. These techniques will be displayed using clear example problems, and you will have opportunities to practice and master the techniques on over 650 practice problems.

(!) You may have noticed that there are no practice tests in this tutorial. At KlassTutoring, we believe that students will benefit from taking *real* SATs, not ones made up by a test-prep company. **In order for this tutorial to be most effective, you should purchase** *The Official SAT Study Guide, 2nd Edition** **by The College Board.** This is the only official source of *real* SAT tests and problems. While most of our competitors decided to create their own tests, we decided against this for two reasons: (1) it is next to impossible to create accurate and appropriate problems that truly reflect the ones you will find on the SAT, and (2) we don't have to—there is an excellent book written by the folks who created the SAT.

So why do you need *The Ultimate SAT Tutorial*? Why not just buy the College Board book? The College Board book is an excellent source of SAT problems and tests but not a great source of SAT *techniques*. That's where we come in—we provide the techniques, and you can practice and perfect them on real SAT tests. *The Ultimate SAT Tutorial* contains references to all 1,700 test questions in the College Board book. You will see these as you complete the lessons.

There are ten tests in the College Board book. **We recommend using the first four tests (Tests 1-4) as a source of *practice problems*.** Practice-problem assignments are at the end of each chapter in the *The Ultimate SAT Tutorial*. You will usually complete these practice problems untimed and sometimes out of order. **The last six tests (Tests 5-10)—let's call them *practice tests*—should be taken *timed*.** These tests will give you the practice and experience you will need before tackling the real test on "game day." More test-taking information can be found on the following pages.

THE ULTIMATE SAT SUPPLEMENT

Our companion book, *The Ultimate SAT Supplement*, contains over 400 pages of clear and complete solutions to every problem in *The Official SAT Study Guide*. Our KlassTutoring techniques can help you solve nearly every problem on the SAT. This book proves it—a must buy if you are looking for the highest score possible. Visit our website for more information.

*SAT is a registered trademark of the College Board, which was not involved in the production of and does not endorse this book.

PROGRAMS AND HOUR SYMBOLS

There are three typical programs that you may follow as you work your way through the tutorial: a 20-hour program, a 30-hour program, and a 40-hour program. The hours are estimates of *actual tutoring time* (including learning techniques, taking quizzes, and completing lesson problems). **The hours do *not* include time for completing homework and taking practice tests.** To determine the program that is right for you, consider: (1) how much time you have before you plan to take the SAT and (2) your desired level of mastery.

40-HOUR PROGRAM

If you are looking for the highest score possible and if time permits, look at every topic in the tutorial, which includes topics marked with the 40-hour symbol (see below). 40-hour topics are sometimes more difficult than the other material found in the tutorial, or they may require considerable time to master, such as memorizing long lists of items. These topics may also test a relatively obscure rule that doesn't show up very often on the SAT (but still *may* show up). Students with high starting scores should definitely consider this program.

30-HOUR PROGRAM

For many students, we recommend the 30-hour program. This program covers well over 90% of the questions you will find on the SAT. This is our most popular program at KlassTutoring. To complete this program, go through the tutorial and **skip all topics marked with the 40-hour symbol**.

20-HOUR PROGRAM

Our shortest standard program should take about 20 hours of lesson time. As you work through the tutorial, **skip all topics marked with the 40-hour and 30-hour symbols (see below)**. Rest assured that in the 20-hour program, you will still cover *most* of the important SAT topics.

(40) Topics or questions marked with the 40-hour symbol should be covered if you are in the 40-hour program.

(30) Topics or questions marked with the 30-hour symbol should be covered if you are in the 30-hour *or* the 40-hour program.

If you need help determining a program, check out the Lesson Plan page of our website (www.KlassTutoring.com/LessonPlan.htm).

SCHEDULES

As you may have noticed in the Table of Contents, *The Ultimate SAT Tutorial* is divided into three main parts: Writing, Critical Reading, and Math. You should *not* work straight through this tutorial. The following schedules should give you an idea of how to plan your work. Students have different strengths and weaknesses and work at different paces, so treat the schedules as general guides. You may choose to spend extra time on more difficult topics or skip entire sections with which you are already comfortable.

The lessons are indicated in the far left column. Each lesson takes an average of two hours. As described before, these hours are estimates of *actual tutoring time* (including learning techniques, taking quizzes, and completing lesson problems). The hours do *not* include time for completing homework and taking practice tests. For most students, completing one to two lessons per week is a realistic pace. Obviously, consider your final test date as you plan your lessons.

LESSON	20-HOUR			30-HOUR			40-HOUR		
	WRITING	CRITICAL READING	MATH	WRITING	CRITICAL READING	MATH	WRITING	CRITICAL READING	MATH
1	Grammar	Vocab.	Basics	Grammar	Vocab. and Word Parts	Basics	Grammar	Vocab. and Word Parts	Basics
2			Arithmetic			Arithmetic			Arithmetic
3									
4		Reading Questions	Algebra			Algebra			Algebra
5					Reading Questions			Reading Questions	
6	IS*	Practice	Geometry						
7	ISE**	Sentence Competion		IS*			IS*		
8	The Essay			ISE**	Reading-Questions Practice		ISE**	Reading-Questions Practice	
9			Functions/ Probability/ Review	IS and ISE Practice		Geometry	IS and ISE Practice		
10	Review	Review							Geometry
11				IP***			IP***		
12				IP Practice	Sentence Competion	Functions	IP Practice	Sentence Competion	
13				The Essay		Probability	The Essay		
14						Practice			Functions
15				Review	Review	Review		Critical Reading Practice	
16							Writing Practice		Probability
17									
18									Math Practice
19									
20							Review	Review	Review

*IS = Improving Sentences **ISE = Identifying Sentence Errors ***IP = Improving Paragraphs

SCHEDULING GUIDELINES FOR EACH SECTION

WRITING

- In the 40-hour program, use some of the grammar quiz and practice problem assignments to review topics that you covered earlier in the program. These assignments are found at the ends of lessons and chapters throughout the tutorial. The 40-hour program is a long one, so you should plan to occasionally go back and review earlier topics.

- **Practice Tests**: If you have time to take three tests during the program, take Test 5 (in the College Board book) at the beginning, Test 6 after you complete the Improving Sentences chapter, and Test 7 at the end. (Recall that you will be using Tests 1-4 as a source of *practice problems*.) If you don't have time to take three tests, take two tests: one at the beginning of the program and one at the end. If you are in the 30 or 40-hour program, you should strive to take at least three tests. **Don't forget to go back and correct past tests as you complete chapters in the tutorial.**

CRITICAL READING

- The vocabulary and word part sections take a while to complete. Don't wait until you have completed them before starting the Reading chapter. Just make sure to complete the vocabulary and word parts material before starting the Sentence Completion chapter (where you will apply your vocabulary and word-part knowledge).

- The 40-hour program offers considerable time to practice Reading passages. Take advantage of this extra time, and cover as many passages as you can.

- **Practice Tests**: Again, assuming you have time for three tests, take Test 5 at the beginning, Test 6 after you complete the Reading Questions chapter, and Test 7 at the end. **Don't forget to go back and correct past tests as you complete chapters in the tutorial.**

MATH

- In the longer programs, particularly the 40-hour one, you might periodically work on practice problems from earlier sections. As mentioned above, don't get rusty with the topics that you worked on early in the program.

- **Practice Tests**: Take Test 5 at the beginning, Test 6 after you complete the Algebra chapter, and Test 7 at the end. **Don't forget to go back and correct past tests as you complete chapters in the tutorial.**

TAKING THE PRACTICE TESTS

Because you will be completing a significant amount of SAT homework as you work your way through the tutorial, it may be desirable to complete only one of the SAT's three parts (Writing, Critical Reading, or Math) at a time rather than completing an entire test. **You should still *always* time yourself, and never take a break in the middle of a section.**

As mentioned before, strive to complete at least two or three practice tests during the program, with the last one taken at the end of the program. **To closely simulate the actual test-taking experience, take this last test in *one sitting* and use the full amount of time available for each section.** This will help you prepare for the actual test day when you will spend over four hours completing the test. You may take a short break every hour or so, but remember, never stop in the middle of a section. If you have time, take any additional practice tests at the end of the program. The more tests you take, the more comfortable you will feel on the actual test day.

Complete the essays on the lined pages provided and show all work in the College Board book. For practice, use the answer sheets provided for each test by the College Board. **Do not look back to the tutorial while taking the practice tests.**

TIMING STRATEGIES

Because the criteria for ordering the questions varies on each test (Writing, Critical Reading, Math), the timing strategies will also vary. For example, when you are completing the Reading questions on the Critical Reading test (questions that are *not* arranged in order of difficulty), it is important to try to get to the end of each section—the last question may be the easiest one on the test. On the other hand, when you are completing the questions on a Math test (questions that *are* arranged in order of difficulty), it is important to spend time on the questions that you can answer correctly, even if that means leaving some of the harder questions blank at the end of the section.

Specific details on timing strategy for each test will be discussed later.

ELIMINATING ANSWER CHOICES AND GUESSING

Eliminating answer choices is a very important part of the SAT, particularly on the Writing and Critical Reading tests. **If you can eliminate TWO answers, you should always guess.** Since you only lose ¼ of a point when you miss a question, even random guessing should increase your score when two answers are eliminated. If you cannot eliminate two answers, leave the question blank.

Some students may not know when to eliminate an answer choice and when to keep it. In general, you should be *very sure* that the answer choice is wrong before eliminating it. But what does *very sure* mean? The best approach is to look at your test and practice problem corrections. If you often eliminate the correct answers, then become more careful and selective in your eliminations. If you generally do *not* eliminate several answer choices for each question and therefore leave a number of questions blank, try to become more aggressive with your eliminations. Find the right balance as you work your way through the tests and practice problems.

FLASH CARDS

There are many opportunities throughout this tutorial to create flash cards. Many of the important and more specific items that should be memorized are indicated with a flash card symbol:

```
FLASH
CARDS
```

There are different ways to create flash cards, but, in general, there should be some form of a question on the front of the card and the answer on the back. Create flash cards for any items that you are worried you may forget before taking the test. And, of course, don't forget to study them frequently.

———

THE ULTIMATE GUARANTEE

At KlassTutoring, we believe in our unique approach to SAT tutoring, and we are committed to your success and satisfaction. If, after completing our standard 30-hour program, your SAT score does not increase by at least 150 points, we will refund you 150% of the purchase price of the tutorial (not including tax, shipping, and handling). To qualify for a refund, please send us *all* of the following items:

☐ The original receipt or proof-of-purchase, clearly showing the purchase date, the purchase price, and the name of the tutorial (*The Ultimate SAT Tutorial*)

☐ Your copy of *The Ultimate SAT Tutorial*, with all of the 30-hour program's lesson problems, homework problems, quizzes, and other assignments clearly completed

☐ Photo copies of your official scores of actual SATs, before and after using the tutorial, or, if you had not taken the SAT before purchasing this tutorial, you may substitute the official scores of an actual PSAT. In case of the latter, the essay score of your final SAT will not be considered. The date of the first SAT (or PSAT) must be before the date of the tutorial purchase.

☐ Your mailing address (where we will send the refund)

Claims for refunds must be received within 90 days of the purchase date of the tutorial, as printed on the original receipt. Incomplete claims will not be processed. Send materials to:

The Ultimate Guarantee

c/o KlassTutoring

3125 Curts Ave., Suite 1000

Los Angeles, CA 90034

Please allow 6-8 weeks to receive your refund in the mail. Limit one refund per customer.

QUESTIONS? COMMENTS? WANT YOUR NAME ON OUR NEXT COVER?

If you have any questions or comments, please email us at:

UltimateSATTutorial@KlassTutoring.com. We appreciate all testimonials. If you would not mind having your testimonial printed on our next cover, please include in your email: "I give KlassTutoring permission to use this testimonial and my name on the cover of *The Ulitimate SAT Tutorial* (or its equivalent) and any related promotional materials."

COLLEGE COUNSELING

This tutorial is *not* intended to replace your college counselor. It has only one goal: to help you achieve the highest score possible on the SAT. Many students have questions such as:

- How do I sign up for the SAT?
- What do my SAT scores mean?
- To what colleges should I apply?
- Do I even have to take the SAT?
- What about the ACT?

There are a number of places where you can find helpful information:

- The College Board website (www.collegeboard.com) can answer a number of your questions about signing up for the test and what your scores mean.
- Your school's college guidance counselor should be able to help you make difficult decisions regarding school selections and what tests you need to take.
- Our website (www.klasstutoring.com) can assist you in determining likely score increases. There is also a handy guide that shows the average SAT scores for some selected colleges. See the Frequently-Asked-Questions (FAQ) section.
- Many students seek the advice of private college counselors in their areas.
- You can contact colleges directly to discuss their expectations and requirements, or just review their websites—usually a great source of information.

- Buy or check out a book that specializes in college selection and enrollment.

———————

THE FIRST ASSIGNMENT

OK—it's time to get started. If you are working with a tutor, practice tests will be assigned. If you are working on your own, now is a good time to take your first practice test. This will give you an idea of your starting score and will perhaps allow you to create a sensible program that focuses on your weaknesses. As you make your way through the tutorial and cover relevant topics, you will frequently go back and correct this practice test.

☐   Take Test 5 in the College Board book. Review Taking Practice Tests in this Introduction.

PART 1

WRITING

I WRITING INTRODUCTION

The Writing Tutorial is divided into seven chapters:

    I.   Introduction

    II.   Grammar

    III. Improving Sentences

    IV. Identifying Sentence Errors

    V.   Improving Paragraphs

    VI. The Essay

    VII. Writing Answers

TYPES OF QUESTIONS

There are three types of multiple choice writing questions on the SAT:

    1. Improving Sentences questions

    2. Identifying Sentence Errors questions

    3. Improving Paragraphs questions

Since you will be taking practice SATs before these questions are discussed in the tutorial, read the test instructions carefully to understand how to answer these questions. The Writing portion of the SAT also includes an essay question.

TEST LAYOUT

There is one essay question requiring you to write about a given topic in 25 minutes. There are a total of 25 Improving Sentences questions (a little over 50% of the total multiple choice questions), 18 Identifying Sentence Errors questions (about 37% of the questions), and six Paragraph Improvement questions (only about 12% of the questions). The total test time is 60 minutes. The tests may have some variations, but they generally adhere to the following layout:

- 25-minute essay
- 25-minute section (35 questions)
  - 11 Improving Sentences questions
  - 18 Identifying Sentence Errors questions
  - 6 Improving Paragraphs questions (*not* arranged in order of difficulty)
- 10-minute section (14 questions)
  - 14 Improving Sentences questions

TIMING STRATEGY

For our purposes, assume that the questions on the Writing test are generally *not* arranged in order of difficulty. Even though the order of the questions may be based to some extent on difficulty, it is not as significant as on the Math test or the Sentence Completion sections of the Critical Reading test. In addition, the techniques in this tutorial will oftentimes make the last several questions seem as easy as the first several questions. Thus, it is important to try to get to every problem on the Writing test. If you find that you are not able to complete the sections, then obviously you must increase your speed. The best way to do this is to learn the techniques in this tutorial and practice diligently.

TECHNIQUE IDENTIFICATION

Often, there are clues that will help you figure out what technique is being tested by a specific question. Throughout the tutorial, look for the magnifying glass for information about identifying techniques:

HAPPY FACE TOPICS

Topics that are indicated with the symbol below may be a review for many students. You may choose to move quickly through this material or (for advanced students) skip it altogether and go straight to lesson problems. If you struggle on any lesson problems, go back and review the relevant material.

II
GRAMMAR

The key to the multiple choice sections of the Writing test, which include the *Improving Sentences,* *Identifying Sentence Errors,* and *Improving Paragraphs* questions, is to learn the basic rules of grammar. There is a relatively small number of grammar topics that the College Board actually tests, at least compared to the huge number of grammar topics in the English language, and we will obviously cover only the ones you need to worry about. These grammar topics will also help you in your writing, so try to keep them in mind while you are practicing the essays.

1. VERB TENSE

The tense of a verb describes *when* a verb "happens." If events occur at the same time, the verb tenses must be the same. If events occur at different times, the verb tenses should reflect the order of these events.

VERB-TENSE TERMINOLOGY ☺*

Verb – The part of speech that expresses existence, action, or occurrence in a sentence.

TENSE

While there are many different tenses, it is helpful to be familiar with the five most important verb tenses found on the SAT. Since you will not be tested on their official names (such as *past participle*), we will refer to them by the *times* that they occur, as shown on the time-line below:

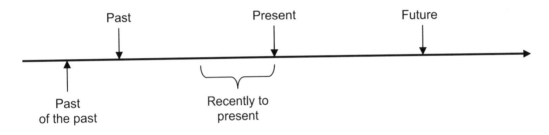

First, let's look at the easy ones. You are probably comfortable with these already. ☺

Present: Today, I *study* with my tutor for the SAT.

Past: Yesterday, I *studied* for several hours for the SAT.

Future: Tomorrow, I *will study* several more hours for the SAT.

Now, for the harder ones—from now on, we'll call these the *other verb tenses*:

Past of the past: This tense always uses the word **had**. For example:

> Before Aimee took the SAT last year, she *had studied* for several months. (The studying took place *before* Aimee took the SAT; hence, the *past of the past*).

*See Happy Face Topics in Writing Introduction

Recently to present: This tense uses the word **has** for *he*, *she*, *it*, or any *singular* thing performing the action and **have** for *I*, *we*, *they*, *you*, or any *plural* thing performing the action.

I *have studied* for the SAT for what seems like an eternity. (This has been going on for a while, and it sounds like it still is.)

TO SUMMARIZE

Past-of-the-past tense → use the word **had**
Recently-to-present tense → use the word **has** or **have**

TO BE ☺

The *to be* verb is an irregular verb. Most of its forms don't even resemble the word itself. Luckily, your ear will probably pick up on its correct and incorrect uses. You are probably already comfortable with the following:

Yesterday, I *was* sick.
Today, I *am* feeling great.
They *were* the best in the class last year, but now they *are* struggling.
She has *been* here for hours.

-ING WORDS

(!) Words in the -*ing* form can be used to express continuous action. **However, a word in the -*ing* form—on its own—does not function as a verb.** Your ear probably knows this already. For example:

Incorrect: John *running* to the store.

To correctly use an -*ing* word as part of a verb phrase, you must use a *to be* verb. The following are some examples:

Past: Yesterday, we *were emptying* out the cupboard.
Present: Today, John *is running* to the store while we finish the work.
Recently-to-present: John *has been working* as a handyman this summer.
Past-of-the-past: John *had been working* two jobs before he had enough money to buy the bike.

IRREGULAR VERBS

Irregular verbs behave the same way as ordinary verbs for *future* and all *-ing* forms, but for the *other tenses*, the form of the verb may change in unpredictable ways. For example:

present: Today, I *lie* on my bed.

past: Last night, I *lay* on my bed.

past of the past: Before I woke up this morning, I had *lain* on my bed.

recently to present: I have *lain* on my bed all morning.

As you can see, it can get a little tricky. The good news is that the College Board does not put too much emphasis on these irregular verbs, but they *do* occasionally show up.

The list of irregular verbs on the following pages includes the *past tenses* and *other tenses* for a number of irregular verbs. Recall that the *other tenses* are the tenses you would use *has, have, or had* with, such as *past of the past*. The table is divided into four sections:

1. A-U

Many verbs follow the (*a-u*) pattern. For example:

I *ran* yesterday.

I had *run* for weeks before the track meet.

2. NO CHANGE

Most irregular verbs have no change between the past tense and the other tenses (just like regular verbs), but the past tense may be tricky. For example:

Before the girls *brought* in the groceries, they had *brought* in their backpacks.

3. ADD -EN TO PAST TENSE FOR THE OTHER TENSES

Several verbs are formed this way. For example:

Yesterday, he *spoke* with no reservations while in custody.

He had *spoken* for some time before he found out that he was being taped.

4. OTHER

Many of the verbs, unfortunately, do not follow a particular pattern, or they are a combination of some of the patterns above. For example:

I *wrote* a letter to my aunt last week, but she thought I *had written* it months ago.

LIST OF IRREGULAR VERBS

The best approach to learning the irregular verb tenses is to make flash cards for the verbs you are not familiar with and study a few at a time. Quizzes will be assigned if you are in the 40-hour program. If you are in a different program, there may not be enough time for quiz assignments, but you are still encouraged to study the irregular verbs on your own.

Present	Past	Other tenses (add *have*, *has*, or *had*)
1. A-U		
begin	began	begun
drink	drank	drunk
ring	rang	rung
run	ran	run
sing	sang	sung
sink	sank	sunk
spring	sprang	sprung
swim	swam	swum
2. NO CHANGE BETWEEN PAST AND OTHER TENSES		
bring	brought	brought
burn	burnt or burned	burnt or burned
burst	burst	burst
catch	caught	caught
dream	dreamt or dreamed	dreamt or dreamed
drown	drowned	drowned
dwell	dwelt or dwelled	dwelt or dwelled
fight	fought	fought
flee	fled	fled
fling	flung	flung
hang (a thing)	hung	hung
hang (a person)	hanged	hanged
lay	laid	laid
lead	led	led
lend	lent	lent
lie (to tell an untruth)	lied	lied
put	put	put
set	set	set
shine (intransitive)	shone	shone
shut	shut	shut
sit	sat	sat
spit	spit or spat	spit or spat
sting	stung	stung
swing	swung	swung

Present	Past	Other tenses (add *have, has,* or *had*)

3. ADD -EN TO THE PAST TENSE FOR OTHER TENSES

beat	beat	beaten
bite	bit	bitten
break	broke	broken
choose	chose	chosen
freeze	froze	frozen
speak	spoke	spoken

4. OTHER

awake	awoke or awaked	awoke, awaked, or awoken
bear	bore	borne
bid (to command)	bade	bidden
come	came	come
dive	dived or dove	dived
get	got	got or gotten
lie (to recline)	lay	lain
rise	rose	risen
shrink	shrank or shrunk	shrunk or shrunken
slay	slew	slain
strive	strove or strived	striven or strived
swear	swore	sworn
tear	tore	torn
tread	trod	trod or trodden
wake	woke or waked	woken or waked
wear	wore	worn
write	wrote	written

Look carefully at all verbs on the Writing test. If a sentence has **two or more verbs**, think about the times that these verbs "occur." Make sure the tenses agree with these times.

LESSON PROBLEMS

Correct the underlined verb in each sentence (if necessary). The answers to all lesson and homework problems for the Writing tutorial start on page 185. You may want to mark this page for future reference.

1. Built at the turn of the century, the mansion <u>displaying</u> some of the oldest styles of architecture seen in the region today.

2. The scientists were sure they had uncovered an ancient human skeleton, but they <u>had not been sure</u> of its origin.

_____

3. Since last night, Paul <u>worked</u> on his history paper, and he will probably still be working on it until tonight.

_____

4. Before Patrick won the diving medal, he <u>has dove</u> since he was old enough to swim.

_____

5. If you <u>got</u> here on time, you would have known it was a surprise party.

_____

(HW)

1. The majestic sun <u>shined</u> through the clouds like I had never seen before.

_____

2. Before I finish my research paper, I <u>have read</u> three books on the subject.

_____

3. The boys play outside every day without coats on, so it's not surprising that they <u>have catched</u> practically every illness known to man.

_____

4. Before the rocket was launched, Ken <u>written</u> dozens of articles about its expected path.

_____

The following quizzes are found in the Grammar Quizzes section at the end of this chapter. The quizzes will be assigned by your tutor. If you are working on your own, take the quizzes after you have studied the irregular verb lists. If you struggle on the quizzes, go back and review the material.

(40) □ Irregular Verb Tense Quiz 1 (*a-u* and no change)

(40) □ Irregular Verb Tense Quiz 2 (*-en* and other)

2. SUBJECT-VERB AGREEMENT

Subject-verb agreement is one of the most commonly tested (and most commonly missed) topics on the SAT. Subjects must always agree with their respective verbs in number. In other words, if the subject is singular then the verb must be singular, and if the subject is plural then the verb must be plural.

There are two challenges to this topic. The first one is identifying the subject and its verb in the sentence. The second one is deciding whether the subject is singular or plural.

SUBJECT-VERB-AGREEMENT TERMINOLOGY ☺

Subject – consists of a noun, noun phrase, or noun substitute which often refers to the one performing the action or being in the state expressed by the rest of the sentence.

Preposition – A word that locates things in *time, place,* or *movement.* ⎫ See examples below.
Prepositional Phrase – A preposition followed by a noun or pronoun. ⎭

Modifying Phrase – We'll get more into modifying phrases later. For now, you should know that a modifying phrase is part of a sentence that can be removed without greatly altering the grammatical correctness of the sentence. A modifying phrase is separated from the rest of the sentence with commas. This makes it easy to spot.

PREPOSITIONS

Since removing *prepositional phrases* will help you find subjects and verbs, first let's look at a lesson on prepositions. If a word sounds correct in *either one* (not necessarily both) of the following sentences, the word is probably a preposition. Memorize these sentences.

(!) **The professor walked _____ the desk.**
The professor talked _____ the class.

Here are some examples of prepositions. Try them out in one or both of the sentences above.

about	beneath	in front of	throughout
across	beside	into	to
after	between	like	toward
against	by	next to	under
around	concerning	**of***	until
at	during	off	upon
before	except	on	without
before	for	past	
behind	in	through	

*The word "of" is probably the most common preposition.

IDENTIFYING THE SUBJECT AND THE VERB

BARE-BONES SENTENCES

! **Since the subject of a sentence will never show up in a prepositional or modifying phrase, get rid of these phrases when looking for the subject.** After these phrases are removed, you will be left with the **bare-bones sentence**. For example:

> The number of calories recommended for the average person by the Food and Drug Administration, according to a report last year, depend on the age and size of the individual.

First, remove the modifying phrase: "according to a report last year." Notice the commas on either side of the phrase. Next, remove the prepositional phrases. You should be left with the following sentence. The subject (and verb) become much easier to see.

> The number ~~of calories~~ recommended ~~for the average person~~ ~~by the Food and Drug~~ ~~Administration, according to a report last year,~~ depend ~~on the age and size of the individual.~~

> The number recommended depend.

The subject is *number* and the verb is *depend*. Since *number* is singular and *depend* is plural, the subject and verb do not agree (more on this on the next page). The correct sentence should read:

> The *number* of calories recommended for the average person by the Food and Drug Administration, according to a report last year, *depends* on the age and size of the individual.

VERBS BEFORE SUBJECTS

Sometimes, the verb comes *before* the subject. When you spot a verb, ask yourself what or who is *performing* the verb, and be prepared to look beyond the verb in the sentence. Watch out for the word "there," especially at the beginning of a sentence:

> There remain questions about the cause of the fire.

Remain is the verb and *questions* is the subject.

> Never before has Bill been so successful.

Has is the verb and *Bill* is the subject.

IDENTIFYING THE NUMBER OF THE VERB ☺

Verbs behave in strange ways, as we've already seen in the previous section. In general, the rules that define the number of a verb are the opposite of those for nouns. When a verb is singular, it generally has an *s* at the end:

He eats by himself.

When a verb is plural, it generally does not have an *s* at the end.

They eat together.

If you're ever in doubt, just try out the verb in question with *he, she,* or *they*, and trust your ear.

IDENTIFYING THE NUMBER OF THE SUBJECT

A NOSE SUBJECTS

FLASH CARDS

(!) **The most commonly missed subjects can be remembered using the acronym:** *A NOSE.*
These are all *singular* in number:

A   anybody, anyone

N   nobody, no one, neither, none

O   one

S   somebody, someone

E   everybody, everyone, either, each, every

Again, these subjects are all *singular*.

COLLECTIVE NOUNS

Collective nouns are almost always *singular* on the SAT, even though they may seem plural.

If you can add an *s* to a collective noun to make it plural (for example: *group → groups*), then you know that without the *s*, it is singular:

number	team
amount	any company or corporation
audience	any city, state, or country
group	

SUBJECTS WITH "AND" OR "OR/NOR"

Linking two subjects with *and* will usually make the linked subject *plural*. Linking two subjects with *or* or *nor* will make the linked subject *singular* if the word closest to the verb (usually the last word) is singular and *plural* if the word closest to the verb is plural. Make sure you are comfortable with these rules.

> Elizabeth *and* Jasmine are going to drink coffee. (*plural*)
> Elizabeth or Jasmine is going to pay for the coffee. (*singular*)
> Andy *or* the girls are going to the museum. (*plural*)
> There is one can of soup *or* bagels in the pantry. (*singular*)

There is an exception to the *and* rule. If the subjects are linked by *and* but are really expressing one thing, then the linked subject is *singular*:

> *Rock and Roll* is still popular today.
> The *long and short of it* is I lost my job.

———

The following steps outline the method for working with subject-verb agreement errors:

1. Identify the subject and its verb. Find the barebones sentence, if necessary.
2. Determine the number of the subject (singular or plural).
3. Make sure the number of the verb matches the number of the subject.

There are several items to look for that will help you identify these errors:
1. Long sentences where the subject is separated from its verb by prepositional phrases or other modifying phrases
2. Subjects that *follow* their verbs; look for the word "there."
3. ANOSE subjects
4. Collective nouns
5. Linked subjects (using "and" or "or")

LESSON PROBLEMS

Underline and correct the verb error in each sentence (if necessary):

1. Each member of the group of scholars have taken a number of courses at the university.

    _____

2. Ryan or Mike, no matter what you may have heard, are going to be at the dance.

    _____

3. The team of representatives, many from as far away as China and India, are assembled in the banquet room.

    _____

4. One of the students is going to the city finals for his or her success in the spelling bee.

    _____

5. I counted numerous boats at the docks, but there was not as many boats as the year before.

    _____

(HW)

1. Either football or basketball are my favorite sport.

    _____

2. Everyone on the team, even the goalies, are in great shape.

    _____

3. The audience, mostly made up of rich businessmen and politicians, pay top-dollar for events like this.

    _____

4. Every nut, bolt, and tool were stolen from the tool shed.

    _____

5. The feeling I got after listening to the lecture about the city's traffic jams were that nothing is going to be done about them anytime soon.

   _____

3. PRONOUN CASE

PRONOUN TERMINOLOGY ☺

Pronoun – A word that generally stands for or refers to a noun or nouns whose identity is made clear earlier in the text.

CASES OF PRONOUNS

The two general *cases* of pronouns are *subject* pronouns and *object* pronouns. Subject pronouns perform the actions in the sentence. Object pronouns are the recipients of the actions. **If you are ever unsure of the case of a pronoun, plug the pronoun into a simple *performer-recipient* sentence and trust your ear**, for example: *He* threw the ball to *them*. *He* is performing the action and *them* is receiving the action. Thus, *he* is a subject pronoun and *them* is an object pronoun.

Subject pronouns		Object pronouns
I	→	*me*
he	→	*him*
she	→	*her*
they	→	*them*
we	→	*us*
it	→	*it*
who	→	*whom*
you	→	*you*

FLASH CARDS

The following rules will help you choose the correct case for a pronoun.

PRONOUNS AND PREPOSITIONS

(!) **Use *object* pronouns when the pronoun shows up in a phrase with a preposition.** For examples:

...between *you* and *me*...

...to Sherry and *her*...

...among *us* students...

...from *him* and *her*...

IF PRONOUN EQUALS SUBJECT, USE SUBJECT CASE

Usually, use *subject* pronouns if the pronoun identifies, defines, or means the same as the subject of the sentence. For example:

> The person in the photo is *I*. (*I* has the same meaning as the subject *the person*)
> The instructors in the course were *he* and Donald.

PLUG IN *I*, *ME*, *WE*, OR *US*

A good way to check many pronoun case questions is to replace the pronoun(s) in the sentence with *I*, *me*, *we*, or *us* and trust your ear. For example:

> Elvis asked that *him and her* practice handshakes.

Replace *him and her*, which are object pronouns, with the object pronoun *us*:

> Elvis asked that *us* practice handshakes.

This sentence clearly sounds incorrect. The object case is incorrect, so the original pronouns should be changed to *subject* pronouns. The correct sentence should read:

> Elvis asked that *he and she* practice handshakes.

COMPARISONS

When you are comparing something to a pronoun, it is difficult to hear what case is correct for the pronoun. For example:

> Kyle is more helpful than *him*.

To decide whether this case is correct, add the logical *to be* verb after the pronoun and trust your ear.

> Kyle is more helpful than *him is*.

This sentence clearly sounds incorrect. You are implying the *is*, so **the correct pronoun case for comparisons is the *subject* case.** The correct sentence should read:

Kyle is more helpful than *he (is)*.

Another way to remember this rule is to always *compare apples to apples*. The comparison is between "Kyle" and "he." Since "Kyle" is the subject of the sentence, it makes sense for "he" to be in the subject case.

Any time a pronoun is part of a comparison, watch out for a pronoun error.

A PRONOUN LINKED WITH A NOUN

When a pronoun is side-by-side with a noun (*we* seniors, *us* students), **eliminate the noun to determine which type of pronoun to use.** For example:

(*We, Us*) seniors decided to take the day off.

We is the correct pronoun since *us* is clearly incorrect when *seniors* is removed.

The award was presented to (*we, us*) students.

Us is the correct pronoun since *we* is clearly incorrect when *students* is removed.

This approach can also help you when a pronoun is part of a linked subject or object. For example:

Toby and me decided to take the day off.

Remove the noun (*Toby*) and you will "hear" the error in the sentence.

Me decided to take the day off.

The pronoun should be in the subject case. The correct sentence reads:

Toby and *I* decided to take the day off.

WHO VERSUS WHOM

Recall that *who* is the subject pronoun and *whom* is the object pronoun. For example:

My mom, *who* has the day off, is going to the store.

With *whom* are you speaking?

I am speaking to the telephone repair man, about *whom* I'm sure you've heard a lot.

THAT VERSUS WHICH

While *who* or *whom* refers to people, as described above, *that* and *which* are pronouns that refer to groups or things. There is often confusion about whether to use *that* or *which*. There are distinct differences between the two.

***That* is used as a pronoun to introduce essential information that you absolutely need to understand what particular thing is being referred to.** For example:

Heather likes bananas *that* are still green.

Out of all the types of bananas in the world, Heather likes the particular ones that are still green. Since the information *are still green* is essential to understand what kind of bananas Heather likes, use *that*. In addition, since this information could not be removed without greatly altering the sentence, do not use a comma.

***Which* is used as a pronoun to introduce nonessential, added information, which may be helpful but is not totally necessary to understand what particular thing is being referred to.** For example:

Heather likes bananas, which are high in potassium.

The fact that bananas are high in potassium is added information that isn't essential to understand what kind of bananas Heather likes (since all bananas are high in potassium). ***Which* is usually preceded by a comma because it introduces information that could be removed without drastically changing the desired meaning of the sentence.**

Pronoun errors are common on the SAT. Make sure to look carefully at every pronoun.

LESSON PROBLEMS

Correct the pronoun error in each sentence (if necessary):

1. I will play the song for Dorothy and <u>he</u>.

   _____

2. After the fire, Margaret and <u>her</u> decided it was time to move to the city.

   _____

3. Colby is better than <u>him</u> in math and science subjects.

   _____

4. The speaker, about <u>who</u> we had been talking for weeks, spoke with grace and eloquence.

   _____

5. The Nile River, <u>that</u> spans 3473 miles, is the longest river in the world.

   _____

(HW)

1. <u>We</u> seniors are proud to be graduates of such a fine school.

   _____

2. The best people for the job were Elizabeth and <u>him</u>.

   _____

3. Waiting for over an hour, we wondered what had happened to <u>she</u> and Daniel.

   _____

4. You are obviously happier than <u>me</u> about the results of the election.

   _____

5. The card <u>that</u> you picked is not the correct one.

   _____

4. PRONOUN AGREEMENT

NUMBER AGREEMENT

In a sentence, the pronoun must agree in number with the noun or nouns it is replacing.

> Everyone who plays an instrument knows *they* must practice for hours everyday to master the craft.

This sentence sounds fine, but it is incorrect. The pronoun *they* is referring to the noun *everyone*, the subject of the sentence, which we know is singular. Therefore, *they* should be replaced with a singular pronoun.

> Everyone who plays an instrument knows *he or she* must practice for hours everyday to master the craft.

PRONOUN AGREEMENT

If pronouns are referring to the same thing in a sentence, make sure they are the same pronoun type. Watch out for illogical changes to the pronouns as a sentence develops.

> When *one* prepares for a concert, *you* should visualize a standing ovation at the end.

Both pronouns should be *one* or *you*, such as:

> When *one* prepares for a concert, *one* should visualize a standing ovation at the end.

———

The following steps will help you work with pronoun-agreement errors:
1. Identify the pronoun in the sentence.
2. Identify the noun that the pronoun is referring to. Usually the noun will precede the pronoun in the sentence.
3. Make sure the pronoun and the noun agree in number.

Once again, look carefully at all pronouns, especially when they are referring to ANOSE subjects and collective nouns.

LESSON PROBLEMS

Correct the underlined pronoun error in each sentence (if necessary):

1. The after school programs have given the students something to do with <u>his or her</u> free time.

   _____

2. Nobody I know who has gone to the water park thinks <u>they</u> will go again.

   _____

3. The company was given financial support until <u>it</u> pulled out of debt.

   _____

4. After watching the evening news, I think <u>they are</u> more concerned with ratings than content.

   _____

5. Anyone starting ninth grade knows that <u>they were</u> thrown from the frying pan into the fire.

   _____

(HW)

1. The team wins so many games because <u>it is</u> more concerned about winning than individual achievement.

   _____

2. When you stand near the conductor, <u>one</u> must be careful not to get hit by his baton.

   _____

3. Each member of the baseball team thought it was <u>their</u> turn to bat.

   _____

4. Parents change jobs frequently just as young people often make changes to <u>his or her</u> career choices while in school.

   _____

5. The curator of the museum indicated that most of <u>their</u> paintings had been donated.

   _____

5. AMBIGUOUS PRONOUNS

Pronouns must clearly refer to the noun or nouns they replace. For example:

> The early marching music of New Orleans was probably the earliest form of jazz, and *they* used musical elements from both the African and European continents.

In the sentence, *they* is an ambiguous pronoun because there are no groups mentioned in the sentence to which *they* logically refers. The sentence could be corrected by either adding a group of people to the first part of the sentence or replacing *they* appropriately:

> The *musicians* of early marching music in New Orleans were probably playing the earliest form of jazz, and *they* used musical elements from both the African and European continents.
> Or:
> The early marching music of New Orleans was probably the earliest form of jazz, and *these musicians* used musical elements from both the African and European continents.

Another ambiguous pronoun problem occurs when it is unclear what noun is being referred to in the sentence. For example:

> Thomas told Jason that *he* was responsible for studying the origins of jazz for their report on American music.

It may sound strange, but for the sentence to be totally clear and unambiguous, it should read:

> Thomas told Jason that *Jason* (or *Thomas*) was responsible for studying the origins of jazz for the report on American music.

THEY

The pronoun *they* is commonly used when some form of *experts* is intended; this is also ambiguous:

> *They* say that jazz was originally a combination of African and European musical elements.

The correct sentence should read:

Musical historians say that jazz was originally a combination of African and European musical elements.

IT

The pronoun *it* is also used frequently in ambiguous ways. For example:

The musicians combined African musical traditions with the use of classical European instruments, and *it* was a sound unlike any that had been heard before.

To what exactly is *it* referring? The pronoun *it* is ambiguous, and the sentence could be corrected to read:

The musicians combined African musical traditions with the use of classical European instruments, and *the sound* was unlike any that had been heard before.

If the pronoun *it* clearly refers to the singular subject of the sentence or another singular noun in the sentence, its use is probably correct. The following examples are correct:

The *music* of early New Orleans had strong rhythmic characteristics because *it* was played in parades, marches, and other processions.

Many contemporary musicians study *jazz* because *it* is the foundation of American music.

––––––––––

 Look for the pronouns "they" and "it." These pronouns are often ambiguous.

LESSON PROBLEMS

Underline the ambiguous pronouns (if any) and correct the sentences on the lines provided (if necessary):

1. After recent experiments with sick volunteers, they determined that the drug had no effect on the virus.

   _____

2. There are over one thousand cable channels available on some viewers' televisions, and it is the main reason why the three networks' ratings have decreased in recent years.

   _____

3. The president of the company told the employee that he would have to fly to Orlando for the conference.

   _____

(HW)

1. The Polish accordion tradition known as *polka* has a recognizable rhythmic pattern because of their consistent use of a triplet meter.

   _____

2. Jake thought he would beat Matt because he had spent the summer practicing in hot and humid Miami.

   _____

3. Rob told Brian that his mom would throw a fit when she sees the mess in the kitchen.

   _____

6. PARALLELISM

BASIC PARALLELISM

When you are expressing two or more series of ideas or actions, they should be *parallel* in form. In other words, they should be constructed in the same way. For example:

> An excellent employee is open to new ideas, responsive to company needs, and he complies with the company rules of business.

Notice the three phrases that describe the employee:
1. ...open to new ideas... (*adjective-preposition-object*)
2. ...responsive to company needs... (*adjective-preposition-object*)
3. ...he complies with the company rules of business. (*pronoun-verb-preposition-object*)

The first two phrases are similar. In each, an *adjective* ("open" and "responsive") is followed by a *preposition* ("to" in both cases) is followed by an *object* ("new ideas" and "company needs"). In the third phrase, the structure is different. A *pronoun* is followed by a *verb* is followed by a *preposition* is followed by an *object* ("the company rules of business"). The sentence is not parallel in construction.

To correct the sentence, replace "he complies" with the appropriate adjective ("compliant") to match the first two phrases. The words "compliant with" are parallel to "open to" and "responsive to," and the correct sentence reads:

> An excellent employee is *open to* new ideas, *responsive to* company needs, and *compliant with* the company rules of business.

DIFFICULT PARALLELISM

The following example illustrates another common and trickier parallelism mistake:

> The new advertisers were more concerned about the company's image than about either its profits or growth.

The use of "either" indicates that two items will be mentioned. Generally speaking, let's say that "either" is followed by *this* or *that*. These two items, *this* and *that*, must be parallel. In the sentence above, *this* is equivalent to "its profits" and *that* is equivalent to "growth." The sentence is not parallel since "its" is part of only one of the items. Below is the best way to correct the error:

The new advertisers were more concerned about the company's image than about either its profits or *its* growth.

———

For parallelism problems, watch out for the following:
1. A series of two or more actions or items
2. Lists, especially when there are distracting phrases thrown in between the items
3. Comparisons (because they always include at least two items)

LESSON PROBLEMS

Underline the part of the sentence that is incorrect (if any) and correct it. If part of the sentence is underlined, correct this part:

1. Lillian's living room displayed a nineteenth century grand piano, a classic antique coffee table, and there were paintings from the early 1920s on the walls.

   ———

2. The audience listened carefully and <u>with compassion</u> to the composer's last symphony, which he composed shortly before his death.

   ———

3. Completing an undergraduate education will prepare you for both the challenges of <u>working</u> and of further study.

   ———

4. While Nick hides in the basement, Louie <u>is looking</u> in the attic.

   ———

5. For most great artists, creative freedom is more important than <u>being financially comfortable</u>.

   ———

6. Ted would prefer <u>to watch</u> grass grow to finishing his homework.

(HW)

1. Mike developed new layouts for the Viking Journal and as a result a professional and easy-to-read paper was created.

---

2. To call The Darkening an important new rock band is like calling Buster Wallace a pioneer in jazz.

---

3. Jess likes to take the bus more than driving her car because she can read, sleep, or talk to interesting new people.

---

4. Jackie became known as the best writer in town after covering the riots and offering solutions to social unrest.

---

5. For most great artists, <u>creative freedom</u> is more important than being financially comfortable.

---

6. Not surprisingly, the larger new engine increased both <u>the car's performance and fuel consumption</u>.

---

7. NOUN AGREEMENT

Nouns must agree in number (plural or singular) with the number of the noun or nouns they are referring to. For example:

Dave and Scott are looking for *a girlfriend*.

Obviously, Dave and Scott are not looking for one girlfriend. *Girlfriend* must be plural so it agrees with the plural subject of the sentence. The correct sentence should read:

Dave and Scott are looking for *girlfriends*.

LESSON PROBLEMS

Underline the part of the sentence that is incorrect (if any) and correct it:

1. Once considered a place to meet people and drink coffee, bookstores are now generally used just to buy books.

    _____

2. To become a better reader, students are urged to read everything they can get their hands on, including newspapers and magazines.

    _____

3. The cookies all come in a different box, so you should have no trouble separating the chocolate chunk ones from the peanut toffee ones.

    _____

4. Frank has a wide and varied course load, taking a subject as diverse as History of Nepal, Thermodynamics, and South American Literature.

    _____

1. The vibraphone, melodic and percussive instruments used mostly in jazz, can be played with two or four mallets.

   _____

2. There are so many great bands, but each year, only two are inducted as a member of the Rock and Roll Hall of Fame.

   _____

3. The visual simplicity of the piano keyboard and the ubiquity of the piano in the modern household are a reason why so many children learn to play the piano before they study other instruments.

   _____   _____

Now is a good time to review sections 1-7. The following quiz on these sections is found in the Grammar Quizzes section at the end of this chapter. It will be assigned by your tutor. If you are working on your own, take the quiz after you have reviewed sections 1-7. If you struggle on the quiz, you should probably review the material further.

☐   Grammar Quiz 1 (Sections 1-7)

8. COMPARISONS

THE *NUMBER* OF A COMPARISON

The *number* of a comparison refers to the number of items being compared. There are grammatical differences between comparing two things and comparing three or more things.

When comparing **two** things, you will use the *-er* form of an adjective (words such as happi*er* or stron*ger*) or the word *more* prior to an adjective (such as *more* beautiful).

When comparing **three or more** things, you will use the *-est* form of an adjective (happi*est* or strong*est*) or the word *most* prior to an adjective (such as *most* beautiful). For example:

> Jason is *better* than I am at shooting with his left hand. (two people)
> Jason is the *best* player on the team at shooting with his left hand. (three or more people)

MAKING COMPARING ADJECTIVES ☺

It is helpful to understand how these *comparing adjectives* are made.

> 1) For most one-syllable words, add *-er* or *-est*:
> *brave → braver, bravest*

> 2) For most two-syllable words, use *more* or *most* (or *less* or *least*):
> *famous → more famous, most famous*

> Some two-syllable words follow the guidelines for one-syllable words:
> *pretty → prettier, prettiest*

> It would also be correct, however, to apply the previous rule:
> *more pretty, most pretty*

> 3) For three-syllable words and all words ending in *-ly*, usually use *more* or *most* (or *less* or *least*):
> *beautiful → more beautiful, most beautiful*
> *happily → more happily, most happily*

Some words deviate from the rules above:

adjective	two things	three or more things
good	better	best
well	better	best
bad	worse	worst
little	less	least
much	more	most
many	more	most

DOUBLE COMPARISONS ☺

Make sure to never create a *double comparison* by putting words like *more* or *most* in the same phrase with words in the *-er* or *-est* form. For example, avoid:

more friendlier, most friendliest

> To find comparison errors, watch out for words in the *-er* and *-est* form and the words *more* and *most*.

LESSON PROBLEMS

Underline the part of the sentence that is incorrect (if any) and correct it:

1. An oil candle is both brighter and more longer-burning than a conventional wax candle.

    _____

2. On our track team, Evan may have long legs, but he is definitely not the faster of the group.

    _____

3. Since he spends all day and night studying, Brian, not surprisingly, is the intelligentest student in the class.

    _____

1. Amanda is definitely the more outspoken of the twins.

   _____

2. When deciding whether to take the high road or the low road, the best choice is often elusive.

   _____

3. Chris is more than happy to hear himself speak in the company of others.

   _____

9. ILLOGICAL COMPARISONS

The saying goes that *you can't compare apples to oranges*. For example:

> The science department's projects are much more interesting than the English department this year.

The sentence is incorrect because the science department's *projects* are being compared to the English *department*. The correct sentence should read:

> The science department's projects are much more interesting than the English department's *projects* this year.

You don't always have to restate the noun being compared, as above. Using an *apostrophe-s* (*'s*) or the word *that* (singular) or *those* (plural) is usually acceptable.

> The science department's projects are much more interesting than the English department*'s* this year.

> The projects of the science department are much more interesting than *those* of the English department this year.

––––––––

When you spot a comparison, ask yourself: what items are being compared? You might want to underline the two items. **Always compare "apples to apples."**

Always look at all comparisons carefully to make sure they are logical.

LESSON PROBLEMS

Underline the part of the sentence that is incorrect (if any) and correct it:

1. Similar to Wayne's modern chord progressions, David is often even more complex.

   _____

2. The history of Hawaii, like other Pacific islands, is primarily concerned with the ocean.

   _____

3. The rules of rugby are different from Australian football, even though the sports look similar.

   _____

4. Our school's students are much stronger in math and science than the average school.

   _____

5. I hate to admit it, but that restaurant is much better than my mom's food.

   _____

(HW)

1. I must admit that your school's badminton team, after winning seven games in a row, is better than our school.

   _____

2. A recent study suggests that eating fish twice a week is healthier than eating other meats.

   _____

3. Gregg's new car, which his generous parents bought him after graduation, is not surprisingly much sleeker than his other friends.

   _____

4. Daniel's score on this test, after diligent study and practice, is much better than his last test.

   _____

5. Our newspaper's new format is much easier to read than last year's.

   _____

10. DOUBLE NEGATIVES ☺

Double negatives must be avoided, not only because they're redundant, but also because two negatives would technically cancel each other out, changing the intended meaning of the sentence. For example:

I *can't hardly* wait for summer to arrive.

Can't and *hardly* are both negative, so one must be removed. The correct sentence should read:

I can *hardly* wait for summer to arrive.
Or:
I *can't* wait for summer to arrive.

Hopefully, your ear will easily pick up on these, but pay attention to sentences involving the words *hardly, scarcely,* or *barely*. These are all negative and should not be combined with *not* or another negative word.

LESSON PROBLEMS

Underline or eliminate the part of the sentence that is incorrect and correct the sentence (if necessary):

1. After spending several hours trying to figure out how to use the internet, Irving decided that it is not scarcely as easy to use as people say it is.

   _____

2. No matter how hard the committee tries to raise awareness about what happens to dogs in pounds, there are hardly no families willing to adopt these dogs as pets.

   _____

3. The coach was unable to offer no reasons for the team's let-down in the fourth quarter.

   _____

1. Mick explained multiple times, "I can't get no satisfaction!"

   _____

2. Christina, unable to sleep a wink, couldn't barely wait for the morning to arrive so she could open her presents.

   _____

3. To not pay attention in class is hardly the way to overcome your incomplete homework.

   _____

11. PUNCTUATION

This section focuses on punctuation errors relating to commas and semicolons. Other punctuation topics, such as apostrophes, dashes, and colons, are not tested on the SAT, but if you choose to incorporate them in your essay writing, make sure you understand their correct uses.

First, let's cover some basic terminology. You do not have to memorize any of these terms; they merely aid in teaching the material.

SENTENCE BUILDING BLOCKS

Sentences are generally made up of up to three distinct parts: *independent clauses*, *dependent clauses*, and *phrases*. Let's look at an example to illustrate these parts.

As he looked up at the blimp, William tripped on the curb.

Clause – a sequence of words that contains a subject and its verb

Independent clause – a clause that can stand on its own and make sense

Dependent clause – a clause that cannot stand on its own because it *depends* on the rest of the sentence to make sense

In the example above, *William tripped on the curb* is the *independent clause*, and *As he looked up at the blimp* is the *dependent clause*.

Phrase – a sequence of two or more words that does not contain a finite (non-*ing*) verb and its subject

By changing the first part of the sentence slightly, we can turn the dependent clause into a *phrase*. The *-ing* form of a verb is the most common way to do this.

Looking up at the blimp, William tripped on the curb.

Because there is no subject in the first part of the sentence, *Looking up at the blimp* is a phrase. This phrase is modifying *William* by adding information about what he was doing when he tripped.

! **Sentences must have at least one independent clause.** Good writers will add different combinations of dependent clauses and phrases to these independent clauses to make interesting-sounding sentences.

COMMAS

SEPARATING DEPENDENT CLAUSES FROM INDEPENDENT CLAUSES

Commas must be used to separate a dependent clause from a following independent clause of a sentence. For example:

As he looked down at his untied shoe, Gregg missed the UFO that flew over his head.

            dependent clause   independent clause

When a dependent clause comes *after* an independent clause, the comma is unnecessary. Notice that there is no need to *pause* between the clauses in this situation, which is a good reminder that the comma is not needed. For example:

Gregg missed the UFO flying over his head as he looked down at his untied shoe.

         independent clause   dependent clause

Or:

Gregg missed the UFO because he was looking down at his untied shoe.

     independent clause   dependent clause

SEPARATING MODIFYING PHRASES FROM INDEPENDENT CLAUSES

Commas must be used to separate modifying phrases from the independent clause of a sentence. This topic was introduced in the Subject-Verb lesson.

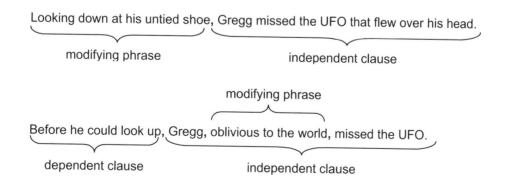

Looking down at his untied shoe, Gregg missed the UFO that flew over his head.

      modifying phrase   independent clause

                            modifying phrase

Before he could look up, Gregg, oblivious to the world, missed the UFO.

      dependent clause   independent clause

SEPARATING TWO INDEPENDENT CLAUSES

Some sentences will have two independent clauses separated by a conjunction, such as *and*, *or*, or *but* (more on conjunctions later). **A comma must come before the conjunction**, as shown in the following example:

Gregg looked down at his untied shoe, and he missed the UFO flying over his head.

independent clause   independent clause

ONE INDEPENDENT CLAUSE WITH TWO ACTIONS

Make sure there are indeed two distinct independent clauses. The following example does not need a comma because the sentence has only one independent clause containing two actions.

Gregg looked down at his untied shoe and missed the UFO flying over his head.

SEMICOLONS

Semicolons (;) function similarly to periods, except the sentences that they separate must be closely related. **Semicolons are used to separate independent clauses**, which, if you recall, could stand alone as complete sentences. The following example illustrates the correct use of a semicolon:

Gregg looked down at his untied shoe; he missed the UFO flying over his head.

independent clause   independent clause

LESSON PROBLEMS

Correct the following sentences (if necessary) by adding punctuation. Circle any added punctuation:

1. After spending several years trying to grow a garden Linda decided she'd rather just buy her produce from the store.
2. Daniel not a large man by any means somehow seems to dominate our basketball games.
3. You should watch the road but you should occasionally check your mirrors, as well.
4. She skated with amazing skill and finesse as though she had wings on her back.

1. Tommy friendly as always offered to assist the confused tourist.
2. Skipping through the sprinklers and rolling through the grass Katie became a wet and grassy mess.
3. Even though many voters apparently unaware of the country's many problems are happy with the incumbent I feel we are ready for a new leader.
4. George rocked the boat many people fell out.

12. CONJUNCTIONS

Conjunction – A word that links the parts of a sentence together.

There are several different types of conjunctions. Once again, you do not have to memorize the terminology.

FANBOYS CONJUNCTIONS

The following conjunctions are also called *coordinating* conjunctions:

> *for, and, nor, but, or, yet, so*

To help remember them, use the acronym **FANBOYS**: **F**or-**A**nd-**N**or-**B**ut-**O**r-**Y**et-**S**o. You might also notice that each conjunction is either two or three letters long. (Many other conjunctions are longer.)

(!) **The FANBOYS conjunctions, listed above, are the only conjunctions that can link two independent clauses.** As explained in the previous section, when they link independent clauses, they should be preceded by a comma. For example:

> In his books and essays, Thoreau challenged the traditional ideas of society, **and** he was thus both criticized and praised by his readers.

ILLOGICAL CONJUNCTIONS

In addition to the FANBOYS conjunctions, there are many other conjunctions that can link parts of sentences together. Words like *because*, *even though*, and *rather than* are examples of conjunctions. Watch out for conjunctions that are used illogically. For example:

> Driving with a friend can save time *so that* you can use the carpool lane on the freeway.

Saving time does not allow you to *use the carpool lane*. *Using the carpool lane* allows you to *save time*. Therefore, replace *so that* with *because*:

Driving with a friend can save time *because* you can use the carpool lane on the freeway.

The following is another example:

I practiced the piece for hours, *and* I still made a number of embarrassing mistakes.

The conjunction *and* is definitely not the best choice here. The more logical sentence reads:

I practiced the piece for hours, *but* I still made a number of embarrassing mistakes.

THEN

Then is a conjunction, but it is not a FANBOYS conjunction, and it cannot link two independent clauses. For example:

I practiced for hours while I taped myself, *then* I listened back to see how I sounded.

This sentence could be corrected several ways:

I practiced for hours while I taped myself, *and then* I listened back to see how I sounded.
Or:
I practiced for hours while I taped myself; *then* I listened back to see how I sounded.
Or:
I practiced for hours while I taped myself, *and* I *then* listened back to see how I sounded.

Watch out for the word "then" at the beginning of the second independent clause in a sentence.

PAIRED CONJUNCTIONS

These conjunctions or phrases, which always come in pairs, are also called *correlative* conjunctions.

- **both...and** — *Both* the lions *and* the tigers were putting on a show at the zoo.

- **not only...but also** — The new electric car is *not only* more efficient than a gasoline-powered car *but also* much quieter.

- **not...but** — The movie is *not* light-hearted or trivial *but* dark and disturbing in the ways it portrays drug-use.

- **either...or** — You can be *either* for him *or* against him; there is no in between.

- **neither...nor** — He is *neither* as large *nor* as strong as his father, but he is much faster.

- **whether...or** — *Whether* you go to a good university *or* straight to the work force is up to you.

- **as...as** — Amy was not *as* scholastic *as* her older sister, but she was much more sociable.

- **not so much...as** — It is *not so much* the sound of the breaking waves *as* (not *but*) the smell of the sea that characterizes my beach house.

- **so...that** — It is *so* hot today *that* I'm afraid to go outside.

To identify paired-conjunction errors, look for the *first* part of each pair. (The second part will often be incorrect or missing altogether).

LESSON PROBLEMS

Correct the following underlined words (if necessary):

1. Michael drove as fast as he could, <u>but</u> he arrived in plenty of time to see the start of the movie.

2. The new documentary is not only an important educational film <u>but</u> a pleasurable viewing experience.

3. I ate nothing but fruits, vegetables, and <u>protein, then</u> I had the urge for a piece of chocolate cake.

_____

4. Both the pencil <u>or</u> the pen are mightier than the sword.

_____

(HW)

1. Howard brought over the automatic screwdriver, and <u>then</u> he proceeded to show me how to use it.

_____

2. Neither your muddy shoes <u>or</u> your rain soaked jacket will be allowed in this house.

_____

3. Frank, while frightening in his own ways, was not as gruesome or as sinister <u>compared to</u> Drake.

_____

4. I know you are angry not so much by your choice of words <u>but</u> by the tone of your voice.

_____

13. FRAGMENTS

Fragments are some of the most common errors found on the SAT. There are several types of fragments that show up. You can identify them by looking for the specific parts described below.

DEPENDENT CLAUSE

Some fragments are dependent clauses. Dependent clauses are usually just independent clauses preceded by words called **subordinate conjunctions**, listed below:

after	even though	though
although	if	unless
as	if only	until
as if	in order that	when
as long as	now that	whenever
as though	once	where
because	rather than	whereas
before	since	wherever
even if	so that	while

All of these words turn an independent clause into a dependent clause. When you spot one of them, if the sentence does not have a clear independent clause, then it is a fragment. For example:

Fragment: *As* the forest fire burned, bellowing smoke into the air.

The sentence lacks an independent clause.

-*ING* WORD USED AS A VERB

As taught in the Verb Tense lesson, a word in the -*ing* form—on its own—does not function as a verb. When the subject of a sentence lacks a verb, the sentence is a fragment. For example:

Fragment: The firefighters, many from hundreds of miles away, *preparing* to fight the fire.

The subject "firefighters" lacks a verb.

PRONOUN PHRASE

Watch out for phrases that begin with pronouns such as *that*, *which*, *who*, or *whom*. Especially watch out for *that*; the others are easier to identify because they will usually be preceded by a comma. The following are all fragments because the subjects ("fire," "fire," and "residents") lack verbs:

> The fire *that* burned over 1,000 acres last summer.
> The forest fire, *which* was likely started when someone threw a cigarette from his car.
> The residents, *who* lived in the small mountain town all their lives.

"THAT" CLAUSE

Sometimes the word *that* indicates a clause within a clause. This so-called *"that" clause* must have its own subject and verb. For example:

> Fragment: The newspaper reporter said *that* residents returning to their homes.

The subject of the "that" clause ("residents") lacks a verb.

While less common, *question* words such as *why*, *where*, *who*, *what*, *how*, etc. can also create their own clauses, so watch out for them.

MODIFYING PHRASE

The College Board will often use long modifying phrases to disguise fragments. Try removing modifying phrases to find the bare-bones sentence.

> The fire captain, one of the most experienced firefighters in the county and not surprisingly the first on the scene.

The subject "captain" lacks a verb.

SEMICOLON

Watch out for fragments when two clauses are separated by a semicolon. As taught in the Punctuation section, a semicolon (like a period) separates two *independent clauses*.

> Incorrect: Jerry enjoys tree climbing; but quick to warn of its potential dangers.
> Incorrect: Jerry enjoys tree climbing; however warning of its potential dangers.

The second clause in each of the previous examples is a fragment.

_____

A fragment usually contains one of the following:
1. Dependent clause (look for a subordinate conjunction)
2. *-ING* word used as a verb
3. Pronoun phrase
4. "That" clause
5. Modifying phrase
6. Semicolon

FRAGMENT LESSON PROBLEMS

If a sentence below is a fragment, write "F" on the line provided.

____ 1. Bertrand Russell's *The Problems of Philosophy*, often one of the first books assigned in introductory Philosophy courses because of its ability to make the abstruse comprehendible.

____ 2. After the committee released its findings on the widespread use of cell phones, scientists warned that there may be a link between cell-phone use and brain tumors.

____ 3. Although better known as a movie star, Austrian actress Hedy Lamarr, who became a pioneer in the field of wireless communications following her emigration to the United States.

____ 4. When choosing a health insurance company; choose carefully.

____ 5. The sculptor, carefully shaping with his hands, transformed clay into art.

(HW)

____ 1. Jerry said that climbing trees, an activity not for everyone because of its inherent risks.

____ 2. Most people showing little concern for agriculture and farming, even though these fields were keys to the rise of human civilization.

____ 3. Possibly the first car, which used a machine similar to a windmill to drive gears, which in turn drove the wheels, designed by Guido da Vigevano in 1335.

____ 4. At the end of the last day of school, the students celebrated; however, the teachers, with stacks of ungraded tests on their desks, had much work ahead.

____ 5. Most of the overnight campers know that the ghost stories being told to scare them from leaving their bunks in the middle of the night.

14. RUN-ONS

> **Recall from the Punctuation section that two independent clauses must be separated by (1) a comma *and* a FANBOYS conjunction or (2) a semicolon—otherwise, the sentence is a run-on.** On the SAT, there are two common types of run-on sentences related to this rule:

COMMA BUT NO CONJUNCTION

The first one, called a *comma splice*, involves two independent clauses separated by a comma but lacking a conjunction. For example:

Yoshio thought that his printer was broken, it simply was out of ink.

          independent clause   independent clause

To correct this run-on, simply add an appropriate conjunction:

Yoshio thought that his printer was broken, *but* it simply was out of ink.

CONJUNCTION BUT NO COMMA

The second type of run-on also has two independent clauses. This one correctly includes a conjunction but is lacking a comma before the conjunction. For example:

Yoshio thought that his printer was broken and this was because the page came out white.

          independent clause   independent clause

Since the second part of the sentence is an independent clause, it must have a comma before the conjunction. The correct sentence should read:

Yoshio thought that his printer was broken**,** and this was because the page came out white.

A more eloquent and succinct way to correct the error is to turn the second clause into a dependent clause or modifying phrase. The College Board often corrects run-ons in this way:

Yoshio thought that his printer was broken because the page came out white.
Or:

Because the page came out white, Yoshio thought that his printer was broken.

Finally, recall that two independent clauses can be separated by a semicolon with no conjunction:

The page came out white; Yoshio, thus, thought that his printer was broken.

TWO SUBJECTS

Some run-ons will have two subjects separated by a modifying phrase.

Yoshio, although he thought that his printer was broken, he discovered that it was simply out of ink.

Which word is the subject: *Yoshio* or *he*? To correct this sentence, remove one of the subjects:

Although he thought that his printer was broken, *Yoshio* discovered that it was simply out of ink.

_____

The following steps will help you correct run-on errors:

1. If the sentence contains two independent clauses, make sure they are separated with either (1) a comma *and* a FANBOYS conjunction or (2) a semicolon.
2. If a sentence contains two subjects separated by a modifying phrase, remove one of the subjects.

As the steps above suggest, look for sentences with two independent clauses or two subjects.

_____

LESSON PROBLEMS

Correct the following sentences (if necessary) by adding punctuation or logical words. Circle any added punctuation. Various answers are possible.

1. Most people rarely get to see the sunrise they are asleep that early in the morning.

_____

2. Kevin had run slowly at first, he then accelerated quickly to avoid the pursuing tacklers who, to the delight of the crowd, fell harmlessly at Kevin's feet.

_____

3. Most health experts agree that young people are not active enough and this inactivity is likely a result of the temptations of such sedentary activities as watching television or working on the internet.

   _____

4. Tickets to the museum are discounted to students; just showing your school I.D. at the ticket window.

   _____

5. Todd, although hardly the best athlete on the team, he continues to impress the coaches with his effort.

   _____

(HW)

1. Playing a sport and learning an instrument offer good analogies for effective studying, because these activities involve considerable practice to master, one can see the obvious benefits of hard work and persistence.

   _____

2. The book was written without regard to punctuation or paragraphs this unconformity made it difficult to understand.

   _____

3. I have no plans to see the movie, but my brother, he plans to wait in line for hours to see the premier.

   _____

4. He spoke with his hands but his voice was silent.

   _____

5. He worked tirelessly to finish the experiment on the health benefits of soy beans, the health conference was only a few weeks away.

   _____

15. IMPROPER MODIFIERS

As we've seen in the previous sections, dependent clauses and phrases can act as modifiers for a noun or nouns in the sentence. On the SAT, *improper modifiers*, which are usually at the beginning of a sentence, appear to modify an illogical noun because of this noun's closeness to the modifying phrase. **You must make sure that the noun meant to be modified is as close as possible to the modifying phrase.** For example:

> With power and skill, the volleyball was spiked over the net by Jill.

The modifying phrase in this sentence is *With power and skill*. It is obviously meant to modify *Jill*, but it seems to modify *the volleyball*. It may be obvious what the intended meaning of the sentence is, but the sentence should be corrected to read:

> With power and skill, Jill spiked the volleyball over the net.

Sometimes, the noun intended to be modified is not found in the sentence. For example:

> Hailed as a pioneer in volleyball, Randy's techniques have been imitated by just about everyone who plays the sport.

Hailed as a pioneer in volleyball is obviously meant to modify *Randy*, but only *Randy's techniques* are mentioned in the sentence; the actual person *Randy* is not mentioned. The correct sentence could read:

> Hailed as a pioneer in volleyball, *Randy* used techniques that have been imitated by just about everyone who plays the sport.

Watch out for any sentence that begins with a *modifying phrase* or a *dependent clause*. Remember, modifying phrases usually have *-ing* words (review the Punctuation section, if necessary). Dependent clauses usually begin with subordinate conjunctions (review the previous section, if necessary).

LESSON PROBLEMS

Correct the following sentences (if necessary) by rewriting the underlined parts in a logical way:

1. After he snuck out the window to play games with his friends, <u>his parents were the last people Sean expected to run into at the arcade</u>.

2. A creature with a great natural defense, <u>the blow fish's body can grow to several times its normal size when danger is sensed</u>.

3. By using his fingers to create an extremely fast hammering-effect on the guitar, <u>electric guitar techniques were raised to a new level by Eddie</u>.

4. Although he had great work experience and an amazing resume, <u>the boss overlooked Kevin for the job</u>.

5. After sleeping through the entire semester, <u>the A was a shock to Chrissie</u>.

HW

1. Getting paid by the word, <u>it's no wonder Charles's books are so long</u>.

2. From the window of the airplane, <u>the farms looked like small green squares</u>.

3. After hearing the CD of the live performance, <u>our disappointment in having missed the show was unbearable</u>.

4. With strength and endurance not found among any of the other competitors, <u>Lance rode to victory yet again</u>.

_____

5. Using rhythmic ideas to create the illusion of changing time-signatures, <u>the playing of Tony inspired a generation of jazz drummers</u>.

_____

16. ADJECTIVES AND ADVERBS ☺

ADJECTIVES AND ADVERBS TERMINOLOGY

Adjective – a word that describes or modifies a person or thing in a sentence (such as *blue*, *old*, *calm*, or *happy*).

Adverb – a word that modifies a verb, adjective, or other adverb in a sentence (such as *quickly*, *happily*, or *stubbornly*). Adverbs describe *how* something happens.

INCORRECT ADJECTIVES

Adjectives only modify nouns. On the SAT, adjective and adverb errors occur when an adjective is used incorrectly in place of an adverb. As you read the example below, first identify the adjective. If you can't identify the noun for the adjective to modify, the adjective is incorrect; replace it with an adverb.

I was surprised how quick she walked to the store.

The adjective is "quick." Ask yourself: what is "quick" modifying? Since it's modifying "how…she walked," it should be an adverb:

I was surprised how *quickly* she walked to the store.

GOOD VERSUS WELL AND BAD VERSUS BADLY

The words *good* and *bad* are adjectives, and the words *well* and *badly* are adverbs. Following the rules above, if a noun is being modified, use *good* or *bad*, and if a verb is being modified, use *well* or *badly*. For example:

He performed *well* on the test. (*Well* describes how he *performed*.)
He received a *good* score on the test. (*Good* modifies the noun *score*.)

When dealing with any of the five senses, there is an exception to these rules. Use the word *good* or *bad* to modify verbs. For example:

After sketching with a new type of charcoal, the drawing looks *good* (not *well*).
The burnt bread made dinner smell *bad* (not *badly*).
After my team lost, I felt *bad* (not *badly*).

Since adjective/adverb errors usually involve the incorrect use of an adjective in place of an adverb, look carefully at all **adjectives** in a sentence.

LESSON PROBLEMS

Underline and correct the adverb or adjective error in each sentence (if necessary):

1. He was cautious about how he backed the car out of the driveway.

    _____

2. Trying to find the source of the rumor, he moved quite rapid from one group to another.

    _____

3. Despite a pulled leg muscle, he did a good job of swimming.

    _____

4. No matter how careful tax returns are checked, there is always a good chance of mistakes.

    _____

(HW)

1. Pete bade his dinner guests good night, asking them to drive safe.

    _____

2. The speaker once again showed her skills with one of her typical brilliant dissertations.

    _____

3. She received accolades for doing a real good job on the science project.

    _____

4. After enjoying a meal at McDonald's, Jeffrey often indulged in its fresh baked cookies.

    _____

Now is a good time to review sections 8-16. The following quiz on these sections is found in the Grammar Quizzes section at the end of this chapter. It will be assigned by your tutor. If you are working on your own, take the quiz after you have reviewed sections 8-16. If you struggle on the quiz, you should probably review the material further.

☐   Grammar Quiz 1 (Sections 8-16)

17. *IDIOM*

Idiom has to do with the manner or style of a language. The rules for idiom are less predictable and consistent (and, thus, more difficult to remember) than most of the other grammar rules in this tutorial. The good news is that many of the idiom errors will simply sound wrong to your ear. For others, however, you will have to memorize.

PREPOSITIONAL IDIOMS

Many idiom mistakes have to do with an incorrect preposition following an adjective or verb. For example:

> We only wanted to look at the paintings; we were *indifferent **of*** the sculpture exhibit.

Idiom dictates that, in general, the preposition *to* (not *of*) should be used after *indifferent.* There is no real way to predict this rule—the choice seems arbitrary. This is why these idiom rules can be difficult. You must either memorize from a long list of rules or (hopefully) rely on your ear. The correct sentence should read:

> We only wanted to look at the paintings; we were *indifferent **to*** the sculpture exhibit.

Here is another common mistake:

> The oil paintings don't look *different **than*** the acrylic ones.

Idiom dictates that the preposition *from* should follow *different*:

> The oil paintings don't look *different **from*** the acrylic ones.

SAME WORD, DIFFERENT PREPOSITIONS

Complicating matters, sometimes the same word can take different prepositions depending on the context. For example:

> We *agreed **to*** go to the museum together, but we could not *agree **on*** how to get there. I hope you *agree **with*** me that walking is out of the question.

Fortunately, most of these rules will sound natural to your ear. For example, you probably would never say: we could not *agree* **to** how to get there. It just sounds wrong.

Here are some other examples of the same word taking different prepositions:

- You might be *angry* **at** (or **about**) the weather (a thing), but please don't be *angry* **with** me (a person) because I forgot the umbrella.
- The paintings of Vincent van Gogh *correspond* **to** the Impressionism style (a thing). Van Gogh continued to *correspond* **with** his brother (a person) throughout his life.
- Michelangelo deserves a *reward* **for** painting the Sistine Chapel. I hear he was *rewarded* **with** an adequate commission.
- Being *surrounded* **with** all of these amazing works of art (things) was quite an experience. It's no wonder that I was *surrounded* **by** so many other excited visitors (people).

TAKE OUT THE PREPOSITIONAL-IDIOM PHRASE

The College Board may make a prepositional idiom question more difficult by putting a phrase between the idiom pair. For example:

She was worried, perhaps because it was raining or perhaps because she had a sprained ankle, of walking all the way to the museum.

When you suspect a prepositional idiom error, try taking the word pair away from the sentence and "listen" to it in your head—trust your ear:

She was *worried...of* walking all the way to the museum.

The preposition *of* is incorrect. One worries *about* something, not *of* something. The correct preposition is *about*.

She was *worried...about* walking all the way to the museum.

SYNONYMS AND PREPOSITIONS

Another approach that may help you when you are not familiar with the correct preposition involves using a synonym of the verb or adverb. For example:

He was *prohibited from* watching television until he finished his art-history paper.

If you are not sure about the preposition *from*, think of a word similar to *prohibited*—maybe *grounded*.

He was *grounded from* watching television...

This sentence sounds fine using *from*, so the original sentence is probably correct, as well. Of course there are exceptions, but, **often, when two words mean about the same thing, they take the same preposition**, as displayed in the following examples:

Example: We were *excited **about*** seeing the Dali exhibit.

enthusiastic about	happy about	pleased about

Example: We were *anxious **about*** getting to every exhibit before the museum closed.

concerned about	furious about	upset about
depressed about	nervous about	worried about
doubtful about	uneasy about	wrong about

Example: We were *amazed **at*** the skill of the Realist painters.

alarmed at	shocked at	surprised at

Example: We were *frightened **by*** Edward Munch's painting, The Scream.

annoyed by	embarrassed by
confused by	irritated by

Example: The modern paintings were clearly *different **from*** the classic ones.

detached from	isolated from	removed from
distinct from	kept from	resigned from
far from	protected from	safe from

Example: He was *accused **of*** leaving a fingerprint on the display case.

suspected of	suspicious of

Example: The paintings of Piet Mondrian look *similar **to*** those of Theo van Doesburg.

akin to	equal to	relevant to
comparable to	parallel to	suited to
essential to	relative to	

Example: The style of Cubism is usually *associated **with*** Pablo Picasso.

in accordance with	affiliated with
acquainted with	preoccupied with

Example: It is interesting to *look **at*** that painting from across the room.

aim at	glare at	shoot at
frown at	point at	

Example: I *long **for*** more hours in the day.

beg for	pray for	wish for
mourn for	search for (but *in search **of***)	yearn for

Example: I'd like to become an *expert **in*** Andy Warhol and Pop Art.

engaged in	involved in
interested in	proficient in

Example: After today, I hope to *develop **into*** one of my school's best painters.

dive into	divide into	pry into
dip into	grow into	sink into

Example: I can't wait to *pounce **on*** my new art history books when I get home.

intrude on	reflect on	spy on
jump on	report on	

Example: Claude Monet *belongs **to*** the Impressionist movement.

commit to	correspond to	subscribe to
conform to	pertain to	
contribute to	similar to	

Example: Perhaps my friend will *collaborate **with*** me on a giant-size painting of the city.

agree with	comply with	share with
assist with	communicate with	sympathize with
combine with	cooperate with	

COMMON PREPOSITIONAL-IDIOM ERRORS

The following list, while lengthy, is just a partial list of the hundreds of possible prepositional-idiom rules. It would be futile to include all of them, and memorizing would be next to impossible anyway. Hopefully reading over these common errors and memorizing *some* of them will help you become comfortable with the types of preposition errors that show up on the test.

Try to recognize synonyms from the previous pages as you work on memorizing. Also, remember that some of these verbs and adverbs may use different prepositions depending on the context of the sentence. When needed for clarification, examples are written in brackets.

LIST OF COMMON PREPOSITIONAL-IDIOM ERRORS

abide **by** (not **to**)

ability **to** [make] (not **for** [making])

accompanied **by** (not **with**)

according **to** (not **with**—but *in accordance* **with**)

accused **of** (not **over** or **with**)

acquainted **with** (not **to**)

afraid **of** (not **about**)

agree **on**, **to**, or **with** (not **about**)

aim **at** (not **on** or **against**)

alarmed **at** (not **about**)

amazed **at** (not **about**)

amused **by** (better than **at**)

angry **with** or **about** (not **against**)

annoyed **by** (not **about** or **at**)

anxious **about** (not **for**)

argue **about** (not **on**)

arrive **at** (not **to**)

ashamed **of** (not **over** or **with**)

belong **to** (not **with**)

benefit **from** (not **by**)

bored **by** or **with** (not **of**)

careful **of** or **with** (not **for**)

combine **with** (not **to**)

comply **with** (not **to**)

concentrate **on** (not **over** or **in**)

concerned **about** (not **of**)

confident **in** (not **about**)

conform **to** (not **in** or **with**)

confused **by** (not **over**)

congratulated **on** (not **about**)

consistent **with** (not **to**)

curious **about** (not **with**)

delighted **with** (not **about**)

depart **for** (not **to**)

dependent **on** (not **of**)

deprived **of** (not **from**)

detrimental **to** (not **for**)

die **of** (not **from**)

different **from** (not **than**)

dip **into** (not **in**)

dive **into** (not **in**)

divide **into** (not **in**)

disapprove **of** (not **with**)

distinct **from** (not **of**)

embarrassed **by** (not **about**)

essential **to** [succeed] (not **for** [succeeding])

exception **to** (not **of**)

excited **about** (not **at** or **over**)

an expert **in** (not **about** or **of**)

familiar **with** (not **to**)

famous **for** (not **in**)

fired **from** (not **off of**)

frightened **by** or **of** (not **at**)

furious **about** (not **over**)

good **at** (not **in**)

guard **against** (not **from**)

happy **about** (not **of**)

hopeless **at** (not **in**)

ignorant **of** (not **with**)

independent **of** (not **from**)

indifferent **to** (not **of** or **with**)

insight **into** (not **to**)

intent **on** (not **with**)

interested **in** (not **about**)

intrude **on** (not **in**)

involved **in** (not **with**)

irritated **by** (not **from**)

knowledge **of** (not **about**)

leave **for** (not **to**)

live **in** [a city] (not **at**)

live **at** [a hotel] (not **in**)

live **on** [a street] (not **at**)

look **at** (not **toward**)

married **to** (not **with**)

mourn **for** (not **over**)

necessary **for** (not **in**) [understanding] (not **to** [understand])

oblivious **to** (not **of**)

opposed **to** (not **over**)

part **with** (not **from**)

planning **to** [work] (not **on** [working])

point **at** (not **to** or **toward**)

popular **with** (not **among**)

pray **for** (not **about**)

preoccupied **with** (not **in**)

prohibited **from** (not **to**)

proud **of** (not **about**)

pry **into** (not **in**)

punished **for** (not **over**)

relevant **to** (not **for**)

responsible **for** (not **about**)

satisfied **with** (not **about**)

shocked **at** (not **about**)

shoot **at** (not **toward**)

similar **to** (not **with**)

sorry **for** (not **about**)

succeed **in** (not **with** or **at**)

suffer **from** (not **with**)

suited **to** (not **for**)

surprised **at** or **by** (not **about**)

sure **of** (not **about**)

suspicious **of** (not **with**)

suspected **of** (not **with**)

tendency **to** [work] (not **of** [working])

tremble **with** [cold] (not **from**)

upset **about** (not **at**)

wary **of** (not **about**)

worried **about** (not **over** or **with**)

HW

First, try these problems without looking back to the lesson. If you miss several of them, you may have to spend some time making flash cards and memorizing. If you got most of them correct, your ear is probably in good shape and hopefully you won't have to put significant time into this lesson.

Underline and correct any errors in each sentence:

1. If you expect to play in the game, you must abide to the coach's rules.

    _____

2. After studying for hours, Bill was amazed about his low test score.

    _____

3. After buying a new wardrobe and getting a much needed haircut, Craig now belongs with the "in" crowd at school.

    _____

4. After eight hours straight, I think I'm finally bored of this new video game.

    _____

5. I was curious about what was inside the abandoned house, so I decided to take a look.

    _____

6. Sir Arthur Conan Doyle is famous for his Sherlock Holmes mystery novels.

    _____

7. Angie was furious over not being selected to the advisory board.

    _____

8. After years of struggle, the country of Kosovo is finally independent from Serbia.

    _____

9. Are you interested about signing up for the new debate team?

    _____

10. The students mourned over their venerable English teacher, who died last week at the age of 98.

COMMON IDIOM MISTAKES

There are hundreds of common mistakes that relate to the rules of idiom. Again, these rules are not necessarily as predictable as the other grammar rules in this tutorial, and the best way to memorize them is to create flash cards for the ones you are not familiar with. Here is an example:

The reason I can't compete in the track meet today is because I have a sprained ankle.

This sentence may sound OK, but it is actually idiomatically incorrect because *is because* is following *reason*. The sentence would be correct with *that* in place of *is because*:

The *reason* I can't compete in the track meet today is *that* I have a sprained ankle.

There is no universal rule here—just an idiom rule that you may have to memorize.

The following common mistakes are violations of idiom rules that may show up on the multiple choice sections of the SAT.

a lot → very much
Incorrect: I like track and field events *a lot*.
Correct: I like track and field events *very much*.

around → about
Avoid *around* to designate time, distance, or any other quantity.
Incorrect: The meet starts at *around* noon.
Correct: The meet starts at *about* noon.

at

    Incorrect: Where is the pole *at* for the pole vault?

    Correct: Where is the pole for the pole vault?

at once

The words "at once" are generally used with the conjunction "and" in the following way: something is "at once (this) *and* (that)."

    Incorrect: The book was *at once* unsophisticated because of its everyday writing and themes,
        but it's certainly enjoyable because of its interesting characters.

    Correct: The book was *at once* simple-minded because of its everyday writing and themes *and*
        enjoyable because of its interesting characters.

badly → desperately

    Incorrect: She *badly* wants to win the decathlon.

    Correct: She *desperately* wants to win the decathlon.

because (used after *reason*) **→ that**

    Incorrect: The reason she runs so quickly is *because* she trains hard.

    Correct: The reason she runs so quickly is *that* she trains hard.

being as/being that → because

    Incorrect: *Being that* she trains so hard, she is difficult to beat.

    Correct: *Because* she trains so hard, she is difficult to beat.

bunch → group

Do not use *bunch* when referring to people.

    Incorrect: There is a *bunch* of athletes getting ready for the marathon.

    Correct: There is a *group* of athletes getting ready for the marathon

center around → center on

A center is a single, fixed point and as such cannot move or exist *around* something.

    Incorrect: The news conference *centered around* the Iraq war.

    Correct: The news conference *centered on* the Iraq war.

doubt but/help but → doubt/help

Incorrect: I have no *doubt but* that you are the best high jumper on the team.

Correct: I have no *doubt* that you are the best high jumper on the team.

Incorrect: I could not *help but* notice the height of the bar.

Correct: I could not *help* noticing the height of the bar.

flunk → fail

Incorrect: He may be the best at pole vaulting, but he *flunked* his history quiz.

Correct: He may be the best at pole vaulting, but he *failed* his history quiz.

former/latter

Former and *latter* should only be used when choosing between *two* things.

Incorrect: After visiting Paris, Madrid, and London, I prefer the *latter*.

Correct: After visiting Paris, Madrid, and London, I prefer London.

graduate

Graduate should be followed by *from*.

Incorrect: He will probably win 20 tournaments before he *graduates* high school.

Correct: He will probably win 20 tournaments before he *graduates from* high school.

in regards to → in regard to

Incorrect: *In regards to* the javelin throw, I'll stay as far away as possible.

Correct: *In regard to* the javelin throw, I'll stay as far away as possible.

inside of → in less than

Incorrect: He ran the mile *inside of* four minutes.

Correct: He ran the mile *in less than* four minutes.

irregardless → regardless

Incorrect: *Irregardless* of what he says, it looks dangerous.

Correct: *Regardless* of what he says, it looks dangerous.

is when/is where → is/occurs when

Incorrect: The shot put *is when* you throw a heavy metal ball called a shot as far as possible.

Correct: The shot put *is* throwing a heavy metal ball called a shot as far as possible.

Incorrect: A false start is *where* you leave before the gun sounds.

Correct: A false start *occurs when* you leave before the gun sounds.

kind of/sort of → somewhat or rather

Incorrect: She was *kind of* disappointed with her javelin throw.

Correct: She was *somewhat* disappointed with her javelin throw.

like/maybe → approximately, perhaps, or about

Incorrect: There were *maybe* one thousand fans in the stands.

Correct: There were *approximately* one thousand fans in the stands.

lots of → many

Incorrect: There are *lots of* athletes on the field.

Correct: There are *many* athletes on the field.

more … and not → more … than

Incorrect: She is known *more* for her jumping *and not* for her running.

Correct: She is known *more* for her jumping *than* for her running.

most → almost

Incorrect: He runs *most* every day of the week.

Correct: He runs *almost* every day of the week.

nor → or (see the conjunction section)

Incorrect: If she expects to win, she cannot start late *nor* early.

Correct: If she expects to win, she cannot start late *or* early.

plenty → very

Incorrect: You could tell from his long stride that he was *plenty* fast.

Correct: You could tell from his long stride that he was *very* fast.

plus → and

    Incorrect: He has huge arms, *plus* his legs are also strong.

    Correct: He has huge arms, *and* his legs are also strong.

reason is/was because (see *because*)

so → very

    Incorrect: It is *so* difficult to jump over hurdles.

    Correct: It is *very* difficult to jump over hurdles.

so as to → to

    Incorrect: He uses chalk *so as to* grip the shot more firmly.

    Correct: He uses chalk *to* grip the shot more firmly.

try and → try to

    Incorrect: *Try and* see if you can run one lap without collapsing.

    Correct: *Try to* see if you can run one lap without collapsing.

use to/suppose to → used to/supposed to

    Incorrect: He *use* to be the fastest sprinter at our school.

    Correct: He *used* to be the fastest sprinter at our school.

    Incorrect: She was *suppose* to win the decathlon, but she sprained her ankle.

    Correct: She was *supposed* to win the decathlon, but she sprained her ankle.

OK

Some grammar situations may sound wrong but are actually correct. The following are a few common examples:

alike

    Correct: Liberals and conservatives *alike* are in favor of passing the new tax law.

This may sound redundant (more on redundancies later), but it's correct.

drop

> Correct: The box *dropped* off the back of the truck.
>
> Correct: The box fell off the back of the truck.

The second example sounds better, but both are correct.

sit

> Correct: The bag I had been looking for was *sitting* in the corner of the room.

whether/whether or not

There does not seem to be a clear rule for this. It is important to realize that *whether* used without *or not* is not necessarily incorrect, but if it sounds very awkward, then trust your ear and add the *or not*. For example:

> Correct: *Whether* you want to go to the store is up to you.
>
> Correct: *Whether or not* you want to go to the store is up to you.
>
> Incorrect: I'm going to the store *whether* you want to join me.
>
> Correct: I'm going to the store *whether* you want to join me *or not*.

Again, there is no real strong rule here; just trust your ear.

———

The following Idiom quizzes are found in the Grammar Quizzes section at the end of this chapter. They will be assigned by your tutor. If you are working on your own, take the quizzes after you have reviewed this section. If you struggle on the quizzes, you should probably review the material further.

(40) ☐   Idiom Quiz 1 (Prepositions)

(40) ☐   Idiom Quiz 2 (Common Mistakes)

18. CONFUSED WORDS

Words are often confused because of similar meanings. For example:

You can only pay here if you have ten items or less.

Believe it or not, this sentence is incorrect. *Less* should be used when referring to things that cannot be counted, like mashed potatoes or water. *Fewer* should be used in place of *less* when the items can be counted:

You can only pay here if you have ten items or *fewer*.

The following words are commonly interchanged even though they have different meanings or uses:

aggravate/irritate

Aggravate means to add to an already troublesome condition; *irritate* means to annoy.

Your refusal to do your homework is just *aggravating* your already poor reputation at school, and your stubbornness is beginning to *irritate* me.

allude/refer

To allude is to make an indirect reference (that is, not specifically mention); to refer is make a direct reference (mention by name).

The speaker was *alluding* to the war when he discussed the effects of budgetary cutbacks on departments not related to defense. He then *referred* to the actual budgets of each department.

between/among

Between is usually used for two items or people; *among* is used for more than two.

Just *between* you and me, I don't think the money was distributed properly *among* all the players at the poker table.

bring/take

You *bring* something to the person speaking; you *take* something away from the person speaking.

Please *take* away this cold cup coffee and *bring* me a fresh cup.

borrow/lend

You *borrow* from; you *lend* to.

Since I *lent* you my bicycle last week, can I *borrow* your Porsche?

each other/one another

Each other refers to two; *one another* refers to more than two.

While the happy couple kissed *each other* in the darkened room, the people still at the party wished *one another* a happy New Year.

fewer/less

Fewer is for things that can be counted; *less* is for things that cannot be counted.

I would like *fewer* peas and *less* mashed potatoes.

into/in

Into refers to the motion of going from outside to inside; *in* means within.

After jumping *into* the lake, you will be *in* over your head.

like/as

Like means: of the same form, appearance, or kind; *as* means: to the same degree or in the same manner. *Like* is not an acceptable substitute for *as*, *as if*, or *as though*. A good rule of thumb is to replace *like* with *as* whenever the sentence still sounds correct.

Adam fouls frequently, just *as* (not *like*) Andrew does.
The dog scratched on the door *as if* (not *like*) it wanted to come in.
Nick is *like* his brother in many ways. (*As* sounds incorrect here).

number/amount

Number is for things that can be counted; *amount* is for things that cannot be counted.

Bill had a *number* of hundred-dollar bills in his wallet—the *amount* of money stolen is just a guess.

Underline and correct the error in each sentence (if necessary):

1. The company's surplus was divided evenly between all twenty hardworking employees.

   _____

2. If you don't bring the movie back to the store by midnight, you'll have to pay for another day.

   _____

3. After Matt walked in the theater, his eyes took several minutes to adjust to the dark.

   _____

4. Spooked by the moonless dark night and the eerily silent alley, we ran like we were being chased by a mob of zombies.

   _____

5. I don't want to sound like my parents, but my neighbor's late night parties are beginning to aggravate me.

   _____

6. The members of the internet company had been a bit premature in congratulating each other since just a few months later their company was nothing more than unpaid bills and worthless stock.

   _____

19. REDUNDANCIES

Redundancy means using more words than necessary. On the multiple choice section of the SAT, as well as in your own writing, watch out for words that are clearly unnecessary. If you can remove words without changing the meaning of a sentence, those words may be redundant. For example:

That school's water polo team is favored to repeat again as state champions.

To *repeat* implies that something is happening *again*, so these words are redundant. The correct sentence should read:

That school's water polo team is favored to *repeat* as state champions.

The following examples are a number of common redundancies. There may be more than one correct answer.

a.m. this morning/p.m. this afternoon
Incorrect: The game is at ten *a.m. this morning*.
Correct: The game is at ten *a.m.*

approximate guess
Incorrect: My best *approximate guess* is that it will take an hour to get to the pool.
Correct: My best *guess* is that it will take an hour to get to the pool.

anyone else/no one else
Sometimes the *else* adds nothing to the sentence and is therefore redundant.
Incorrect: Don't go to the game with *anyone else* but me.
Correct: Don't go to the game with *anyone* but me.

biography of his/her life
Incorrect: He is such a dominant player that I'm sure we'll some day read the *biography of his life*.
Correct: He is such a dominant player that I'm sure we'll some day read his *biography*.

both alike

Incorrect: The two brothers are *both alike* in their style of play.

Correct: The two brothers are *alike* in their style of play.

circle around

Incorrect: Notice how the defenders *circle around* the ball carrier.

Correct: Notice how the defenders *circle* the ball carrier.

consensus of opinions

Incorrect: The *consensus of opinions* is that we have a better goalie.

Correct: The *consensus* is that we have a better goalie.

cooperate together

Incorrect: To win, our team must *cooperate together*.

Correct: To win, our team must *cooperate*.

each and every

Incorrect: *Each and every* player has been contributing all season long.

Correct: *Each* player has been contributing all season long.

end result

Incorrect: The *end result* is a trip to the championship game.

Correct: The *result* is a trip to the championship game.

free gift

Incorrect: These tickets were a *free gift* from my teacher.

Correct: These tickets were a *gift* from my teacher.

good chance ... probably

Incorrect: There's a *good chance* we will *probably* win the game.

Correct: There's a *good chance* we will win the game.

he is a man/she is a woman/is a person who

Incorrect: *He is a man* who can tread water for hours.

Incorrect: *He is a person* who can tread water for hours.

Correct: *He* can tread water for hours.

natural instinct

Incorrect: Our goalie relies on *natural instincts*.

Correct: Our goalie relies on *instincts*.

new innovations

Incorrect: He has created *new innovations* in the sport with his unique style.

Correct: He has created *innovations* in the sport with his unique style.

one and the same

Incorrect: It's hard to believe that our star player and the guy who struggles in math class are *one and the same*.

Correct: It's hard to believe that our star player and the guy who struggles in math class are *the same*.

Correct: It's hard to believe that our star player is the *same* guy who struggles in math class.

period of time

Incorrect: It has been a long *period of time* since our last championship.

Correct: It has been a long *time* since our last championship.

personally, I

Incorrect: *Personally, I* really dislike the other team.

Correct: *I* really dislike the other team.

plan ahead for the future

Incorrect: Next time I will *plan ahead for the future* and get my tickets in advance.

Correct: Next time I will *plan ahead* and get my tickets in advance.

repeat again/return again/revert back

Incorrect: Do you think we will *return* to the championship game *again* next year or *revert back* to old habits?

Correct: Do you think we will *return* to the championship game next year or *revert* to old habits?

shorter or longer in length/small or large in size

Incorrect: Water polo would be easier if the pool were *shorter in length*.

Correct: Water polo would be easier if the pool were *shorter*.

think … opinion

Incorrect: I *think* our team, in my *opinion*, has a great chance to go all the way.

Correct: I *think* our team has a great chance to go all the way.

two twins

Incorrect: Surprisingly, the *two twins* have very different playing styles.

Correct: Surprisingly, the *twins* have very different playing styles.

unexpected surprise

Incorrect: It was an *unexpected surprise* to win so easily.

Correct: It was a *surprise* to win so easily.

usual habit/usual custom

Incorrect: It is our *usual custom* to eat at Bob's after a game.

Correct: It is our *custom* to eat at Bob's after a game.

year … 1972

Incorrect: The last time our school won a championship in water polo was in the *year 1972*.

Correct: The last time our school won a championship in water polo was in *1972*.

REDUNDANCIES FOR TWO THINGS

Another form of redundancy occurs when two things are referred to more than once. Watch out for words like: *both*, *too*, *also*, *in addition*, *furthermore*, and *besides*. These errors are best explained with examples:

Incorrect: *Both* hockey *as well as* basketball share aspects of water polo.

Correct: *Both* hockey and basketball share aspects of water polo.

Incorrect: In *addition* to water polo, our school is *also* very good at swimming.

Correct: In *addition* to water polo, our school is very good at swimming.

Incorrect: He is a strong swimmer. *Furthermore*, he is a smart player, *too*.

Correct: He is a strong swimmer. *Furthermore*, he is a smart player.

———

The following Redundancies quiz is found in the Grammar Quizzes section at the end of this chapter. It will be assigned by your tutor. If you are working on your own, take the quiz after you have reviewed this section. If you struggle on the quiz, you should probably review the material further.

 ☐   Redundancies Quiz

20. AMBIGUITIES

We've already discussed how pronouns can be used ambiguously, but sometimes ambiguities can occur simply because of the order of words in the sentence. For example:

There was a scratch on the new wood table right in the center.

This sentence literally suggests that the wood table is "in the center." Likely, this is not the intended meaning. Move the related words together in the sentence to remove the ambiguity, as in the corrected version below:

There was a scratch *right in the center* of the new wood table.

Here is another example:

The ice cream competition will be the largest ever with ice-cream samples from over 100 contestants kept in a large freezer.

Our hearts go out to those poor contestants in the freezer. The following sentences remove the ambiguity:

The ice cream competition will be the largest ever with over 100 contestants. The ice-cream samples will be kept in a large freezer.

LESSON PROBLEMS

Rewrite the following sentences to remove any ambiguities:

1. You can use this phone card to call your sister and tell her about the fine dinner you had for less than a dollar.

_____

_____

2. Corporations are more likely to hire college graduates with advanced degrees than smaller companies.

    _____

    _____

HW

1. The writer discussed the negative impact of graffiti in the last chapter of his book.

    _____

    _____

2. The new amendment to the state's constitution, which has come under fire recently, may be repealed in the election.

    _____

    _____

3. The new navigation system will speak directions to the driver when pressing a button on the steering wheel.

    _____

    _____

21. GRAMMAR QUIZZES

The following quizzes test all of the grammar topics. **Do not look back to the tutorial while taking these quizzes.** Answers to all quizzes start on page 191.

Grammar quizzes:

- GRAMMAR QUIZ 1 (SECTIONS 1-7)
- GRAMMAR QUIZ 2 (SECTIONS 8-16)
- GRAMMAR QUIZ 3 (ALL SECTIONS, INCLUDING 40-HOUR TOPICS)
- GRAMMAR QUIZ 4 (ALL SECTIONS, INCLUDING 40-HOUR TOPICS)

Grammar quizzes on 40-hour topics:

- IRREGULAR VERB TENSE QUIZ 1 (A-U & NO CHANGE)
- IRREGULAR VERB TENSE QUIZ 2 (-EN AND OTHER)
- IDIOM QUIZ 1 (PREPOSITIONS)
- IDIOM QUIZ 2 (COMMON MISTAKES)
- REDUNDANCIES QUIZ

GRAMMAR QUIZ 1 (SECTIONS 1-7)

Underline and correct any errors in each sentence. Add or delete words if necessary:

1. Played in a 1989 chess tournament in Belgrade, the longest game in history ends in a 269-move draw.

   _____

2. Before I won first place at the Halloween contest yesterday, I worked for hours on my costume.

   _____

3. He reads actively, but when he has to talk in front of a group he spoke like someone unfamiliar with the standard rules of grammar.

   _____

4. Everyone on the bus, even the shy and uncomfortable freshmen, were laughing and singing all the way to the museum.

   _____

5. We wanted to give the package to she and Marcus, but they had already left town.

   _____

6. The country was largely ignored until they decided to build long-range weapons.

   _____

7. The new gasoline-powered blowers have no smog-reducing equipment or mufflers, and it leads to unhealthy air and angry residents in the once peaceful community.

   _____

8. To enjoy time with family and friends is more important than working all day and night.

   _____

9. He was not only kind to his own children but also showed kindness to the children of others.

   _____

10. Apprentices at the computer factory must observe experienced experts for months before becoming an independent technician.

    _____

GRAMMAR QUIZ 2 (SECTIONS 8-16)

Underline and correct any errors in each sentence. Add or delete words or punctuation if necessary:

1. After training all summer, he is the stronger of all the linemen on our school's football team.

   _____

2. No game has rules as simple as the ancient Chinese game Go, which is played on a simple board of small squares and involves capturing your opponent's stones.

   _____

3. The weather is not only hot, as the thermometer indicates, and it's humid, as you can see from the perspiration on my shirt.

   _____

4. Now that you understand the basics of electricity, particularly the dangers involved when you are working with bare wires, and you will take precautions so as not to hurt yourself.

   _____

5. The storm hit last night and the electricity was out for over eight hours.

   _____

6. Places to shop, eat, and socialize, people flock to malls for a variety of reasons.

   _____

7. Considered an expert in her field, the doctor's research papers were widely read and studied.

   _____

8. Slow, like thick molasses, the mud slid down the side of the hill and threatened the village.

   _____

9. I almost fell asleep as the raft floated lazy in the still waters.

   _____

10. Since surfing involves riding a thin board on sometimes violent and unpredictable waves, balance is more important than many other sports.

   _____

GRAMMAR QUIZ 3 (ALL SECTIONS)

Underline and correct any errors in each sentence. Add or delete words or punctuation if necessary:

1. Because he hits so many game winning shots, he was considered last season's best closer.

   _____

2. The investor bought stock and then had shrewdly sold it before the market collapsed.

   _____

3. The number of times that I have had to reprimand my employees for wasting time playing on their computers are approaching the hundreds.

   _____

4. Each of the three witnesses were wary of testifying against the frightening gang leader.

   _____

5. Those citizens which refuse to vote should be the last to complain about the government.

   _____

6. The new gardener is better than him at keeping the grass green.

   _____

7. Everybody who went to the game came away knowing they had just witnessed history.

   _____

8. Elephants, a surprisingly fast creature, have been known to run forty miles per hour.

   _____

9. Martin and Sid have similar running styles, but Sid is definitely the fastest of the two.

   _____

10. She could not scarcely conceal her excitement after the promotion.

    _____

11. He thought the math class would be easy, then his class started working on limits.

Quiz continued on next page →

   _____

12. After getting into the college of her choice, studying for finals was a chore for Vivian.

_____

(30) 13. There are less people on the beach each year because of the erosion caused by the high surf.

_____

(40)

14. Ted was surprised by how badly he wanted to publish another book after tasting success with his first one.

_____

15. It is the usual custom at our family gatherings to toss the ball around a little after dinner, even though we are usually too full to run.

_____

16. As a reader, she has an ability for making even the most mundane prose come alive.

_____

17. I understood the material when I read the math book but was confused by my teacher's lengthy and boring lectures.

_____

18. Because she was having such a great time, the little girl was opposed of leaving the theme park early.

_____

19. To ensure that the piece will fit, please try and hold the wood still while I'm sawing.

_____

20. He is a man who has always relied on instincts when playing the game, but if he intends to coach, he'll have to understand the methods behind his greatness.

_____

GRAMMAR QUIZ 4 (ALL SECTIONS)

Underline and correct any errors in each sentence. Add or delete words or punctuation if necessary:

1. The craftsman is working on the desk since early this morning but isn't close to done.

   _____

2. The knight was satisfied after he had slew the supposedly indomitable dragon.

   _____

3. The fireman or the policeman are often great role models for young people.

   _____

4. Have you seen the book which I had left on the table before the house was cleaned?

   _____

5. I have started exercising regularly because of all the warnings they continue to publish in health journals and magazines about obesity.

   _____

6. After graduating from design school and by observing the strengths and weaknesses of popular ads in magazines, Amy became an amazing graphic designer.

   _____

7. Last year's company party, which was catered by the best cook in town, was much better than this year, when the boss's mom made casseroles and lentil soup.

   _____

8. He is ambivalent about his favorite team going to the finals, both happy about the chance to win it all but sad about the fact that he can't afford tickets.

   _____

9. The old man treasured a life of freedom and travel, he walked from one coast to the other accompanied only by his trusty walking stick.

   _____

10. Despite their apparent intelligence, dogs' ability to reason pales in comparison to that of primates or humans.

   _____

Quiz continued on next page →

(30) 11. The amount of gifts I had to buy this year has taken away any holiday cheer I once had.

_____

(40)

12. The class was annoyed about the way the teacher kept putting questions on the tests that were not part of the homework assignment.

_____

13. When the thermometer hit zero degrees, I was literally trembling from cold.

_____

14. I was accepted to Harvard, Yale, and Stanford, and because I wanted to stay in California, I chose the latter.

_____

15. Being that you are the tallest guy on the team, don't be surprised if you have to play center.

_____

16. The members of the home team and the visiting team alike are in favor of postponing the game until after the thunderstorm passes.

_____

17. She was suppose to follow the instructions to the letter, so it's not surprising that the couch she had assembled collapsed when she sat down.

_____

18. It is important to plan ahead for the future and start depositing money into a savings account.

_____

19. Modern lizards are smaller in size and certainly more docile than their distant cousins, the dinosaurs.

_____

20. The meeting will introduce the new president, a grandson of the founder, who knows everything there is to know about the business.

_____

(40) IRREGULAR VERB TENSE QUIZ 1 (A-U & NO CHANGE)

Underline and correct any errors in each sentence:

1. He had drunken the entire bottle of Coke before the movie was even half over.

   _____

2. The choir sung with such passion and conviction that one couldn't help clapping and singing along.

   _____

3. The lucky rabbit springed away from the hungry coyote.

   _____

4. It is no surprise you catch so many colds and missed so many days of school last semester.

   _____

5. The bandit, finally caught by the sheriff, was hanged as the sun went down.

   _____

6. The sun shined upon the tiny vessel as it sailed across the blue immensity.

   _____

7. He had spat out his gum before it lost all of its flavor.

   _____

8. The criminal fleed the scene shortly before the police arrived, but he left behind a surfeit of evidence.

   _____

9. The bee stang the farmer and flew away to apparent safety, unaware that bees die shortly after stinging a victim.

   _____

10. The phone had rang for several minutes before she woke up and answered it.

   _____

40) IRREGULAR VERB TENSE QUIZ 2 (-EN AND OTHER)

Underline and correct any errors in each sentence:

1. Elvin had beat the drum for hours before the head finally broke.

   _____

2. The spoiled girl had got every thing she ever asked for.

   _____

3. All his life he had froze his meats outside his igloo, unaware of the existence of electric freezers.

   _____

4. We had awoke in the middle of the night to the sound of thunder and flash of lightning.

   _____

5. After the rains, the river risen to its highest level since the ice age.

   _____

6. After seeing their performance, I think it is obvious that they have strived to become the best dancers in the country.

   _____

7. He took the old man's advice and trod lightly past the sleeping bear.

   _____

8. I have wrote all morning, and my hand is starting to cramp.

   _____

9. After spreading malicious rumors, your classmates have came to ask for your forgiveness.

   _____

10. In the mountains, I had woke before the sun rose and had been amazed at the silence.

   _____

Underline and correct any errors in each sentence:

1. After hours of heated arguing, the panel finally agreed about the plan for the new park.

    _____

2. The soldiers hid in the brush and aimed their guns against the oncoming enemy.

    _____

3. The committee argued on the benefits of increasing the number of trashcans at the park.

    _____

4. The politician benefited by a clever campaign that focused on his own strengths rather than his competitor's weaknesses.

    _____

5. You must conform with the master's strict rules if you expect him to teach you the art of the Samurai.

    _____

6. Many poor children in this country are deprived from a good high school education.

    _____

7. Notice how the amoeba reproduces by dividing in two parts.

    _____

8. The children were excited about their first visit to Disneyland.

    _____

9. You should get a flu shot to guard from catching the flu this winter.

    _____

10. The old woman lived at New Orleans in one of the oldest houses in America.

    _____

11. We were planning on attending the play, but our car got a flat tire on the way there.

    _____

12. To the relief of everyone, the researchers succeeded at finding a cure to the new disease.

    _____

IDIOM QUIZ 2 (COMMON MISTAKES)

Underline and correct any errors in each sentence:

1. Children lined the street for the parade that was supposed to start at around noon.

   _____

2. The reason for my late arrival is because the train was running behind schedule due to the demonstration downtown.

   _____

3. I couldn't help but notice the smell of cigarettes on your clothes when you returned from the library.

   _____

4. Since Josh studied hard, it's no surprise he graduated high school with an A+ average.

   _____

5. Winning the lottery is a matter of luck, irregardless of what the fortune teller may say.

   _____

6. I decided to bring my umbrella because the sky looked kind of dark and foreboding.

   _____

7. The grandfather clock was more for decoration and not really meant for time keeping.

   _____

8. You should not wear a jacket nor long pants on the raft because they will just get soaked.

   _____

9. Because the music gets plenty loud at the concert, make sure to bring ear plugs.

   _____

10. He proofread his resume several times, double checked his tie, and polished his shoes to a mirror so as to ensure the best possible chance of getting the coveted job.

    _____

(40) REDUNDANCIES QUIZ

Underline and correct any errors in each sentence:

1. The bus is late; it should have been here at seven a.m. this morning.

   _____

2. The biography of his life, which was published before he won the Nobel Prize, may have been written a few years too soon.

   _____

3. Hockey and Lacrosse are both alike in that they involve using sticks to get a small object into a net.

   _____

4. The first step in developing a successful management team is to begin cooperating together.

   _____

5. Each and every fan, all 52,000 of them, was given a set of trading cards at the game.

   _____

6. To increase business, the shoe salesmen decided to offer a free gift to anyone who bought two or more pairs of shoes.

   _____

7. The Laker great Kareem Abdul-Jabbar and the Bruin great Lew Alcindor are one in the same.

   _____

8. The period of time between the start of school and graduation seems interminable.

   _____

9. She has an unexpected surprise waiting for her when she gets home and finds that I have washed and waxed her car.

   _____

10. I am frightened by both horseback riding and also swimming, so it is no wonder why I don't like going to that camp every summer.

   _____

III
IMPROVING SENTENCES

Improving Sentences questions test your ability to recognize clear, effective, and grammatically correct sentences. At this point, you should feel fairly comfortable with the grammar rules of chapter II. There are only a few other guidelines with which you should become comfortable.

Make sure you are familiar with the directions, as found on the actual SAT (printed below). What the directions do not make clear (although it is perhaps obvious) is the fact that, while there may be mistakes in the *underlined* portion of the sentence, **any part of the sentence that is *not* underlined is considered correct**. You may have to use the correct part of the sentence to find the correct answer.

The following sentences test correctness and effectiveness of expression. Part of each sentence or the entire sentence is underlined; beneath each sentence are five ways of phrasing the underlined material. Choice A repeats the original phrasing; the other four choices are different. If you think the original phrasing produces a better sentence than any of the alternatives, select choice A; if not, select one of the other choices.

In making your selection, follow the requirements of standard written English; that is, pay attention to grammar, choice of words, sentence construction, and punctuation. Your selection should result in the most effective sentence—clear and precise, without awkwardness or ambiguity.

EXAMPLE:

Laura Ingalls Wilder published her first book <u>and she was sixty-five years old then</u>.

(A) and she was sixty-five years old then
(B) when she was sixty-five
(C) at age sixty-five years old
(D) upon the reaching of sixty-five years
(E) at the time when she was sixty-five

1. BE AGGRESSIVE

(!) **The first step in Improving Sentences questions is to aggressively look for grammar errors by carefully reading the sentence and thinking about the grammar rules from the previous chapter.** This is by far the most important aspect of these questions—now you see why we spent so much time on the grammar rules in chapter II. If your understanding of grammar is in tip-top shape, you will often be able to identify an obvious grammar error before you look at the answer choices. This will make it much easier for you to identify the correct answer or eliminate answers that do not successfully correct the error. You will often sense obvious awkwardness when you read the sentence, but if you can identify a specific error, you will be ahead of the game.

While all of the grammar rules in chapter II are fair game on Improving Sentences questions, the rules that focus on **sentence structure** are emphasized. These include:

- Parallelism
- Punctuation
- Conjunctions
- Fragments
- Run-ons
- Improper modifiers

Also showing up with regularity are:

- Ambiguous pronouns

Make sure you are very comfortable with these grammar rules. Review these topics in chapter II if necessary, and aggressively look for sentence structure and ambiguous pronoun errors on the Improving Sentences questions. Answers are on page 193.

Try to identify and correct errors in the underlined portions of the following examples:

1. The artist painted <u>landscapes and they express</u> the fragility and beauty of the land.

2. Alex captured an amazing number of different insects during his field study and <u>these he used in a presentation</u> for his school.

3. By creating freedom in phrasing and harmonic interpretation, <u>the standards of improvisation were raised by Brad</u> on his most recent recording.

_____

4. Many people who <u>start training to become a firefighter are surprised by</u> the physical and mental intensity of the training programs.

_____

5. Because the deadline was fast approaching, the reports were made too hastily, <u>without enough thought or research behind it.</u>

_____

2. LOOK AT EVERY ANSWER CHOICE

On Improving Sentences questions, you may identify a grammar error in the original sentence and then identify an answer choice that corrects the error, but don't stop there—**you should always look at *every answer choice*.** Often more than one of the answer choices corrects the error. Sometimes, new grammar errors are introduced in the answer choices, so simply correcting the original error, while extremely helpful in eliminating *some* of the answer choices, may not be enough. Hopefully, you will spot new grammar errors or use the other rules in this chapter to identify the correct answer.

A note about example problems: If you are working on your own, you will see an italicized solution following each example problem. For this and all future example problems in the Writing section, try to complete the problem *before* looking at the solution. You may want to cover the correct answer with a sheet of paper.

(EX) Eating right and getting enough sleep, perhaps as much as exercise and physical training, <u>help students to become a better athlete</u>.

    (A) help students to become a better athlete

    (B) are helpful to students who want to be a better athlete

    (C) helps students to become better athletes

    (D) are helpful to students in becoming a better athlete

    (E) help students to become better athletes

*You hopefully notice that the noun agreement grammar rule is broken: "a better athlete" does not agree in number with "students." Answer choices (A) and (B) don't correct the error, so eliminate them. You may be tempted to choose answer choice (C), the first answer that corrects the error, **but remember to check all the answer choices**. Answer choice (D) doesn't correct the original error, so eliminate it. Answer choice (E) corrects the error, so we're left with (C) and (E). Notice that a new grammar error has been introduced in (C): the subject "eating right and getting enough sleep," which is plural, does not agree with the verb "helps," which is singular. The correct answer is (E).*

    *(A) help students to become **a better athlete** − [noun agreement]*
    *(B) are helpful to students who want to be **a better athlete** − [noun agreement]*
    *(C) **helps** students to become better athletes − [subject-verb agreement]*
    *(D) are helpful to students in becoming **a better athlete** − [noun agreement]*
    (E) help students to become better athletes

3. ANSWER CHOICE (A)

The previous section said to read every answer choice, but remember that answer choice (A) is exactly the same as the underlined portion of the sentence, so don't waste any time reading it twice.

Answer choice (A) is the correct answer about as often as each of the other answer choices (about one-fifth of the time), so don't be afraid to select it. Students have a tendency to find an error in the sentence at all costs, but often the sentence is correct as written. If you are comfortable with the grammar rules from the previous chapter and can't identify an obvious error, the sentence may be correct, even if it sounds somewhat awkward. As you know, you should check every answer choice, so hopefully you can identify grammar errors in the other answer choices before choosing (A).

(EX) The idea that radio was as important a media as television prevailed during most of the twentieth century.

    (A) The idea that radio was as important a media as television prevailed during most of the twentieth century.

    (B) The idea that prevailed about radio during most of the twentieth century was that of being as important a media as television.

    (C) During most of the twentieth century, they had a prevalent idea that radio was as important a media as television.

    (D) Prevalent as an idea during most of the twentieth century was for radio to be as important a media as television.

    (E) Prevalent during most of the twentieth century, they thought that radio was as important a media as television.

Even though the sentence may sound somewhat awkward, it is grammatically correct. A quick read of the other answer choices reveals that none of them improve the sentence; in fact (C) and (E) have obvious grammar errors, and (B) and (D) have glaring awkwardness. The correct answer is (A).

    *(A) **The idea that radio was as important a media as television prevailed during most of the twentieth century.***
    (B) The idea that prevailed about radio during most of the twentieth century was that of being as important a media as television.
    *(C) During most of the twentieth century, **they** had a prevalent idea that radio was as important a media as television. − [ambiguous pronoun]*
    (D) Prevalent as an idea during most of the twentieth century was for radio to be as important a media as television.
    *(E) Prevalent during most of the twentieth century, **they** thought that radio was as important a media as television. − [ambiguous pronoun]*

4. BE CAREFUL OF -ING WORDS

(!) **Answer choices that use words in the *-ing* form are usually incorrect.** These *-ing* words often create fragments or other awkwardness. It is important to remember that, as taught in the Verb Tense lesson, a single word (on its own) in the *-ing* form does not function as an active verb:

> Fragment: John *running* to the store.
>
> Correct: John *runs* to the store.
>
> Correct: John *has been running* to the store.

Be especially wary of the words *being* and *having*, which show up in wrong answers with considerable frequency.

(EX) The professor argued that although many universities have excelled at training future scientists, <u>the failure is in their not educating</u> humanities majors in the methods of scientific thought.

  (A) the failure is in their not educating
  (B) the failure they have is in their not educating
  (C) they failed not to educate
  (D) they have failed to educate
  (E) having failed to educate

*As you go through the answer choices, answer choices (A), (B), and (E) can probably be eliminated because of the -ing words, so you're left with (C) and (D). You may recognize that answer choice (C) has a double negative ("failed not"). The correct answer must be **(D)**.*

> (A) the failure is in their not educat**ing** − [-ing]
> (B) the failure they have is in their not educat**ing** − [-ing]
> (C) they **failed not** to educate − [double negative]
> **(D) they have failed to educate**
> (E) **having** failed to educate − [having creates a sentence fragment]

EXCEPTIONS

GRAMMATICALLY-CORRECT USES

The *-ing* form of a word is not *necessarily* incorrect, as we have seen in some of the previous grammar lessons. The College Board will sometimes intentionally use an *-ing* word in a correct answer choice just to make sure that you're not mindlessly avoiding all *-ing* words. Thus, **it is essential that you are able to recognize *-ing* words that *are* used correctly**. As covered in the grammar chapter, there are two common grammatically-correct uses of *-ing* words:

1. Recall that the *-ing* form of a verb can be used to express continuous action over a period of time, for example:

Bob *has been working* at the mini-mart since he was in high school.
Bob *is* certainly *gaining* the respect of his boss.

2. Modifying phrases often contain *-ing* words, as displayed in the punctuation section. For example:

Using both hands, Bob has become the fastest bagger in the store.
Having the most experience, Bob is certain to become the store manager before long.

PARALLELISM

If you have to maintain parallel construction with *-ing* words that are not underlined (which means they must be correct), then an *-ing* word will be part of the correct answer.

(EX) For many a great artist, <u>being free to innovate is more important</u> than being well paid.

    (A) being free to innovate is more important

    (B) having freedom of innovation is more important

    (C) there is more importance in the freedom to innovate

    (D) freedom to innovate has more importance

    (E) to have the freedom to innovate is more important

Notice that the word "being," usually a clear indicator of an incorrect answer, is found in a part of the sentence that is not underlined. The only answer choice that maintains a parallel construction is (A):

    ... ***being*** <u>*free to innovate is more important*</u> than ***being*** *well paid.*

        (A) being free to innovate is more important
        (B) having freedom of innovation is more important − [parallelism]
        (C) there is more importance in the freedom to innovate − [parallelism]
        (D) freedom to innovate has more importance − [parallelism]
        (E) to have the freedom to innovate is more important − [parallelism]

-ING IN EVERY ANSWER CHOICE

Another situation where an -*ing* answer is correct occurs when there are -*ing* words in every answer choice. Obviously, one of them must be correct. You should still probably avoid answer choices that have more -*ing* words than the others or ones that contain *being* or *having*.

(EX) No two of the papers <u>were sufficiently alike to warrant them being given</u> the same grade.

    (A) were sufficiently alike to warrant them being given

    (B) were sufficiently alike in warranting the giving of them

    (C) were sufficiently alike to warrant their being given

    (D) were sufficiently alike to warrant the giving of them

    (E) were sufficiently alike to warrant giving them

*Notice that every answer choice includes an -ing word. Eliminate (A) because of the word "being," (B) because there are two -ing words, and (C) because of the word "being." The correct answer is **(E)**, which is more succinct than (D).*

    *(A) were sufficiently alike to warrant them **being** given − [being]*
    *(B) were sufficiently alike in warrant**ing** the giv**ing** of them − [two -ing words]*
    *(C) were sufficiently alike to warrant their **being** given− [being]*
    (D) were sufficiently alike to warrant the giving of them
    (E) were sufficiently alike to warrant giving them

In summary, answer choices with -*ing* words are usually incorrect, but, as illustrated, there are exceptions. Just make sure that you are very careful if you pick an answer choice containing an -*ing* word.

5. AVOID WORDY ANSWERS

As you will learn in the essay part of this tutorial, good writing is usually as concise and clear as possible, with no needless words. Besides being grammatically correct, the correct answers on the Improving Sentences section are usually the clearest and often the shortest of the answer choices.

(!) In fact, **roughly half of the correct answers on the Improving Sentences sections of the SAT are the shortest answer choices available**.

(EX) <u>The company, once close to laying off all of its workers, is</u> now a successful and competitive enterprise.

    (A) The company, once close to laying off all of its workers, is

    (B) The company was once close to laying off all of its workers, it is

    (C) The company that once having been close to laying off all of its workers is

    (D) The company, because it was once close to laying off all of its workers, is

    (E) The company was once close to laying off all of its workers, and it is

Answer choice (A) is the shortest answer choice. To check if it is correct, try eliminating other answer choices. Every answer choice has an -ing word, but we know we can't eliminate all of them. (B) is a run-on sentence because it lacks a conjunction. (C) can probably be eliminated because of the additional -ing word "having." (D) and (E) have illogical conjunctions ("because" and "and"). (A) is the correct answer.

> **(A)** **The company, once close to laying off all of its workers, is** − *[shortest]*
> ~~(B)~~ *The company was once close to laying off all of its workers, it is* − *[run-on]*
> ~~(C)~~ *The company that once* **having** *been close to laying off all of its workers is* − *[having]*
> ~~(D)~~ *The company,* **because** *it was once close to laying off all of its workers, is* − *[conjunctions (illogical conjunctions)]*
> ~~(E)~~ *The company was once close to laying off all of its workers,* **and** *it is* − *[conjunctions (illogical conjunctions)]*

Of course, you should use the rules of grammar to eliminate answer choices and identify correct

(!) answers, but be careful before choosing a long and perhaps wordy answer choice. Also, **if you find yourself in a guessing situation, guess the shortest answer choice**.

In the Eloquence section at the end of the Essay chapter, two important lessons discuss succinct writing, specifically and most importantly the elimination of prepositional phrases and avoiding *to be* verbs. See pages 156 and 159.

6. AVOID THE PASSIVE VOICE

The passive voice means that the performer of the action in the sentence is *not* the subject of the sentence. For example,

>   The books were carefully arranged on the shelf by Dan, a self-proclaimed neat-freak.

The subject of this sentence is *books*, but the books are obviously not performing the action of arranging—*Dan* is. This sentence is in the *passive voice*. To rewrite the sentence in the *active voice*, make *Dan* the subject of the sentence:

>   Dan, a self-proclaimed neat-freak, arranged the books on the shelf.

Look to eliminate answer choices in the passive voice in the following example:

(EX) <u>Dan arranged the books on the shelf, he</u> proceeded to proclaim himself a neat-freak.

    (A) Dan arranged the books on the shelf, he

    (B) The books, which were arranged on the shelf by Dan, who

    (C) The books were first arranged on the shelf by Dan, who then

    (D) After arranging the books on the shelf, Dan

    (E) Dan, having arranged the books on the shelf, he

*The original sentence (answer choice (A)) is a run-on, because it lacks a conjunction. Answer choices (B) and (C) should be eliminated because they are both in the passive voice. Answer choice (E) could probably be eliminated because of the word "having." It is also a run-on (two subjects). The correct answer is **(D)**. Dan is the subject of the sentence and performs the action in the sentence; he "proceeded to proclaim himself a neat-freak."*

>   *(A) Dan arranged the books on the shelf, he − [run-on]*
>   *(B) The books, which were arranged on the shelf by Dan, who − [passive. (also a fragment)]*
>   *(C) The books were first arranged on the shelf by Dan, who then − [passive]*
>   **(D) After arranging the books on the shelf, Dan**
>   *(E) Dan, **having** arranged the books on the shelf, he − [-ing (having)/run-on]*

Note: If you ever have to make a choice between avoiding an improper modifier and avoiding the passive voice, avoid the improper modifier. The following sentence is correct, even though it is in the passive voice:

>   Organized alphabetically by authors' last names, the books were arranged on the shelf by Dan.

7. AVOID UNCOMMON CONJUNCTIONS

Recall that a conjunction links parts of a sentence together. On the SAT, a conjunction will usually be the most common—and often the shortest—appropriate choice available. For example:

Inasmuch as the rain would not let up, we decided to take a cab.

"Inasmuch as" is a relatively uncommon conjunction phrase. The writers of the SAT would much prefer a more common conjunction, such as "because":

Because the rain would not let up, we decided to take a cab.

The following list shows some of the less common conjunctions and conjunction phrases. These will usually not be part of a correct answer. Possible alternate (and more common) conjunctions are shown:

Cause and Effect Conjunctions	Contrast Conjunctions
being that → since or because	notwithstanding → despite
for the reason that → since or because	whereas → although or while
inasmuch as → since or because	even though → although or while
insofar as → since or because	in spite of → despite
the fact that → since or because	
the fact being that → since or because	
by reason of → because of	
in view of → because of	
on account of → because of	
through → because of	
in order that → so that	
whereby (avoid it)	

Watch out for uncommon conjunctions in the following example:

(EX) In spite of a brilliant defense team for the accused, he was found guilty.

    (A) In spite of a brilliant defense team for the accused

    (B) Inasmuch as a brilliant defense team could help the accused

    (C) Whereas the accused had a brilliant defense team

    (D) Although the accused, having a brilliant defense team

    (E) Although the accused had a brilliant defense team

In the original sentence (answer choice (A)), the words "In spite of" function as a conjunction, but the more common (and shorter) choice would be "despite." You might not eliminate (A) at this point, but definitely look for a better answer. Answer choices (B) and (C) should be eliminated because they both contain uncommon conjunctions: "Inasmuch" and "Whereas," respectively. Answer choice (D) could probably be eliminated because of the word "having." It is also a fragment of sorts because the dependent clause, "Although the accused...," is lacking a verb. The best answer is (E).

    *(A) **In spite of** a brilliant defense team for the accused – ["In spite of" is less common than "despite" or "although."]*

    *(B) **Inasmuch** as a brilliant defense team could help the accused – [uncommon conjunction]*

    *(C) **Whereas** the accused had a brilliant defense team – [uncommon conjunction]*

    *(D) Although the accused, **having** a brilliant defense team – [-ing (having) / fragment]*

    *(E) **Although the accused had a brilliant defense team***

8. IMPROVING SENTENCES SUMMARY

As stated before, your knowledge of the grammar rules from chapter II is the most important aspect of the Improving Sentences section. If you remember the additional guidelines below, you should be comfortable with these questions.

- Be aggressive
- Look at every answer choice
- Don't read answer choice (A)
- Don't be afraid to select answer choice (A)
- Be careful of answer choices containing *-ing* words
- Avoid wordy (long) answer choices
- Avoid the passive voice
- Avoid uncommon conjunctions

MOST COMMON GRAMMAR ERRORS:

- Parallelism
- Punctuation
- Conjunctions
- Fragments
- Run-ons
- Improper modifiers
- Ambiguous pronouns

9. IMPROVING SENTENCES PROBLEMS

PRACTICE PROBLEMS

The following assignments are from *The Official SAT Study Guide** by the College Board (2nd Edition). Do not time yourself on these problems and look back to the KlassTutoring tutorial as you learn and master the techniques. You are encouraged to review the techniques of the Improving Sentences chapter (summarized on the previous page) and the grammar topics before and during the completion of these problems. If you do not identify the correct answer, either eliminate at least two answer choices and guess or leave the problem blank.

- ☐ Test 1, Section 6 (1-11) and Section 10 (1-14)
- ☐ Test 2, Section 6 (1-11) and Section 10 (1-14)
- ☐ Test 3, Section 6 (1-11) and Section 10 (1-14)
- ☐ Test 4, Section 7 (1-11) and Section 10 (1-14)

TEST CORRECTIONS

After each practice test is graded, you should correct Improving Sentences problems that you missed or left blank. (The practice tests are found in *The Official SAT Study Guide*.) Go back to the tutorial and review the techniques as you correct the problems. The idea is to: (1) identify techniques that have given you trouble, (2) go back to the tutorial so you can review and strengthen these techniques, and (3) apply these techniques to the specific problems on which you struggled.

- ☐ Test 5, Section 6 (1-11) and Section 10 (1-14)
- ☐ Test 6, Section 6 (1-11) and Section 10 (1-14)
- ☐ Test 7: Section 4 (1-11) and Section 10 (1-14)
- ☐ Test 8: Section 4 (1-11) and Section 10 (1-14)
- ☐ Test 9: Section 3 (1-11) and Section 10 (1-14)
- ☐ Test 10: Section 3 (1-11) and Section 10 (1-14)

*SAT is a registered trademark of the College Board, which was not involved in the production of and does not endorse this book.

Reminder: If you are working on your own in the 30 or 40-hour program, now is a good time to take your second practice test. After you grade your test, make sure you go back and correct it as you complete the chapters in the tutorial.

☐   Take Test 6 (Writing sections only) in the College Board book. Review Taking Practice Tests in the Introduction.

IDENTIFYING SENTENCE ERRORS

Identifying Sentence Errors questions ask you to identify grammar errors in sentences (as the name implies). Your knowledge of the grammar rules of chapter II is the key to this chapter, even more so than with the Improving Sentences questions.

Make sure you are familiar with the directions, as found on the actual SAT:

> The following sentences test your ability to recognize grammar and usage errors. Each sentence contains either a single error or no error at all. No sentence contains more than one error. The error, if there is one, is underlined and lettered. If the sentence contains an error, select the one underlined part that must be changed to make the sentence correct. If the sentence is correct, select choice E. In choosing answers, follow the requirements of standard written English.
>
> **EXAMPLE:**
>
> <u>The other</u> delegates and <u>him immediately</u>
>   A   B   C
> accepted the resolution <u>drafted by</u> the
>   D
> neutral states. <u>No Error</u>
>   E

Once again, the directions do not make clear the important fact that **any part of the sentence that is *not* underlined is considered correct**. As with the Improving Sentences questions, you may have to use the correct part of the sentence to find the correct answer.

1. LOOK FOR COMMON GRAMMAR ERRORS

Unlike the Improving Sentences questions, Identifying Sentence Errors questions do not focus on sentence structure errors. Once again, all of the grammar rules are commonly tested on these questions, but the following rules show up the most frequently:

- Verb tense
- Subject-verb agreement
- Pronoun case
- Pronoun agreement

LOOK AT EVERY UNDERLINED VERB AND PRONOUN

Make sure you are very comfortable with these grammar rules. Review these topics in chapter II if necessary.

On Identifying Sentence Errors questions, make sure to look carefully at every underlined verb. Check its tense and make sure it agrees with its subject.

Also, look carefully at every underlined pronoun. Make sure it is in the correct case (subject or object) and agrees with the noun it is referring to.

CORRECT THE SENTENCE

If you are comfortable with the grammar rules, you should be able to not only *identify* the grammar errors but also *correct* them. This is a great way to make sure that you are not selecting answer choices that are actually grammatically correct. **If you can *not* correct an answer choice, there is a good chance that the answer choice is OK.** Try the following examples and write your corrections for your selected answer choices. Answers are on page 193.

For each question, circle your answer and write your correction on the line provided:

1. The white leopards <u>drew</u> huge crowds
A

at the zoo, <u>for</u> <u>it</u> had <u>never been seen</u>
B CD

anywhere outside of the Tibet region

of Asia before. <u>No error</u>
E

_____

2. Aerospace engineers were employed <u>to perform</u>
A

one small part of one process in one department,

and so <u>having</u> no sense <u>of</u> the process <u>as a whole</u>.
BCD

<u>No error</u>
E

_____

3. Many historians <u>have written</u> about America's
A

involvement in the Vietnam war, but <u>never before</u>
B

<u>has</u> the contributions of American soldiers, both
C

positive and negative, been <u>so completely</u> analyzed.
D

<u>No error</u>
E

_____

4. There has always been a <u>great deal of</u> tension
A

between <u>Jill and I</u> <u>because we</u> have opposing political
BC

views <u>about which</u> we are very passionate. <u>No error</u>
DE

_____

5. None of the candidates <u>are suited</u> <u>to lead</u>
AB

a democracy or deal with the pressures involved

<u>with</u> the <u>day to day</u> management of a nation.
CD

<u>No error</u>
E

_____

Remember to look at all underlined verbs and pronouns, and make sure you can correct an answer choice before you select it.

2. ANSWER CHOICE (E)

Just as with the Improving Sentences section, the sentence is sometimes correct as written. **Answer choice (E), the *No Error* answer, is the correct answer about as often as each of the other answer choices (about one-fifth of the time), so don't be afraid to select it.** If you are comfortable with the grammar rules from the grammar chapter and can't identify an obvious error, the sentence may be correct, even if it sounds somewhat awkward.

(EX) A possible first step <u>in developing</u> a simple
                             A

    vocabulary <u>with which</u> to discuss the writings <u>of</u> the
                  B   C

    brilliant physicist Stephen Hawking would

    be <u>to cease</u> using terms found only in physics
          D

    books. <u>No Error</u>.
            E

This may sound like an awkward sentence. Think about the grammar rules of chapter II. Can you put your finger on any obvious grammar errors?

LOOK AT THE BARE BONES SENTENCE

A good first step is to find the subject and verb of the sentence's independent clause. As discussed in the Subject-Verb Agreement section, get rid of prepositional and modifying phrases and **look at the bare bones sentence**:

    A possible first step ~~in developing a simple~~
                            A

    ~~vocabulary with which to discuss the writings~~ ~~of~~ the
                  B   C

    ~~brilliant physicist Stephen Hawking~~ would

    be <u>to cease</u> using terms found only in physics
          D

    books. <u>No Error</u>.
            E

The bare-bones sentence reveals agreement between the subject "step" and the verb "would be."

    A possible first *step would be…*

ELIMINATE ANSWER CHOICES YOU KNOW ARE OK

Now look back to the original sentence. There is clearly nothing wrong with answer choice (C) (*of*), so eliminate it.

THE WORD *WHICH* IS OFTEN OK

As discussed in the *pronoun case* section, there is nothing inherently wrong with the word *which* (even though many students indiscriminately mark it as incorrect). Answer choice (B) is grammatically correct.

-ING WORDS ARE NOT NECESSARILY WRONG

By now, you may be wary of all *-ing* words, but **-ing words in the Identifying Sentence Errors questions are not incorrect as often as they are in the Improving Sentences questions**. You should still look at them carefully, but don't assume that they are automatically wrong. In this question, the alternative to *in developing* (answer choice (A)) would be *to develop*. This doesn't sound any better than the original form:

> A possible first step *to develop* a vocabulary … would be to cease using terms found only in physics books.

DIFFICULT VOCABULARY IS NOT NECESSARILY WRONG

You may not be comfortable with the word *cease*, but you should not assume that (D) is the correct answer. The Writing section tests *grammar*, not word choices or difficult vocabulary; in fact, **answer choices with difficult words are often traps and should be avoided**. The words *to cease* are parallel to the words *to discuss*, which are not underlined and are therefore correct. *To cease* means *to stop*, and this makes perfect sense in the sentence.

There are no errors in the sentence. The correct answer is **(E)**.

A possible first step <u>in developing</u> a simple
                A

vocabulary <u>with which</u> to discuss the writings <u>of</u> the
          B   C

brilliant physicist Stephen Hawking would

be <u>to cease</u> using terms found only in physics
    D

books. <u>No Error</u>.
      E

3. IDIOM ERRORS

The most difficult questions on the Identifying Sentence Errors section test *idiom*. Idiom has to do with the manner or style of language. The rules for idiom are less predictable and consistent than most of the other grammar rules in this tutorial. The good news is that many of the idiom errors will simply sound wrong to your ear. If something sounds awkward, but you can't put your finger on exactly *why* it's awkward, it may be an idiom error. However, as stated before, the College Board makes things difficult because many of the awkward-sounding sentences have no errors (the answer is (E)). The following approach will hopefully help.

FIRST TIME THROUGH

While working through an Identifying Sentence Errors section, you will likely come across sentences that you suspect contain idiom errors. Put marks next to these sentences and leave them blank for now. (Don't forget to leave the relative numbers blank on your answer sheet.) Answer the other questions, including ones where you are fairly certain that the answer is (E).

GO BACK

(!) **Usually, each Identifying Sentence Errors section has <u>2 or 3</u> questions containing idiom errors and <u>3 to 5</u> questions that have no errors (E).**

When you go back to the questions that you left blank, expect two or three of them to be idiom errors—probably the questions that sound the most awkward to your ear. The other questions that you left blank likely have no errors—pick (E). However, if you end up with more than five (E)'s, you're probably missing some other, more-obvious grammar errors.

To summarize, when you finish an Identifying Sentence Errors section and before you move on to the next section, make sure you consider the number of idiom errors and (E)'s that you have chosen. Again, expect 2 or 3 idiom errors and 3 to 5 (E)'s per section.

GRAMMAR RULES VERSUS YOUR EAR

Using the approach above only works when you have identified most—if not all—of the more common grammar errors found in each section. Obviously, if you incorrectly mark (E) a number of times or have to leave many questions blank, your count will be inaccurate. You may be missing more-obvious grammar errors. While it is not necessarily a bad idea to trust your ear, if you are relying on your ear too often, your knowledge of the grammar rules from chapter II may be weak and should be reviewed.

4. IDENTIFYING SENTENCE ERRORS SUMMARY

As you can see, there's not much to these questions. As stated before, your knowledge of the grammar rules from chapter II is the most important aspect of the Identifying Sentence Errors section. Keep in mind the additional rules below:

- Look carefully at underlined verbs
- Look carefully at underlined pronouns
- Correct the sentence
- Don't be afraid to select answer choice (E) (No Error)
- Eliminate answer choices that you know are OK
- The word *which* is often OK
- *-ING* words are not necessarily wrong
- Difficult vocabulary is not necessarily wrong
- Watch out for idiom errors

MOST COMMON GRAMMAR ERRORS:

- Verb tense
- Subject-verb agreement
- Pronoun case
- Pronoun agreement

5. IDENTIFYING SENTENCE ERRORS PROBLEMS

PRACTICE PROBLEMS

The following assignments are from *The Official SAT Study Guide** by the College Board (2nd Edition). Do not time yourself on these problems and look back to the KlassTutoring tutorial as you learn and master the techniques. You are encouraged to review the techniques of the Identifying Sentence Errors chapter (summarized on the previous page) and the grammar topics before and during the completion of these problems. **In addition to identifying the errors, for practice, try to correct any errors in the sentences.** If you do not identify the correct answer, either eliminate at least two answer choices and guess or leave the problem blank.

- ☐ Test 1, Section 6 (12-29)
- ☐ Test 2, Section 6 (12-29)
- ☐ Test 3, Section 6 (12-29)
- ☐ Test 4, Section 7 (12-29)

TEST CORRECTIONS

After each practice test is graded, you should correct Identifying Sentence Errors problems that you missed or left blank. (The practice tests are found in *The Official SAT Study Guide*.) Go back to the tutorial and review the techniques as you correct the problems. The idea is to: (1) identify techniques that have given you trouble, (2) go back to the tutorial so you can review and strengthen these techniques, and (3) apply these techniques to the specific problems on which you struggled.

- ☐ Test 5, Section 6 (12-29)
- ☐ Test 6, Section 6 (12-29)
- ☐ Test 7: Section 4 (12-29)
- ☐ Test 8: Section 4 (12-29)
- ☐ Test 9: Section 3 (12-29)
- ☐ Test 10: Section 3 (12-29)

*SAT is a registered trademark of the College Board, which was not involved in the production of and does not endorse this book.

Now is a good time to review all topics from the Grammar chapter. The following quiz on these sections is found in the Grammar Quizzes section at the end of the Grammar chapter. It will be assigned by your tutor. If you are working on your own, take the quiz after you have reviewed the Grammar topics. If you struggle on the quiz, you should probably review the material further.

☐   Grammar Quiz 3 (All Sections)

V

IMPROVING PARAGRAPHS

Improving Paragraphs questions ask you to revise the first draft of a short passage. You will have to combine sentences and alter structures within sentences to improve the paragraphs.

Make sure you are familiar with the directions, as found on the actual SAT:

Directions: The following passage is an early draft of an essay. Some parts of the passage need to be rewritten.

Read the passage and select the best answers for the questions that follow. Some questions are about particular sentences or parts of sentences and ask you to improve sentence structure or word choice. Other questions ask you to consider organization and development. In choosing answers, follow the requirements of standard written English.

1. THE PASSAGE

Just as with the Reading questions (from the Critical Reading section), **the first step is to read the paragraphs and consider the main idea and tone of the passage.** Each passage is usually fairly simple, so it should be relatively easy to get a feel for its main idea and tone. **Remember, do *not* read the questions first**; they will only distract you from getting the main idea of the passage.

Read the following passage. It will be used to teach the techniques on the following pages:

(1) At one point in the movie *Raiders of the Lost Ark*, the evil archaeologist Bellocq shows the heroic Indiana Jones a cheap watch. (2) If the watch were to be buried in the desert for a thousand years and then dug up, Bellocq says, it would be considered priceless. (3) I often think of this scene whenever I consider the record album collection phenomenon, it being one of the more remarkable aspects of popular culture in the United States. (4) Collecting record albums gives us a chance to make a low-cost investment. (5) It just might pay dividends in the future.

(6) When my aunt collected them in the mid-sixties, nobody regarded them as investments. (7) A young fan shelled out dollar after dollar at the corner record store for no other reason than to assemble a complete collection of her favorite musical groups — in my aunt's case, the Beatles and the Supremes. (8) These were two of the most popular bands of the time. (9) By committing so much of her allowance each week to the relentless pursuit of that one group not yet in her collection — the immortal Yardbirds, let us say — she was proving her loyalty to her superstars.

(10) Just as everyone has heard of the exorbitant prices being paid for the Beatles' first album in mint condition, so everyone is certain that a payoff is among each stack of old records. (11) If that album was buried somewhere in my aunt's closet full of dusty records, my aunt will never know. (12) Long before she learned it, she had thrown them out.

2. GRAMMAR AND PAST TOPICS

GRAMMAR

Just as with Improving Sentences and Identifying Sentence Errors questions, knowledge of the grammar topics from chapter II of this tutorial is essential. The most common grammar errors on Improving Paragraphs questions are *fragments* and *run-ons*. *Ambiguous pronouns* also show up frequently. Make sure you are very comfortable with these grammar topics. Review them in chapter II if necessary.

PAST TOPICS

You will likely be able to use some of the techniques from the Improving Sentences chapter and the Reading chapter (from Critical Reading) on Improving Paragraphs questions:

BE CAREFUL OF ANSWER CHOICES CONTAINING -*ING* WORDS

As taught in the Improving Sentences chapter, answer choices that use words in the -*ing* form are usually incorrect. This is a great way to eliminate answer choices. Be especially wary of the words *being* and *having*.

AVOID WORDY (LONG) ANSWER CHOICES

Just as on Improving Sentences questions, be careful before choosing a long and perhaps wordy answer choice. Also, if you find yourself in a guessing situation, guess the shortest answer choice.

ANSWER QUESTIONS IN THE CONTEXT OF THE PASSAGE

As defined in the Critical Reading part of the tutorial,

> *context* means: the parts before or after a statement that can influence its meaning, or the circumstances that surround a particular situation.

You must answer questions *in the context of the paragraphs*, or *contextually*. This means you should always be aware of the sentences before and after the sentence in question.

ELIMINATE FALSE OR SENSELESS ANSWER CHOICES

This sounds obvious, but don't forget that you may be able to get rid of some answer choices that, after reading the paragraphs, you know to be false, or that simply don't make any sense in answering the question, even out of the context of the paragraphs.

On the SAT, the Improving Paragraphs questions are arranged based on the organization of the paragraphs. For our example paragraphs, however, the questions will be put in a logical order for teaching the techniques and topics of this chapter.

(EX) 1. In the context of the first paragraph, which revision is most needed in sentence 3?

    (A) Insert "As a matter of fact" at the beginning.
    (B) Omit the word "scene."
    (C) Omit the words "it being."
    (D) Change the comma to a semicolon.
    (E) Change "think" to "thought" and "consider" to "considered."

*Answer choice (A) may be hard to eliminate, so keep it for now. In answer choice (B), if the word "scene" is eliminated, "this" becomes an ambiguous pronoun. (C) is a contender, so keep it. In answer choice (D), changing the comma to a semicolon would create a fragment since the second part of the sentence is not an independent clause. Answer choice (E) changes the verb tense that has been established throughout this paragraph. Perhaps you noticed the awkward words "it being" while reading the sentence. Certainly, answer choice **(C)** is the most needed revision.*

    (A) Insert "As a matter of fact" at the beginning.
    (B) Omit the word "scene." – [ambiguous pronoun]
    (C) Omit the words "it being." – [–ing]
    (D) Change the comma to a semicolon. – [fragment]
    (E) Change "think" to "thought" and "consider" to "considered." – [tense]

(EX) 2. In context, which of the following is the best version of sentence 12 (reproduced below)?

Long before she learned it, she had thrown them out.

    (A) (As it is now)
    (B) Long before she learned that the records could be valuable, she had thrown them out.
    (C) Long before she has learned about the records, she throws them out.
    (D) It was long before she learned about the records that she threw them out.
    (E) She throws the records out long before she hears about them.

*The word "it" is an ambiguous pronoun, so you could eliminate answer choice (A). Since she threw the records out before she learned if they could be valuable, the tense of the verb **throw** must be past of the past, as in answer choice (B), so keep it. The previous sentence sets the verb tense as past, so you could eliminate answer choice (C) because it's in the present tense. (D) is not in the past of the past, so eliminate it. Answer choice (E), like (C), is in the present tense and can be eliminated. The correct answer is **(B)**.*

    (A) (As it is now) – [ambiguous pronoun]
    (B) Long before she learned that the records could be valuable, she had thrown them out. – notice the past of the past tense for "had thrown"
    *(C) Long before she **has learned** about the records, she **throws** them out. – [verb tense]*
    *(D) It was long before she learned about the records that she **threw** them out. – [verb tense]*
    *(E) She **throws** the records out long before she **hears** about them. – [verb tense]*

3. SENTENCES

Many of the Improving Paragraphs questions will deal with sentence revisions. You will usually not have to worry about main ideas of the paragraphs on these questions.

TRANSITIONS BETWEEN SENTENCES

You will often have to find sensible transitions between sentences. Make sure to answer these questions in context, as described before; carefully read the sentences in question, as well as perhaps the preceding sentence to get an idea of the intended flow of the sentences. The following words are examples of *contrast, support,* and *cause and effect* transitions:

CONTRAST TRANSITIONS

although	however	nevertheless	rather than
but	in contrast	on the contrary	still
despite	in spite of	on the other hand	yet
even though	instead of		

SUPPORT TRANSITIONS

additionally	Besides	likewise	(semicolon) ;
also	furthermore	moreover	(colon) :
and	in addition		

CAUSE AND EFFECT TRANSITIONS

accordingly	for	so...that	thus
because	hence	therefore	when...then
consequently	in order to		

(EX) 3. Which of the following is the best revision of the underlined portion of sentence 11 (reproduced below)?

If that album was buried somewhere in my aunt's closet full of dusty records, my aunt will never know.

    (A) And if that album was buried
    (B) Because that album was buried
    (C) That album was buried
    (D) Buried as the album was
    (E) But if that album was buried

Since the previous sentence discusses the "certain ... payoff" of old records, and sentence 11 mentions that the aunt did **not** receive this payoff, the sentence needs a **contrast** transition. Answer choice (A) has a **support** transition. Answer choice (B) may make sense in the context of the sentence, but it is not the best answer when considering the context of the essay (particularly the previous sentence). Answer choices (C) and (D) both lack sensible transitions. The correct answer is **(E)**.

(A)̶ And if that album was buried – [improper transition]
(B)̶ Because that album was buried– [improper transition]
(C)̶ That album was buried– [lacking a transition]
(D)̶ Buried as the album was– [lacking a transition]
(E) But if that album was buried

COMBINING SENTENCES

When you are asked to combine sentences, consider the transitions discussed above. Also, watch out for fragments and run-ons, which commonly show up on these questions. **You will usually *not* have to focus on the context of the paragraphs while tackling these questions; rather, focus on the context of the sentences you are combining.**

(EX) 4. What is the best version of the underlined portion of sentences 4 and 5 (reproduced below)?

Collecting record albums gives us a chance to make a low-cost <u>investment. It just might pay</u> dividends in the future.

(A) investment so it just might pay
(B) investment and it just might pay
(C) investment that might pay
(D) investment paying
(E) investment; consequently, it just might pay

Answer choice (A) has an illogical transition: "so." Technically, the investment is not causing the dividends. Rather, the second sentence is **describing** the "investment," so a cause and effect transition is inappropriate here. In addition, answer choice (A) is a run-on (no comma before the conjunction). Answer choice (B) is also a run-on. Answer choice (D) has an -ing word. Answer choice (E) also has an illogical (cause and effect) transitions: "consequently." The correct answer is **(C)**.

(A)̶ investment so it just might pay – [illogical transition and run-on]
(B)̶ investment and it just might pay – [run-on]
(C) investment that might pay
(D)̶ investment paying – [-ing]
(E)̶ investment; consequently, it just might pay– [illogical transition]

4. PARAGRAPHS

MAIN IDEAS OF PARAGRAPHS

Many questions require you to understand the *main idea* of a particular paragraph. Think about the main idea of each paragraph while reading the passage. The first and last sentences of a paragraph often help you identify its main idea, but remember that these paragraphs are in need of revision and may be lacking clear and effective topic sentences. Therefore, you will likely have to look at details within the paragraph as well.

It is a good idea to quickly jot down the main idea of each paragraph before answering Improving Paragraphs questions. Go back to the example paragraphs and briefly write down the main idea of each paragraph. See page 194 for possible answers.

¶ I: _____

_____

¶ II: _____

_____

¶ III: _____

_____

Paragraph main idea questions may ask you to:
- Add a topic sentence to the beginning of a paragraph.
- Add a logical concluding sentence to the end of a paragraph.
- Divide a paragraph with two main ideas into two separate paragraphs.
- Delete a sentence because it contains unrelated information.

For all of these question types, **always consider the main idea of the paragraph in question**.

(EX) 5. Which sentence should be deleted from the essay because it contains unrelated information?

    (A) Sentence 2
    (B) Sentence 3
    (C) Sentence 7
    (D) Sentence 8
    (E) Sentence 12

*Think about the main idea of each paragraph. Sentence 8, which points out the popularity of the Beatles and the Supremes, has little to do with the main idea of the second paragraph. **(D)** is the answers.*

(EX) 6. Which of the following is the best sentence to insert at the beginning of the third paragraph?

    (A) Finally, like the capitalist enterprise of recording, record collecting will be transformed.
    (B) It is said that the recording industry has been transformed into a capitalist enterprise, much like this hobby.
    (C) The recording industry is similar to record collecting.
    (D) My aunt may have lacked a capitalistic attitude, but she loved her music.
    (E) Like the recording industry itself, this hobby has become a capitalist enterprise.

*The main idea of the third paragraph is the reality of making money on old records. There is no mention of the **transformation** in (A) and (B). It may be helpful to know that the independent clause of a sentence is its most important part. Notice that the independent clauses of answer choices (B) and (C) focus on the **recording industry** (not **record collecting**), so they can be eliminated. Answer choice (D) discusses the main idea of the second paragraph, not the third one. The correct answer is **(E)**.*

    *(A) Finally, like the capitalist enterprise of recording, record collecting will be **transformed**.*
    *(B) It is said that the **recording industry** has been transformed into a capitalist enterprise, much like this hobby.*
    *(C) The **recording industry** is similar to record collecting.*
    *(D) My aunt may have lacked a capitalistic attitude, but she loved her music. − [main idea of **second** paragraph]*
    (E) Like the recording industry itself, this hobby has become a capitalist enterprise.

TRANSITIONS BETWEEN PARAGRAPHS

Paragraphs should logically flow together. Once you are familiar with the main ideas of the paragraphs, they may be effectively connected using the transitions in the previous section or other logical words.

(EX) 7. Which of the following sentences is best inserted at the beginning of the second paragraph, before sentence 6?

    (A) Not everyone, however, starts collecting records to make a profit.
    (B) It is obvious that these early investments pay off.
    (C) No two experiences are exactly alike when it comes to collecting records.
    (D) Allow me to tell you about my aunt's attempt to achieve wealth.
    (E) Many hobbies have advantages that are not readily apparent to you in the beginning.

*Since the first paragraph discusses making money on an investment and the second paragraph discusses another reason for buying records, there should be a contrast transition. Only answer choice (A) has one ("however"). Answer choices (B) and (C) have nothing to do with the main idea of the second paragraph. Answer choice (D) is simply false; the aunt was not trying to achieve wealth. While true and perhaps tempting, answer choice (E) lacks a contrast transition and really doesn't discuss the main idea of the paragraph. The answer is **(A)**.*

    ***(A) Not everyone, however, starts collecting records to make a profit.** – [contrast transition]*
    (B) It is obvious that these early investments pay off. – [main idea]
    (C) No two experiences are exactly alike when it comes to collecting records. – [main idea]
    (D) Allow me to tell you about my aunt's attempt to achieve wealth. – [false]
    (E) Many hobbies have advantages that are not readily apparent to you in the beginning. – [no contrast transition; wrong main idea]

5. MAIN IDEA OF THE PASSAGE

You should probably save these questions for last. Hopefully, after reading the paragraphs, thinking about the main idea of each paragraph, and answering the more specific questions, you will have a good feel for the main idea of the paragraphs as a whole. **Make sure your main idea is not too broad or too specific.** Again, looking at the main idea of each paragraph should help.

(EX) 8. Which of the following sentences best states the main idea of the passage?

(A) Sentence 1
(B) Sentence 2
(C) Sentence 3
(D) Sentences 4 and 5
(E) Sentences 6 and 7

The main idea of the paragraphs as a whole has to do with the possibility of making money by investing in records. Answer choice (A), which introduces the movie reference, has nothing to do with this main idea. Answer choice (B), which refers to the "watch," is too specific. Answer choice (C) says that record collecting is a "remarkable" aspect of "pop culture." This is too broad. Answer choice (E), which discusses the aunt's motives for record collecting, also has nothing to do with the main idea. Only answer choice (D) effectively states the main idea of the paragraphs.

(A) Sentence 1
(B) Sentence 2 – [too specific]
(C) Sentence 3 – [too broad]
(D) Sentences 4 and 5
(E) Sentences 6 and 7

6. IMPROVING PARAGRAPHS SUMMARY

The rules below, in combination with the grammar rules from chapter II, should help you on Improving Paragraphs questions.

GRAMMAR AND PAST TOPICS:

- Look out for fragments and run-ons
- Look out for ambiguous pronouns
- Be careful of answer choices containing -*ing* words
- Avoid wordy (long) answer choices
- Answer questions in the context of the passage
- Eliminate false or senseless answer choices

SENTENCES:

- Make sure transitions between sentences are logical
  - Contrast transitions
  - Support transitions
  - Cause and effect transitions
- Combining sentences
  - Watch out for fragments and run-ons
  - Focus on the context of the sentences to be combined

PARAGRAPHS:

- Always consider the *main idea* of the paragraph or paragraphs in question

MAIN IDEA OF THE PASSAGE:

- Consider the main idea of each paragraph
- Don't be too broad or too specific

7. IMPROVING PARAGRAPHS PROBLEMS

PRACTICE PROBLEMS

The following assignments are from *The Official SAT Study Guide** by the College Board (2nd Edition). Do not time yourself on these problems and look back to the KlassTutoring tutorial as you learn and master the techniques. You are encouraged to review the techniques of the Improving Paragraphs chapter (summarized on the previous page) and the grammar topics before and during the completion of these problems. If you do not identify the correct answer, either eliminate at least two answer choices and guess or leave the problem blank.

- ☐ Test 1, Section 6 (30-35)
- ☐ Test 2, Section 6 (30-35)
- ☐ Test 3, Section 6 (30-35)
- ☐ Test 4, Section 7 (30-35)

TEST CORRECTIONS

After each practice test is graded, you should correct Improving Paragraphs problems that you missed or left blank. (The practice tests are found in *The Official SAT Study Guide*.) Go back to the tutorial and review the techniques as you correct the problems. The idea is to: (1) identify techniques that have given you trouble, (2) go back to the tutorial so you can review and strengthen these techniques, and (3) apply these techniques to the specific problems on which you struggled.

- ☐ Test 5, Section 6 (30-35)
- ☐ Test 6, Section 6 (30-35)
- ☐ Test 7: Section 4 (30-35)
- ☐ Test 8: Section 4 (30-35)
- ☐ Test 9: Section 3 (30-35)
- ☐ Test 10: Section 3 (30-35)

*SAT is a registered trademark of the College Board, which was not involved in the production of and does not endorse this book.

Now is a good time to review all topics from the Grammar chapter. The following quiz on these sections is found in the Grammar Quizzes section at the end of the Grammar chapter. It will be assigned by your tutor. If you are working on your own, take the quiz after you have reviewed the grammar topics. If you struggle on the quiz, you should probably review the material further.

☐   Grammar Quiz 4 (All Sections)

VI
THE ESSAY

Make sure you are familiar with the instructions for writing the essay. The following instructions are for a sample essay:

ESSAY

Time − 25 minutes

The essay gives you an opportunity to show how effectively you can develop and express ideas. You should, therefore, take care to develop your point of view, present your ideas logically and clearly, and use language precisely.

Your essay must be written on the lines provided on your answer sheet − you will receive no other paper on which to write. You will have enough space if you write on every line, avoid wide margins, and keep your handwriting to a reasonable size. Remember that people who are not familiar with your handwriting will read what you write. Try to write or print so that what you are writing is legible to those readers.

You have twenty-five minutes to write an essay on the topic assigned below. DO NOT WRITE ON ANOTHER TOPIC. AN OFF-TOPIC ESSAY WILL RECEIVE A SCORE OF ZERO.

Think carefully about the issue presented in the following excerpt and the assignment below.

> Western civilization is largely based on a linear view of the world. It is exemplified by *Aristotle's Poetics*, in which a story is seen as something with a beginning, a middle, and an ending. Once the story has ended, it's over. However, there is evidence to suggest that the history of the world is in fact cyclical, like the four seasons of the annual calendar. In the annual calendar, the seasons never "end." Autumn is followed by winter, which is followed by spring, which is followed by summer, and then we're into autumn again, and so on.

Assignment: Is the history of the world cyclical? Plan and write an essay in which you develop your point of view on this issue. Support your position with reasoning and examples taken from your reading, studies, experience, or observations.

1. INTRODUCTION

The essay is written during a separate 25-minute section of the test. It will test your ability to understand and discuss some given topic, express your ideas and opinions in an effective and clear way, organize your thoughts according to a sensible plan, and write correctly and tastefully—following the rules of standard English.

LENGTH

There is no required length for the essay question. In general, *quality* is far more important than *quantity*. An essay written succinctly and to the point will always score better than a needlessly wordy one. However, it is unlikely that a single-paragraph essay will score well. **The essay should generally be between three and five paragraphs long.**

HANDWRITING

It is obviously important to write neatly and legibly. You cannot effectively convey your points and opinions if the reader is not able to understand what you have written. In addition, a neatly written essay may put the judges in a better frame of mind, perhaps gaining you a point or two.

SCORING

The essay is scored on a scale or 1 (worst) to 6 (best) by two graders, so your total score will be between 2 and 12 (assuming you write on the assigned topic). The following is an excerpt from the scoring guide given to the graders. The excerpt lays out the criteria for an excellent essay (score of 6). Focus on the items in bold.

SCORE OF 6
An essay in this category is *outstanding*, demonstrating *clear and consistent mastery*, although it may have a few minor errors. A typical essay

- effectively and insightfully **develops a point of view on the issue** and demonstrates outstanding critical thinking, using **clearly appropriate examples**, reasons, and other evidence to support its position
- is **well organized** and **clearly focused**, demonstrating clear coherence and smooth progression of ideas
- exhibits **skillful use of language**, using a varied, accurate, and apt vocabulary
- demonstrates meaningful **variety in sentence structure**
- is **free of most errors in grammar**, usage, and mechanics

2. PREWRITING

THE THREE STAGES

There are three basic stages in writing the essay. It is important to practice writing essays with these stages in mind so that when you take the actual test you will be comfortable and confident, both in terms of *what* you write and *how long* to take writing it.

1. Prewriting (3-5 minutes)
   - Reading and analyzing the topic
   - Deciding what your argument, or thesis will be
   - Preparing an outline
2. Writing the Essay (17-20 minutes)
   - Introduction
   - Body: supporting your thesis with examples and other evidence
   - Conclusion
3. Revising and Proofreading (2-3 minutes)
   - Checking for errors in grammar, spelling, etc.
   - Minor rearranging of ideas or sentences

The prewriting stage includes: understanding the topic, developing a thesis, thinking of specific examples to support your thesis, and creating a brief outline. **You have approximately 3 to 5 minutes to do this.**

THE TOPIC

The first step is to read and understand the given topic. The topic will be introduced with an *excerpt* in the form of a brief quotation or statement, followed by an *assignment*, which clearly summarizes the topic using a simple question. You should read the excerpt (you may get some ideas from it), but if you find it confusing focus on the question.

THE THESIS

Once you understand the given topic, it is time to take a position. **A *thesis* clearly defines your opinion on the topic, and it is what you must support and defend in the body of your essay.** You must take a position on the topic, even if you have no strong opinion about it or you aren't interested in it. While you may not care deeply about the topic, you must create the appearance to the reader that you do. You will not be graded down for having an unpopular or politically incorrect opinion; it is how you support your opinion that will be graded.

FOCUS THE THESIS

$\left(\,!\,\right)$ **You should strive to *focus* your thesis by *narrowing* your discussion of the topic.** Look at the following topic:

> Think carefully about the issue presented in the following excerpt and the assignment below.
>
> | |
> |---|
> | Western civilization is largely based on a linear view of the world. It is exemplified by *Aristotle's Poetics*, in which a story is seen as something with a beginning, a middle, and an ending. Once the story has ended, it's over. However, there is evidence to suggest that the history of the world is in fact cyclical, like the four seasons of the annual calendar. In the annual calendar, the seasons never "end." Autumn is followed by winter, which is followed by spring, which is followed by summer, and then we're into autumn again, and so on. |
>
> **Assignment:**   Is the history of the world cyclical? Plan and write an essay in which you develop your point of view on this issue. Support your position with reasoning and examples taken from your reading, studies, experience, or observations.

A general essay might take several varied examples to illustrate that history repeats. A more *focused* essay, in contrast, might look at a *specific* way in which history repeats, such as *one* of the following:

- Death leading to rebirth in nature
- Wars throughout history
- Team sports

It is usually advantageous to focus your essay, but be aware that when you use a more specific or narrow thesis, you will have less evidence and fewer examples available to support it. For example, it would be inappropriate to discuss *team sports* in an essay focusing on the reoccurrence of *wars between nations*. While most exceptional essays are based on an effectively focused thesis, if you feel as if you will run out of supporting evidence, keep your thesis broader. Many excellent essays have broad theses.

Write your thesis down and stick with it throughout the essay. Because of time constraints, you probably won't have time to change your thesis, even if you think of a better one. **It is important to always keep your thesis in mind while you write the essay. Let it guide you from your introduction to your last sentence, and eliminate any information that wanders from your main argument.**

SUPPORT FOR YOUR THESIS

A clear thesis is obviously only the beginning of creating an excellent essay. You must provide evidence to effectively and sensibly support your thesis. This should include examples, facts, ideas, or observations from any of the following:

- literature
- history
- science
- current events
- specific personal experiences
- anything else that effectively supports your thesis

You must strive to think of *specific* examples. Don't write about wars in general. Write about *World War II* or, perhaps, *D-day*. Don't write about a typical loving relationship. Write about *Romeo and Juliet*. Don't write about courage in general. Write about the courage of *Martin Luther King* or *the firemen at the World Trade Center*.

Literary and historical examples are probably the strongest examples, assuming they effectively and appropriately give support to your thesis. Personal examples are also very good; just remember to be specific. Examples relating to pop culture, such as television, movies, and music, are probably the least effective, but these are still better than using general explanations rather than specifics to support your thesis.

(40) EXAMPLE PREPARATION

To come up with sensible specific examples during the prewriting stage in less than five minutes is one of the most difficult aspects of writing the essay. It will be very helpful to perform some research in the areas above, particularly literature, history, and current events.

The topics of the essay are usually based on a broad idea or quality. Some examples include:

love	historical growth	money
hate	historical change	peace
personal growth	jealousy	courage
personal change	greed	etc...

Your job is to find literary, historical, or current examples that are related to broad ideas or qualities such as the ones listed above.

LITERATURE

Summarize *five* books that you have read. Select books with clear and universal themes. The books may or may not be considered classics, but they certainly should be highly regarded. Books read for your high school studies are usually fine. Include all of the following information in your summary:

- Author
- Protagonists (the good guys)
- Antagonists (the bad guys)
- Three universal themes within the book, with supporting evidence for each one
- One or two important specific events

You may choose to speak with your English teacher, visit a library, or search the Internet for assistance.

HISTORICAL EVENTS

Write about at least *five* important historical events that you have studied in school. Choose events that triggered or marked important changes in the world. You should generally include the following information:

- Approximate years
- Names of people associated with the event
- Names of places associated with the event
- Causes and effects of the event

HISTORICAL PEOPLE

Write about at least *five* important historical people that you have studied in school. Choose people that have exhibited some of the universal qualities described above, such as courage or greed. Include the following information:

- Several important specific events associated with the person
- Approximate years
- Results of these events
- Characteristic qualities associated with the person

CURRENT EVENTS

Keep track of current events that interest you. These can include topics ranging from wars and terrorism to business and technology. Remember to be specific. Newspapers and magazines are obviously great sources for current events. When you come across something in the news that interests you, write down the specific information that could be used in an essay. Remember to think about universal themes and broad effects of the events. Write about at least *five* current events.

THE OUTLINE

Before writing the essay, it is important to have a plan. Writing as ideas pop into your head is hardly a good way to create a well organized essay. Rather, take a few minutes to jot down your ideas in the form of an outline. Use the following steps:

1. **Brainstorm**: Write down your ideas in a simple outline with bullets (•) or dashes (−), but not numbers. (Use the space in your test booklet beneath the assignment.) You will not always construct the outline in the eventual order of the essay, and that's fine. The outline is a chance for you to brainstorm. Remember, no one but you will read the outline, so just jot down any ideas and examples you can think of and worry about organization later. Also, you don't have to use all of the ideas you think up in your essay; it is better to have too many ideas in the outline than not enough.

2. **Paragraphs**: Your essay will be divided into an introduction, a body of one or more paragraphs, and a conclusion. Look at the examples and ideas you have written, and think about possible main ideas for each paragraph, particularly the ones in the body of your essay.

3. **Organize**: Decide where your ideas and examples would fit best, and label each with a number corresponding to the appropriate paragraph. Label the first body paragraph as paragraph 1. A good rule of thumb is to have your most effective body paragraph last and your least effective body paragraph in the middle.

The following example-outline is based on the topic introduced earlier:

> Intro paragraph — Thesis: History repeats itself everywhere and in many different ways.
> paragraph 1 — Entropy: "big bang"
> paragraph 2 — Wars: Vietnam and Iraq. Trying (and failing) to spread democracy to strange foreign lands.
> paragraph 3? — Fashion: Retro styles. Bell bottoms...
> paragraph 3? — Business: stock market crash.

Notice that the writer decided to "focus" the essay by intentionally *not* focusing on one specific aspect of history repeating itself. His thesis is based on the omnipresent and inescapable nature of history's repetition. Also notice that the writer is not sure if he will have time for the topics in paragraph 3; he should be prepared to use the last two points as part of a concluding paragraph if time is running short (or not use them at all).

☐ Go to the essay topic of Test 1 in the College Board book. Read and analyze the topic, develop a thesis, and create a brief outline for an essay. Use the space at the bottom of the assignment page (as you will have to do on the real test). Remember, your goal is to accomplish these tasks in 3-5 minutes. You will eventually complete this essay for HW, so keep track of your time—you might want to make a note of the time you have left near your outline.

3. WRITING THE ESSAY

You have 17 to 20 minutes to write, revise, and proofread your essay, depending on how much time you spent on the prewriting stage.

The following essay is a first draft written in 25 minutes based on the topic introduced in the previous section.

History most certainly repeats itself. From the cosmic to the microcosmic, from wars to fashion, and even in business, there are clear examples of the cyclical nature of the world.

Entropy is a term used to describe the nature of the universe's expansion—everything is slowly moving away from everything else. But what is particularly interesting is evidence showing that this rate of expansion is slowing down. This suggests that the expansion of the universe will eventually stop and lead to a contraction. Because of the forces of gravity, all matter will "fall" closer and closer to a point that, in theory, would contain everything. Scientists believe a huge, or "big," bang will occur, just like the one that happened a few billion years ago, and everything will begin expanding again.*

We may have no control over entropy and "big bangs," but what about our own human history? Forty years ago, in an effort to spread democracy, the U.S. sent tens of thousands of soldiers to a strange foreign land called Vietnam. Amidst anti-war protests, both at home and abroad, the effort proved fruitless, and thousands of American and Vietnamese lives were lost. Nearly forty years after the end of that war, in an effort to spread democracy, the U.S. has once again sent thousands of troops to a strange foreign land—this time, it's Iraq. Once again met with protests in the states and around the world, and faced with a violent and unstable country, it seems we may be walking down the same path we found ourselves forty years ago. Unfortunately, history repeats.

Even in fashion, where bell-bottoms from the '70s, Izod-style polo shirts from the '80s, and retro-style cars from the 60's are all the rage, we see the cyclical nature of our history. And those who have lost money in the most recent stock market crash should not worry; it will come back up. It always does. From the huge to the small and from the weighty to the mundane, we are incapable of escaping the truth that history repeats.

* Is this true? Don't be frightened—it's based on an unlikely theory. Does this lack of certainty matter? Probably not. The graders are more interested in how well you support your argument than the accuracy of your details. While it's not a good idea to make things up—if a grader is knowledgeable in the field you are discussing, your errors will certainly create a negative impression and likely hurt your score—but you shouldn't worry too much if you get a few details wrong.

THE INTRODUCTION

The introduction is usually a short paragraph that states the thesis and grabs the reader's interest. The introduction should not drag on; remember, you must save plenty of time for the important body of the essay. While the thesis should be clear to the reader, don't phrase it as an announcement, such as: "In this essay, I will..." It is usually a good idea to **give some general idea of how you will support your thesis**, but don't go into too much detail.

SIMPLE INTRODUCTION

The introduction in the essay above clearly and succinctly announces the thesis and mentions the existence of numerous and wide-ranging examples, hinting at how the thesis will be supported.

History most certainly repeats itself. From the cosmic to the microcosmic; from wars to fashion; and even in business, there are clear examples of the cyclical nature of the world.

EXPANDED INTRODUCTION

There are of course many options for the length and content of the introduction. Let's assume that the writer of the essay above is concerned about his ability to provide sufficient content in his essay. He may choose to *expand* the introduction:

History most certainly repeats itself. The cyclical nature of the natural world can be seen in many ways, such as the four seasons of the year, consistently repeating weather patterns, or even the physical nature of the entire universe. There are also countless examples beyond the uncontrollable forces of nature, such as with the reoccurrence of wars or the resurgence of fashion trends from bygone times. From the cosmic to the microcosmic; from wars to fashion; and even in business, there are clear examples of the repetition of history.

FOCUSED INTRODUCTION

If the writer had decided to *focus* the essay on a more specific topic, the introduction would reflect this focus:

History most certainly repeats itself. This can be easily seen by observing how Mother Nature changes not only the earth, but also the entire universe. Everything is cyclical. Whether studying the life and death of the world's organisms and how the death of one member provides for the eventual birth of another, or observing the consistent reoccurrence of the seasons and other weather patterns, or even the physical nature of the entire universe, there are clear examples of the cyclical nature of the natural world.

COUNTERPOINT INTRODUCTION

Another option is to start the introduction with a *counterpoint*. Once again, this expanded introduction should probably be used only when there is some question about the amount of content you have available for the body of the essay.

Many people believe that history is linear, like a book, with a beginning, a middle, and an end. They look at their own lives in a similar way. Clearly, we are born, we grow old, and we eventually die. But lost in this linear view of the world is the bigger picture. Yes, we die, but our death leads to new life. Yes, a book comes to an end, but there it waits for a new reader to begin the journey again. The history of the world is not linear. Rather, it is cyclical. History repeats itself. From the cosmic to the microcosmic; from wars to fashion; and even in business, there are clear examples of this cyclical nature of the world.

In all the examples above, the introduction clearly states the thesis and hints at how it will be supported by the essay. The introduction can be expanded by briefly describing the topic as illustrated in several of the example introductions above.

THE BODY

The *body* is the most important part of the essay. **The body's function is to support the thesis**—to convince the reader that your argument is appropriate and sound. The best way to do this is with **specific evidence, examples, facts, data, arguments, or whatever else you can think up**.

You should already have an idea of the content of the paragraphs you will write in the body (from the prewriting section). Two or three paragraphs are probably best, but one good paragraph can get the job done as well. Make sure each paragraph has a main idea. Don't throw related ideas into separate paragraphs in an effort to make your essay look more impressive. Remember, it's about *quality,* not quantity. If you're going to have only one paragraph, make sure it is filled with related evidence and examples that effectively support your thesis. **If you use two paragraphs, put your best one last. If you use three, put your best one last and your least effective paragraph in the middle. Always work towards your best point, not away from it.**

The first body-paragraph in the essay example above describes a "huge" and "cosmic" example of history repeating, one that we have no control over. The writer makes it very clear that he is supporting the thesis when he states: a "'big,' bang will occur, just like the one that happened a few billion years ago, and everything will begin expanding again." (The use of the word "again" is important.) The second paragraph discusses a "weighty" example closer to home that we may have some control over. Once again, the example clearly supports the thesis: "...it seems we may be walking down the same path we found ourselves forty years ago. Unfortunately, history repeats."

CONCLUSION

The concluding paragraph should review your essay's thesis and needs only to be two or three sentences long. **An easy way to do this is to restate the introduction with different words.**

If you can, find a creative way to end your essay unforgettably. This can be done with humor, a quote, a metaphor, or any other creative idea, but remember that the conclusion's main purpose is to wrap up the essay by confirming your thesis one final time.

If you are running out of time, you may choose to include a new idea or two in your concluding paragraph that you were not able to include in a separate paragraph in the body of the essay. It is probably best *not* to do this, but if you choose to include a new detail, do not emphasize the new information; treat it like an afterthought that assists in wrapping up the essay.

Notice that the writer of the example essay chose to include examples related to fashion and business in his conclusion. He was most likely running out of time and did not feel he could create a third structurally-sound paragraph in the body of the essay. Once again, these examples clearly support the thesis.

> Even in fashion, where bell-bottoms from the '70s, Izod-style polo shirts from the '80s, and retro-style cars from the 60's are all the rage, we see the cyclical nature of our history. And those who have lost money in the most recent stock market crash should not worry; it will come back up. It always does. From the huge to the small and from the weighty to the mundane, we are incapable of escaping the truth that history repeats.

By adding the extra information, the writer was able to use one sentence to conclude the essay. Notice how this last sentence is similar to the last sentence of the introduction:

Conclusion:
> From the huge to the small and from the weighty to the mundane, we are incapable of escaping the truth that history repeats.

Introduction:
> From the cosmic to the microcosmic; from wars to fashion; and even in business, there are clear examples of the cyclical nature of the world.

CONCLUSION WITH NO NEW EXAMPLES

If you have time, try to avoid a one-sentence paragraph for the conclusion. The following examples add one simple sentence to the last sentence of the original conclusion.

> The history of the world is clearly cyclical. From the huge to the small and from the weighty to the mundane, we are incapable of escaping the truth that history repeats.

> Examples taken from such varied subjects as the universe, wars, fashion, and business show that the history of the world is cyclical, and not linear, as many believe. From the huge to the small and from the weighty to the mundane, we are incapable of escaping the truth that history repeats.

CREATIVE CONCLUSION

If you really want to end the essay unforgettably, get creative. For example, you may use a quote in your conclusion:

> Joni Mitchell wrote: "we're captive on the carousel of time," and this is certainly true. The history of the world goes "round and round" in a cyclical nature. From the huge to the small and from the weighty to the mundane, we are incapable of escaping the truth that history repeats.

Or, you may include a brief personal anecdote or experience in your conclusion.

> As I continue my journey toward college, I can't help recognizing the cyclical nature of the world. I realize that, just like my parents and my parents' parents, I prepare to take a step that has been taken countless times in the past. It's amazing to me that even in my own life, I see how history repeats. From the huge to the small and from the weighty to the mundane, we are incapable of escaping this basic truth.

TRANSITIONS

As you move from paragraph to paragraph, make sure you use sensible and effective transitions. The most common transition problems occur between body paragraphs, particularly when the paragraphs have very different main ideas. Look at the main ideas of the two body paragraphs in the sample essay:

Main idea of body-paragraph 1: entropy and the big bang
Main idea of body-paragraph 2: the repetition of wars

Notice how the author transitioned from the first paragraph to the second:

> We may have no control over entropy and "big bangs," but what about our own human history?

This sentence, the first sentence of the second body paragraph, logically and effectively moves the reader to the next idea of the essay. Try reading the essay without this sentence, and you will see the importance of a good transition.

There is more than one way to create transitions:

1. The example above shows that mentioning the previous subject ("entropy and the big bang") and then the next subject ("human history") can be effective. Often these examples have contrasts (notice "not" in the first example below and "While" in the second):

    The universe does not hold a monopoly on history repeating—our own history is filled with examples, many unfortunate.

    While the universe provides a good example of history repeating, our own human history provides even more compelling cases.

2. You could create a simple topic sentence with a word such as *also* or *similarly*:

    History also repeats much closer to home.

No matter which approach you take, **make sure to have effective transitions between your paragraphs, especially if the paragraphs have very different main ideas**.

AVOID "I"

Unless you are discussing a personal example, you should usually keep yourself out of it—avoid the use of *I* and *me*. Using these pronouns usually creates redundancy and wordiness while decreasing the strength of your ideas. Consider the following examples:

Weak: I agree with the statement that the history of the world is cyclical.
Strong: The history of the world is cyclical. (Keep *I* out of your thesis.)

Weak: I believe teachers should be paid more.
Strong: Teachers should be paid more. (Of course you believe this; you wouldn't write it otherwise.)

Weak: I will conclude with...
Strong: To conclude... (Don't tell the reader what you're going to do—just do it.)

4. REVISING AND PROOFREADING

Always leave yourself **two to three minutes** to read over your essay when you have completed it. Look for mistakes in spelling and grammar that are a common result of hurried writing. You may also decide to rearrange some ideas or sentences if you notice obvious awkwardness. Remember, you only have a few minutes, so there will probably not be enough time for major revisions; however, if you catch a few spelling or grammar errors, your essay will likely give a better impression to the reader.

Quickly read through the following paragraph and see how many grammar errors you can find. (The eight errors can be found on page 194.)

Entropy is a term used to describe the nature of of the universes expansion—everything is slowly moving away from everything else. But what is particuly interesting are evidence showing that this rate of expansion is slowing down. This suggests that the expansion of the universe will eventually stopped and lead to a contraction. Because of the forces of gravity. Everything will "fall" closer and closer to a point that, in theory, would contain everything. Scientists believes a huge, or "big," bang will occur, just like the one that happened a few billion years ago and everything will begin expanding again.

5. GRAMMAR AND MULTIPLE CHOICE REVIEW

The primary reason the Essay chapter is at the end of the Writing tutorial is to ensure that all grammar topics have been studied and practiced before the essay is discussed in detail. Hopefully, at this point you are comfortable *identifying* grammar errors, but now you must be *proactive*, and avoid them altogether. As you read over your practice essays, look for grammar errors the same way you have been on the multiple choice questions. Try to determine which grammar errors you have a tendency to make, and work on avoiding them on future essays.

In addition to the many grammar rules discussed in chapter II of this tutorial, don't forget about the specific rules that relate to the multiple choice questions, particularly Improving Sentences questions and Improving Paragraphs questions (30 and 40-hour programs). Some of these will be discussed in further detail in the Eloquence section:

- When possible, avoid -*ing* words, especially *being* and *having*. While not always incorrect, -*ing* words are often awkward.
- Avoid needless words. Write succinctly and watch out for redundancies.
- Avoid the passive voice. Make sure the subjects of your sentences are performing the actions.
- Make sure transitions between sentences are logical. If necessary, review the following transitions in the Improving Paragraphs chapter:
  - Contrast transitions
  - Support transitions
  - Cause and effect transitions
- Each paragraph should have a clear main idea.
- As discussed, make sure your transitions between paragraphs are logical.
- Each paragraph should support your thesis.

6. IMPROVING YOUR ESSAY SCORE, NOW

All of the previous techniques have one thing in common: they can be applied to your essay writing *now*. The next section will discuss *writing style*, which will take some time to develop, but for now just focus on the techniques discussed on the previous pages. The best way to become comfortable with these techniques is to practice them. There are several example essay topics at the end of this chapter. **By following these techniques and guidelines as you practice writing the essays, most students will quickly see immediate and sometimes dramatic score increases.**

The following summarizes the previous pages:

THE THREE STAGES:

1. Prewriting (3-5 minutes)
   - Reading and analyzing the topic
   - Deciding what your argument, or thesis will be
     - Support for your thesis
       - literature
       - history
       - science
       - current events
       - specific personal experiences
       - anything else that effectively supports your thesis
   - Preparing an outline
2. Writing the Essay (17-20 minutes)
   - Introduction
     - Simple
     - Expanded
     - Focused
     - Counterpoint
   - Body: supporting your thesis with examples and other evidence

- Conclusion
  - With new examples
  - With no new examples
  - Creative
- Transitions
- Avoid "I"

3. Revising and Proofreading (2-3 minutes)
   - Checking for errors in grammar, spelling, etc.
   - Minor rearranging of ideas or sentences

GRAMMAR AND REVIEW OF PAST TOPICS:

- Avoid *-ing* words
- Avoid needless words.
- Avoid the passive voice.
- Make sure transitions between sentences are logical.
  - Contrast transitions
  - Support transitions
  - Cause and effect transitions
- Each paragraph should have a clear main idea.
- Make sure your transitions between paragraphs are logical.
- Each paragraph should support your thesis.

7. ELOQUENCE

Eloquence is what separates a good essay from an average essay. An eloquent essay will support the thesis in extremely clear and effective ways, and it will be enjoyable to read, smoothly and logically moving from one sentence to the next. This section will explore a number of topics that relate to eloquence. It is these topics that allow you to create a personal writing style, to let a bit of *you* come through in your writing, and to create an essay that stands out as a welcome oasis in a monotonous desert of drab and dreary writing that the SAT graders must certainly face.

The following topics are roughly in order of importance. If you do not have time to cover all them, start with the first topic and go in order. You could also look over your past essays with a tutor and identify the topics that would benefit you the most.

VARY SENTENCE STRUCTURE

Many beginning writers use several sentences of similar structure in repetition. For example:

> I hadn't yet seen a science fiction movie. I didn't know what to expect. The lights dimmed. The movie started. I knew immediately I was in for something special. I was hooked from the first scene.

Another example would include nothing but compound sentences with two independent clauses:

> I hadn't yet seen a science fiction movie, and I didn't know what to expect. The lights dimmed, and the movie started. I knew immediately I was in for something special, and I was hooked from the first scene.

To create interest, avoid excess mechanical symmetry by *varying your sentence structure*. Besides simple sentences, include sentences with dependent clauses and modifying phrases, as well as compound sentences with more than one independent clause. Turn back to the punctuation section, if necessary, to review these topics. The following paragraph displays a variety of sentence structures:

> Because I hadn't yet seen a science fiction movie, I didn't know what to expect. As the lights dimmed, the movie started, and I knew immediately I was in for something special. I was hooked from the first scene.

Rewrite the following short passage using a variety of sentence structures. For the following, and all writing exercises in this section, you are encouraged to be creative with your revisions. Possible answers start on page 194:

Star Wars was released in 1977. Star Wars was the most popular movie of its kind. The success of Star Wars brought on a barrage of toys and other movie-related merchandise. Young fans collected countless items. These items included action figures, coloring books, lunch boxes, and anything else bearing the Star Wars logo. These fans are much older now. Some of these fans have kept their Star Wars toys in pristine condition. They can sell some of these items to collectors for thousands of dollars.

_____

_____

_____

_____

_____

_____

_____

_____

_____

_____

WRITE SUCCINCTLY

It is important to write in a concise and succinct manner, avoiding all needless words. This can be accomplished in a number of ways:

COMBINE SENTENCES

Writing succinctly does not mean sentences must be short and simple; in fact, succinct writing often includes combining simple sentences into complex ones through the use of dependent clauses and modifying phrases.

Wordy:

The Wizard of Oz is a story that tells of the adventures of Dorothy and her dog Toto. It was one of a series of books written by L. Frank Baum.

Succinct:

The Wizard of Oz, one of a series of books written by L. Frank Baum, is a story that tells of the adventures of Dorothy and her dog Toto.

MINIMIZE THE USE OF PREPOSITIONAL PHRASES

When possible, eliminating prepositional phrases will lead to more succinct writing.

Wordy:

Jordan was delighted about his boss's decision to end the day by closing the doors of the factory and letting everyone go home early.

Succinct:

Jordan was delighted that his boss closed the factory doors and let everyone go home early.

In the example above, four prepositional phrases were removed, yielding a much more succinct sentence.

USE YOUR VOCABULARY TO SHORTEN PHRASES

Many common expressions can be easily shortened using different words in place of wordy phrases.

Wordy: In spite of the fact that it is raining out, I think I'll leave my umbrella at home.
Succinct: Although it is raining out, I think I'll leave my umbrella at home.

Wordy: The fact that he had not succeeded in raising his test scores can be attributed to a death in his family.
Succinct: His failure to raise his test scores can be attributed to a death in his family.

Wordy: Let me call your attention to the matter at hand.
Succinct: Focus on the matter at hand.

There are countless ways to use new vocabulary to shorten wordy phrases. Look for opportunities to do this in your writing.

AVOID REDUNDANCIES

The redundancy section of this tutorial offers numerous examples of common redundancy errors. Avoiding redundancies will certainly help your writing become more succinct.

WRITE SUCCINCTLY, A SUMMARY:

- Combine sentences
- Minimize the use of prepositional phrases
- Use your vocabulary to shorten phrases
- Avoid redundancies

Try using any of the preceding succinct-writing rules to improve the following wordy examples:

1. Steve was a rich man. He gave generously to charity. He still had millions to his name when he died last February.

   _____

   _____

2. My attempt to run to the top of the Haleakala volcano on the island of Maui was cut short by blisters on the soles of my feet.

   _____

   _____

3. The fact that Elliot is not present with us today should not sway your vote toward his competitor.

   _____

   _____

4. Collin is usually a quiet man. The fact that he missed the shot at the end of the last game of the championship series caused him to scream like I've never heard before.

   _____

   _____

USE THE ACTIVE VOICE

This topic was introduced in the Improving Sentences chapter. In general, you should make sure the subject of the sentence is performing the action. For example:

Passive: The first time I saw Star Wars is something I will always remember.
Active: I will always remember the first time I saw Star Wars.

Passive: There were many excited fans at the theater.
Active: Excited fans filled the theater.

Passive: As the curtain opened, the cheer of the audience could be heard.
Active: As the curtain opened, the audience cheered.

There are two other advantages of writing in an active voice:
- Sentences become shorter and more succinct.
- Action verbs (such as *remember, filled,* and *cheered*) take the place of weaker *to be* verbs (such as *is, were,* and *could be*).

Rewrite the following sentences in an active voice:

1. The rebels' decision to attack the Death Star was greeted with approval by the audience.

_____

2. There were more than a few fans waiting outside the theater for tickets to the next show.

_____

USE CONCRETE LANGUAGE

To use *concrete language* means to be specific and definite rather than general and vague. The best writers are successful because they write about particular things and report details that create pictures in the minds of their readers. The following examples are first written with general and vague words and then using concrete language. Notice how the concrete examples, which are taken from the previous example-essay, are far more effective at conveying information and creating interest for the reader:

Vague:

Many times in our history, the U.S. has gone to war. Many people disagree about the reasons for war, and the war-efforts often prove fruitless. Many troops die.

Concrete:

Forty years ago, in an effort to spread democracy, the U.S. sent tens of thousands of soldiers to a strange foreign land called Vietnam. Amidst anti-war protests, both at home and abroad, the effort proved fruitless, and thousands of American and Vietnamese lives were lost.

Vague:

Even in fashion, where items of the past are reappearing today, we see the cyclical nature of our history.

Concrete:

Even in fashion, where bell-bottoms from the '70s, Izod-style polo shirts from the '80s, and retro-style cars from the 60's are all the rage, we see the cyclical nature of our history.

Using concrete language involves *showing* your readers rather than *telling* them. The following examples illustrate the point:

Telling: The weather was unfavorable.
Showing: Rain fell from dark storm clouds.

Telling: I was happy about my grade.
Showing: Thinking about my A, I skipped all the way home.

Practice using concrete language by rewriting the following vague sentences. Feel free to be creative. Remember to *show*; don't tell:

1. The movie we saw was great.

_____

_____

2. The swordsman showed courage while battling the beast.

_____

_____

3. Ellie's mom was angry about the mess in the kitchen.

_____

_____

4. I really enjoyed the song on the radio.

_____

_____

USE THE POSITIVE FORM

It is often advantageous to avoid the word *not*. Readers are not interested in what is *not*; they want to know what *is*. Create sentences in a *positive* form. For example:

Negative: She did *not* remember to bring her books to school.
Positive: She forgot to bring her books to school.

Negative: He did *not* think the movie was as good as advertised.
Positive: The movie failed to meet his expectations.

You may choose to use negative phrases when they are in clear opposition to a positive phrase:

Ask *not* what your country can do for you—ask what you can do for your country.

Rewrite the following sentences in a positive form:

1. The speeding driver did not pay any attention to the police car parked at the side of the road.

_____

2. Marshall is not the player he once was.

_____

AVOID REPEATING WORDS

Unless you are intentionally trying to create an exaggerated emphasis, you should avoid frequent repetition of key words in your writing. Often, you can use pronouns to take the place of important nouns.

> *The Wizard of Oz is a story that tells of the adventures of Dorothy and her dog Toto. The Wizard of Oz was one of a series of books written by L. Frank Baum.*

Use the pronoun *it* in the second sentence:

> *The Wizard of Oz is a story that tells of the adventures of Dorothy and her dog Toto. It was one of a series of books written by L. Frank Baum.*

Make sure you don't overuse pronouns. At some point you must reintroduce the noun to avoid ambiguity.

In other cases, you can hopefully use words in your vocabulary to avoid awkward repetition. The following is similar to the introduction of the example-essay:

> *History most certainly repeats itself. From the cosmic to the microcosmic; from wars to fashion; and even in business, there are clear examples of history repeating itself.*

This introduction is greatly improved by replacing *history repeating itself* at the end with a phrase that means the same thing: *the cyclical nature of the world.*

> *History most certainly repeats itself. From the cosmic to the microcosmic; from wars to fashion; and even in business, there are clear examples of the cyclical nature of the world.*

Improve the following brief passages that contain awkward repetition:

1. *Scott was passionate about the characters in his writing. He was passionate about developing realistic characters, but he was also passionate about creating characters that were heroic in almost superhuman ways.*

_____

_____

_____

_____

_____

2. Courage is a quality that is not often seen in the world today. It is too often when a man lacks the courage to speak up for what he believes. The courage to fight for one's principles seems to frequently be replaced with an attitude of apathy and laziness. People are too busy or too tired to be courageous.

_____

_____

_____

_____

_____

_____

AVOID *-ING* WORDS

As introduced in the Improving Sentences chapter, *-ing* words are often awkward and should be avoided when possible. For example:

By having the best grades in his class, he is being persistently courted by several universities.

By rewriting the sentence without the awkward words *having* and *being*, a much more eloquent sentence is created:

Since he has the best grades in his class, he has been persistently courted by several universities.

Underline and rewrite the parts of the following sentences containing awkward *-ing* words:

1. The committee's job was maintaining harmony between the developers and the environmentalists.

_____

2. Completing your own taxes is a relatively easy task, but the difficulty being that the time involved is usually quite great.

_____

3. It being the hottest day of the year, I decided to go to the beach.

_____

4. The company is divided into several departments, each having a specific duty to fulfill.

_____

ADD IMPORTANCE TO WORDS (WORD-PLACEMENT IN SENTENCES)

The word or words that the writer considers most important should usually be placed at *the end* of the sentence.

Bob walked into his boss's office and calmly quit at a little after noon.

The writer likely wants to emphasize the fact that Bob quit. By placing these words at the end of the sentence, they are made more prominent:

At a little after noon, Bob walked into his boss's office and calmly quit.

In contrast, another effective way to add importance to words is to place them at the *beginning* of the sentence, particularly if the words are not the subject of the sentence. For example:

Deceit and lies I could never forgive.

Home is the sailor.

Add importance to prominent words by changing their placement in the following sentences:

1. Jerry came in last even after training over the summer and wearing new, lighter, and supposedly faster running shoes.

_____

_____

2. I noticed sadness and longing in your eyes.

_____

_____

AVOID QUALIFIERS

The use of words like *very*, *rather*, *little*, *bit*, and *pretty* detract from the power of eloquent language.

Weak: It was a very hot day.
Strong: It was a scorching day.

Weak: I knew something was wrong because she was acting a little strange.
Strong: I knew something was wrong because she was restless and fidgety.

Rewrite the following weak sentences:

1. The waiter was rather rude as he coolly ignored my request for more soup.

_____

2. Anna did pretty well on the exam, but she knew she could do better.

_____

USE FIGURES OF SPEECH (SPARINGLY)

The use of a figure of speech, such as a metaphor or synonym, is a valuable tool that you are encouraged to use, but it is one that should be used with caution. Repeated and disparate figures of speech sound awkward at best and illogical and confusing at worst. A good rule of thumb is to use no more than *one* figure of speech in your essay.

An effective essay may introduce a metaphor in the introduction and come back to that same metaphor in the conclusion. For example:

Introduction:
Joni Mitchell wrote: "we're captive on the carousel of time," and this is certainly true. The history of the world goes "round and round" in a cyclical nature. From the cosmic to the microcosmic, from wars to fashion, and even in business, there are clear examples of history repeating.

Conclusion:
Like the painted horses of a carousel, history most certainly goes round and round. From the huge to the small and from the weighty to the mundane, we are incapable of escaping the truth that the history of the world repeats.

The conclusion above, which restates the metaphor introduced in the introduction, is much more effective than the following conclusion, which introduces three new metaphors:

Like a spinning top, history most certainly goes round and round. From the huge to the small and from the weighty to the mundane, we are incapable of jumping off the merry-go-round of life, a ride that circles endlessly like the planets about the sun.

SUMMARY OF ELOQUENCE TOPICS

- Vary sentence structure
- Write succinctly
  - Combine sentences
  - Minimize the use of prepositional phrases
  - Use your vocabulary to shorten phrases
  - Avoid redundancies
- Use the active voice
- Use concrete language
- Use the positive form
- Avoid repeating words
- Avoid *-ing* words
- Add importance to words (word-placement in sentences)
- Avoid qualifiers
- Use figures of speech (sparingly)

8. ESSAY PRACTICE TOPICS

PRACTICE PROBLEMS

The following topics are from *The Official SAT Study Guide** by the College Board (2nd Edition). You may choose to practice the first few essays untimed until you are comfortable with the essay-writing techniques taught in this tutorial, but make sure to practice several essays with the 25-minute time limit so you are comfortable with the time constraints of the SAT. Review the essay summaries on the previous pages before you complete these assignments.

- ☐ Topic 1: Test 1, Section 1
- ☐ Topic 2: Test 2, Section 1
- ☐ Topic 3: Test 3, Section 1
- ☐ Topic 4: Test 4, Section 1

(40) Additional topics are found on the following pages. Use the blank lined pages following Topic 10.

- ☐ Topic 5
- ☐ Topic 6
- ☐ Topic 7
- ☐ Topic 8
- ☐ Topic 9
- ☐ Topic 10

*SAT is a registered trademark of the College Board, which was not involved in the production of and does not endorse this book.

─────────

Reminder: At the end of the program, don't forget to take your final practice test. Make sure you have completed all required practice problems in the College Board book. In addition, you should have gone back to Test 5 (and Test 6, if applicable) and corrected missed and skipped problems using the Test Correction assignments at the end of the chapters in this tutorial.

- ☐ Take Test 7 in the College Board book. Review Taking Practice Tests in the Introduction. After grading, go back and correct missed and blank problems using the Test Correction assignments.

ESSAY TOPIC 5

> **Turn to page 2 of your answer sheet to write your ESSAY.**

The essay gives you an opportunity to show how effectively you can develop and express ideas. You should, therefore, take care to develop your point of view, present your ideas logically and clearly, and use language precisely.

Your essay must be written on the lines provided on your answer sheet − you will receive no other paper on which to write. You will have enough space if you write on every line, avoid wide margins, and keep your handwriting to a reasonable size. Remember that people who are not familiar with your handwriting will read what you write. Try to write or print so that what you are writing is legible to those readers.

You have twenty-five minutes to write an essay on the topic assigned below. DO NOT WRITE ON ANOTHER TOPIC. AN OFF-TOPIC ESSAY WILL RECEIVE A SCORE OF ZERO.

Think carefully about the issue presented in the following excerpt and the assignment below.

The principle is this: each failure leads us closer to deeper knowledge, to greater creativity in understanding old data, to new lines of inquiry. Thomas Edison experienced 10,000 failures before he succeeded in perfecting the light bulb. When a friend of his remarked that 10,000 failures was a lot, Edison replied, "I didn't fail 10,000 times; I successfully eliminated 10,000 materials and combinations that didn't work."

Myles Brand. "Taking the Measure Your Success"

Assignment: What is your view on the idea that it takes failure to achieve success? Plan and write an essay in which you develop your point of view on this issue. Support your position with reasoning and examples taken from your reading, studies, experience, or observations.

DO NOT WRITE YOU ESSAY IN YOUR TEST BOOK. You will receive credit only for what you write on your answer sheet.

BEGIN WRITING YOUR ESSAY ON PAGE 2 OF THE ANSWER SHEET.

**If you finish before time is called, you may check your work on this section only.
Do not turn to any other section in the test.**

Note: blank lined pages can be found following Topic 10.

ESSAY TOPIC 6

Turn to page 2 of your answer sheet to write your ESSAY.

The essay gives you an opportunity to show how effectively you can develop and express ideas. You should, therefore, take care to develop your point of view, present your ideas logically and clearly, and use language precisely.

Your essay must be written on the lines provided on your answer sheet − you will receive no other paper on which to write. You will have enough space if you write on every line, avoid wide margins, and keep your handwriting to a reasonable size. Remember that people who are not familiar with your handwriting will read what you write. Try to write or print so that what you are writing is legible to those readers.

You have twenty-five minutes to write an essay on the topic assigned below. DO NOT WRITE ON ANOTHER TOPIC. AN OFF-TOPIC ESSAY WILL RECEIVE A SCORE OF ZERO.

Think carefully about the issue presented in the following excerpt and the assignment below.

A sense of happiness and fulfillment, not personal gain, is the best motivation and reward for one's achievements. Expecting a reward of wealth or recognition for achieving a goal can lead to disappointment and frustration. If we want to be happy in what we do in life, we should not seek achievement for the sake of winning wealth and fame. The personal satisfaction of a job well done is its own reward.

Assignment: Are people motivated by personal satisfaction rather than by money or fame? Plan and write an essay in which you develop your point of view on this issue. Support your position with reasoning and examples taken from your reading, studies, experience, or observations.

DO NOT WRITE YOU ESSAY IN YOUR TEST BOOK. You will receive credit only for what you write on your answer sheet.

BEGIN WRITING YOUR ESSAY ON PAGE 2 OF THE ANSWER SHEET.

**If you finish before time is called, you may check your work on this section only.
Do not turn to any other section in the test.**

Note: blank lined pages can be found following Topic 10.

ESSAY TOPIC 7

ESSAY
Time − 25 minutes

Turn to page 2 of your answer sheet to write your ESSAY.

The essay gives you an opportunity to show how effectively you can develop and express ideas. You should, therefore, take care to develop your point of view, present your ideas logically and clearly, and use language precisely.

Your essay must be written on the lines provided on your answer sheet − you will receive no other paper on which to write. You will have enough space if you write on every line, avoid wide margins, and keep your handwriting to a reasonable size. Remember that people who are not familiar with your handwriting will read what you write. Try to write or print so that what you are writing is legible to those readers.

You have twenty-five minutes to write an essay on the topic assigned below. DO NOT WRITE ON ANOTHER TOPIC. AN OFF-TOPIC ESSAY WILL RECEIVE A SCORE OF ZERO.

Think carefully about the issue presented in the following excerpt and the assignment below.

The passion for change causes conflict between those who want change and those who want to keep the status quo.

Assignment: Does change cause conflict between those who want change and those who are happy the way things are? Plan and write an essay in which you develop your point of view on this issue. Support your position with reasoning and examples taken from your reading, studies, experience, or observations.

DO NOT WRITE YOU ESSAY IN YOUR TEST BOOK. You will receive credit only for what you write on your answer sheet.

BEGIN WRITING YOUR ESSAY ON PAGE 2 OF THE ANSWER SHEET.

**If you finish before time is called, you may check your work on this section only.
Do not turn to any other section in the test.**

Note: blank lined pages can be found following Topic 10.

ESSAY TOPIC 8

ESSAY
Time − 25 minutes

Turn to page 2 of your answer sheet to write your ESSAY.

The essay gives you an opportunity to show how effectively you can develop and express ideas. You should, therefore, take care to develop your point of view, present your ideas logically and clearly, and use language precisely.

Your essay must be written on the lines provided on your answer sheet − you will receive no other paper on which to write. You will have enough space if you write on every line, avoid wide margins, and keep your handwriting to a reasonable size. Remember that people who are not familiar with your handwriting will read what you write. Try to write or print so that what you are writing is legible to those readers.

You have twenty-five minutes to write an essay on the topic assigned below. DO NOT WRITE ON ANOTHER TOPIC. AN OFF-TOPIC ESSAY WILL RECEIVE A SCORE OF ZERO.

Think carefully about the issue presented in the following excerpt and the assignment below.

"The best things in life are free," says a refrain from an old song.

Assignment: Do you agree with this sentiment? Plan and write an essay in which you develop your point of view on this issue. Support your position with reasoning and examples taken from your reading, studies, experience, or observations.

DO NOT WRITE YOU ESSAY IN YOUR TEST BOOK. You will receive credit only for what you write on your answer sheet.

BEGIN WRITING YOUR ESSAY ON PAGE 2 OF THE ANSWER SHEET.

**If you finish before time is called, you may check your work on this section only.
Do not turn to any other section in the test.**

Note: blank lined pages can be found following Topic 10.

ESSAY TOPIC 9

ESSAY

Time – 25 minutes

Turn to page 2 of your answer sheet to write your ESSAY.

The essay gives you an opportunity to show how effectively you can develop and express ideas. You should, therefore, take care to develop your point of view, present your ideas logically and clearly, and use language precisely.

Your essay must be written on the lines provided on your answer sheet – you will receive no other paper on which to write. You will have enough space if you write on every line, avoid wide margins, and keep your handwriting to a reasonable size. Remember that people who are not familiar with your handwriting will read what you write. Try to write or print so that what you are writing is legible to those readers.

You have twenty-five minutes to write an essay on the topic assigned below. DO NOT WRITE ON ANOTHER TOPIC. AN OFF-TOPIC ESSAY WILL RECEIVE A SCORE OF ZERO.

Think carefully about the issue presented in the following excerpt and the assignment below.

> After rescuing a child from a burning building, Jim Smith, a fireman, commented, "Courage is just a matter of luck – of being in the right place at the right time. Courage is common to most of us, but most of us never have an opportunity to show it."

Assignment: Is physical courage a common trait? Plan and write an essay in which you develop your point of view on this issue. Support your position with reasoning and examples taken from your reading, studies, experience, or observations.

DO NOT WRITE YOU ESSAY IN YOUR TEST BOOK. You will receive credit only for what you write on your answer sheet.

BEGIN WRITING YOUR ESSAY ON PAGE 2 OF THE ANSWER SHEET.

**If you finish before time is called, you may check your work on this section only.
Do not turn to any other section in the test.**

Note: blank lined pages can be found following Topic 10.

ESSAY TOPIC 10

ESSAY
Time – 25 minutes

Turn to page 2 of your answer sheet to write your ESSAY.

The essay gives you an opportunity to show how effectively you can develop and express ideas. You should, therefore, take care to develop your point of view, present your ideas logically and clearly, and use language precisely.

Your essay must be written on the lines provided on your answer sheet – you will receive no other paper on which to write. You will have enough space if you write on every line, avoid wide margins, and keep your handwriting to a reasonable size. Remember that people who are not familiar with your handwriting will read what you write. Try to write or print so that what you are writing is legible to those readers.

You have twenty-five minutes to write an essay on the topic assigned below. DO NOT WRITE ON ANOTHER TOPIC. AN OFF-TOPIC ESSAY WILL RECEIVE A SCORE OF ZERO.

Think carefully about the issue presented in the following excerpt and the assignment below.

Most of us go through life handicapped by old myths rather than inspired by current realities.

Assignment: Do you agree with this observation of human behavior? Plan and write an essay in which you develop your point of view on this issue. Support your position with reasoning and examples taken from your reading, studies, experience, or observations.

DO NOT WRITE YOU ESSAY IN YOUR TEST BOOK. You will receive credit only for what you write on your answer sheet.

BEGIN WRITING YOUR ESSAY ON PAGE 2 OF THE ANSWER SHEET.

**If you finish before time is called, you may check your work on this section only.
Do not turn to any other section in the test.**

Note: blank lined pages can be found following Topic 10.

Begin your essay on this page. If you need more space, continue on the next page. Do not write outside of the essay box.

Continuation of ESSAY from previous page. Write below only if you need more space.

176 ● THE ULTIMATE SAT TUTORIAL

Begin your essay on this page. If you need more space, continue on the next page. Do not write outside of the essay box.

Begin your essay on this page. If you need more space, continue on the next page. Do not write outside of the essay box.

Begin your essay on this page. If you need more space, continue on the next page. Do not write outside of the essay box.

Begin your essay on this page. If you need more space, continue on the next page. Do not write outside of the essay box.

VII
WRITING ANSWERS

The following answers are to all lesson problems, homework problems, quizzes, and any other questions in the previous chapters.

II. GRAMMAR
1. VERB TENSE
LESSON PROBLEMS:
1. *displays OR has displayed OR has been displaying (note the word "today")*
2. *were not sure*
3. *has worked OR has been working*
4. *had been diving OR had dived*
5. *had gotten*

HW PROBLEMS:
1. *shone*
2. *will have read OR will read*
3. *have caught*
4. *had written*

2. SUBJECT-VERB AGREEMENT
LESSON PROBLEMS:
1. *have → has*
2. *are → is*
3. *are → is*
4. *no error*
5. *was → were (the subject is "boats"; notice the word "there.")*

HW PROBLEMS:
1. *are → is*
2. *are → is*
3. *pay → pays*
4. *were → was*
5. *were → was*

3. PRONOUN CASE
LESSON PROBLEMS:
1. *him*
2. *she your*
3. *he OR he is*
4. *whom*
5. *which*

HW PROBLEMS:
1. *no error*
2. *he*
3. *her*
4. *I OR I am*
5. *no error*

4. PRONOUN AGREEMENT
LESSON PROBLEMS:
1. *their*
2. *he or she*
3. *no error*
4. *it is*
5. *he or she was*

HW PROBLEMS:
1. *no error*
2. *you*
3. *his or her*
4. *their*
5. *its*

5. AMBIGUOUS PRONOUNS
LESSON PROBLEMS:
1. *they → doctors (for example)*
2. *it → this (other answers possible)*
3. *he → the president OR the employee*

HW PROBLEMS:
1. *their → the tradition's OR the pattern's, etc.*
2. *(2nd) he → Jake*
3. *his → Rob's OR Brian's*

6. PARALLELISM
LESSON PROBLEMS:
1. *eliminate "there were"*
2. *compassionately*
3. *work*
4. *looks*
5. *financial comfort*
6. *watching*

HW PROBLEMS:
1. *a professional... → created a professional and easy-to-read paper*
2. *To call → Calling*
3. *to take → taking*
4. *no error*
5. *creative freedom → being creatively free*
6. *the car's performance and its fuel consumption*

7. NOUN AGREEMENT
LESSON PROBLEMS:
1. *a place → places OR bookstores are → a bookstore is*
2. *a better reader → better readers*
3. *a different box → different boxes*
4. *a subject → subjects*

HW PROBLEMS:
1. *The vibraphone → Vibraphones; OR melodic ... instruments → a melodic ... instrument*
2. *a member → members*
3. *a reason → reasons*

8. COMPARISONS
LESSON PROBLEMS:
1. *eliminate "more"*
2. *faster → fastest*
3. *intelligentest → most intelligent*

HW PROBLEMS:
1. *no error*
2. *best → better*
3. *no error*

9. ILLOGICAL COMPARISONS
LESSON PROBLEMS:
1. *David is → David's chord progressions are OR David's are*
2. *other → the histories of other OR those of other*
3. *from → from the rules of OR from those of*
4. *average school → average school's (students)*
5. *restaurant → restaurant's food*

HW PROBLEMS:
1. *school → school's (badminton team)*
2. *no error*
3. *friends → friend's (cars)*
4. *his last test → his score on his last test*
5. *no error*

10. DOUBLE NEGATIVES
LESSON PROBLEMS:
1. *eliminate "not" or "scarcely"*
2. *no → any*
3. *no → any*

HW PROBLEMS:
1. *no → any*
2. *couldn't → could*
3. *no error*

11. PUNCTUATION
LESSON PROBLEMS:

1. *After spending several years trying to grow a garden, Linda decided she'd rather just buy her produce from the store.*
2. *Daniel, not a large man by any means, somehow seems to dominate our basketball games.*
3. *You should watch the road, but you should occasionally check your mirrors, as well.*
4. *no error*

HW PROBLEMS:

1. *Tommy, friendly as always, offered to assist the confused tourist.*
2. *Skipping through the sprinklers and rolling through the grass, Katie became a wet and grassy mess.*
3. *Even though many voters, apparently unaware of the country's many problems, are happy with the incumbent, I feel we are ready for a new leader.*
4. *George rocked the boat; many people fell out.*

12. CONJUNCTIONS

LESSON PROBLEMS:
1. *and*
2. *but also*
3. *protein, and then OR protein; then*
4. *and*

HW PROBLEMS:
1. *no error*
2. *nor*
3. *as*
4. *as*

13. FRAGMENTS

LESSON PROBLEMS:

The following numbers are fragments.
1. *Modifying phrase—the subject "The Problems of Philosophy" lacks a verb.*
3. *Pronoun phrase—the subject "Hedy Lamarr" lacks a verb.*
4. *Semicolon—the first clause is a dependent clause.*

HW PROBLEMS:
1. *"That" clause—the subject of the "that" clause, "climbing trees," lacks a verb.*
2. *-ING word used as a verb—the word "showing" is not a verb.*
3. *Pronoun phrase—the subject "car" lacks a verb. Note that "designed" functions as an adjective here.*
5. *"That" clause—the subject of the "that" clause, "stories," lacks a verb.*

14. RUN-ONS

LESSON PROBLEMS:
1. *add "because" after "sunrise" (no comma)*
2. *add a period or semicolon after "first"*
3. *add a comma after "enough"*
4. *showing → show (this removes the fragment following the semicolon)*
5. *Although hardly the best athlete on the team, Todd...*

HW PROBLEMS:
1. *add a semicolon after "studying"*
2. *add ", and" after "paragraphs" (note the need for a comma) / A more eloquent way to correct number 2 is to turn the second clause into a modifying phrase: The book was written without regard to punctuation or paragraphs, an unconformity that made it difficult to understand.*
3. *my brother, he plans → my brother plans*
4. *add a comma after "hands"*
5. *remove the comma and add "because" OR change the comma to a semicolon*

15. IMPROPER MODIFIERS

LESSON PROBLEMS:
1. *Sean least expected to run into his parents at the arcade*
2. *the blow fish has a body that can grow... OR the blow fish can grow...*
3. *Eddie raised electric guitar techniques*
4. *Kevin was overlooked for the job by the boss*
5. *Chrissie was shocked by the A*

HW PROBLEMS:

1. *Charles, not surprisingly, writes long books*
2. *no error*
3. *we were unbearably disappointed about missing the show*
4. *no error*
5. *Tony inspired a generation of jazz drummers*

16. ADJECTIVES AND ADVERBS

LESSON PROBLEMS:

1. *no error*
2. *rapid → rapidly*
3. *no error*
4. *careful → carefully*

HW PROBLEMS:

1. *safe → safely*
2. *typical → typically*
3. *real → very or really*
4. *fresh → freshly OR fresh baked → fresh, baked*

17. IDIOM

HW PROBLEMS:

1. *(2nd) to → by*
2. *about → at*
3. *with → to*
4. *of → with*
5. *no error*
6. *no error*
7. *over → about*
8. *from → of (The correct answer is "of" even though words similar to "independent" take "from.")*
9. *about → in*
10. *over → for*

18. CONFUSED WORDS

HW PROBLEMS:

1. *between → among*
2. *bring → take*
3. *in → into*
4. *like → as if*
5. *aggravate → irritate*
6. *each other → one another*

20. AMBIGUITIES

LESSON PROBLEMS:

1. *You can use this phone card to call your sister for less than a dollar and tell her about the fine dinner you had.*
2. *Corporations are more likely than smaller companies to hire college graduates with advanced degrees.*

HW PROBLEMS:

1. *In the last chapter of his book, the writer discussed the negative impact of graffiti.*
2. *The new amendment to the state's constitution, an amendment that has come under fire recently, may be repealed in the election.*
3. *The new navigation system will speak directions to the driver when a button is pressed on the steering wheel. OR ...when the driver presses a button on the steering wheel.*

21. GRAMMAR QUIZZES
GRAMMAR QUIZ 1 (SECTIONS 1-7)

1. *ends → ended (verb tense)*
2. *worked → had worked (verb tense)*
3. *spoke → speaks (verb tense)*
4. *were → was (subject-verb agreement)*
5. *she → her (pronoun case)*
6. *they → it (pronoun agreement)*
7. *and it leads → a condition that leads OR leading (other answers possible) (ambiguous pronouns)*
8. *To enjoy → Enjoying (parallelism)*
9. *showed kindness → kind (parallelism)*
10. *an independent technician → independent technicians (noun agreement)*

GRAMMAR QUIZ 2 (SECTIONS 8-16)

1. *stronger → strongest (comparisons)*
2. *put "the rules of" OR "those of" before "the ancient Chinese game Go" (illogical comparisons)*
3. *and it's → but it's also (conjunctions – paired)*
4. *eliminate "and" (other answers possible) (fragments)*
5. *add "," before "and" (run-ons)*
6. *people flock to malls → malls attract people (improper modifiers)*
7. *doctor's research papers → doctor wrote research papers that (improper modifiers)*
8. *slow → slowly (adjectives and adverbs)*
9. *lazy → lazily (adjectives and adverbs)*
10. *put "it is in" before "many" (compare "balance" to "balance") (illogical comparisons – compare "balance" to "balance")*

GRAMMAR QUIZ 3 (ALL SECTIONS)

1. *hits → hit (verb tense)*
2. *put "had" before "bought" OR eliminate "had" before "shrewdly" (verb tense)*
3. *are → is (subject-verb agreement)*
4. *were → was (subject-verb agreement)*
5. *which → who (pronoun case – use "who" for people)*
6. *him → he (pronoun case – comparisons)*
7. *they → he or she (pronoun agreement)*
8. *a surprisingly fast creature → surprisingly fast creatures (noun agreement)*
9. *fastest → faster (comparisons)*
10. *eliminate "not" (double negatives)*
11. *easy, then → easy; then OR easy, but then (run-ons)*
12. *studying... → Vivian found studying for finals to be a chore (improper modifiers)*
13. *less → fewer (confused words)*
14. *badly → desperately (idiom – common mistakes)*
15. *eliminate "usual" (redundancies)*
16. *for making → to make (idiom – prepositional)*
17. *no error*
18. *of → to (idiom – prepositional)*
19. *and → to (idiom – common mistakes)*
20. *eliminate "is a man who" (redundancies)*

GRAMMAR QUIZ 4 (ALL SECTIONS)

1. *is → has been (verb tense)*
2. *slew → slain (verb tense)*
3. *or → and OR are great role models → is a great role model (subject-verb agreement)*
4. *which → that (pronoun case)*
5. *they → doctors (ambiguous pronouns)*
6. *eliminate "by" (parallelism)*
7. *year → year's OR year's party (illogical comparisons)*
8. *but → and (conjunctions – paired)*
9. *travel, he → travel; he OR travel. He (run-ons)*
10. *dogs' ability to reason → dogs have an ability to reason that (improper modifiers)*
11. *amount → number (confused words)*
12. *about → by (idiom – prepositional)*
13. *from → with (idiom – prepositional)*
14. *the latter → Stanford (idiom – common mistakes)*
15. *Being that → Since (idiom – common mistakes)*
16. *no error (idiom – OK)*
17. *suppose → supposed (idiom – common mistakes)*
18. *eliminate "for the future" (redundancies)*
19. *eliminate "in size" (redundancies)*
20. *The meeting will introduce the new president, who knows everything there is to know about the business. He is a grandson of the founder. (ambiguities)*

IRREGULAR VERB TENSE QUIZ 1 (A-U & NO CHANGE)

1. *drunken → drunk*
2. *sung → sang*
3. *springed → sprang*
4. *catch → caught*
5. *no error*
6. *shined → shone*
7. *no error ("had spit" is also correct)*
8. *fleed → had fled or fled*
9. *stang → stung*
10. *rang → rung*

IRREGULAR VERB TENSE QUIZ 2 (-EN AND OTHER)

1. *beat → beaten*
2. *got → gotten*
3. *froze → frozen*
4. *no error ("had awoken" and "had awaked" are also correct)*
5. *risen → rose*
6. *no error ("have striven" is also correct)*
7. *no error*
8. *wrote → written*
9. *came → come*
10. *woke → woken OR waked*

IDIOM QUIZ 1 (PREPOSITIONS)

1. *about → on*
2. *against → at*
3. *on → about*
4. *by → from*
5. *with → to*
6. *from → of*
7. *in → into*
8. *no error*
9. *from → against*
10. *at → in*
11. *on attending → to attend*
12. *at → in*

IDIOM QUIZ 2 (COMMON MISTAKES)

1. *around → about*
2. *because → that*
3. *eliminate "but"*
4. *put "from" after "graduated"*
5. *irregardless → regardless*
6. *kind of → somewhat*
7. *and not really meant → than*
8. *nor → or*
9. *plenty → very*
10. *eliminate "so as"*

REDUNDANCIES QUIZ

1. *eliminate "a.m." or "this morning"*
2. *The biography of his life → His biography*
3. *eliminate "both"*
4. *eliminate "together"*
5. *eliminate "and every"*
6. *eliminate "free"*
7. *eliminate "one in"*
8. *eliminate "period of"*
9. *an unexpected → a*
10. *eliminate "also"*

III. IMPROVING SENTENCES
1. BE AGGRESSIVE

1. *landscapes that express OR landscapes, and they express (run-ons)*
2. *used them in a presentation (run-ons; note that there is no comma before "and")*
3. *Brad raised the standards of improvisation (improper modifiers)*
4. *a firefighter → firefighters (noun agreement)*
5. *it → them (pronoun agreement)*

IV. IDENTIFYING SENTENCE ERRORS
1. LOOK FOR COMMON GRAMMAR ERRORS

1. *C: it → they (pronoun agreement)*
2. *B: having → they had (verb tense/punctuation)*
3. *C: has → have (subject-verb agreement)*
4. *B: Jill and I → Jill and me (pro. case)*
5. *A: are suited → is suited (subject-verb agreement)*

V. IMPROVING PARAGRAPHS
4. PARAGRAPHS
¶ I: The first paragraph introduces the idea that something nearly worthless today (such as a watch or a record album) could make money in the future.

¶ II: The second paragraph discusses the fact that the writer's aunt was not thinking about records as an investment when she bought them in the sixties.

¶ III: The third paragraph discusses the reality of making money on these old records and points out that the aunt did not take advantage of her investment.

VI. THE ESSAY
4. REVISING AND PROOFREADING
Errors:
Line 1 - eliminate second "of."
Line 1 - universes → universe's
Line 2 - particuly → particularly
Line 2 - are → is
Line 4 - stopped → stop
Line 5 - gravity. Everything → gravity, everything
Line 6 - believes → believe
Line 7 - ago and → ago, and

6. ELOQUENCE
Answers may vary in this section.

VARY SENTENCE STRUCTURE
Star Wars, released in 1977, was the most popular movie of its kind. The success of Star Wars brought on a barrage of toys and other movie-related merchandise. Young fans collected countless items, including action figures, coloring books, lunch boxes, and anything else bearing the Star Wars logo. These fans are much older now. Because many of them have kept their Star Wars toys in pristine condition, they can sell some of these items to collectors for thousands of dollars.

WRITE SUCCINCTLY
1. *Although Steve, a rich man, gave generously to charity, he still had millions to his name when he died last February.*
2. *My attempt to ascend Maui's Haleakala volcano was cut short by blisters on my feet.*
3. *Elliot's absence today should not sway your vote toward his competitor.*
4. *Collin, usually a quiet man, missed the last shot of the championship series' last game and screamed like I've never heard before.*

USE THE ACTIVE VOICE
1. *The audience **greeted** the rebels' decision to attack the Death Star with approval.*
2. *More than a few fans **waited** outside the theater for tickets to the next show.*

USE CONCRETE LANGUAGE
1. *The movie was a brilliant collage of colors and sounds − I couldn't stop smiling as I left the theater.*
2. *The swordsman, bloody and exhausted, never wavered as he battled the monstrous beast.*
3. *Steam rose from her head, her face turned a deep crimson, and her temples pulsed when Ellie's mom noticed the mess in the kitchen.*
4. *Melodies soaring like eagles, relentless rhythms pounding like the heartbeats of the gods, harmonies richer than kings − I wanted the song to never end.*

USE THE POSITIVE FORM

1. The speeding driver ignored the police car parked at the side of the road.
2. Marshall is a shadow of his former self.

AVOID REPEATING WORDS

1. Scott was **passionate** about the people in his writing. His **primary concern** was the development of realistic **characters**, but he also worked to create those that were heroic in almost superhuman ways.
2. **Courage** is a quality that is not often seen in the world today. It is too often when a man lacks the **strength** to speak up for what he believes. The **bravery** to fight for one's principles seems to frequently be replaced with an attitude of apathy and laziness. People are too busy or too tired to be **courageous**

AVOID -ING WORDS

1. The committee's job was **to maintain** harmony between the developers and the environmentalists.
2. Completing your own taxes is a relatively easy task, but the time involved is usually quite great.
3. **Since** it was the hottest day of the year, I decided to go to the beach.
4. The company is divided into several departments, each **with** a specific duty to fulfill.

ADD IMPORTANCE TO WORDS (WORD-PLACEMENT IN SENTENCES)

1. Even after training over the summer and wearing new, lighter, and supposedly faster running shoes, Jerry came in last.
2. Sadness and longing I noticed in your eyes. OR I noticed in your eyes sadness and longing.

AVOID QUALIFIERS

1. The waiter acted like a boor as he coolly ignored my request for more soup.
2. Anna performed reasonably well on the exam, but she knew she could do better.

PART 2
CRITICAL
READING

I
CRITICAL READING INTRODUCTION

The Critical Reading tutorial is divided into five chapters:

   I.   Introduction

   II.   Vocabulary and Word Parts

   III.   Reading questions

   IV.   Sentence Completion questions

   V.   Critical Reading Answers

TYPES OF QUESTIONS

There are two types of Critical Reading questions on the SAT:

1. Sentence Completion questions
2. Reading questions

TEST LAYOUT

There are a total of 19 Sentence Completion questions (about 28% of the total Critical Reading questions) and 48 Reading questions (about 72% of the questions). The total test time is 70 minutes. The tests may have some variations, but they generally adhere to the following layout:

- 25-minute section (24 questions)
  - 8 Sentence Completion questions (arranged in order of difficulty)
  - 16 Reading questions (*not* arranged in order of difficulty)
- 25-minute section (24 questions)
  - 5 Sentence Completion questions (arranged in order of difficulty)
  - 19 Reading questions (*not* arranged in order of difficulty)
- 20-minute section (19 questions)
  - 6 Sentence Completion questions (arranged in order of difficulty)
  - 13 Reading questions (*not* arranged in order of difficulty)

TIMING STRATEGY

Since the questions of each of the three Sentence Completion sections are arranged in order of difficulty, the last few questions are likely difficult, but the last few questions on the reading sections could very well be easy since these questions are *not* arranged in order of difficulty. **If you have trouble finishing the test, try to always look at every Reading question, even if you have to leave some of the harder Sentence Completion questions blank.** This way, you know that the problems you're not getting to are difficult and commonly-missed. If you find that you are not able to complete the sections, then obviously you must increase your speed. The best way to do this is to learn the techniques in this tutorial and practice diligently.

II

VOCABULARY AND WORD PARTS

Your knowledge of vocabulary words and word parts will have a definite impact on your Critical Reading scores, particularly on the Sentence Completion sections. These Sentence Completion questions will be discussed in chapter IV, but to make sure you are prepared when you get there, begin your study of vocabulary and word parts now. **Be prepared to spend considerable time on your own with these topics. Keep in mind that while most of the techniques throughout this tutorial are very SAT-specific, a working knowledge of vocabulary and word parts will provide benefits that go far beyond the scope of the SAT, both in your future studies and in your reading for pleasure.**

1. VOCABULARY

There are 10 vocabulary lists, each containing about 50 words. The words on the first five lists may be easier to memorize because they contain recognizable word parts or have some other built-in memorizing hints. The words on lists 6-10 may be more difficult, but they are perhaps more useful on harder SAT problems. Lists 6-10 are generally only covered in the 40-hour program and are thus indicated with a 40-hour symbol:

If your vocabulary is already in good shape, work quickly through the first five lists so you can spend extra time on the more difficult, and potentially more valuable, words on the last five lists.

THE FLASH-CARD APPROACH

To get the most out of this section, make flash cards. Definitions for the words are provided on the following pages. **For the words you don't know, write the definition on the *upper half* of the back of a flash card.** Make sure you understand the words in the definitions—defining a word you don't know with words you don't know will not help you. Use a dictionary if necessary.

Use the *bottom half* of the back of the card to write a memorizing *hint* that will help you memorize the word. Usually, the hint should be visible within the vocab word, as displayed in the example on the next page. Word parts, which are discussed in the next section, are often great hints. **The idea is to use the hint as a *bridge* between the vocabulary word and its definition. This is the key to the KlassTutoring approach.** While quizzing yourself, if you can't remember a word's definition, try looking at your hint first, before you look at the definition. Does your hint lead you to the definition? If not, try to think of a better hint.

Hopefully, you will begin to remember your hints when you see the words, which will help you remember the definitions. Of course, for some words, especially the advanced words on lists 6-10, you may have to simply memorize.

Remember, if you are sure you know a word, do not make a flash card for it.

The following is an example of how you might study the word *aggregate*:

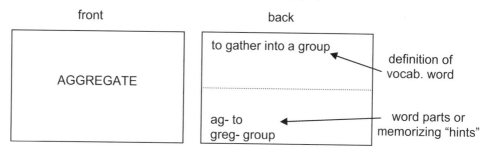

The first few times that you look at the flash card, you may not know the definition. Look at your hint. Since the prefix *ag* means *to* and the root word *greg* means *group*, you will hopefully remember that *aggregate* means *to gather into a group*. (What if you aren't comfortable with the word parts yet? Maybe you have a friend named *Greg* who likes to hang out in groups. This would be a good hint—try to be creative. Any hint that works for you is fine. Just make sure you can *see* the hint when you look at the vocab word.)

Eventually, if you have been studying diligently, you will start to *see* and remember your hint when you look at the vocab word (without having to look at the back of the card). This will lead you to the definition.

STUDYING

To successfully learn the vocabulary words, you must study your flash cards frequently. If you are working with a tutor, you will be given vocabulary assignments one list at a time. Make flash cards for the words you don't know. As you successfully learn a particular word, set aside this word's flash card so you can focus on the more difficult words. As you continue to learn the words, your stack of cards will get smaller and smaller, thereby allowing you to spend even more time on the words with which you are struggling.

Once you feel comfortable with a list of words, bring back your flash cards from previous lists to make sure you continue to remember these words.

(!) **You must study the flash cards at least once or twice a day.** These study sessions may only take fifteen minutes to a half hour, but this sort of repetition is the best way to get the definitions into your *long-term* memory. Students who try to cram the words right before a quiz may do well on the quiz but tend to forget the words by the time they take the SAT, which of course does them no good. Create a schedule that works for you and find time to study the words every day.

In addition to the words on the vocabulary lists, add unknown words to your flash cards as you complete the practice tests and work through this tutorial. Remember, the more words you learn, the more prepared you will be for the SAT.

VOCABULARY ASSIGNMENTS

If you are working on your own, create a schedule that works for you. Typically, you should strive to learn one vocabulary list a week. Take the appropriate quiz before moving on to the next list:

- ☐ VOCAB. LIST 1
- ☐ VOCAB. LIST 2
- ☐ VOCAB. LIST 3
- ☐ VOCAB. LIST 4
- ☐ VOCAB. LIST 5
- ☐ VOCAB. LIST 6
- ☐ VOCAB. LIST 7
- (40) ☐ VOCAB. LIST 8
- ☐ VOCAB. LIST 9
- ☐ VOCAB. LIST 10
- ☐ VOCAB. LISTS 1-5 (Review)
- (40) ☐ VOCAB. LISTS 6-10 (Review)

VOCABULARY LIST 1

abridge - shorten

abstract - apart from concrete realities; difficult to understand

accessible - capable of being reached

acclaim - applaud

acknowledge - to recognize the rights, authority, or status of

acquiesce - agree without protest

acrid - sharp or bitter

adversary - opponent

adverse - unfavorable

advocate (v.) - to plead in favor of

affirmation - a positive assertion

agenda - a plan or program

aggregate (v.) - gather, accumulate

altruistic - unselfishly generous

ambiguous - capable of being understood in two or more possible ways

ambivalence - the state of having contradictory emotions

amorphous - lacking shape

analogous - comparable

anarchist - a person who rebels against authority

antagonism - actively expressed opposition or hostility

antediluvian - extremely primitive or outmoded

antidote - a remedy to counteract the effects of poison; something that relieves

antiquated - outmoded or discredited by reason of age

apathy - lack of caring

appease - pacify

apprehension - suspicion or fear especially of future evil

archaic - characteristic of an earlier or more primitive time

artifact - an object remaining from a particular period

artisan - craftsperson

ascendance - domination

aspire - seek to attain

authoritarian - relating to a concentration of power in a leader

autonomous - self-governing

aversion - firm dislike

avert - to turn away

aviary - a place for keeping birds confined

belie - give a false impression

benevolent - marked by or disposed to doing good

bequeath - to hand down, especially by a will

braggart - a loud arrogant boaster

brevity - shortness of duration

buttress - support

candor - honesty

censorious - critical

certitude - certainty

circumlocution - the use of an unnecessarily large number of words to express an idea

compile - to put together in one book or work

complacency - self-satisfaction, often while unaware of some potential danger

complementary - serving to fill out or complete

compliance - a disposition to yield to others

concede - to accept as true, often grudgingly or hesitantly

conciliatory - soothing

concise - marked by brevity

VOCABULARY LIST 2

concur - approve or agree with

confluence - flowing together

conjecture - a conclusion deduced by surmise or guesswork

constraint - limitation or restrictions

contentious - quarrelsome

contract (v.) - to reduce to smaller size

converge - to come together

conviction - a strong persuasion or belief

cordial - gracious

credulity - gullibility

cursory - casual, hastily done

curtail - shorten

cynical - distrusting or disparaging the motives of others

debilitate - to impair the strength of

defame - to harm the reputation of by libel or slander

degradation - humiliation

dehydrate - to remove water from

deleterious - harmful

delineate - to describe, portray, or set forth with accuracy or in detail

denounce - to pronounce to be blameworthy or evil

depose - dethrone

deride - ridicule

derivative - not original, secondary, something derived

despondent - depressed

detached - separate, apart; indifferent, disinterested

deterrent - something that discourages or turns aside

diffuse - wordy, spread out

digression - a turning aside especially from the main subject

diminution - the act of diminishing or decreasing

discerning - mentally quick

disclose - reveal

discordant - disagreeing, quarrelsome

disinclination - unwillingness

dismiss - to permit or cause to leave

disparage - belittle

disparity - difference; unlikeness; incongruity

dispassionate - not affected by personal or emotional involvement

disputatious - inclined to dispute

dissent - disagree

dissonance - discord

distend - expand

divergent - diverging; differing; deviating

doctrine - a body or system of teachings

document (v.) - to provide with factual or substantial support for statements made

efface - rub out

elaboration - an expansion of something in detail

eloquence - expressiveness

elucidate - explain

elusive - hard to express or define

endorse - to approve, support, or sustain

enmity - hatred, hostility

enunciate - to utter or pronounce esp. in an articulate manner

erratic - wandering; characterized by lack of consistency, regularity, or uniformity

erroneous - mistaken

VOCABULARY LIST 3

erudite - learned, scholarly

eulogy - a speech or writing in praise of a person

euphemism - mild expression in place of unpleasant one

evanescent - fleeting, vanishing

exacerbate - to increase the severity, bitterness, or violence of

exalt - to praise

execute - to carry out; accomplish

exemplary - outstanding

explicit - fully and clearly expressed

facilitate - to make easier; help forward

fallacious - false

fanaticism - excessive zeal

fell (v.) - to knock, strike, shoot, or cut down

fervor - intensity of feeling

florid - reddish, flowery

foolhardy - recklessly or thoughtlessly bold

frivolous - lacking seriousness or sense

frugality - thrift

glutton - one who overeats

gratify - to satisfy; indulge

gratuitous - given freely

gravity - seriousness

gregarious - fond of the company of others; sociable

gullible - easily deceived or cheated

hardy - sturdy; strong

homogeneous - of the same kind

ignominy - deep disgrace

illicit - illegal

illusory - deceptive; misleading

immutable - unchangeable

impede - obstruct; hinder

implausible - unlikely

implication - something suggested as naturally to be inferred or understood

implicit - implied, rather than expressly stated

incisive - penetrating, cutting; clear and direct, sharp, keen

inclusive - including a great deal, or including everything concerned

incongruous - not fitting, absurd

inconsequential - of little or no importance; insignificant

incontrovertible - not open to question or dispute

incorrigible - bad beyond correction or reform

indefatigable - tireless

indelible - not able to be erased

indict - to charge with an offense or crime

indifferent - unmoved, unconcerned

induce - to bring about, produce, or cause

inert - having no inherent power of action

infamous - having an extremely bad reputation

ingenious - clever

inherent - existing in someone or something as a permanent and inseparable element

innate - existing in one from birth; inborn; native

innocuous - harmless

innovation - something new or different introduced

insolvent - bankrupt

instigate - to urge, provoke, or incite to some action

VOCABULARY LIST 4

insuperable - insurmountable

intervene - to come between disputing people; intercede; mediate

intimidate - to make timid; fill with fear

intractable - not easily controlled or directed; stubborn

inundate - to cover with a flood; overwhelm

invert - to turn upside down

irreproachable - blameless

irresolute - not resolute; doubtful; infirm of purpose

jocular - characterized by joking or jesting

laconic - brief, to the point

languish - to become weak or feeble; droop; fade

laud - praise

levity - lack of seriousness

linger - to remain in a place longer than is usual or expected

lofty - of imposing height; exalted in rank, dignity, or character

luxuriant - producing abundantly, as soil; fertile; fruitful; productive

magnanimous - great-hearted

malicious - hateful

materialism - preoccupation with or emphasis on material objects

methodical - systematic; orderly

misanthrope - hater of man

miserly - stingy, mean

misnomer - a misapplied or inappropriate name or designation

negate - to deny the existence or truth of

notoriety - the state of being widely known

novelty - something new

nullify - to render or declare legally void or inoperative

nurture - to feed and protect

obdurate - stubborn

obstinate - firmly or stubbornly adhering to one's purpose, opinion, etc.

ominous - threatening

opportunist - one who takes advantage of opportunities as they arise

optimist - one who usually expects a favorable outcome

orator - public speaker

ostentatious - characterized by pretentious show to impress others

pacifist - a person who is opposed to war or violence

parody - humorous imitation

penury - poverty; stinginess

perfunctory - performed merely as a routine duty; hasty and superficial

peripheral - outer

perpetuate - to preserve from extinction or oblivion

pervasive - spread throughout

philanthropist - a person who engages in charitable giving

pitfall - any trap or danger for the unwary

pithy - concise, meaningful

placate - pacify, conciliate

ponderous - of great weight; heavy; massive

prattle - to talk in a foolish or simple-minded way; chatter

preclude - make impossible

predecessor - a person who precedes another in an office, position, etc.

predilection - partiality, preference

presumptuous - arrogant

prevalent - widespread

VOCABULARY LIST 5

profane - irreverent, blasphemous

profusion - abundance; a great quantity or amount

proliferation - a rapid and often excessive spread or increase

prolific - abundantly fruitful

protract - to draw out or lengthen, esp. in time

provoke - to incite to anger or enrage

quandary - dilemma

quiescent - at rest; quiet; still

ramble - to wander around in a leisurely, aimless manner

rancor - bitterness

raze - to tear down; demolish

recant - retract previous statement

recluse - loner

recount - to relate or narrate; tell in detail

repel - to drive or force back

replete - filled to the brim

resolution - a resolve or determination

resolve (n.) - firmness of purpose or intent

respite - interval of relief

resplendent - shining brilliantly; gleaming; splendid

restraint - reserve in feelings, behavior, etc.

retract - to draw back; to withdraw a promise, vow, etc.

sanction - approve

satirical - mocking

seclusion - solitude; isolation

servile - slavishly submissive or obsequious; fawning

spurn - reject

steadfast - firm in purpose

strident - loud and harsh

subordinate - placed in or belonging to a lower order or rank

substantiate - to establish by proof or competent evidence

superficial - trivial, on the surface

superfluous - being more than is sufficient or required; excessive

susceptible - subject to some influence; impressionable

sustain - to keep up or keep going

tantamount - equivalent in effect or value

tenacity - persistence in maintaining, adhering to, or seeking something; courage

threadbare - shabby or poor

tranquility - calmness; peacefulness

transient - temporary

trifling - of very little importance; trivial; insignificant

undermine - to attack by indirect, secret, or underhand means

uniformity - overall sameness, homogeneity, or regularity

unkempt - uncared for in appearance

unobtrusive - not blatant

unprecedented - without previous instance; unparalleled

vaporize - to cause to change into vapor

verbose - wordy

viable - practicable; workable

vigor - active strength

virulent - hostile, bitter

whimsical - capricious, unpredictable

zealot - fanatic

abate - subside, lessen

abstemious - sparing in eating or drinking

abstruse - obscure, hard to understand

accolade - any award, honor, or laudatory notice

acquire - get as one's own

adroit - skillful

adulation - excessive flattery or admiration

aesthetic - pertaining to a sense of the beautiful

affable - easily approachable

alleviate - to make easier to endure; lessen

aloof - apart, reserved

anecdote - a short account of a particular incident

anomaly - irregularity

apocryphal - untrue

arable - capable of producing crops

arbitrary - depending on individual discretion and not fixed by law

arbitrator - judge

arid - being without moisture; extremely dry

arrogance - offensive display of superiority or self-importance; overbearing pride

articulate (adj.) - uttered clearly in distinct syllables

ascetic - practicing self-denial

assuage - soothe

astute - of keen penetration or discernment

atrophy - wasting away

attribute (v.) - to explain by indicating a cause

audacious - extremely bold or daring; recklessly brave

austere - forbiddingly stern

avarice - insatiable greed for riches

banal - commonplace

beguile - mislead

bleak - bare; desolate

blighted - destroyed; deteriorated

bolster - to add to, support, or uphold

cacophonous - having a harsh or discordant sound

cajole - coax; persuade w/ pleasing words

calculated - carefully thought out or planned

capricious - impulsive, unpredictable

caricature - exaggeration by means of ludicrous distortion

carping - finding fault

censure - strong disapproval

charlatan - a fraud (person)

clemency - disposition to show compassion or forgiveness in judging or punishing; leniency

cliché - a trite, stereotyped expression

coalesce - to grow together or into one body

coercion - use of force to get someone to obey

composure - mental calmness

comprehensive - of large scope; covering or involving much; inclusive

concede - to acknowledge as true, just, or proper; admit

condone - to give tacit approval to

conflagration - a destructive fire

confound - to perplex or amaze; bewilder; confuse

contend - to struggle in opposition

corroborate - to make more certain; confirm

corrode - to wear away gradually

corrugated - wrinkled; furrowed

criterion - standard used in judging

cryptic - secret, hidden

culpable - deserving blame

daunt - intimidate

debunk - to expose as being pretentious, false, or exaggerated

decorum - dignified propriety of behavior

deference - courteous regard for another's wishes

deplore - to regret deeply or strongly; lament

depravity - wickedness

deprecate - to express earnest disapproval of

desiccate - dry up

detrimental - damaging; harmful

devious - not straightforward; shifty or crooked

devise - to contrive, plan, or elaborate

diligence - constant and earnest effort to accomplish what is undertaken

discount - to leave out of account; disregard

discrepancy - difference; inconsistency

discrimination - the power of making fine distinctions; discriminating judgment

disdain - view with scorn

disperse - to drive or send off in various directions; scatter

disseminate - spread

dogmatic - opinionated

dormant - sleeping

dubious - of doubtful quality or propriety; questionable

dupe - to fool; someone easily fooled

duplicity - double-dealing, hypocrisy

duration - the length of time something continues or exists

ebullient - showing excitement

eccentric - deviating from the recognized or customary character, practice, etc.; irregular; erratic; peculiar; odd

eclectic - from disparate sources

edify - to instruct and improve morally

elated - very happy or proud; jubilant

elegy - sad poem or song, especially at someone's death

elicit - to draw or bring out or forth

emaciated - thin by a gradual wasting away of flesh

embellish - to ornament or adorn

emulate - to try to equal or excel; imitate with effort to equal or surpass

enervate - weaken

engender - to produce, cause, or give rise to

enhance - increase; improve

enigma - a puzzling or inexplicable occurrence or situation

ephemeral - short lived

equivocal - ambiguous, intentionally misleading

esoteric - limited to the understanding of a select few

excerpt - a passage or quotation taken from a book, etc.

exemplify - serve as an example

exhaustive - comprehensive; thorough

exhilaration - animation, joyousness, jollity, hilarity

exonerate - free from guilt or blame

expedient - suitable for achieving a particular end in a given circumstance

expedite - to execute promptly

exploit - to use selfishly for one's own ends

extol - praise

extraneous - not pertinent; irrelevant

extricate - free

exuberance - the state of being joyously unrestrained and enthusiastic

fallow - uncultivated

falter - to hesitate or waver in action or purpose

fastidious - difficult to please

feasible - capable of being done

fitful - intermittent

flagrant - blatant

furtive - sneaky

garrulous - wordy, talkative

guile - crafty or artful deception; duplicity

hackneyed - made commonplace or trite; stale

hamper - to hold back; hinder; impede

haughtiness - overbearing pride evidenced by a superior manner toward inferiors

heed - to give careful attention to

heresy - opinion contrary to popular belief

hyperbole - obvious and intentional exaggeration

hypocritical - feigning to be what one is not

hypothetical - assumed by hypothesis; supposed

iconoclastic - attacking cherished traditions

idiosyncrasy - strange trait

impair - weaken or damage

impeccable - faultless; flawless; irreproachable

impecunious - without money

implement (v.) - to put into effect

impudence - offensively bold behavior

inane - silly, senseless

inception - beginning; start

incidental - incurred casually and in addition to the regular or main amount

incite - to stir, encourage, or urge on

indigenous - native

indiscriminate - lacking in care, judgment, selectivity, etc.

indolent - lazy

infer - to derive by reasoning

insipid - lacking flavor

insularity - narrow-mindedness; isolation

integrity - adherence to moral and ethical principles; soundness of moral character

ironic - conveying a meaning that is the opposite of its literal meaning

judicious - characterized by sound judgment

labyrinth - any confusingly intricate state of things or events

lament - grieve

lampoon - to ridicule

lavish - expended or produced in abundance

lethargic - drowsy, dull

listless - lacking spirit or energy

lurid - gruesome; horrible; revolting

marred - damaged or spoiled to a certain extent

meager - deficient in quantity or quality

meander - to wander aimlessly; ramble

mercenary - working or acting merely for money

meticulous - taking or showing extreme care about minute details; precise

mitigate - appease

mock - to attack or treat with ridicule, contempt, or derision

mollify - soothe

morose - gloomily or sullenly ill-humored

mundane - common; ordinary; banal; unimaginative

munificent - very generous

nefarious - very wicked

nonchalance - cool indifference or lack of concern; casualness

objective (adj.) - not influenced by personal feelings, interpretations, or prejudice

obliterate - to remove or destroy all traces of

oblivion - the state of being completely forgotten or unknown

obscure (v.) - to conceal (by confusing)

opaque - dark, not transparent

opulence - extreme wealth

ornate - elaborately or excessively decorated

parsimony - extreme or excessive economy or frugality; stinginess

partisan - an adherent or supporter of a person, group, party, or cause

paucity - scarcity

pessimism - the tendency to see only bad or undesirable outcomes

phenomena - facts, occurrences, or circumstances observed (plural of phenomenon)

piety - reverence for God or devout fulfillment of religious obligations

pragmatic - practical (not idealistic)

precarious - uncertain; unstable; insecure

precocious - pertaining to uncharacteristically early development, esp. in maturity

predator - any organism that exists by preying upon other organisms

pretentious - ostentatious, making excessive claims

prodigal - wasteful (w/ money)

prodigious - marvelous

profligate - recklessly prodigal or extravagant

profound - deep, important

propriety - conformity to established standards of good or proper behavior or manners

provincial - unsophisticated

proximity - nearness in place or time

prudent - wise or judicious in practical affairs

qualified - having the qualities that fit a person for some function, office, etc.

ratify - formally approve

rebuff - snub; beat back

rebuttal - refutation, denial, confutation

rectify - to make, put, or set right; remedy; correct

redundant - characterized by verbosity or unnecessary repetition in expressing ideas

refute - to prove to be false

relegate - to send or consign to an inferior position, place, etc.

relevant - applicable; appropriate; suitable; fitting

remorse - deep and painful regret for wrongdoing

renounce - to give up or put aside voluntarily

reprehensible - deserving blame

reprove - censure

repudiate - disown, disavow

rescind - cancel

reserve (n.) - restraint or caution in one's words and actions

resigned - unresisting

reticence - inclination to silence; reluctance; restraint

(40) VOCABULARY LIST 10

reverent - deeply respectful

rhetorical - concerned with mere style or effect

rigor - strictness, severity, or harshness

robust - strong and healthy; hardy; vigorous

ruthless - without pity or compassion; cruel; merciless
sage - wise man

saturate - to soak, impregnate, or imbue thoroughly or completely
savory - pleasant or agreeable in taste or smell

scanty - meager

scrupulous - extremely thorough

scrutinize - to examine in detail with careful or critical attention
sedentary - sitting

skeptic - a person who maintains a doubting attitude
sluggish - lacking in energy; lazy; indolent

somber - gloomy, depressing, or dismal

soporific - sleep-causing

sporadic - appearing or happening at irregular intervals in time; occasional
spurious - false

squander - waste

stagnant - motionless, stale

static (adj.) - fixed or stationary

stoic - unmoved by joy or grief

stolid - dull

stupefy - to put into a state of little or no sensibility; astound; astonish
submissive - inclined or ready to submit; unresistingly or humbly obedient
subside - decline; descend; settle

subtlety - delicacy of character or meaning

succinct - brief

surpass - to go beyond

surreptitious - secret, furtive

sycophant - servile flatterer; a yes-man

taciturn - habitually silent

taint - to infect, contaminate, corrupt, or spoil

temper (v.) - to moderate; to mitigate; to soften

tentative - unsure; uncertain; not definite or positive
terse - concise; brief; pithy

thrive - prosper

tirade - a prolonged outburst of bitter, outspoken denunciation
torpor - sluggishness

trepidation - fear

trite - lacking in freshness or effectiveness because of excessive repetition; hackneyed; stale
truncate - to shorten by cutting off a part; cut short
turbulence - violent disorder or commotion

turmoil - a state of great commotion, confusion, or disturbance
unwarranted - having no justification; groundless

usurp - seize another's power

vacillate - waiver, fluctuate

venerate - revere, respect

vilify - to speak ill of; defame

vindicate - clear from blame

virtuoso - a person who has special knowledge or skill in a field
volatile - changeable; explosive

voluble - fluent; talkative

㉚ 2. WORD PARTS

Word parts are the basic building blocks that make up many of the words in the English language. In particular, these are *prefixes*, *roots*, and *suffixes*. We will focus only on the prefixes and roots; suffixes have more to do with word *usage* than meaning.

There are two important reasons to study word parts:

1. **By memorizing many of the basic word parts, you can discover the meanings of unfamiliar words—words you would otherwise have no way of knowing.**
2. **It becomes easier to memorize vocabulary words by identifying familiar word parts that make up these words.**

The word part lists contain the most common prefixes and root words. For each word part, there are several example words. Define these words using a dictionary. These example words are intended to help you learn the word parts, so you must **use the word part's meaning in your definitions**.

It is important to create flash cards to help study the word parts. **Write the word part on the front of the card and its meaning on the *upper half* of the back. On the *lower half* of the back, write an example word that you think will help you remember the word part's meaning.** For example, the prefix *bi-* is easy to remember because it makes up the familiar word *bi*cycle, a *two-wheeled* vehicle. As with the vocabulary words, **the idea is to use a familiar example word as a bridge between the word part and its meaning**. While quizzing yourself, if you can't remember a word part's meaning, try looking at the example word first. Of course, for some word parts, you may have to simply memorize.

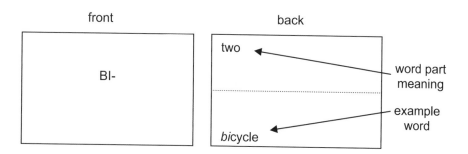

STUDYING

! **Just as with the vocabulary words, frequent repetition is the only way to learn the word parts.** The word parts will be assigned by lists. Create a schedule and study your flash cards every day.

WORD-PARTS ASSIGNMENTS

If you are working on your own, create a schedule that works for you. Typically, you should strive to learn two word-parts lists a week. Take the appropriate quiz before moving on to the next lists:

- ☐ PREFIX LISTS 1 AND 2
- ☐ PREFIX LISTS 3 AND 4
- ☐ R.W. (ROOT WORD) LISTS 1 AND 2
- ☐ R.W. LISTS 3 AND 4
- ☐ R.W. LISTS 5 AND 6
- ☐ R.W. LISTS 7 AND 8
- ☐ R.W. LISTS 9 AND 10
- ☐ ALL WORD PARTS

PREFIX LIST 1

AB, ABS – from, away from

    abandon

    abduct

    abjure

    abject

    abstain

    abstemious

AC, AD, AF, AG, AP, AR, AS, AT – to, forward

    accord

    act

    admit

    aggregation

    appoint

    assign

    attain

    attract

AMBI – both

    ambidextrous

    ambiguous

    ambivalent

AN, A – without

    anarchy

    anemia

    amoral

ANTE – before

    antecedent

    antediluvian

ANTI – against, opposite

    antipathy

    antiseptic

ARCH – chief

    archangel

    archbishop

    archenemy

ARCH – first

    archeology

    archetype

BI – two

    biennial

    bicycle

CIRCUM – around

    circumnavigate

    circumspect

    circumscribe

COM, CO, COL, CON, COR – with, together

    coeditor

    colony

    combine

    communicate

    conference

    congruent

    corroborate

    correlate

PREFIX LIST 2

CONTRA, CONTRO — against

    contravene

    controversy

DE — down, away

    debase

    decline

    decrease

    degenerate

    deplane

    destroy

    deteriorate

DI — two

    dichotomy

    dilemma

DIA — across

    diagonal

    diameter

DIS — not

    disapprove

    discord

    disparity

DYS — faulty, bad

    dyslexia

    dystopia

    dysfunction

EX, E — out

    eject

    exit

    expel

EXTRA, EXTRO — beyond, outside

    extracurricular

    extraneous

    extraterrestrial

    extrovert

HOMO — alike

    homogeneous

    homophone

    homonym

HYPER — above, excessively

    hyperbole

    hyperventilate

IN, IL, IM, IR — not

    illegible

    improper

    inefficient

    inarticulate

    irrevocable

IN, IM — in, on, upon

    impression

    incision

    invite

PREFIX LIST 3

INTER — between, among

    interjection

    intermission

    intervene

INTRA, INTRO — within

    intramural

    introvert

MEGA — great, million

    megadose

    megaton

META — involving change

    metabolism

    metamorphosis

MICRO — small

    microcosm

    microscopic

MIS — bad, improper

    misanthrope

    misbehave

    misnomer

MONO — one

    monarchy

    monologue

    monotheism

MULTI — many

    multiply

    multitude

NEO — new

    neologism

NON — not

    nonentity

    nonfat

    nonprofit

OB, OC, OP — against

    obtrude

    object (verb)

    occlude

    oppose

    oppression

PAN — all, every

    panacea

    panorama

PAR, PARA — related

    parallel

    paramedic

    parody

PER — through, completely

    perambulate

    permeable

    perspire

    pervade

PERI — around

    perimeter

    periscope

PREFIX LIST 4

POLY – many

    polygamy

    polygon

POST – after

    posthumous

    postscript

PRE – before

    prefix

    premonition

PRIM – first

    primordial

    primary

PRO – forward, in favor of

    pro-choice

    propel

    proponent

PSEUDO – false

    pseudonym

RE – again, back

    reiterate

    rewind

RETRO – backward

    retrospect

    retrofit

SEMI – half, partly

    semicircle

    semifinal

SUB – under, less

    subdue

    subway

SUPER, SUR – over, above

    supernatural

    superstar

    surfeit

    surtax

SYN, SYM, – with, together

    synchronize

    sympathize

TRANS – across

    transport

    transpose

ULTRA – beyond, excessive

    ultramodern

    ultrasound

UN – not

    unkempt

    untie

UNI – one

    unison

    unicycle

WITH – against

    withhold

    withstand

ROOT WORD LIST 1

AC, ACR — sharp, bitter

    acrimonious

    acerbity

    acid

AGRI, AGRARI — field

    agriculture

    agrarian

ALT — high

    altitude

    altimeter

ALTER, ALTRU — other

    altruistic

    alter ego

    alternate

AM — love

    amorous

    amicable

ANN, ENN — year

    annuity

    annual

    biennial

ANTHROP — man

    anthropology

    philanthropy

AQUA — water

    aquarium

    aqueduct

ASTER — star

    astronomy

    asterisk

AUD, AUDIT — hear

    audible

    auditorium

    audience

AUTO — self, on its own

    autobiography

    automobile

    autonomous

BELLI — war

    bellicose

    belligerent

BEN — good

    benevolent

    benign

BIBLIO — book

    Bible

    bibliography

    bibliophile

BIO — life

    biography

    biology

ROOT WORD LIST 2

CAPT, CEPT, CIP — to take

 capture

 except

 intercept

 participate

CAPIT, CAPT — head

 capital

 captain

 decapitate

CARN — flesh

 carnage

 carnivorous

CED, CESS — to go

 antecedent

 process

 proceed

 recede

CELER — swift

 accelerate

 celerity

CENT — one hundred

 bicentennial

 cent

 century

CHRON — time

 chronology

 anachronism

CID — kill

 fratricide

 homicide

 suicide

CIS — cut

 incision

 scissors

CLAM — to cry out

 acclamation

 acclaim

 clamorous

 exclamation

CLAUS, CLOS, CLUD, CLUS — to close

 claustrophobia

 conclude

 closet

 enclose

 exclusive

 reclusive

CORD — heart

 accord

 discord

ROOT WORD LIST 3

CORP, CORPOR — body

    incorporate

    corpse

    corporation

CRED — to believe

    credo

    credulity

    incredulous

CUR — to care

    curator

    secure

CURR, CURS — to run

    excursion

    cursory

    precursor

    curriculum

DEI, DIV — God, god

    deify

    deity

    divine

DEM — people

    demagogue

    democracy

    epidemic

DERM — skin

    dermatitis

    dermatology

DI, DIURN — day

    diary

    diurnal

DIC, DICT — to say

    contradiction

    dictate

    diction

    predict

DOCT, DACT — teach

    didactic

    doctrine

    doctor

DOM, DOMIN — to rule

    domain

    dominate

    dominion

    indomitable

DUC, DUCT — to lead

    aqueduct

    induce

    reduce

    viaduct

EGO — I

    ego

    egocentric

ROOT WORD LIST 4

ERR — to wander or err

    error

    erratic

    errant

EU — good, beautiful

    euphemism

    eulogy

FALL, FALS — to deceive, to err

    fallacy

    false

    infallible

FID — belief, faith

    infidel

    confide

    confident

FIN — limit

    confine

    finish

    finite

FLECT, FLEX — bend

    deflection

    flexible

    reflect

FORT — luck

    fortunate

    fortune

FORT — strong

    comfort

    fort

    fortitude

    fortress

FRAG, FRACT — break

    fractious

    fracture

    fragile

    fragment

GAM — marriage

    monogamy

    polygamy

GEN, GENER — class, race

    gender

    generation

    genre

    genus

    heterogeneous

GRAD, GRESS — go, step

    gradual

    graduate

    regress

GREG — group

    gregarious

    aggregate

ROOT WORD LIST 5

IT, ITINER — journey, way

    exit

    itinerant

    itinerary

JAC, JACT, JEC — to throw

    ejaculatory

    eject

    interjection

    projectile

    reject

LABOR — to work

    labor

    laboratory

    collaborate

LOG — word

    dialogue

    logbook

    monologue

LOG — study

    astrology

    logic

    theology

LOQU, LOCUT — to talk

    circumlocution

    eloquent

    loquacious

    soliloquy

LUC — light, clarity

    elucidate

    lucid

    translucent

MAGN — great

    magnificent

    magnify

    magnanimity

MAL — bad

    dismal

    maladroit

    malevolent

    malfunction

    malicious

    malignant

MAR — sea

    marine

    maritime

    submarine

MATER, MATR — mother

    maternal

    matriarch

    matron

ROOT WORD LIST 6

MIT, MISS — to send

    admit

    dismiss

    missile

    transmit

MOB, MOT, MOV — move

    mobile

    motivate

    motor

    move

MON, MONIT — warn

    admonish

    monitor

    premonition

MORI, MORT — death

    immortal

    moribund

    mortuary

MORPH — shape, form

    amorphous

    metamorphosis

MUT — change

    immutable

    mutate

NAT — born

    innate

    prenatal

    nativity

NAV — ship

    navigate

    navy

    unnavigable

NOM, NOWN, NAM, NYM — name

    anonymous

    ignominy

    misnomer

    name

    nomenclature

    renown

OMNI — all

    omnipotent

    omniscient

    omnivorous

PATER, PATR — father

    paternal

    patriarch

    patriot

ROOT WORD LIST 7

PATH, PAS — feeling

    antipathy

    compassion

    empathy

    passion

    pathos

    sympathy

PED, POD — foot

    pedal

    pedestrian

    quadruped

    tripod

PEL, PULS — to drive

    compel

    expel

    impulse

    propeller

    propulsion

PHIL — love

    philander

    philanthropist

PHON — sound

    microphone

    phonograph

    telephone

PORT, PORTAT — to carry

    export

    import

    portable

    transport

POTEN — able, powerful

    impotent

    potent

    potential

PSYCH — mind

    psychic

    psychology

    psychopath

QUE, QUI — to ask

    inquire

    inquisition

    query

    question

RUPT — to break

    corrupt

    interrupt

    rupture

SACR, SANC — holy

    sacred

    sanctuary

    sanctify

ROOT WORD LIST 8

SCOP – to see

    scope

    telescope

SCRIB, SCRIPT – to write

    circumscribe

    inscription

    scribe

    scribble

    script

SECT – cut

    bisect

    intersect

    secant

    section

    sector

SENT, SENS – to think, to feel

    consent

    sensory

    sensitive

    sensual

SEQU, SEC – to follow

    consecutive

    consequence

    obsequious

    second

    sequel

SOMN, SO – sleep

    insomnia

    somnambulist

    soporific

SPEC, SPECT – to look at

    inspect

    perspective

    spectator

    spectrum

    spectacle

STRING, STRICT – bind

    constrict

    strict

    string

    stringent

TELE – from far

    television

    telephone

    telegraph

TEMPOR – time

    contemporary

    tempo

    temporary

ROOT WORD LIST 9

TEN, TENT, TAIN – to hold, to stretch, thin

    distend

    retain

    tenable

    tension

    tent

    tentacle

TERM – end

    interminable

    terminal

    terminate

TERR – land

    subterranean

    terrain

    terrestrial

    territory

THERM – heat

    thermal

    thermodynamics

    thermometer

TRACT – drag, pull

    intractable

    subtract

    traction

    tractor

VAC – empty

    vacuum

    vacant

    vacuous

VERB – word

    verbiage

    verbose

    verbatim

VERS, VERT – turn

    aversion

    controversy

    convert

    diversion

    inversion

    revert

VITA – life

    revitalize

    vital

    vitality

    vitamin

VIA – way

    deviation

    via

    viaduct

ROOT WORD LIST 10

VINC, VICT, VANQ — to conquer

    invincible

    vanquish

    victory

VOC, VACAT — to call

    avocation

    irrevocable

    provocation

    vocal

    vocation

    vociferous

3. VOCABULARY AND WORD-PART QUIZZES

VOCABULARY QUIZZES

The vocabulary quizzes list several words taken from the indicated vocabulary lists. For each word, write a brief definition. There is a quiz for each of the following vocabulary lists. The answers to all quizzes can be found in the Answers chapter starting on page 305.

- VOCAB. LIST 1
- VOCAB. LIST 2
- VOCAB. LIST 3
- VOCAB. LIST 4
- VOCAB. LIST 5
- VOCAB. LISTS 1-5

(40)
- VOCAB. LIST 6
- VOCAB. LIST 7
- VOCAB. LIST 8
- VOCAB. LIST 9
- VOCAB. LIST 10
- VOCAB. LISTS 6-10

(30) WORD-PART QUIZZES

The word-part quizzes list several words containing word parts taken from the prefix or root word lists. Underline and define all word parts in each word; some words will contain more than one word part. **It is not necessary to define the words—only the word parts. These quizzes are cumulative, so look for word parts from previous word part lists.**

For a given word, if you see more than one word part for the same part of the word and are not sure which one to put, put all possible answers. If you write the correct answer, give yourself credit, even if you wrote incorrect answers as well. For example, in the word *amoral*, you might see the following possible word parts: *a - without* or *am - love*. If you're not sure which one to put, put them both. Usually, on the SAT, you will know which word part to focus on. (The correct answer for *amoral* is *a - without*.)

There is a quiz for each of the following word part lists:

- PREFIX LISTS 1 AND 2
- PREFIX LISTS 3 AND 4
- R.W. (ROOT WORD) LISTS 1 AND 2
- R.W. LISTS 3 AND 4
- R.W. LISTS 5 AND 6
- R.W. LISTS 7 AND 8
- R.W. LISTS 9 AND 10
- ALL WORD PARTS

QUIZ: VOCAB. LIST 1

1. abridge
2. acclaim
3. acquiesce
4. acrid
5. adverse
6. altruistic
7. ambivalence
8. amorphous
9. analogous
10. apathy
11. aspire
12. autonomous
13. aversion
14. belie
15. buttress
16. censorious
17. certitude
18. circumlocution
19. complacency
20. conciliatory

QUIZ: VOCAB. LIST 2

1. confluence
2. contentious
3. credulity
4. curtail
5. cynical
6. deleterious
7. depose
8. deride
9. despondent
10. diffuse
11. discerning
12. disinclination
13. disparage
14. dissent
15. distend
16. efface
17. eloquence
18. elucidate
19. enmity
20. erroneous

QUIZ: VOCAB. LIST 3

1. erudite
2. evanescent
3. exemplary
4. fallacious
5. fanaticism
6. fervor
7. frugality
8. glutton
9. gratuitous
10. gravity
11. homogeneous
12. ignominy
13. implausible
14. incisive
15. indefatigable
16. indelible
17. indifferent
18. ingenious
19. innocuous
20. insolvent

QUIZ: VOCAB. LIST 4

1. insuperable
2. intractable
3. irreproachable
4. laconic
5. laud
6. levity
7. magnanimous
8. malicious
9. miserly
10. obdurate
11. orator
12. penury
13. peripheral
14. pervasive
15. philanthropist
16. pithy
17. placate
18. predilection
19. presumptuous
20. prevalent

QUIZ: VOCAB. LIST 5

1. profane
2. prolific
3. quandary
4. quiescent
5. rancor
6. recluse
7. replete
8. respite
9. sanction
10. satirical
11. strident
12. superficial
13. tantamount
14. transient
15. unkempt
16. unobtrusive
17. verbose
18. vigor
19. whimsical
20. zealot

(40) QUIZ: VOCAB. LIST 6

1. abstemious
2. abstruse
3. adroit
4. aloof
5. anomaly
6. apocryphal
7. arbitrator
8. ascetic
9. assuage
10. austere
11. banal
12. beguile
13. blighted
14. cajole
15. capricious
16. carping
17. charlatan
18. clemency
19. coercion
20. composure

(40) QUIZ: VOCAB. LIST 7

1. criterion
2. cryptic
3. culpable
4. deference
5. depravity
6. desiccate
7. disdain
8. disseminate
9. dogmatic
10. dupe
11. duplicity
12. ebullient
13. eclectic
14. edify
15. enervate
16. enhance
17. ephemeral
18. equivocal
19. exemplify
20. exonerate

(40) QUIZ: VOCAB. LIST 8

1. extricate
2. fallow
3. fastidious
4. flagrant
5. furtive
6. garrulous
7. hackneyed
8. hyperbole
9. iconoclastic
10. idiosyncrasy
11. impecunious
12. impudence
13. inane
14. indolent
15. insipid
16. insularity
17. lament
18. lampoon
19. lethargic
20. listless

40 QUIZ: VOCAB. LIST 9

1. mitigate
2. mollify
3. munificent
4. nefarious
5. opaque
6. opulence
7. parsimony
8. paucity
9. pragmatic
10. pretentious
11. prodigal
12. profound
13. provincial
14. ratify
15. rebuff
16. reprove
17. repudiate
18. rescind
19. resigned
20. reticence

40 QUIZ: VOCAB. LIST 10

1. scanty
2. scrupulous
3. sedentary
4. soporific
5. spurious
6. stoic
7. stolid
8. succinct
9. surreptitious
10. sycophant
11. taciturn
12. temper
13. terse
14. torpor
15. turmoil
16. usurp
17. vacillate
18. vindicate
19. volatile
20. voluble

QUIZ: VOCAB. LISTS 1-5

1. adversary
2. aggregate
3. appease
4. candor
5. cordial
6. cursory
7. degradation
8. dissonance
9. euphemism
10. florid
11. illicit
12. incongruous
13. misanthrope
14. novelty
15. ominous
16. parody
17. recant
18. spurn
19. susceptible
20. virulent

(40) QUIZ: VOCAB. LISTS 6-10

1. abate
2. affable
3. atrophy
4. coercion
5. daunt
6. dormant
7. elegy
8. esoteric
9. extol
10. fitful
11. heresy
12. indigenous
13. ornate
14. precocious
15. prodigious
16. reprehensible
17. sage
18. stagnant
19. trepidation
20. venerate

Review the Word Part instructions on page 231.

QUIZ: PREFIX LISTS 1 AND 2

1. abstain
2. act
3. attain
4. ambidextrous
5. amoral
6. antediluvian
7. antipathy
8. archenemy
9. archetype
10. biennial
11. circumspect
12. combine
13. controversy
14. decline
15. dichotomy
16. diameter
17. disparity
18. dysfunction
19. exit
20. extraterrestrial
21. homonym
22. hyperventilate
23. inefficient
24. irrevocable
25. incision

QUIZ: PREFIX LISTS 3 AND 4

1. intermission
2. introvert
3. metabolism
4. microcosm
5. misbehave
6. monologue
7. multitude
8. neologism
9. obtrude
10. occlude
11. oppose
12. panacea
13. parody
14. permeable
15. perimeter
16. postscript
17. primordial
18. propel
19. retrospect
20. surfeit
21. synchronize
22. transpose
23. ultrasound
24. unison
25. withstand

Remember, some words have more than one word part. Each word part is worth one point.

QUIZ: R.W. LISTS 1 AND 2

1. acrimonious
2. agrarian
3. altimeter
4. alternate
5. amorous
6. annuity
7. anthropology
8. aquarium
9. asterisk
10. auditorium
11. autobiography
12. belligerent
13. bibliography
14. bibliophile
15. intercept
16. decapitate
17. carnivorous
18. proceed
19. celerity
20. cent
21. anachronism
22. suicide
23. scissors
24. exclamation
25. exclusive

QUIZ: R.W. LISTS 3 AND 4

1. corporation
2. credo
3. secure
4. curriculum
5. divine
6. demagogue
7. dermatology
8. diurnal
9. didactic
10. doctrine
11. doctor
12. indomitable
13. induce
14. egocentric
15. euphemism
16. fallacy
17. confide
18. finish
19. reflect
20. fortunate
21. fortress
22. fractious
23. monogamy
24. genre
25. regress

QUIZ: R.W. LISTS 5 AND 6

1. itinerant
2. projectile
3. collaborate
4. logbook
5. astrology
6. soliloquy
7. lucid
8. magnify
9. maladroit
10. maritime
11. matron
12. transmit
13. mobile
14. premonition
15. moribund
16. metamorphosis
17. immutable
18. prenatal
19. unnavigable
20. anonymous
21. nomenclature
22. renown
23. omnivorous
24. paternal
25. patriot

QUIZ: R.W. LISTS 7 AND 8

1. compassion
2. sympathy
3. quadruped
4. tripod
5. compel
6. impulse
7. philander
8. phonograph
9. portable
10. potential
11. psychopath
12. inquisition
13. corrupt
14. sanctuary
15. scope
16. scribe
17. secant
18. consent
19. consequence
20. somnambulist
21. perspective
22. stringent
23. telephone
24. contemporary
25. tempo

QUIZ: R.W. LISTS 9 AND 10

1. distend
2. retain
3. tenable
4. terminal
5. terrestrial
6. thermodynamics
7. intractable
8. vacuous
9. verbatim
10. controversy
11. convert
12. vitamin
13. deviation
14. vanquish
15. irrevocable

QUIZ: ALL WORD PARTS

1. amicable
2. autonomous
3. benevolent
4. capture
5. incision
6. accord
7. credulity
8. excursion
9. contradiction
10. error
11. infidel
12. deflection
13. gender
14. gregarious
15. interjection
16. missile
17. admonish
18. mutate
19. pathos
20. transport
21. rupture
22. inscription
23. bisect
24. sequel
25. tension

III
READING QUESTIONS

Over 70% of the questions on the Critical Reading section are Reading questions. Unlike Sentence Completion questions, **Reading questions are *not* arranged in order of difficulty.** Rather, they are arranged based on the organization of the equivalent passage. **You should always look at every Reading question because you never know where the easy ones may be; the last question could very well be the easiest one.**

Answering the Reading questions involves three stages:
1. THE PASSAGE
2. THE QUESTIONS
3. THE ANSWER CHOICES

Techniques and approaches for each stage will be discussed below.

1. THE PASSAGE

READ THE INTRODUCTION

The first step is to read the italicized introduction at the beginning of most of the passages. This will give you a head start toward understanding the passage and may help you answer some of the questions.

READ CAREFULLY

After reading the introduction, read the passage. With few exceptions, **do *not* read the questions first**—they will distract you from getting the main ideas of the passage. Some educators argue that reading the questions first and then skimming the passage is the best approach, and if time is a major issue, this might work. However, this approach almost guarantees that you will struggle through the harder main-idea questions. In addition, the easier, more specific questions become no easier. So even if at first you are not able to finish the Critical Reading sections, through practice, it is important to work toward the goal of reading the passages completely and *then* answering the questions. If you don't practice this approach, you can never reach this ideal goal.

MAIN IDEAS OF PARAGRAPHS

As you read each paragraph, try to determine its main idea. **Focus on the first and last sentences of a paragraph.** One or both of these sentences are often *topic* sentences—sentences that reveal the topic of a paragraph.

MAIN IDEA OF THE PASSAGE

After you finish reading the passage, you should have an idea of its main idea. **Usually, the main ideas of each paragraph will tie into the main idea of the passage.**

FIRST THIRD

The main idea will almost always be introduced in the first third of the passage. Don't wait until the end of the passage to start thinking about its main idea.

STRAW-MAN APPROACH

Some writers will intentionally introduce an argument "made of straw"—one that is easily *blown away*. This is sometimes called the *straw-man approach*. The author intends to introduce an argument, one with which he or she probably disagrees, and then completes the passage by showing why his or her *counter* argument is better. Watch out for this approach as you consider main ideas.

LAST PARAGRAPH

Pay close attention to the last paragraph. Writers usually work *toward* their most important points, so what comes at the end of the passage will often help you confirm the author's main idea.

Sometimes, an author will throw a *twist* into this last paragraph. Perhaps the author questions a point made earlier, acknowledges a lack of certitude, or introduces an alternate viewpoint. Take note of how this twist affects the main idea.

TONE

It is important to consider the author's *tone* while you read the passage. This will often be the author's argument—his or her opinion on the topic. The author's tone may range from one of obvious passion to one of passive indifference. It is important to consider the author's tone in order to develop a solid understanding of the passage's main idea. In addition, **frequently one or two answer choices for a question can be easily eliminated because they contradict the author's tone**.

TONE WORDS

While reading the passage, always underline *tone words*. These are words or phrases that convey feeling, sometimes positive and sometimes negative.

CONTRAST SIGNALS

Perhaps the best way to recognize the author's tone is to look for *contrast signals*. Contrast signals are words that signal a change in the flow of a sentence. The following are examples:

although	in contrast	on the other hand
but	in spite of	rather than
despite	instead of	still
even though	nevertheless	yet
however	on the contrary	

What comes *after* these words is usually something that the author feels is very important— this will help you determine his or her tone.

TONE AND THE SAT

As you might guess, the passages in the SAT will never take a *negative* tone toward a minority or disadvantaged group. These minorities may be based on ethnicity, nationality, economics, or gender. You can be confident that any answer choice that negatively reflects one of these groups is incorrect.

TYPES OF PASSAGES

Passages will cover subjects in the humanities, social studies, natural sciences, and literary fiction. The following specific points may be helpful. For the most part, however, you don't have to approach different types of passages in different ways. Just read each passage carefully and focus on its main idea and tone.

FICTION PASSAGES

These passages are sometimes more difficult to understand because they are often written in a stylized prose. Furthermore, things are not always as they seem in these passages. Be on the lookout for literary tools such as sarcasm, satire, and metaphor as you read fiction passages. These are ways that an author may say one thing but mean something else.

> **Sarcasm** – A form of irony in which apparent praise conceals another, scornful meaning
> **Satire** – The use of witty and sometime humorous language to convey insults or scorn
> **Metaphor** – a figure of speech in which a word or phrase literally denoting one kind of object or idea is used in place of another to suggest a likeness or analogy between them (as in *drowning in money*)

Tone is particularly important in fiction passages. Think about how the author feels toward the characters. Also consider how the characters feel about themselves and the other characters in the passage.

SCIENCE PASSAGES

These passages are often difficult to read. The questions, however, are usually easier than those of other types of passages because they are based on clear facts in the passage. Be aggressive with these passages, even if you find the reading challenging.

DOUBLE PASSAGES

(!) Sometimes, Reading questions will be based on *two* passages. **It is important to concentrate on one passage at a time.** Read the first passage and then answer the questions related to this passage (usually the first several questions). Then do the same for the second passage. Finally, answer the questions related to both of the passages (usually the last several questions and sometimes the first one or two).

(!) Every test will have one double passage that includes two short passages and **four** questions. Often, all four questions will relate to both passages, so on these short double passages plan to read both passages before looking at the questions. In these double passages, **the authors will agree on one point and disagree on another**; look for this as you read.

———

Take a moment now to read Passage 1 on the next page. Underline all tone words or phrases. Pay attention to the contrast signals. As stated earlier, these words will help you identify the author's tone. Stop after reading the first passage and move on to the next page.

Questions 1-13 are based on the following passages.

These passages present two perspectives of the prairie, the grasslands that covered much of the central plains of the United States during the nineteenth century. In Passage 1, a young English journalist writes about his visit to the prairie on a sight-seeing tour in the 1840's. In Passage 2, an American writer describes the area near his childhood home of the early 1870's.

Passage 1

We came upon the Prairie at sunset. It would be difficult to say why, or how − though it was possibly from having heard and read so much about it −
Line but the effect on me was disappointment. Towards
(5) the setting sun, there lay stretched out before my view a vast expanse of level ground, unbroken (save by one thin line of trees, which scarcely amounted to a scratch upon the great blank) until it met the glowing sky, wherein it seemed to dip,
(10) mingling with its rich colors and mellowing in its distant blue. There it lay, a tranquil sea or lake without water, if such a simile be admissible, with the day going down upon it: a few birds wheeling here and there, solitude and silence reigning
(15) paramount around. But the grass was not yet high; there were bare black patches on the ground and the few wild flowers that the eye could see were poor and scanty. Great as the picture was, its very flatness and extent, which left nothing to the
(20) imagination, tamed it down and cramped its interest. I felt little of that sense of freedom and exhilaration that the open landscape of a Scottish moor, or even the rolling hills of our English downlands, inspires. It was lonely and wild, but oppressive in
(25) its barren monotony. I felt that in traversing the Prairies, I could never abandon myself to the scene, forgetful of all else, as I should instinctively were heather moorland beneath my feet. On the Prairie I should often glance towards the distant
(30) and frequently receding line of the horizon, and wish it gained and passed. It is not a scene to be forgotten, but it is scarcely one, I think (at all events, as I saw it), to remember with much pleasure or to covet the looking-on again, in after
(35) years.

Passage 2

In herding the cattle on horseback, we children came to know all the open prairie round about and found it very beautiful. On the uplands a short, light-green grass grew, intermixed with various
(40) resinous weeds, while in the lowland grazing grounds luxuriant patches of blue joint, wild oats, and other tall forage plants waved in the wind. Along the streams, cattails and tiger lilies nodded above thick mats of wide-bladed marsh grass.
(45) Almost without realizing it, I came to know the character of every weed, every flower, every living thing big enough to be seen from the back of a horse.

Nothing could be more generous, more
(50) joyous, than these natural meadows in summer. The flash and ripple and glimmer of the tall sunflowers, the chirp and gurgle of red-winged blackbirds swaying on the willow, the meadowlarks piping from grassy bogs, the peep
(55) of the prairie chick and the wailing call of plover on the flowery green slopes of the uplands made it all an ecstatic world to me. It was a wide world with a big, big sky that gave alluring hints of the still more glorious unknown wilderness beyond.
(60) Sometimes we wandered away to the meadows along the creek, gathering bouquets of pinks, sweet william, tiger lilies, and lady's slippers. The sun flamed across the splendid serial waves of the grasses and the perfumes of a
(65) hundred spicy plants rose in the shimmering midday air. At such times the mere joy of living filled our hearts with word-less satisfaction.

On a long ridge to the north and west, the soil, too wet and cold to cultivate easily, remained
(70) unplowed for several years. Scattered over these clay lands stood small wooded groves that we called "tow-heads." They stood out like islands in the waving seas of grasses. Against these dark-green masses, breakers of blue joint radiantly
(75) rolled. To the east ran the river; plum trees and crabapples bloomed along its banks. In June immense crops of wild strawberries appeared in the natural meadows. Their delicious odor rose to us as we rode our way, tempting us to dismount.
(80) On the bare upland ridges lay huge antlers, bleached and bare, in countless numbers, telling of the herds of elk and bison that had once fed in these vast savannas. On sunny April days the mother fox lay out with her young on southward-
(85) sloping swells. Often we met a prairie wolf, finding in it the spirit of the wilderness. To us it seemed that just over the next long swell toward the sunset the shaggy brown bison still fed in myriads, and in our hearts was a longing to ride
(90) away into the "sunset regions" of our pioneer songs.

Cut and remove this page ⟶

TONE OF PASSAGE 1

The following is a list of positive and negative tone words from Passage 1:

disappointment (line 4), glowing (l.9), rich (l.10), tranquil (l.11), solitude (l.14), silence (l.14), bare black patches (l.16), poor and scanty (l.18), Great (l.18), lonely and wild (l.24), oppressive (l.24), barren monotony (l.25), not a scene to be forgotten (l.31), scarcely one ... to remember with much pleasure... (l.32)

Determining the author's tone in Passage 1 may be difficult at first. As you see above, he mentions a number of both positive and negative aspects of the prairie. He describes the prairie with the following positive tone words (underlined): "mingling with its <u>rich</u> colors" (line 10), "<u>tranquil</u>" (line 11), "<u>solitude and silence</u>" (line 14), "<u>Great</u> as the picture was" (line18), and "<u>not a scene to be forgotten</u>" (lines 31-32). However, you need to focus on the words that come *after* the four contrast signals found in the passage:

"...**but** the effect on me was <u>disappointment</u>" (line 4)

"**But** the <u>grass was not yet high</u>; there were <u>bare black patches</u> on the ground and the few wild flowers that the eye could see were <u>poor and scanty</u>." (lines 15-18)

"...**but** <u>oppressive</u> in its <u>barren monotony</u>." (lines 24-25)

"...**but** it is <u>scarcely one</u>, I think (at all events, as I saw it), <u>to remember with much pleasure</u> or to covet the looking-on again, in after years." (lines 32-35)

The author's tone is clearly *negative*—any positive points he makes about the prairie are quickly negated by contrast signals and the negative details that follow them.

FOCUS ON THE EASY STUFF

(!) **If the passage is hard to understand or there are phrases or whole sentences that are confusing, focus on the parts you *do* understand.** Many students get discouraged during difficult reading and give up trying to understand the passage. When you start to feel exasperated and have no idea what the passage is saying, look for parts of the passage that *are* clearly written, and focus on these. Underline sentences or parts of sentences that are clear to you and that seem to mention an important point about the passage.

For example, in Passage 1, the first 20 lines or so describe the prairie in potentially confusing ways. Consider this sentence:

"Towards the setting sun, there lay stretched out before my view a vast expanse of level ground, unbroken (save by one thin line of trees, which scarcely amounted to a scratch upon the great blank) until it met the glowing sky, wherein it seemed to dip, mingling with its rich colors and mellowing in its distant blue." (lines 4-11)

This is a long and somewhat complex sentence, with five commas, a parenthetical statement, and no fewer than nine adjectives. But does it really matter? Read the six words preceding this sentence.

"...the effect on me was disappointment." (line 4)

This is a very clear statement. Underline and focus on a statement of such clarity and apparent importance, and don't worry as much about the harder stuff.

TRANSLATE

When part of a passage seems like it's written in a different language, *translate* it. Translating involves searching out the true and clear meaning of a sentence and creating a simple sentence, often in your own words. Consider the last sentence of Passage 1:

"It is not a scene to be forgotten, but it is scarcely one, I think (at all events, as I saw it), to remember with much pleasure or to covet the looking-on again, in after years." (lines 31-35)

This sentence may be somewhat confusing, so let's look at the parts that are clear. Underline these parts. Don't forget to focus on the contrast signal:

"It is not a scene to be forgotten, *but* it is scarcely one, I think (at all events, as I saw it), to remember with much pleasure or to covet the looking-on again, in after years."

The underlined portion above seems simple enough. If you were to eliminate the rest of the sentence, you would be left with a very clear sentence that does indeed reflect the original sentence's intended meaning.

2. THE QUESTIONS

READ THE QUESTIONS CAREFULLY

It is very important to understand and carefully examine a given question before it can be effectively answered. Oftentimes there are answer choices that are absolutely true according to the passage yet don't properly answer the question. In addition, the question may give important hints about the correct answer.

ANSWER QUESTIONS IN THE CONTEXT OF THE PASSAGE

Context – the parts before or after a statement that can influence its meaning, or the circumstances that surround a particular situation

(!) **You must answer questions *in the context of the passage*, or *contextually*.** This is probably the most important technique in the Critical Reading part of the tutorial. The answers must be clearly stated or supported by *the text*. Many students answer questions without looking back to the text, but this is like taking an open-book test and forgetting to open the book, so be prepared to go back to the passage frequently, and diligently use its information. You must use the passage and the passage only to answer the questions.

(!) *TRY TO ANSWER QUESTIONS BEFORE YOU LOOK AT THE ANSWER CHOICES.*
This is one of the best ways to answer questions contextually. This approach will force you to use the text to find your answers, and it will eliminate the temptation of picking answer choices that sound correct *out* of the context of the passage.

Use this approach when questions provide:
1. **line numbers**
2. **passage-location clues**, such as an important word or the mention of a familiar topic

BROAD OR GENERAL QUESTIONS

You will not always be able to answer questions before looking at the answer choices. When the question is broad or if it covers a large part of the passage, you will have to look at the answer choices first and *then* use the context of the passage. See the figure on the next page.

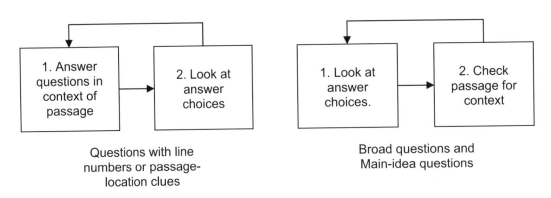

1. Answer questions in context of passage	→	2. Look at answer choices

Questions with line numbers or passage-location clues

1. Look at answer choices.	→	2. Check passage for context

Broad questions and Main-idea questions

(!) **Remember, regardless of whether you look at the answer choices before or after answering the question, you will still answer *all* questions in the context of the passage.**

USE BRACKETS TO KEEP TRACK OF WHAT TO REREAD

If the question gives line numbers, draw a bracket to the left of the passage to keep track of what to reread. (This is faster than underlining and won't interfere with the underlines you may have already drawn.) You must consider the main idea and tone of the part of the passage you are looking at, so be prepared to read **several lines above or below** the given line numbers to find your answer.

———

The following outline summarizes the approach for tackling the *passage* and the *questions*. Next up will be the *answer choices*.

THE PASSAGE:

- Read the introduction
- Read carefully
- Find the main idea of each paragraph
- Find the main idea of the passage
- Discover the author's tone
- Consider the type of passage
  - Tackle double passages one at a time
- Focus on the easy stuff
- Translate

THE QUESTIONS:

- Read the questions carefully
- Answer questions in the context of the passage

3. THE ANSWER CHOICES

Now, it is time to answer the questions for Passages 1 and 2. (You should have already read the first passage). There are a number of techniques that will help you find the correct answers and eliminate incorrect answer choices—we will use the questions from the passages to illustrate these techniques.

It is very important to eliminate answers that you know are wrong, particularly when you don't recognize the correct answer right away—usually there will be anywhere from one to four answer choices that are easy to eliminate. Many of the following techniques will address using this process of elimination to find the correct answer.

ⓘ ELIMINATE ANSWER CHOICES THAT CONTRADICT THE AUTHOR'S TONE

As stated before, often one or more answer choices can be eliminated simply because they disagree with the author's tone. Let's look at question 1:

(EX) 1. In creating an impression of the prairie for the reader, the author of Passage 1 makes use of

This is a broad question. It would be difficult to answer without looking at the answer choices first. Are there any answer choices (see below) that suggest a positive tone?

    (A) reference to geological processes
    (B) description of its inhabitants
    (C) evocation of different but equally attractive areas
    (D) comparison with other landscapes
    (E) contrast to imaginary places

*When you see the hand symbol, stop and answer the question or follow the direction before moving on. You should generally not stop **until** you see this symbol. Make sure to go back to the passage and diligently use context as you make your way through the questions.

If you are working on your own, you will see an italicized solution following each question or direction (see below, for example). Make sure to answer the question or follow the direction *before* looking at the solution. You may want to cover the solution with a sheet of paper.

You will notice that (C) mentions "equally attractive areas", but this suggests the author finds the prairie attractive, which contradicts his tone, so eliminate (C).

! ELIMINATE ANY ANSWER CHOICE THAT MENTIONS SOMETHING <u>SPECIFIC</u> THAT IS NOT MENTIONED IN THE PASSAGE

This is probably the most important and commonly used technique for eliminating answer choices. Make sure you look for *specific* references in the answer choices. Answer choices that are vague or broad are more difficult to eliminate using this concept.

> Do you see any answer choices that are not mentioned in the passage? Use the answer choices below.

(A) reference to geological processes
(B) description of its inhabitants
(C) evocation of different but **equally attractive** areas – [incorrect tone]
(D) comparison with other landscapes
(E) contrast to imaginary places

*Look at answer choice (A). "Geological processes" is a very specific reference. Since there are no processes of any kind mentioned in the passage, you should eliminate (A). Look at answer choice (E). While the author does mention "imagination" (line 20), he never mentions imaginary **places**. Eliminate (E).*

The last step is to look at the remaining answers and check the context of the passage.

> Does the author describe any of the prairie's inhabitants (B), or does he compare the prairie to other landscapes (D)? Go back to the passage and look for evidence to support your choice.

(A) reference to **geological processes** – [not mentioned]
(B) description of its inhabitants
(C) evocation of different but equally attractive areas – [incorrect tone]
(D) comparison with other landscapes
(E) contrast to **imaginary places** – [not mentioned]

! *The only inhabitants he mentions are "a few birds" (line 13), but he only **mentions** them; he does not provide a "description" of them—**EVERY WORD COUNTS**, so eliminate (B). Go back to the passage and you will notice that he compares the prairie to "the open landscape of a Scottish moor, or even the rolling hills of our English downlands..." (lines 22-23), so answer choice (D) is the correct answer.*

(A) reference to geological processes – [not mentioned]
(B) description of its inhabitants – [no "description" of the birds]
(C) evocation of different but equally attractive areas – [incorrect tone]
(D) comparison with other landscapes
(E) contrast to imaginary places – [not mentioned]

LOOK FOR MAIN-IDEA QUESTIONS

> Main-idea questions are identifiable by such words as *primarily*, *essentially*, and *mainly*.

These questions may be referring to part of the passage, as in question 2 below, or to the whole passage. When you see these words in the question, you must watch out for answers that may be *partially* correct yet don't reflect the author's main idea.

(EX) 2. In line 13, the author includes the detail of "a few birds" primarily to emphasize the

The author of Passage 1 may have mentioned the "birds" to give the reader an idea of (for example) what kind of wildlife can be found on the prairie, but this would not be the author's *primary* reason for mentioning the birds.

> The question gives a line number, so go back to the passage and answer the question using context. (Don't look at the answer choices first.)

In the sentence preceding the one mentioning the "birds," the author describes the prairie as "a tranquil sea or lake without water" (lines 11-12). The sentence with "a few birds" mentions "solitude and silence" (line 14). So your answer must have something to do with tranquility (calmness), solitude (state of aloneness), and silence.

> Use your contextual answer, and try to identify the correct answer, or eliminate answer choices that you know are incorrect. The answer choices are below.

(A) loneliness of the scene
(B) strangeness of the wildlife
(C) lateness of the evening
(D) dominance of the sky
(E) infertility of the land

*Only **(A)** should work with your contextual answer.*

(A) loneliness of the scene
(B) strangeness of the wildlife − [not **primary** reason]
(C) lateness of the evening − [not mentioned]
(D) dominance of the sky − [not **primary** reason]
(E) infertility of the land − [tone is correct, but not **primary** reason]

USE CONTEXT TO SOLVE VOCABULARY QUESTIONS

Vocabulary questions test your ability to define a word or group of words in context.

These questions are identifiable by the words *most nearly means*.

There are three steps to these problems:

1. **Define the original word.** Read the sentence from the passage that contains the word or phrase in question, and define the word or phrase. Keep your definitions short and simple. **Make sure to use context: these questions usually deal with words that have several meanings, and the correct answer is almost *never* the most common of these definitions.**

2. **Eliminate answer choices.** If you do not spot the correct answer right away, eliminate the answer choices that do not match your definition from step 1. If you are not sure about an answer choice, plug it into the actual sentence and trust your ear—when you read the passage with the answer choices plugged in, incorrect answer choices will often sound awkward or obviously wrong. You might also eliminate answer choices that disagree with the author's tone.

3. **Choose an answer and check.** Substitute your answer for the original word, and read the original sentence. The correct answer should sound correct.

(EX) 3. In line 20, "tamed" most nearly means

Here is the sentence from the passage: "Great as the picture was, its very flatness and extent, which left nothing to the imagination, **tamed** it down and cramped its interest."

Define the word "tamed" using context.

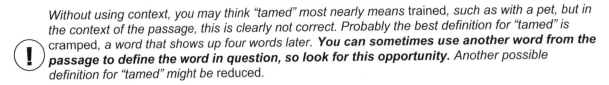

Without using context, you may think "tamed" most nearly means trained, *such as with a pet, but in the context of the passage, this is clearly not correct. Probably the best definition for "tamed" is* cramped, *a word that shows up four words later.* **You can sometimes use another word from the passage to define the word in question, so look for this opportunity.** *Another possible definition for "tamed" might be* reduced.

Continue this example on the next page.

Now look at the answer choices (below). Sometimes, you will feel confident that you have identified the correct answer. Frequently, however, it is a good idea to eliminate the incorrect answer choices. **Eliminate answer choices that don't match your definition from above. Also, eliminate answer choices that sound awkward or obviously incorrect when read in the original sentence.**

    (A) composed
    (B) trained
    (C) subdued
    (D) captured
    (E) befriended

Answer choice (B) doesn't mean cramped or reduced. In addition, "trained" is probably the most common definition of "tamed," and thus an unlikely answer. Eliminate (B). It doesn't make sense to "capture" something down, so (D) could be eliminated. "Befriended" certainly doesn't mean cramped or reduced. It also sounds positive, which is the wrong tone, so eliminate (E). You're left with (A) and (C).

Which remaining answer choice works better with your original definition? Consider the tone of the passage before choosing an answer.

*One definition of "compose" is to calm or to quiet, usually oneself or one's mind. "Subdue" means to reduce the intensity of. The definition for "subdue" works better in the passage. In addition, it has a more negative tone. The new sentence becomes: "Great as the picture was, its very flatness and extent, which left nothing to the imagination, **subdued** it down and cramped its interest." This sentence sounds fine. The answer is (C).*

    (A) composed
    (B) trained – [most common definition]
    (C) subdued – [more negative tone than (A)]
    (D) captured – [sounds awkward]
    (E) befriended – [tone is incorrect]

4. In line 26, "abandon myself" most nearly means

"... I could never **abandon myself** to the scene, forgetful of all else, as I should instinctively were heather moorland beneath my feet."

This seems like a difficult problem, but if you notice the tone of "abandon myself," and if you plug in the answer choices and trust your ear, the problem is not bad.

 Define the phrase "abandon myself" using context. Is this phrase positive or negative?

*Remember that the author's tone toward the prairie is negative, and **abandoning himself** is something he could "never" do while "traversing the prairie," so logically, "abandon myself" must be positive. You might come up with a definition such as lose myself in or **forget** myself in (remember, try to use other words from the passage when you can). Make sure you think of these definitions in a positive way, such as "losing myself in a book" or "forgetting myself in a summer daydream."*

 Eliminate answer choices (below). Make sure to eliminate answer choices that sound awkward when plugged into the passage.

    (A) dismiss as worthless
    (B) isolate from all others
    (C) overlook unintentionally
    (D) retreat completely
    (E) become absorbed in

*When you plug the answer choices into the sentence, **make sure you plug them in** exactly— don't lose any words. Answer choices (A), (B), and (C) sound awkward and can be eliminated. Both (D) and (E) sound OK, and neither one is too different from your definition above.*

 Are you left with (D) and (E)? Of these two remaining answer choices, which one has the more positive tone?

*To "retreat completely" means to withdraw or run away to, which sounds as though it could a negative tone, so (D) is probably incorrect. Using (E), the new sentence becomes: "... I could never **become absorbed in**to the scene, forgetful of all else, as I should instinctively were heather moorland beneath my feet." This sounds fine. The correct answer is **(E)**.*

    (A) dismiss as worthless − [sounds awkward]
    (B) isolate from all others − [sounds awkward]
    (C) overlook unintentionally − [sounds awkward]
    (D) retreat completely
    (E) become absorbed in

WATCH OUT FOR EYE CATCHERS

Eye catchers are words or phrases that come directly from the passage but have nothing to do with answering the question. Students tend to be attracted to answer choices with eye catchers because they recognize these words or phrases from the passage. **Correct answers, however, will often *not* be written with the exact words of the passage. Before you select an answer choice with an eye catcher, be absolutely sure it answers the question correctly.**

WATCH OUT FOR ANSWER CHOICES THAT ARE TOO STRONG

Sometimes, there are answer choices that are nearly correct but are too strong. An author may be *disappointed* but not *devastated*. He may be *upset* but not *furious*. He may be *surprised* but not *shocked*. **Watch out for answer choices that seem to overly exaggerate the attitude of an author or character in a passage—the College Board may be trying to trick you.** Look at question 5:

(EX) 5. The author of Passage 1 qualifies his judgment of the prairie by

This is a broad question. Broad questions are sometimes more difficult than the more specific ones, which usually offer line numbers. You may choose to skip these broad questions and come back to them if you have time, especially if you found the passage challenging.

> Use any of the previous techniques to eliminate answers choices (below). Especially look to eliminate answer choices that are not specifically mentioned in the passage. Watch out for eye catchers.

    (A) pointing out his own subjectivity
    (B) commenting on his lack of imagination
    (C) mentioning his physical fatigue
    (D) apologizing for his prejudices against the landscape
    (E) indicating his psychological agitation

*Answer choice (A) may sound confusing, but that doesn't mean you can eliminate it. The author mentions that the prairie "left nothing to the imagination" (lines 19-20) but doesn't mention that **he** has a lack of imagination. The word "imagination" is an **eye catcher**. Eliminate (B). The author never mentions that he is physically fatigued, so eliminate (C). In (D), the word "landscape" is an **eye catcher**—it is used in the passage (line 22) and it was part of an answer to a previous question, so the word may be fresh in your head. The author never apologizes for anything, so you can eliminate (D).*

Continue this example on the next page.

You may be left with (A) and (E). Translate (E) to read: indicating that he is mentally disturbed (psychologically agitated).

Do you think the author felt *mentally disturbed*? Use process of elimination to choose an answer.

*The author says that he feels "disappointment" (line 4), but "psychological agitation," or feeling mentally disturbed seems stronger than disappointment. Answer choice (E) is likely **too strong**, so go with answer choice (A). Subjective means personal or reflecting on one's past experiences or thoughts. The author is certainly subjective when he says, "…it was impossible to say why or how — though it was possibly from having heard and read so much about it — but the effect on me was a disappointment." (lines 1-4). The answer is **(A)**.*

> **(A) pointing out his own subjectivity**
> (B) commenting on his lack of imagination — [not mentioned/eye catcher]
> (C) mentioning his physical fatigue — [not mentioned]
> (D) apologizing for his prejudices against the landscape — [not mentioned/eye catcher]
> (E) indicating his psychological agitation — [too strong]

Question 5 was the last question relating only to Passage 1.

———

Turn back to the passages and read Passage 2. Remember to underline tone words.

———

The tone words for Passage 2 include: beautiful (line 38), generous (l.49), joyous (l.50), ecstatic (l.57), alluring (l.58), glorious (l.59), splendid (l.63), joy (l.66), satisfaction (l.67), delicious (l.78)

———

 6. In line 66, "mere" most nearly means

"At such times the **mere** joy of living filled our hearts with word-less satisfaction."

This is another vocabulary question, so go back to the original sentence and define "mere."

*Since the tone is clearly positive, you are looking for a word that **supports** the "joy of living." You might come up with a definition such as pure or effortless or easy.*

Continue this example on the next page.

Do you see the correct answer (below)? If not, eliminate answer choices as you did in the previous vocabulary questions.

(A) tiny
(B) trivial
(C) simple
(D) direct
(E) questionable

*You can eliminate (A), (B), and (E), since "tiny," "trivial," and "questionable" are all non-supportive, negative-sounding words. (D) sounds awkward and makes no sense, so the answer must be **(C)**. The new sentence becomes: "At such times the **simple** joy of living filled our hearts with word-less satisfaction."*

(A) tiny — [wrong tone]
(B) trivial — [wrong tone]
(C) simple
(D) direct — [sounds awkward]
(E) questionable — [wrong tone]

WATCH OUT FOR CAMOUFLAGED ANSWER CHOICES

The College Board likes to *camouflage* the correct answers with words that are different from and often more *difficult* than the words used in the passage. For lack of understanding, students are often tempted to eliminate these answer choices as nonsense.

For example, the author of Passage 2 says, "I came to know the character of every weed, every flower, every living thing big enough to be seen from the back of a horse." (lines 45-48) The answer choice to a question about this author may read: *the author discovered the quintessence of the natural scene of the prairie.* This would be the correct answer even though the words are different from those used in the passage—the answer is *camouflaged.* The correct answer is saying the same thing as the passage, but it uses different, and more difficult, words.

(EX) 7. In Passage 2, the author's references to things beyond his direct experience (lines 57-59 and lines 86-91) indicate the

This is a fairly tricky question. Before going back to the passage, read the question carefully. It says that the author refers to *things beyond his direct experience.* Make sure to look for these things while you're rereading the given lines. Don't forget to bracket the passage so you know exactly what to focus on.

> What part of the first section is beyond the author's direct experience? Is there anything else mentioned in this first section? (Since line numbers are given, look back to the passage before looking at the answer choices.)

The part of the first section that is beyond the author's direct experience is "the glorious unknown wilderness beyond." There is also part of the prairie that the author does experience—the "wide world with a big, big sky."

> Do the same for the second section.

*The word "seemed" hints that the "shaggy brown bison" are not directly experienced. Once again, there is mention of something that the author **does** experience—"the next long swell toward the sunset."*

Continue this example on the next page.

What do both translated sections have in common?

*In each section, you may notice: (1) something that the author experiences (the "sky" and the "sunset") and (2) things **beyond his direct experience** (the "glorious unknown wilderness beyond" and the "bison").*

Now, look at the answer choices (below). Eliminate answer choices that are different from your contextual answers above. As always, look for answer choices that are not mentioned or contradict the author's tone.

    (A) unexpected dangers of life on the unsettled prairie
    (B) psychological interweaving of imagination and the natural scene
    (C) exaggerated sense of mystery that is natural to children
    (D) predominant influence of sight in experiencing a place
    (E) permanence of the loss of the old life of the prairie

*Answer choices (A) and (E) have nothing to do with your contextual answer, and they are negative in tone, which conflicts with the author's positive tone, so eliminate these. Answer choice (C) is tempting but really never mentioned. If everything else gets eliminated, you could guess this one, but it's not a great answer. Answer choice (D) also sounds tempting, but it does not take into account the things beyond [the author's] direct experience, and this is clearly emphasized in the question. However, (B) sounds terrible. What is "psychological interweaving of imagination and the natural scene?" Try translating this answer choice to read: combining imagination and the natural scene in one's mind. Now, this answer sounds good—(B) is correct. The answer was **camouflaged** with tricky words.*

    (A) unexpected dangers of life on the unsettled prairie − [incorrect tone and out of context]
    (B) psychological interweaving of imagination and the natural scene −
       [camouflaged]
    (C) exaggerated sense of mystery that is natural to children − [not explicitly mentioned]
    (D) predominant influence of sight in experiencing a place − [out of context]
    (E) permanence of the loss of the old life of the prairie − [incorrect tone and out of context]

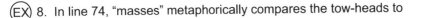

8. In line 74, "masses" metaphorically compares the tow-heads to

This question focuses on a specific part of the passage, so definitely go back to the passage before looking at the answer choices on this one. What are the "masses?" What does the author compare them to?

It is easy to confuse the masses with something else when reading the passage, such as the "seas of grasses." Remember to read questions carefully. In this case, the question itself contains the key: masses = tow-heads. With that clue, the whole chain becomes easier to untangle. The passage says that there are "small wooded groves that we called 'tow-heads'," and these tow-heads were "like islands in the waving seas of grasses." You may also notice that against these "**masses**, breakers…rolled" (lines 71-75). If you don't know what "breakers" are, that's OK. Focus on the easy stuff. Your translated answer might be: the masses are like **islands in the sea** (with breakers rolling against them).

Eliminate answer choices (below) that contradict your contextual answer.

    (A) ships on a stormy ocean
    (B) birds on a pond
    (C) reefs submerged by rising waters
    (D) islands amidst the surf
    (E) islands engulfed by a river

Answer choices (A), (B), and (C) can be easily eliminated since ships, birds, and reefs are not islands. (E) is a possible **eye catcher** since a "river" is mentioned in line 75. You may not have read that far, but if you did, the word "river" may have caught your eye. The "surf" is never literally mentioned. "Surf" is just another name for "breakers," or waves. Answer choice **(D)**, which is **camouflaged**, is the correct answer.

    (A) ships on a stormy ocean − [not in context]
    (B) birds on a pond − [not in context]
    (C) reefs submerged by rising waters − [not in context]
    (D) islands amidst the surf − [camouflaged]
    (E) islands engulfed by a river − [eye catcher]

(EX) 9. One aspect of Passage 2 that might make it difficult to appreciate is the author's apparent assumption that readers will

There's no easy way to answer this question before looking at the answer choices.

Eliminate answer choices (below) that have specific references that are not mentioned in the passage.

(A) have seen nineteenth-century paintings or photographs of the prairie
(B) connect accounts of specific prairie towns with their own experiences of the prairie
(C) be able to visualize the plants and the animals that are named
(D) recognize the references to particular pioneer songs
(E) understand the children's associations with the flowers that they gathered

*There is no mention of "nineteenth-century paintings or photographs" or "specific prairie towns," so get rid of (A) and (B). There is mention of "pioneer songs" (lines 90-91) but no reference to "particular" pioneer songs (remember, **every word counts**), so eliminate (D). Now we need to choose between (C) and (E).*

Are you left with (C) and (E)? Which one sounds better?

*The gathering of "flowers" (E) is mentioned in lines 61-62. The "plants and animals" (C) are mentioned in almost every line of Passage 2. **(C)** is the better answer.*

~~(A)~~ have seen nineteenth-century paintings or photographs of the prairie – [not mentioned]
~~(B)~~ connect accounts of specific prairie towns with their own experiences of the prairie – [not mentioned]
(C) be able to visualize the plants and the animals that are named – [best answer]
~~(D)~~ recognize the references to particular pioneer songs – [not mentioned]
(E) understand the children's associations with the flowers that they gathered

KEEP YOUR ANSWERS CONSISTENT, AND LEARN AS YOU GO

This may be obvious, but as you work your way through the questions, make sure your answers are consistent. For example, if your chosen answers on past questions reflect an author's *negative* tone toward the prairie, make sure your future answers also reflect this tone.

Also, be open to learning about the passage as you answer the questions, thus preparing you for future questions. For example, question 2 on page 255 was a straightforward specific-detail question. By focusing on the specific context of the passage, a student would likely answer this question correctly, even if she lacked a thorough knowledge of the passage. Perhaps she is not clear about the author's tone toward the prairie. Recall that the answer is (A), *loneliness of the scene*. This answer suggests that the author's tone is likely negative. The student has learned something about the passage, something that will certainly help her on future questions, such as question 10 below.

(EX) 10. The contrast between the two descriptions of the prairie is essentially one between

The word *essentially* hints that this is another main-idea question. This main-idea question relates to *both* passages. Think about the main idea of each passage, and remember: the question is asking you to focus on the *descriptions of the prairie*. Hopefully your knowledge of the passages, as well as what you have learned so far while answering the past questions, will help you.

In Passage 1, the author feels "disappointment." But *why* does he feel this way?

Go back to passage 1 and look at the tone words that the author uses to describe the prairie, especially the negative words. How would you summarize his description of the prairie?

Some of the key words are: "vast expanse of level ground, unbroken…" (line 6), "great blank" (line 8), "lake without water" (lines 11-12), "grass was not yet high; there were bare black patches on the ground" (lines 15-16), "the few wild flowers … were poor and scanty" (lines 17-18), "lonely and wild" (line 24), "oppressive" (line 24), and "barren monotony" (line 25). The author clearly feels the prairie is **desolate** *and for the most part* **devoid of life***.*

Continue this example on the next page.

ELIMINATE DOUBLE ANSWERS ONE AT A TIME

When there are two answers in each answer choice, try eliminating one answer at a time. If you can eliminate any *half* of an answer choice, you can eliminate the whole thing.

Eliminate the answer choices (below) that contradict the main idea of Passage 1.

      (A) misfortune and prosperity
      (B) homesickness and anticipation
      (C) resignation and joy
      (D) bleakness and richness
      (E) exhaustion and energy

You will notice that all of the first words are negative, so you can't use the author's tone to help you, but only one is close to **desolate** *or* **lacking life***: "bleakness" in answer choice* **(D)**.

At this point, if you narrowed it down to one answer choice, you're done with the question, but let's look at Passage 2 to be safe. You probably already have a feel for this author's tone. He is clearly happy and content about the prairie. Once again, *why* does he feel this way? If you remember from question 9, the author mentions plants and animals throughout the passage to describe the prairie; in fact, he mentions plants no fewer than thirty times and animals another ten or eleven times. Clearly, the author mainly uses *living things* to describe the prairie. You could probably eliminate (A), (B), and (E) since they are not totally correct. In addition they focus on the *author's emotions* when the question asks about the *descriptions of the prairie*.

      (A) ~~misfortune~~ and ~~prosperity~~
      (B) ~~homesickness~~ and ~~anticipation~~
      (C) ~~resignation~~ and joy
      (D) bleakness and richness
      (E) ~~exhaustion~~ and ~~energy~~

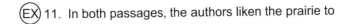

EX 11. In both passages, the authors liken the prairie to

Since this question is broad, you will have to look at the answer choices before answering the question.

Go back and use the context of the passages to eliminate answer choices (below). Make sure you find *concrete evidence* to support you eliminations. You should be left with one answer choice.

(A) a desert
(B) an island
(C) a barren wilderness
(D) a large animal
(E) a body of water

You could eliminate (C) because it contradicts the tone of Passage 2. Answer choice (A) could probably be eliminated for the same reason. Eliminate (D) because "large animal(s)" are not mentioned in either passage. So we're left with (B) and (E). Answer choice (B) is an **eye catcher** because "islands" (line 72) are clearly mentioned in Passage 2 (and this word was part of the correct answer to a previous question). Only **(E)** "a body of water" works for both passages: "a tranquil sea or lake" (line 11) and "waving seas of grasses" (line 73).

(A) a desert — [contradicts tone of Passage 2]
(B) an island — [eye catcher (Passage 2 only)]
(C) a barren wilderness — [contradicts tone of Passage 2]
(D) a large animal — [not mentioned]
(E) a body of water

ELIMINATE FALSE OR SENSELESS ANSWER CHOICES

This sounds obvious, but don't forget that even in confusing questions that have confusing answer choices, you may be able to get rid of some answer choices that you know are false according to the passage.

You may also eliminate answer choices that simply could never make any sense in answering the question, even out of the context of the passage.

(EX) 12. Both authors indicate that the experience of a beautiful landscape involves

This question is probably too broad to answer before looking at the answer choices.

The answer choices are below. Do you see an answer choice that could never sensibly answer the question, even if you were unfamiliar with the passages?

    (A) artistic production
    (B) detached observation of appearances
    (C) emotional turmoil
    (D) stimulation of the imagination
    (E) fanciful reconstruction of bygone times

Do you know that "turmoil" is a very negative word meaning: a state of great commotion, confusion, or disturbance? It certainly doesn't make sense to involve "emotional turmoil" with "the experience of a beautiful landscape." Eliminate (C).

Eliminate answer choices that are false or not mentioned in the passages. Are you left with one answer choice?

*You could probably eliminate (A) and (E) because they are never mentioned in either passage. Answer choice (B) is **false** because both authors are completely involved in what they observe; (they are certainly not "detached," or disconnected). The correct answer must be **(D)**. The Passage 1 author is disappointed because the prairie "left nothing to the imagination" (lines 19-20). This implies that he wishes that his imagination **was** stimulated. Recall from question 7 that the Passage 2 author mentions "things beyond his direct experience" (imagination) in describing the prairie, a landscape we know he finds beautiful.*

    (A) artistic production – [not mentioned]
    (B) detached observation of appearances – [false answer]
    (C) emotional turmoil – [senseless answer]
    (D) stimulation of the imagination
    (E) fanciful reconstruction of bygone times – [not mentioned]

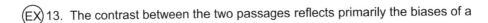 13. The contrast between the two passages reflects primarily the biases of a

This is another main-idea question for both passages. It is not focusing on the prairie but rather the *authors* of the passages. You have your first opportunity to use the italicized introduction to eliminate answer choices.

  What does the introduction specifically tell us about each author?

The introduction tells us that the first author is a "young English journalist" on a "visit" to the prairie and the second author is an "American writer" near his "childhood home."

  Now look at the answer choices (below). Eliminate any false answer choices or answer choices that are not mentioned. Don't forget that since the answers are *double answers*, you may be able to eliminate one at a time.

    (A) grown man and a little boy
    (B) journalist and a writer of fiction
    (C) passing visitor and a local resident
    (D) native of Europe and a native of the United States
    (E) weary tourist and an energetic farm worker

*Once again, remember that **every word counts**. Eliminate (A) (the first author is a young man, not a grown man), (B) (there is no mention of "a writer of fiction"), and (E) (there is no mention of "an energetic farm worker").*

  Both (C) and (D) are true, but which one satisfies the *primary* biases of the two authors?

*Remember that with main idea questions there may be answers that are somewhat correct but don't fully consider the main focus of the passage. Did you even remember that the author of Passage 1 was English? Maybe not, but you probably knew he was a "passing visitor" of the prairie. Answer choice **(C)** would be the better answer.*

    (A) ~~grown man~~ and a little boy − [false answer]
    (B) journalist and a ~~writer of fiction~~ − [not mentioned]
    (C) passing visitor and a local resident
    (D) native of Europe and a native of the United States
    (E) weary tourist and an ~~energetic farm worker~~ − [not mentioned]

_____

4. PRACTICE AND READING

PRACTICE

As you can see, there are numerous techniques that you can use to tackle Reading questions and eliminate answer choices. The only way to remember and perfect all of these techniques and get comfortable enough with them to complete the test without running out of time is to **practice**, so get ready to work on a number of College Board passages.

Even if you're worried that you may forget some of these techniques, always remember that the most important part of answering these questions is to *always use the context of the passage*. Go back to the passage and diligently use its information to answer the questions. Remember, it's an open book test!

READ

Perhaps the best way to raise your Critical Reading scores is to read as much as possible. Read material that is hard to understand at first. Choose a variety of reading materials, such as novels, newspapers, and poetry. While the previous techniques are certainly extremely helpful and will begin to compensate for less-than-great reading skills, no instruction can completely take the place of a solid reading background. For this reason, *reading* is a significant part of improving your Critical Reading scores.

5. READING SUMMARY

As stated before, to improve your Reading scores, you will need to practice. The College Board book contains dozens of reading passages; assignments are found on the next page. Start slowly, try to use the techniques below, and turn back to this chapter frequently. The following summarizes the techniques:

THE PASSAGE:

- Read the introduction
- Read carefully
- Find the main idea of each paragraph
- Find the main idea of the passage
- Discover the author's tone
- Consider the type of passage
  - Tackle double passages one at a time
- Focus on the easy stuff
- Translate

THE QUESTIONS:

- Read the questions carefully
- Answer questions in the context of the passage

THE ANSWER CHOICES:

- Eliminate answers that contradict the author's tone
- Eliminate answer choices that are not mentioned in the passage
- Look for main idea questions
- Plug in answers choices to solve vocabulary questions
- Watch out for eye catchers
- Watch out for answer choices that are too strong
- Watch out for camouflaged answer choices
- Keep your answers consistent, and learn as you go
- Eliminate double answers one at a time
- Eliminate false or senseless answer choices

6. READING PROBLEMS

PRACTICE PROBLEMS

The following assignments are from *The Official SAT Study Guide** by the College Board. Complete (2nd Edition) the first several assignments *untimed*. Look back to the KlassTutoring tutorial as you learn and master the techniques. You are encouraged to review the summary on the previous page before and during the completion of these problems. Eventually, start completing the passages *timed*, using the following formula: **approximate total time (in minutes) = 1.2 × # of questions**. Remember to answer each question *in context*. For each of your answers, be prepared to show support taken from the passage. **Next to each problem, it may be helpful to indicate line numbers from the passage where support for your answer can be found.** If you do not identify the correct answer, either eliminate at least two answer choices and guess or leave the problem blank.

- ☐ Assignment 1: Test 1, Section 2 (6-24)
- ☐ Assignment 2: Test 1, Section 5 (9-24)
- ☐ Assignment 3: Test 1, Section 9 (7-19)
- ☐ Assignment 4: Test 2, Section 4 (9-25)
- ☐ Assignment 5: Test 2, Section 7 (6-24)
- ☐ Assignment 6: Test 2, Section 9 (7-18)
- ☐ Assignment 7: Test 3, Section 4 (9-24)
- ☐ Assignment 8: Test 3, Section 7 (6-24)
- ☐ Assignment 9: Test 3, Section 9 (7-19)
- ☐ Assignment 10: Test 4, Section 2 (9-24)
- ☐ Assignment 11: Test 4, Section 5 (6-24)
- ☐ Assignment 12: Test 4, Section 8 (7-19)

TEST CORRECTIONS

After each practice test is graded, you should correct problems that you missed or left blank. (The practice tests are found in *The Official SAT Study Guide*.) Go back to the tutorial and review the techniques as you correct the problems. The idea is to: (1) identify techniques that have given you trouble, (2) go back to the tutorial so you can review and strengthen these techniques, and (3) apply these techniques to the specific problems on which you struggled.

- ☐ Test 5: Section 3 (6-24), Section 7 (9-24), and Section 9 (7-19)
- ☐ Test 6: Section 3 (6-24), Section 7 (9-24), and Section 9 (7-19)
- ☐ Test 7: Section 2 (6-24), Section 5 (9-24), and Section 8 (7-19)
- ☐ Test 8: Section 2 (6-24), Section 5 (9-24), and Section 8 (7-19)
- ☐ Test 9: Section 4 (9-24), Section 6 (6-24), and Section 9 (7-19)
- ☐ Test 10: Section 4 (9-24), Section 6 (6-24), and Section 9 (7-19)

*SAT is a registered trademark of the College Board, which was not involved in the production of and does not endorse this book.

Reminder: If you are working on your own in the 30 or 40-hour program, now is a good time to take your second practice test. After you grade your test, make sure you go back and correct it as you complete the chapters in the tutorial.

☐ Take Test 6 (Critical Reading sections only) in the College Board book. Review Taking Practice Tests in the Introduction.

SENTENCE COMPLETION QUESTIONS

Sentence completion questions ask you to fill in one or two blanks in a sentence, using appropriate and sensible words. This is the last Critical Reading chapter because it relies heavily on your vocabulary and word-part studies, which required a considerable amount of study time. At this point, you hopefully have progressed through a number of vocabulary and word part lists and feel fairly comfortable with the vocabulary typically found on the SAT. The stronger your vocabulary, the easier the sentence completion questions will be. Continue working on vocabulary and word parts, and you will see the benefits with these questions, especially the higher-numbered questions with difficult vocabulary. **Remember, sentence completion questions are arranged in order of difficulty.**

Make sure you are familiar with the directions:

Each sentence below has one or two blanks, each blank indicating that something has been omitted. Beneath the sentence are five words or sets of words labeled A through E. Choose the word or set of words that, when inserted in the sentence, <u>best</u> fits the meaning of the sentence as a whole.

EXAMPLE:

Hoping to ------- the dispute, negotiators proposed a compromise that they felt would be ------- to both labor and management.

(A) enforce . . useful
(B) end . . divisive
(C) overcome . . unattractive
(D) extend . . satisfactory
(E) resolve . . acceptable

1. PICK A WORD

READ THE SENTENCE

The first step on Sentence Completion questions is to read the sentence slowly and carefully. Try to get a general idea of what the sentence is about. If there are difficult words that you are not familiar with, think about your vocabulary words or try using your knowledge of word parts.

PICK A WORD

(!) **The most important technique on Sentence Completion questions is to read the sentence carefully and pick your own words for the blanks.** Most of the techniques in this chapter will help you get comfortable picking effective words that will lead you to the correct answer. Once you get comfortable at picking these words, you will rely on your vocabulary and word-part knowledge to identify the correct answers or eliminate incorrect answer choices. You will pick words of your own for the blanks *before* looking at the answer choices. **Do not look at the answer choices first. They will only distract you from getting the main idea of the sentence and thinking of an appropriate word.**

Read the sentence → pick a word → look at answer choices

The word you think up does not have to be a difficult or impressive one. A simple word is all that is needed, or sometimes you can just think of a group of words that effectively *describes* the word you

(!) are looking for. **Oftentimes, you should use one of the words or phrases from another part of the sentence.**

In this chapter, assume that the Sentence Completion questions are taken from the eight-question section of the SAT. **This means that a problem 1 should be fairly easy and a problem 8 should be quite difficult**, as discussed in the introduction. Much of the difficulty in Sentence Completion questions occurs when the answer choices contain difficult vocabulary, and since many of the following examples do not show the answer choices, a high-numbered problem may seem quite easy.

A note about example problems: If you are working on your own, you will see an italicized solution following each example problem. For all of the following example problems, try to complete the problem *before* looking at the solution. You may want to cover the solutions with a sheet of paper.

Try picking a word for each the following examples:

(EX) 1. Compared to the excitement of New York, the ------- that prevails in this sleepy mountain resort is quite remarkable.

   picked word*: sleepiness or un-excitement (use words from the sentence when possible)*

(EX) 2. Even after hungrily devouring their entire dinners, the children were still ------- and clamored for more.

   picked word*: hungry*

2. HOW TO PICK WORDS

CONTEXT

Recall the definition of *context* from the Reading Passages chapter:

Context – the parts before or after a statement that can influence its meaning, or the circumstances that surround a particular situation.

The answers to Sentence Completion questions must be clearly stated or supported by *the words of the sentence*. Many students pick answer choices that sound correct, or perhaps go with a familiar answer choice that *partly* works because they can't identify a perfect answer, but on the Sentence Completion questions, **the correct answer will almost always work *perfectly* with the context of the sentence.** For all of the following techniques, you will use important parts of the sentence to pick your word.

TARGET WORDS

Target words are the most important words in the sentence. These key words will help you pick words for the blanks. In fact, **you can frequently use the target word as your picked word, particularly when the target word is a perfect synonym or a perfect antonym to the word you are looking for.**

A good way to identify target words in a sentence is to first focus on the blank. If you can figure out what *type* of word could appropriately fit the blank, then you can look for words of this type in the sentence—these words are probably the target words. Keep in mind that the *parts of speech* of the words (verb, adjective, etc.) do not necessarily have to correlate—just focus on the general meanings of the words.

Try underlining target words in the following examples. Do not pick words for these sentences yet.

(EX) 1. With scant rainfall and a long history of -------, the region is one of the world's most arid.

> The target word or words will describe the "history of the region." What words in the sentence could describe the history of a region? *targets: scant rainfall, arid*

(EX) 2. Oddly, a mere stranger managed to ------- Joanna's disappointment, while even her closest friends remained oblivious.

> The target word or words could do something to "Joanna's disappointment." What can one do to disappointment? One could perhaps cause it, soothe it, notice it, ignore it, and so on. Do you see any words of this type in the sentence? *targets: remained oblivious*

(EX) 5. To her great relief, Tina found that wearing dark sunglasses in bright sunlight helped to ------- her headaches.

> The target word or words will *do* something to a "headache." What can be done to a headache? Perhaps *sooth* it or *aggravate* it. Look for words of this type in the sentence. *targets: relief*

(EX) 6. The blanket served the sleeping child as ------- with seemingly magical powers to ward off frightening phantasms.

> The target word or words could describe the "blanket." *targets: magical, ward off frightening phantasms*

(EX) 8. Unlike sedentary people, ------- often feel a sense of rootlessness instigated by the very traveling that defines them.

> The target word or words will be a group of people or *describe* a group of people. *targets: sedentary people, rootlessness, traveling*

SIGNAL WORDS

Signal words are important words or punctuation that will help you determine *relationships* between parts of the sentences. In particular, these words determine the relationships between target words and the blanks. If you have trouble identifying target words, look for signal words first since they are easier to identify. Because they relate the target words to the blanks, signal words usually fall in between the target words and the blanks—this may help you figure out where to look in the sentence for the target words. Some sentences do not have signal words, but when signal words are present they can be very important.

NEGATIVE SIGNALS

It is important to look for *negative words* (such as *not*, *no*, or *none*) since these words can greatly alter the meaning of the sentence. In the examples on the following pages, remember to look for these negative signal words.

CONTRAST SIGNALS

Contrast signals are words which signal an *opposite* relationship between two parts of the sentence. Oftentimes, the answer is an antonym to the target word or words of the sentence. Whenever possible, use the target word in some way for your picked word. For contrast signal sentences, you will usually put a *not* or *un-* in front of the target word. Be familiar with the following contrast signals:

although	however	nevertheless	rather than
but	in contrast	on the contrary	still
despite	in spite of	on the other hand	yet
even though	instead of		

In the examples below and on the following pages, look for signal words and target words, and pick words for the blanks. Write your words near the blanks—you will come back to them later.

(EX) 1. Eli Lilly did not become a famous philanthropist overnight; on the contrary, the change was -------.

signals: not, on the contrary; ***target:*** *overnight;* ***picked word:*** *not overnight*

(EX) 3. In attempting to reconcile estranged spouses, counselors try to foster a spirit of ------- rather than one of stubborn implacability.

signals: rather than; ***targets:*** *reconcile, stubborn;* ***picked words:*** *reconciliation or un-stubbornness*

(EX) 7. The deference shown to Adam at his birthday party directly contrasted with the ------- shown to Paul at his party.

signal: contrasted; ***target:*** *deference;* ***picked word:*** *lack of deference*

SUPPORT SIGNALS

One part of the sentence may *support* another part of the sentence, and this is usually indicated with a *support signal*. Frequently, the answer is a synonym to the target word or words of the sentence. As mentioned before, try to use some form of the target word as your picked word. Be familiar with the following support signals:

additionally	furthermore	since
also	in addition	(semicolon) ;
and	likewise	(colon) :
besides	moreover	

(EX) 2. Lately there has been a ------- of interest in Patel's writing, and the recent growth in her popularity has made it difficult to buy her books even in specialized secondhand bookstores.

    signal: and; ***target***: recent growth; ***picked word***: recent growth

(EX) 4. I regret that my remarks seemed -------; I never intended to belittle you.

    signal: (;); ***target***: belittle; ***picked word***: belittling

(EX) 8. Lorena, who rose to become the highest-ranking female in the television industry, was ------- recruited: television producers courted her persistently.

    signal: (:); ***target***: persistently; ***picked word***: persistently

CAUSE AND EFFECT SIGNALS

Cause and effect signals are very similar to support signals because one part of the sentence *causes* another part in some way, but **these sentences often lack a clear target word**. Use the context of the sentence to pick a logical word. Be familiar with the following cause and effect signals:

accordingly	in order to
because	so...that
consequently	therefore
for	thus
hence	when...then

(EX) 3. Jasmine suspected her dog of eating the chocolate cake because Fido was ------- under the table.

   signal: because; **target**: none; **picked word**: hiding, etc.

(EX) 4. These regulations are so ------- that we feel we have lost all our privileges.

   signal: so...that; **target**: none; **picked word**: strict, etc.

(EX) 6. The movie was out of theatres in only a week after its opening because critics gave it ------- reviews.

   signal: because; **target**: none; **picked word**: negative, etc.

UNEXPECTED SIGNALS

Unexpected signals indicate that something *unexpected* exists in the sentence. Oftentimes, the unexpected occurrence is a contradiction and the answer may be an antonym to a target word, as with the contrast sentences. Be familiar with the following unexpected signal words.

abnormal	even	paradoxical
actually	illogical	surprising
amazing	incongruous	unexpected
anomalous	ironic	
curious (2nd def.)	odd	

(EX) 2. Paradoxically, Helen, who had been a strict mother to her children, proved a ------- mistress to her cats.

   signal: paradoxically; **target**: strict; **picked word**: un-strict

(EX) 6. It was illogical for someone who appeared so innocuous to commit such a ------- act.

   signal: illogical; **target**: innocuous; **picked words**: not innocuous

POSITIVE VERSUS NEGATIVE

Sometimes you may not be able to identify clear target words, or you may not completely understand the sentence. This will obviously make it difficult to pick a *perfect* word for the blank. If you can recognize *tone* in the sentence, you may be able to at least determine whether the missing word is a *positive* word or a *negative* word. This may allow you to eliminate some answer choices. Try to identify the blanks as positive or negative in the following examples:

(EX) 5. The medical community seemed so divided that medical progress was often accompanied by -------, with each step forward creating new enmities.

   signal: none; **targets**: divided, enmities; **picked word**: negative word

(EX) 7. Stephen was a jocular and even-tempered man; he had none of his brother's -------.

   signals: (;), none; **targets**: jocular, even-tempered; **picked word**: negative word

3. DOUBLE BLANKS

Perhaps close to half of sentence completion questions have two blanks. This may make the sentence more difficult to understand, but it will also give you twice the opportunity to pick words and eliminate answer choices.

ONE BLANK AT A TIME

With double-blank sentences, read the sentence carefully, and then **work on *one blank at a time***:

1. Pick a word for the particular blank that seems easier or is supported by the clearest signals and targets.
2. Look at the appropriate parts of the answers choices (either the first words or the second words) and eliminate all possible answers.
3. Tackle the other blank.

For the following examples, look for target and signal words and pick a word for at least *one* of the blanks:

(EX) 3. Scratching, though a useful self-remedy for an annoying itch, can ------- a problem by harming the skin if performed too -------.

   signal*: though;* ***target****: useful, harming;* ***picked word (blank 1)****: worsen*

(EX) 4. When an already ------- machine is modified to correct existing problems, there is always a chance that the modifications will ------- more problems than they solve.

   signal*: than;* ***target****: solve;* ***picked word (blank 2)****: not solve*

(EX) 4. Weather models do not provide ------- forecasts of what the future will bring; such models serve only as a clouded crystal ball in which a range of ------ possibilities can be glimpsed.

   signals*: not, (;);* ***target****: clouded;* ***picked word (blank 1)****: not cloudy (clear)*

(EX) 8. Because college professors often rely on ------- language, their writings often seem ------- to readers who fail to understand its meaning.

   signal*: because;* ***target****: fail to understand;* ***picked words (blank 1 or 2)****: not understandable*

SYNONYMS AND ANTONYMS

Some double-blank sentences do not have clear signals for either blank but offer clues about the *relationships* of the missing words. For these types of sentences, determine whether the words are *synonyms* or *antonyms*, and eliminate answer choices accordingly.

There are usually two possible answers to these problems in regard to the *tone* of the missing words. If the words are synonyms, either both are *positive* words or both are *negative* words. If the words are antonyms, either the first word is *positive* and the second word is *negative* or vice versa. There will usually be clues in the sentence that help you determine which choice is correct, but when in doubt, check both options with the answer choices.

It is still a good idea to make up some words for each option before looking at the answer choices. In the following examples, decide whether the blanks are synonyms or antonyms and consider possible words for the blanks. If you have a sense for which option is more likely, put this option first.

(EX) 2. Despite their technical -------, the maps of the West Indies provide ------- information for geographers and historians.

Are the missing words synonyms or antonyms?

The missing words are antonyms. Notice the contrast signal word: "Despite."

Option 1: first blank _____, second blank _____

   first blank: *negative word,* **second blank**: *positive (keep it simple)*

Option 2: first blank _____, second blank _____

   first blank: *positive word,* **second blank**: *negative*

(EX) 6. The ------- of the program charged with developing a revolutionary new means of transportation based on fuel cells confidently predicted that there would soon be proof of the fuel cell's -------.

Are the missing words synonyms or antonyms? Hint: the first word describes a *group* of people.

The missing words are synonyms.

Option 1: first blank _____, second blank _____

    first blank: supporters, **second blank**: success

Option 2: first blank _____, second blank _____

    first blank: critics, **second blank**: failure

DOUBLE TARGET WORDS

Often double blank questions (and sometimes single blank questions) will have *double target words*. Usually, these target words are close to each other in the sentence. In these questions, each target word allows you to pick a word for its respective blank, usually in the order that the words are given. (In other words, the first target word usually relates to the first blank and the second target word usually relates to the second blank.) Sometimes the missing words will be synonyms to the target words. Other times the target words will provide information that will allow you to pick logical words for the blanks.

(EX) 2. Body armor had advantages and disadvantages for medieval knights: they helped the warriors to ------- injury, but left them more ------- when trying to move.

signal: (:); *double targets*: advantages and disadvantages; *picked words (blanks 1 and 2)*: avoid, tied-down (other answers possible)

(EX) 5. The famous pianist performs both classical and contemporary works; he is honored both as an active ------- of the new and as a ------- interpreter of the old.

signal: (;); *double targets*: classical and contemporary OR new and old; *picked words (blanks 1 and 2)*: positive word, positive word—the target words are vague, so keep the picked words vague as well. (Note: The order of the targets is opposite to that of the blanks.)

(EX) 6. Since the research in a graduate-level thesis must be a ------- and ------- contribution to the focus of study, care must be given to select a previously unaddressed, though important topic.

signal: since; *double targets*: previously unaddressed, important; *picked words (blanks 1 and 2)*: previously unaddressed, important

(EX) 7. The essay was both ------- and -------: although concise, it was profoundly moving.

signal: (:); *double targets*: concise, profoundly moving; *picked words (blanks 1 and 2)*: concise, profoundly moving

4. DEFINITIONS

It is not uncommon to have the actual *definition* of the missing word somewhere in the sentence. This is the ultimate target. **A general rule on medium or difficult questions is: the easier it is to pick a word for the blank, the more difficult the answer choice vocabulary. Since definition questions tend to be the easiest questions to "pick words" for the blanks, expect the answer choice vocabulary to be difficult.** Underline the definitions of the missing words in the following sentences. These definitions are equivalent to your picked words from the previous sections.

(EX) 6. Shy and timid by nature, Martin became even more ------- when in the presence of his boss.

   definition of picked word: shy and timid

(EX) 8. Through a series of -------, the professor presented a dramatic narrative that portrayed life in the ancient Aztec city.

   definition of picked word: dramatic narrative(s)

(EX) 8. The researchers were ------- in recording stories of the city's Mexican American community during the depression, preserving even the smallest details.

   definition of picked word: preserving even the smallest details

5. ANSWER CHOICES

Finally, it is time to look at the answer choices. Your vocabulary and word-part studies will help you with this final step.

CORRECT ANSWERS ARE PERFECT

(!) As stated earlier, **the correct answers on sentence completion questions will almost always work *perfectly* with the context of the sentence.** All of the previous techniques were designed to help you focus on the context of the sentence and pick a word based on this context. The correct answer must reflect this context. If you are comfortable and effective at picking words, the correct answers and your picked words should be synonyms.

LOOK AT EVERY ANSWER CHOICE

Even if you think you have identified the correct answer, it is a good idea to check every answer choice. Some words may sound correct, but remember, you are looking for the word or words that best fit the meaning of the sentence.

ELIMINATE ANSWER CHOICES

You will often have an excellent picked word, but you can't identify the correct answer. Since you know the answer must be *perfect*, **make sure to eliminate familiar words that are *not* perfect,**
(!) **especially on higher-numbered questions where correct answers are often unfamiliar, difficult words**. Remember, if you can eliminate even two answer choices, you should guess.

WHEN ALL ELSE FAILS...

COMPARE ANSWER CHOICES

You can use this technique when you are struggling with a problem and can't begin to pick a word for the blank. If you're not sure of the intended meaning of a sentence or there is a word or words in the sentence that you can't figure out, try comparing the answer choices. If there are two answer choices that mean about the same thing, there's a good chance that you can eliminate these words. Often, the correct answer is an antonym to these words. Also, see if there is one answer choice that seems to stand out from the rest, such as a *positive* word when all the rest are *negative* words. This word may be the correct answer. The following examples exaggerate a lack of understanding of the sentences. See if you can guess the correct answer by comparing answer choices:

(EX) 3. ???????????????????? -------, ??????????????????????????????????????.

(A) consistent (B) thrilling (C) invigorating (D) overrated (E) scenic

*(B) and (C) are synonyms, and (A), (B), (C), and (E) are all **positive** words. Guess (D): overrated.*

Now, look at the actual sentence and see if your answer is correct:

3. Either the skiing here is -------, or the snowfall this year is way below average.

(EX) 6. ?? ------- ????????????????
???????.

(A) harmonious (B) sensational (C) impeccable (D) vapid (E) esteemed

*(A), (B), (C), and (E) all sound like **positive** words. Guess (D) vapid – dull.*

Now, look at the actual sentence and see if your answer is correct:

6. Her singing style is such that she can invest even the most ------- lyrics with dramatic meaning.

COMPARE ANSWER CHOICES – DOUBLE BLANKS

Here's a trick you can use on double-blank questions. First look at all five blank-1 answer choices. Eliminate any answer choices that have no synonyms or near synonyms among the other blank-1 answer choices. Make sure you only eliminate words that you know. It may be helpful to consider the tones of the words while you do this. If you think two words have similar definitions (but perhaps they are not perfect synonyms), play it safe and don't eliminate them. Then do the same thing for the blank-2 answer choices. You will often be left with just one answer choice—the correct one— without looking at the sentence at all! Try the following example:

(EX) 3. ???
?????????????; ?????? -------- ??????????????????????? -------- ???????????????????????.
(A) advances . . promoting   (B) validates . . segregating   (C) discounts . . evaluating
(D) reaffirms . . exploring   (E) confuses . . diminishing

Blank 1: You might notice that (B) (validates) and (D) (reaffirms) are synonyms; both mean a positive statement of affirmation. Answer choice (A) (advances) is not too far off, so let's keep these three similar words. Answer choices (C) (discounts) and (E) (confuses) are certainly different from the positive, blank-1 answer choices in (A), (B), and (D), and since "discounts" and "confuses" are not synonyms, eliminate them.

Blank 2: The only near synonyms among the blank-2 answer choices are (C) (evaluating) and (D) (exploring). Eliminate (A) (promoting), (B) (segregating), and (E) (diminishing). Note that "segregating" (separating or setting apart) and "diminishing" (reducing or lessening) may both be negative, but they are really not near synonyms. The word "promoting" (encouraging or advancing) is not close enough to exploring or evaluating to be considered a near synonym. You're left with (D).

Now, look at the actual sentence and see if your answer is correct:

3. Artist Chie Fueki invests the traditional Japanese craft technique of Kazari with contemporary themes; thus, he -------- a Japanese practice while -------- current-day Japan.

PLUG ANSWER CHOICES INTO THE SENTENCE

The last technique can be used when you are confused by the sentence, cannot pick a word for the blank, and cannot identify a likely correct answer by comparing the answer choices. Try plugging the answer choices into the sentence. Occasionally, just reading the sentence with the answer choices plugged in will help you get an idea of the sentence's intended meaning. You may also be able to eliminate a few answer choices that sound awkward when read in the sentence.

6. SENTENCE COMPLETION SUMMARY

The following summarizes the sentence completion chapter:

ORDER:

- Read the sentence → pick a word → look at answer choices

HOW TO PICK WORDS:

- Look at the *context* of the sentence
- Look for *target words*
- Look for *signal words*
  - *Negative signals*
  - *Contrast signals*
  - *Support signals*
  - *Cause and effect signals*
  - *Unexpected signals*
- Identify *tone* of the missing words: *positive* versus *negative*

DOUBLE BLANKS:

- Work on one blank at a time
- Look for synonyms and antonyms
- Look for *double target words*

DEFINITIONS:

- Look for the definitions of missing words; watch out for difficult vocabulary.

ANSWER CHOICES:

- Answers are *perfect*
- Look at every answer choice
- Eliminate answer choices
- Compare answer choices when you can't pick a word
- Plug answer choices into the sentence when you can't pick a word

7. COMPLETING THE EXAMPLE PROBLEMS

The following questions are the same ones that were used as examples in the previous sections, but now the answer choices are given. **They are in the order of the topics of this chapter, so look back at your underlined target words, signal words, and picked words on the previous pages while you tackle these problems.** Remember to look at problem numbers to determine the difficulty level of the questions; each question is part of an 8-question section. Answers can be found starting on page 311.

TARGET WORDS AND SIGNAL WORDS

TARGET WORDS:

1. With scant rainfall and a long history of -------, the region is one of the world's most arid.

(A) monsoons   (B) farming   (C) drought   (D) manufacturing   (E) conservation

2. Oddly, a mere stranger managed to ------- Joanna's disappointment, while ever her closest friends remained oblivious.

(A) arouse   (B) perceive   (C) warrant   (D) discredit   (E) misrepresent

5. To her great relief, Tina found that wearing dark sunglasses in bright sunlight helped to ------- her headaches.

(A) ascertain   (B) dislocate   (C) mitigate   (D) extend   (E) propagate

6. While sleeping, the blanket served the child as ------- with seemingly magical powers to ward off frightening phantasms.

(A) an arsenal   (B) an incentive   (C) a talisman   (D) a trademark   (E) a harbinger

8. Unlike sedentary people, ------- often feel a sense of rootlessness instigated by the very traveling that defines them.

(A) athletes   (B) lobbyists   (C) itinerants   (D) dilettantes   (E) idealists

CONTRAST SIGNALS:

1. Eli Lilly did not become a famous philanthropist overnight; on the contrary, the change was -------.

(A) unpopular   (B) unexpected   (C) advantageous   (D) sufficient   (E) gradual

3. In attempting to reconcile estranged spouses, counselors try to foster a spirit of ------- rather than one of stubborn implacability.

(A) disillusionment   (B) ambivalence   (C) compromise   (D) antagonism
(E) independence

7. The deference shown to Adam at his birthday party directly contrasted with the ------- shown to Paul at his party.

(A) obedience   (B) irreverence   (C) collaboration   (D) formality   (E) restraint

SUPPORT SIGNALS:

2. Lately there has been a ------- of interest in Patel's writing, and the recent growth in her popularity has made it difficult to buy her books even in specialized secondhand bookstores.

(A) retention   (B) concealment   (C) moderation   (D) suppression   (E) resurgence

4. I regret that my remarks seemed -------; I never intended to belittle you.

(A) inadequate   (B) justified   (C) unassailable   (D) disparaging   (E) shortsighted

8. Lorena, who rose to become the highest-ranking female in the television industry, was ------- recruited: television producers courted her persistently.

(A) indiscriminately   (B) enigmatically   (C) vicariously   (D) rancorously
(E) assiduously

CAUSE AND EFFECT SIGNALS:

3. Jasmine suspected her dog of eating the chocolate cake because Fido was ------- under the table.

(A) barking   (B) cowering   (C) sleeping   (D) interloping   (E) revolting

4. These regulations are so ------- that we feel we have lost all our privileges.

(A) stringent   (B) aristocratic   (C) redundant   (D) specious   (E) garish

6. The movie was out of theatres in only a week after its opening because critics gave it ------- reviews.

(A) innocuous   (B) caustic   (C) rave   (D) gaudy   (E) contrite

UNEXPECTED SIGNALS:

2. Paradoxically, Helen, who had been a strict mother to her children, proved ------- mistress to her cats.

(A) a harsh   (B) an indolent   (C) an ambivalent   (D) a cautious   (E) a lenient

6. It was illogical for someone who appeared so innocuous to commit such a
------- act.

(A) harmless   (B) fortunate   (C) grateful   (D) destructive   (E) discerning

POSITIVE VERSUS NEGATIVE:

5. The medical community seemed so divided that medical progress was often accompanied
by -------, with each step forward creating new enmities.

(A) sacrifice   (B) astonishment   (C) coordination   (D) conflict   (E) error

7. Stephen was a jocular and even-tempered man; he had none of his brother's -------.

(A) atrophy   (B) joviality   (C) equanimity   (D) hardiness   (E) acerbity

DOUBLE BLANKS

ONE BLANK AT A TIME:

3. Scratching, though a useful self-remedy for an annoying itch, can ------- a problem by
harming the skin if performed too -------.

(A) exacerbate . . vigorously   (B) cure . . carefully   (C) worsen . . refreshingly
(D) clarify . . abrasively   (E) exonerate . . violently

4. When an already ------- machine is modified to correct existing problems, there is always a
chance that the modifications will ------- more problems than they solve.

(A) perfected . . promote   (B) imposing . . curtail   (C) complex . . create
(D) intricate . . eliminate   (E) flawed . . alleviate

4. Weather models do not provide ------- forecasts of what the future will bring; such models serve only as a clouded crystal ball in which a range of ------ possibilities can be glimpsed.

(A) meteorological . . discarded   (B) definitive . . plausible   (C) practical . . impeccable
(D) temporal . . scientific   (E) conventional . . forgotten

8. Because college professors often rely on ------- language, their writings often seem ------- to readers who fail to understand its meaning.

(A) accessible . . abstruse   (B) inscrutable . . unequivocal   (C) esoteric . . unfathomable
(D) hackneyed . . striking   (E) coherent . . raucous

SYNONYMS AND ANTONYMS:

2. Despite their technical -------, the maps of the West Indies provide ------- information for geographers and historians.

(A) inaccuracies . . imaginative   (B) limitations . . abundant   (C) interest . . additional
(D) precision . . great   (E) proficiency . . considerable

6. The ------- of the program charged with developing a revolutionary new means of transportation based on fuel cells confidently predicted that there would soon be proof of the fuel cell's -------.

(A) directors . . redundancy   (B) adversaries . . profitability   (C) originators . . futility
(D) critics . . efficiency   (E) advocates . . feasibility

DOUBLE TARGET WORDS:

2. Body armor had advantages and disadvantages for medieval knights: they helped the warriors to ------- injury, but left them more ------- when trying to move.

(A) evade . . unbounded   (B) avoid . . restricted   (C) dissipate . . liable
(D) practice . . restrained   (E) preserve . . accountable

5. The famous pianist performs both classical and contemporary works; he is honored both as an active ------- of the new and as ------- interpreter of the old.

(A) excluder . . a disciplined   (B) reviler . . an unparalleled   (C) disparager . . a pathetic
(D) champion . . an inadequate   (E) proponent . . an incomparable

6. Since the research in a graduate-level thesis must be a ------- and ------- contribution to the focus of study, care must be given to select a previously unaddressed, though important topic.

(A) novel . . significant   (B) biased . . verbose   (C) succinct . . redundant
(D) scholarly . . mundane   (E) neutral . . opinionated

7. The essay was both ------- and -------: although concise, it was profoundly moving.

(A) meandering . . denigrating   (B) compact . . enervating   (C) fictional . . touching
(D) argumentative . . rationalistic   (E) terse . . poignant

DEFINITIONS

6. Shy and timid by nature, Martin became even more ------- when in the presence of his boss.

(A) boisterous   (B) retiring   (C) oblivious   (D) perturbed   (E) gallant

8. Through a series of -------, the professor presented a dramatic narrative that portrayed life in the ancient Aztec city.

(A) conundrums   (B) vignettes   (C) dynamics   (D) factors   (E) tangents

8. The researchers were ------- in recording stories of the city's Mexican American community during the depression, preserving even the smallest details.

(A) obstreperous   (B) apprehensive   (C) compensatory   (D) radicalized
(E) painstaking

8. PICKING-WORDS PRACTICE

Underline target and signal words, and write your picked word near the blanks in the following sentences. If there are two blanks, fill in at least one of the blanks. For definitions, underline the definition of the missing word. Answers can be found on page 312.

1. The editorial argued that scientific research has become too ------- when excessive rivalry among researchers compromises proper scientific procedures.

2. Journalists present at demonstrations of the telephone in 1876 described the invention as a -------, evoking much wonder and astonishment.

3. She was -------, always ready to fight about something; it is little wonder that such a ------- individual had few friends.

4. David often blurted out suggestions spontaneously; this ------- sometimes got him into trouble.

5. Most of my friends are the reverse of flattering or deferential; they are extremely -------.

6. Too subtle a novelist to be bluntly -------, Beryl Bainbridge nonetheless criticizes certain values implicitly through her characterizations.

7. Trinkets intended to have only ------- appeal can exist virtually forever in landfills because of the ------- of some plastics.

8. Despite years of poverty and -------, the poet Ruth Pitter produced work that is now ------- by a range of critics.

9. Although surfing is often ------- as merely a modern pastime, it is actually ------- practice, invented long ago by the Hawaiians to maneuver through the surf.

10. Fungus beetles are quite -------: they seldom move more than the few yards between fungi, their primary food.

11. Many linguists believe that our ability to learn language is at least in part -------, that it is somehow woven into our genetic makeup.

12. An apparently gratuitous gesture, whether it is spiteful or solicitous, arouses our suspicion, while a gesture recognized to be ------- gives no reason for surprise.

13. The student's feelings about presenting the commencement address were -------; although visibly happy to have been chosen, he was nonetheless ------- about speaking in public.

14. In sharp contrast to the previous night's revelry, the wedding was a ------- affair.

15. Both by ------- and by gender, American painter Mary Cassatt was an -------, because her artistic peers were French men.

16 Despite an affected ------- which convinced casual observers that he was indifferent to his painting, Warhol cared deeply about his art and labored at it -------.

17. He was ------- success, painting not for the sake of fame or monetary reward, but for the sheer love of art.

18. Because he is so -------, we can never predict what course he will take at any moment.

19. Surprisingly enough, it is more difficult to write about the ------- than about the ------ and strange.

20. She was accused of plagiarism in a dispute over a short story, and, though -------, she never recovered from the accusation.

21. The younger members of the company resented the domineering and ------- manner of the office manager.

22. We need both ornament and implement in our society; we need the artist and the -------.

23. Many educators argue that a ------- grouping of students would improve instruction because it would limit the range of student abilities in the classroom.

24. She told the conference that, far from having to be ------- subjects of an -------technology, human beings can actually control the system to improve their collective future.

25. Like a charlatan, Harry tried to ------- the audience with ------- evidence.

9. SENTENCE COMPLETION PROBLEMS

PRACTICE PROBLEMS

The following assignments are from *The Official SAT Study Guide** by the College Board (2nd Edition). Do not time yourself on these problems and look back to the KlassTutoring tutorial as you learn and master the techniques. You are encouraged to review the techniques (summarized earlier) before and during the completion of these problems. **For practice, underline target words, signal words, and definitions, and write your picked words near the blanks for each problem.** If you do not identify the correct answer, either eliminate at least two answer choices and guess or leave the problem blank.

- ☐ Test 1, Section 2 (1-5), Section 5 (1-8), and Section 9 (1-6)
- ☐ Test 2, Section 4 (1-8), Section 7 (1-5), and Section 9 (1-6)
- ☐ Test 3, Section 4 (1-8), Section 7 (1-5), and Section 9 (1-6)
- ☐ Test 4, Section 2 (1-8), Section 5 (1-5), and Section 8 (1-6)

TEST CORRECTIONS

After each practice test is graded, you should correct problems that you missed or left blank. (The practice tests are found in *The Official SAT Study Guide*.) Go back to the tutorial and review the Sentence Completion techniques as you correct the problems. The idea is to: (1) identify techniques that have given you trouble, (2) go back to the tutorial so you can review and strengthen these techniques, and (3) apply these techniques to the specific problems on which you struggled.

- ☐ Test 5, Section 3 (1-5), Section 7 (1-8), and Section 9 (1-6)
- ☐ Test 6, Section 3 (1-5), Section 7 (1-8), and Section 9 (1-6)
- ☐ Test 7: Section 2 (1-5), Section 5 (1-8), and Section 8 (1-6)
- ☐ Test 8: Section 2 (1-5), Section 5 (1-8), and Section 8 (1-6)
- ☐ Test 9: Section 4 (1-8), Section 6 (1-5), and Section 9 (1-6)
- ☐ Test 10: Section 4 (1-8), Section 6 (1-5), and Section 9 (1-6)

*SAT is a registered trademark of the College Board, which was not involved in the production of and does not endorse this book.

Reminder: At the end of the program, don't forget to take your final practice test. Make sure you have completed all required practice problems in the College Board book. In addition, you should have gone back to Test 5 (and Test 6, if applicable) and corrected missed and skipped problems using the Test Correction assignments at the end of the chapters in this tutorial.

☐   Take Test 7 in the College Board book. Review Taking Practice Tests in the Introduction. After grading, go back and correct missed and blank problems using the Test Correction assignments.

V
CRITICAL READING ANSWERS

The following answers are to all quizzes, lesson problems, homework problems, and any other questions in the previous chapters.

II. VOCABULARY AND WORD PARTS
3. VOCABULARY AND WORD PARTS QUIZZES

QUIZ: VOCAB. LIST 1

1. abridge - shorten
2. acclaim - applaud
3. acquiesce - agree w/out protest
4. acrid - sharp or bitter
5. adverse - unfavorable
6. altruistic - unselfishly generous
7. ambivalence - having contradictory emotions
8. amorphous - lacking shape
9. analogous - comparable
10. apathy - lack of caring
11. aspire - seek to attain
12. autonomous - self-governing
13. aversion - firm dislike
14. belie - give a false impression
15. buttress - support
16. censorious - critical
17. certitude - certainty
18. circumlocution - the use of an unnecessarily large number of words to express an idea
19. complacency - self-satisfaction, often while unaware of some potential danger
20. conciliatory - soothing

QUIZ: VOCAB. LIST 2

1. confluence - flowing together
2. contentious - quarrelsome
3. credulity - gullibility
4. curtail - shorten
5. cynical - distrusting or disparaging the motives of others
6. deleterious - harmful
7. depose - dethrone
8. deride - ridicule
9. despondent - depressed
10. diffuse - wordy, spread out
11. discerning - mentally quick
12. disinclination - unwillingness
13. disparage - belittle
14. dissent - disagree
15. distend - expand
16. efface - rub out
17. eloquence - expressiveness
18. elucidate - explain
19. enmity - hatred, hostility
20. erroneous - mistaken

QUIZ: VOCAB. LIST 3

1. erudite - learned, scholarly
2. evanescent - fleeting, vanishing
3. exemplary - outstanding
4. fallacious - false
5. fanaticism - excessive zeal
6. fervor - intensity of feeling
7. frugality - thrift
8. glutton - one who overeats
9. gratuitous - given freely
10. gravity - seriousness
11. homogeneous - of the same kind
12. ignominy - deep disgrace
13. implausible - unlikely
14. incisive - penetrating, cutting; clear and direct, sharp, keen
15. indefatigable - tireless
16. indelible - not able to be erased
17. indifferent - unmoved, unconcerned
18. ingenious - clever
19. innocuous - harmless
20. insolvent - bankrupt

QUIZ: VOCAB. LIST 4

1. insuperable - insurmountable
2. intractable - not easily controlled or directed; stubborn
3. irreproachable - blameless
4. laconic - brief, to the point
5. laud - praise
6. levity - lack of seriousness
7. magnanimous - great-hearted
8. malicious - hateful
9. miserly - stingy, mean
10. obdurate - stubborn
11. orator - public speaker
12. penury - poverty, stinginess
13. peripheral - outer
14. pervasive - spread throughout
15. philanthropist - a person who engages in charitable giving.
16. pithy - concise, meaningful
17. placate - pacify, conciliate
18. predilection - partiality, preference
19. presumptuous - arrogant
20. prevalent - widespread

QUIZ: VOCAB. LIST 5

1. profane - irreverent, blasphemous
2. prolific - abundantly fruitful
3. quandary - dilemma
4. quiescent - at rest; quiet; still
5. rancor - bitterness
6. recluse - loner
7. replete - filled to the brim
8. respite - interval of relief
9. sanction - approve
10. satirical - mocking
11. strident - loud and harsh
12. superficial - trivial, on the surface
13. tantamount - equivalent in effect or value
14. transient - temporary
15. unkempt - uncared for in appearance
16. unobtrusive - not blatant
17. verbose - wordy
18. vigor - active strength
19. whimsical - capricious, unpredictable
20. zealot - fanatic

QUIZ: VOCAB. LIST 6

1. abstemious - sparing in eating or drinking
2. abstruse - obscure, hard to understand
3. adroit - skillful
4. aloof - apart, reserved
5. anomaly - irregularity
6. apocryphal - untrue
7. arbitrator - judge
8. ascetic - practicing self-denial
9. assuage - soothe
10. austere - forbiddingly stern
11. banal - commonplace
12. beguile - mislead
13. blighted - destroyed; deteriorated
14. cajole - coax, persuade w/ pleasing words
15. capricious - impulsive, unpredictable
16. carping - finding fault
17. charlatan - fraud (person)
18. clemency - disposition to show compassion or forgiveness in judging or punishing; leniency
19. coercion - use of force
20. composure - mental calmness

QUIZ: VOCAB. LIST 7

1. criterion - standard used in judging
2. cryptic - secret, hidden
3. culpable - deserving blame
4. deference - courteous regard for another's wishes
5. depravity - wickedness
6. desiccate - dry up
7. disdain - view with scorn
8. disseminate - spread
9. dogmatic - opinionated
10. dupe - to fool or someone easily fooled
11. duplicity - double-dealing, hypocrisy
12. ebullient - showing excitement
13. eclectic - from disparate sources
14. edify - to instruct and improve morally
15. enervate - weaken
16. enhance - increase, improve
17. ephemeral - short lived
18. equivocal - ambiguous, intentionally misleading
19. exemplify - serve as an example
20. exonerate - free from guilt or blame

QUIZ: VOCAB. LIST 8

1. extricate - free
2. fallow - uncultivated
3. fastidious - difficult to please
4. flagrant - blatant
5. furtive - sneaky
6. garrulous - wordy, talkative
7. hackneyed - made commonplace or trite; stale
8. hyperbole - obvious and intentional exaggeration
9. iconoclastic - attacking cherished traditions
10. idiosyncrasy - strange trait
11. impecunious - without money
12. impudence - offensively bold behavior
13. inane - silly, senseless
14. indolent - lazy
15. insipid - lacking flavor
16. insularity - narrow-mindedness, isolation
17. lament - grieve
18. lampoon - ridicule
19. lethargic - drowsy, dull
20. listless - lacking in spirit or energy

QUIZ: VOCAB. LIST 9

1. mitigate - appease
2. mollify - soothe
3. munificent - very generous
4. nefarious - very wicked
5. opaque - dark, not transparent
6. opulence - extreme wealth
7. parsimony - extreme or excessive economy or frugality; stinginess
8. paucity - scarcity
9. pragmatic - practical (not idealistic)
10. pretentious - ostentatious, making excessive claims
11. prodigal - wasteful (w/ money)
12. profound - deep, important
13. provincial - unsophisticated
14. ratify - formally approve
15. rebuff - snub, beat back
16. reprove - censure
17. repudiate - disown, disavow
18. rescind - cancel
19. resigned - unresisting
20. reticence - inclination to silence; reluctance; restraint

QUIZ: VOCAB. LIST 10

1. scanty - meager
2. scrupulous - extremely thorough
3. sedentary - sitting
4. soporific - sleep-causing
5. spurious - false
6. stoic - unmoved by joy or grief
7. stolid - dull
8. succinct - brief
9. surreptitious - secret, furtive
10. sycophant - servile flatterer; a yes-man
11. taciturn - habitually silent
12. temper - to moderate, to mitigate, to soften
13. terse - concise; brief; pithy
14. torpor - sluggishness
15. turmoil - a state of great commotion, confusion, or disturbance
16. usurp - seize another's power
17. vacillate - waiver, fluctuate
18. vindicate - clear from blame
19. volatile - changeable, explosive
20. voluble - fluent, talkative

QUIZ: VOCAB. LISTS 1-5

1. adversary - opponent
2. aggregate - gather, accumulate
3. appease - pacify
4. candor - honesty
5. cordial - gracious
6. cursory - casual, hastily done
7. degradation - humiliation
8. dissonance - discord
9. euphemism - mild expression in place of unpleasant one
10. florid - reddish, flowery
11. illicit - illegal
12. incongruous - not fitting, absurd
13. misanthrope - hater of man
14. novelty - something new
15. ominous - threatening
16. parody - humorous imitation
17. recant - retract previous statement
18. spurn - reject
19. susceptible - subject to some influence; impressionable
20. virulent - hostile, bitter

QUIZ: VOCAB. LISTS 6-10

1. abate - subside, lessen
2. affable - easily approachable
3. atrophy - wasting away
4. coercion - use of force to get someone to obey
5. daunt - intimidate
6. dormant - sleeping
7. elegy - sad poem or song, especially at someone's death
8. esoteric - limited to the understanding of a select few
9. extol - praise
10. fitful - intermittent
11. heresy - opinion contrary to popular belief
12. indigenous - native
13. ornate - elaborately or excessively decorated
14. precocious - pertaining to uncharacteristically early development, esp. in maturity
15. prodigious - marvelous
16. reprehensible - deserving blame
17. sage - wise man
18. stagnant - motionless, stale
19. trepidation - fear
20. venerate - revere, respect

QUIZ: PREFIX LISTS 1 AND 2

1. abstain abs - away from
2. act ac - to, forward
3. attain at - to, forward
4. ambidextrous ambi - both
5. amoral a - without
6. antediluvian ante - before
7. antipathy anti - against
8. archenemy arch - chief
9. archetype arch - first
10. biennial bi - two
11. circumspect circum - around
12. combine com - with, together
13. controversy contro - against
14. decline de - down, away
15. dichotomy di - two
16. diameter dia - across
17. disparity dis - not
18. dysfunction dys - faulty, bad
19. exit ex - out
20. extraterrestrial extra - beyond
21. homonym homo - same
22. hyperventilate hyper - above
23. inefficient in - not
24. irrevocable ir - not
25. incision in - in

QUIZ: PREFIX LISTS 3 AND 4

1. intermission inter - between
2. introvert intro - within
3. metabolism meta - involving change
4. microcosm micro - small
5. misbehave mis - bad
6. monologue mono - one
7. multitude multi - many
8. neologism neo - new
9. obtrude ob - against
10. occlude oc - against
11. oppose op - against
12. panacea pan - all
13. parody par - related
14. permeable per - through
15. perimeter peri - around
16. postscript post - after
17. primordial prim - first
18. propel pro - forward
19. retrospect retro - backward
20. surfeit sur - over, above
21. synchronize syn - with, together
22. transpose trans - across
23. ultrasound ultra - beyond
24. unison uni - one
25. withstand with - against

QUIZ: R.W. LISTS 1 AND 2

1. acrimonious acri - sharp, bitter
2. agrarian agr - field
3. altimeter alti - high
4. alternate alter - other
5. amorous am - love
6. annuity ann - year
7. anthropology anthrop - man
8. aquarium aqua - water
9. asterisk aster - star
10. auditorium audit - hear
11. autobiography auto - self, bio - life
12. belligerent belli - war
13. bibliography biblio - book
14. bibliophile biblio - book
15. intercept inter - between, cept - take
16. decapitate de - down, away; capit - head
17. carnivorous carni - flesh
18. proceed pro - forward; ceed - to go
19. celerity celer - swift
20. cent cent - one hundred
21. anachronism an - without; chron - time
22. suicide cid - kill
23. scissors cis - cut
24. exclamation ex - out; clam - cry
25. exclusive ex - out; clus - close

QUIZ: R.W. LISTS 3 AND 4

1. corporation corpor - body
2. credo cred - believe
3. secure cur - care
4. curriculum curr - run
5. divine div - god
6. demagogue dem - people
7. dermatology derm - skin
8. diurnal diurn - day
9. didactic dact - teach
10. doctrine doct - teach
11. doctor doct - teach
12. indomitable in - not; dom - rule
13. induce in - in; duc - lead
14. egocentric ego - I
15. euphemism eu - good
16. fallacy fall - deceive, err
17. confide con - together; fid - believe
18. finish fin - limit
19. reflect re - again, back; flect - bend
20. fortunate fort - luck
21. fortress fort - strong
22. fractious fract - break
23. monogamy mono - one; gam - marriage
24. genre gen - class
25. regress re - back; gress - step

QUIZ: R.W. LISTS 5 AND 6

1. itinerant itiner - journey, way
2. projectile pro - forward; ject - to throw
3. collaborate col - together; labor - work
4. logbook log - word
5. astrology astr - star; log - study
6. soliloquy loqu - to talk
7. lucid luc - light, clarity
8. magnify magn - great
9. maladroit mal - bad
10. maritime mari - sea
11. matron matr - mother
12. transmit trans - across; mit - send
13. mobile mob - move
14. premonition pre - before; monit - warn
15. moribund mori - death
16. metamorphosis meta - change; morph - shape
17. immutable im - not; mut - change
18. prenatal pre - before; nat - born
19. unnavigable un - not; navi - ship
20. anonymous an - without; nym - name
21. nomenclature nom - name
22. renown nown - name
23. omnivorous omni - all
24. paternal pater - father
25. patriot patr - father

QUIZ: R.W. LISTS 7 AND 8

1. compassion com - with; pas - feeling
2. sympathy sym - with; path - feeling
3. quadruped ped - foot
4. tripod pod - foot
5. compel com - together; pel - drive
6. impulse im - in; puls - drive
7. philander phil - love
8. phonograph phon - sound
9. portable port - to carry
10. potential poten - able, powerful
11. psychopath psych - mind
12. inquisition in - in; qui - to ask
13. corrupt cor - together; rupt - break
14. sanctuary sanc - holy
15. scope scop - to see
16. scribe scrib - to write
17. secant sec - cut
18. consent con - together; sent - think, feel
19. consequence con - with; sequ - follow
20. somnambulist somn - sleep
21. perspective per - through; spect - look
22. stringent string - bind
23. telephone tele - from far; phon - sound
24. contemporary con - together; temp - time
25. tempo temp - time

QUIZ: R.W. LISTS 9 AND 10

1. distend tend - stretch
2. retain re - back; tain - hold
3. tenable ten - hold
4. terminal term - end
5. terrestrial terr - land
6. thermodynamics therm - heat
7. intractable in - not; tract - drag
8. vacuous vac - empty
9. verbatim verb - word
10. controversy contro - against; vers - turn
11. convert con - together; vert - turn
12. vitamin vita - life
13. deviation de - away; via - way
14. vanquish vanq - conquer
15. irrevocable ir - not; re - back; voc - call

QUIZ: ALL WORD PARTS

1. amicable am - love
2. autonomous auto - on its own
3. benevolent ben - good
4. capture capt - take
5. incision in - in; cis - cut
6. accord ac - to; cord - heart
7. credulity cred - believe
8. excursion ex - out; curs - to run
9. contradiction contra - against; dict - to say
10. error err - err
11. infidel in - not; fid - belief, faith
12. deflection de - down, away; flect - bend
13. gender gen - class, race
14. gregarious greg - group
15. interjection inter - between; ject - throw
16. missile miss - to send
17. admonish ad - to; moni - warn
18. mutate mut - change
19. pathos path - feeling
20. transport trans - across; port - carry
21. rupture rupt - break
22. inscription in - in; scrip - write
23. bisect bi - two; sect - cut
24. sequel sequ - follow
25. tension tens - to stretch

IV. SENTENCE COMPLETION QUESTIONS

7. COMPLETING THE EXAMPLE PROBLEMS

In the problems below, KlassTutoring vocabulary words will be indicated with a (V). Definitions for difficult vocabulary will be given. Of course, the answer choices will contain numerous word parts. While most of them will **not** be defined, some important ones will be indicated. You are encouraged to use your word-parts knowledge to help figure out the meanings of words you don't know.

TARGET WORDS:
1. *(C)*
2. *(B)*
5. *(C)*, mitigate (vocab. word (V))
6. *(C)*, talisman (good luck charm), harbinger (one who heralds the approach of something)
8. *(C)*, itinerants (characterized by travel; itiner - journey, way), dilettantes (a person having a superficial interest, a dabbler)

CONTRAST SIGNALS:
1. *(E)*
3. *(C)*, ambivalence (V), antagonism (V)
7. *(B)*, deference (V, respect), irreverence (V), restraint (V)

SUPPORT SIGNALS:
2. *(E)*
4. *(D)*, unassailable (not vulnerable to attack), disparaging (V, belittling)
8. *(E)*, indiscriminately (V), enigmatically (V), rancorously (w/ bitter resentment), assiduously (w/ diligence)

CAUSE AND EFFECT SIGNALS:
3. *(B)*, interloping (intruding)
4. *(A)*, redundant (V), specious (apparently true, but lacking merit), (E) garish
6. *(B)*, innocuous (V), caustic (severely critical), gaudy (tastelessly showy), contrite (showing remorse)

UNEXPECTED SIGNALS:
2. *(E)*, indolent (V, lazy), an ambivalent (V)
6. *(D)*, innocuous (V, harmless), discerning (V, mentally quick)

POSITIVE VERSUS NEGATIVE:
5. *(D)*
7. *(E)*, atrophy (V, wasting away), equanimity (composure, evenness), acerbity (hostility)

DOUBLE BLANKS:
ONE BLANK AT A TIME:
3. *(A)*, exacerbate (V, make worse), vigorously (V, vigor - active strength), exonerate (V)
4. *(C)*, curtail (V), alleviate (V)
4. *(B)*, impeccable (V), temporal (relating to time, as opposed to eternity; temp - time)
8. *(C)*, abstruse (V, obscure, hard to understand), inscrutable (not readily understood), unequivocal (V, equivocal - ambiguous, intentionally misleading), esoteric (V, limited to the understanding of a select few), hackneyed (V, made commonplace or trite; stale), raucous (disagreeably harsh)

2. *(B)*
6. *(E)*, *adversaries (V)*, *advocates (V)*

DOUBLE TARGET WORDS:

2. *(B)*
5. *(E)*, *reviler (one who speaks abusively)*, *disparager (V, one who belittles)*
6. *(A)*, *novel (V)*, *verbose (V)*, *succinct (V)*, *redundant (V)*, *mundane (V)*
7. *(E)*, *meandering (V)*, *denigrating (disparaging, belittling)*, *enervating (V, weakening)*, *terse (V, concise)*

DEFINITIONS:

6. *(B)*, *perturbed (disturbed)*, *gallant (brave)*
8. *(B)*, *conundrums (riddles or puzzles)*
8. *(E)*, *obstreperous (unruly)*, *apprehensive (V)*

8. PICKING-WORDS PRACTICE

The "SAT words" below are the actual SAT answers; it is not necessary to pick these words, but they are good for vocabulary practice.

1. **signal**: *none*; **target**: *excessive rivalry*; **picked word/SAT word**: *competitive*
2. **signal**: *none*; **target**: *wonder and astonishment*; **picked word**: *wonder*; **SAT word**: *marvel*
3. **signal**: *(;)*; **target**: *fight*; **picked words (blanks 1 and 2)**: *fighting, fighting*; **SAT words**: *pugnacious, quarrelsome*
4. **signal**: *(;)*; **target**: *spontaneously*; **picked word**: *spontaneity*; **SAT word**: *impulsiveness*
5. **signal**: *(;)*; **target**: *reverse of flattering or deferential*; **picked word**: *unflattering*; **SAT word**: *caustic*
6. **signal**: *none*; **target**: *criticizes*; **picked word**: *critical*; **SAT word**: *polemical*
7. **signal**: *because*; **target**: *exist ... forever*; **picked word (blank 2)**: *longevity*; **SAT words**: *ephemeral, durability*
8. **signal**: *despite*; **target**: *poverty*; **picked words (blanks 1 and 2)**: *negative, positive*; **SAT words**: *adversity, acclaimed*
9. **signal**: *although*; **targets**: *modern, invented long ago*; **picked word (blank 2)**: *a not modern, an old*; **SAT words**: *dismissed, a time-honored*
10. **signal**: *(:)*; **target**: *seldom move*; **picked word**: *unmoving*; **SAT word**: *sedentary*
11. **signal**: *none*; **target**: *woven into our genetic makeup*; **picked word**: *genetic*; **SAT word**: *innate*
12. *gratuitous (not called for (secondary definition))*, **signal**: *none*; **target**: *while (contrast)*; **picked word**: *not gratuitous*; **SAT word**: *warranted*
13. **signals**: *(;), although*; **target**: *happy*; **picked word (blank 2)**: *unhappy* OR **picked word (blank 1)**: *mixed*; **SAT words**: *ambivalent, anxious*
14. **signal**: *contrast*; **target**: *revelry*; **picked word**: *not a revelry*; **SAT word**: *dignified*
15. **signal**: *none*; **double targets**: *French (blank 1), men ("gender")*; **picked word (blank 1)**: *nationality*; **SAT words**: *nationality, anomaly*
16. **signal**: *despite*; **targets**: *indifferent to, cared deeply*; **picked words (blanks 1 and 2)**: *indifference, with deep care* ; **SAT words**: *nonchalance, diligence*
17. **signal**: *not*; **target**: *fame or monetary reward*; **picked word**: *not concerned with*; **SAT word**: *indifferent to*
18. **signal**: *because*; **target**: *never predict*; **picked word**: *unpredictable*; **SAT word**: *capricious*
19. **signals**: *surprisingly, and*; **target**: *strange*; **picked word (blanks 1 and 2)**: *not strange, strange*; **SAT words**: *commonplace, exotic*
20. **signal**: *though*; **target**: *never recovered*; **picked word**: *positive word, not guilty*; **SAT word**: *exonerated*

21. **signal**: and; **target**: domineering; **picked word**: domineering; **SAT word**: imperious
22. **signal**: (;); **double targets**: ornament ("artist"), implement (blank); **picked word**: one who uses or makes implements (tools); **SAT word**: artisan
23. **signal**: because; **target**: limit the range; **picked word**: range-limiting; **SAT word**: homogeneous
24. **signal**: far from (contrast); **target**: control; **picked words (blanks 1 and 2)**: un-controlling, uncontrollable; **SAT words**: passive, ungovernable
25. **signal**: like (support); **target**: charlatan; **picked words (blanks 1 and 2)**: trick, false; **SAT word**: dupe, spurious

PART **3**

MATH

I
MATH INTRODUCTION AND BASIC CONCEPTS

This chapter will introduce the Math test, including types of questions found on the test, test layout, and timing strategy. It will also cover the use of your calculator and other basic mathematical concepts and terminologies.

1. INTRODUCTION

The math tutorial is divided into seven chapters:

   I.   Introduction and basic concepts
   II. Arithmetic
   III. Algebra
   IV. Geometry
   V.   Functions
   VI. Probability, etc.
   VII. Math Answers

The primary purpose of this part of the tutorial is to teach the mathematical techniques that will allow you to solve the problems found on the SAT. The tutorial will provide detailed explanations of techniques, example problems displaying the application of these techniques, and SAT-like problems that will allow you to practice and master these techniques.

While knowing *how* to apply the techniques in this tutorial is obviously important, knowing *when* to use the techniques is perhaps just as important. You may be an expert at a particular technique, but if you come across a problem on the SAT and do not know to *use* this technique, then your mastery of the technique may not help you. For this reason, the tutorial will also focus on *identifying* the correct technique to use on a particular problem. Throughout the tutorial, look for the magnifying glass for information about identifying techniques.

TYPES OF QUESTIONS

There are two types of math questions on the SAT:

   1. Multiple choice questions
   2. Student Produced Response (SPR) questions

Since you will be taking practice SATs before these questions are discussed in the tutorial, read the instructions in the SATs carefully.

TEST LAYOUT

There are 54 math questions on the SAT. The total test time is 70 minutes. The tests may have some variations, but they generally adhere to the following layout:

- 25-minute section (20 questions)
  - 20 multiple choice questions (arranged in order of difficulty)
- 25-minute section (18 questions)
  - 8 multiple choice questions (arranged in order of difficulty)
  - 10 Student Produced Response (SPR) questions (arranged in order of difficulty)
- 20-minute section (16 questions)
  - 16 multiple choice questions (arranged in order of difficulty)

TIMING STRATEGY

(!) **It is important to realize that the questions on each individual math section are arranged in order of difficulty.** Since each question has the same scoring value, you should never spend too much time on a high-numbered question (with a greater probability of failure) at the expense of lower-numbered problems. If you have a tendency to make careless mistakes (as many students do), don't rush through the easy problems in an effort to complete a section.

Since many of the tips in this tutorial will help make "hard" problems significantly easier, your eventual goal is to at least *look* at every problem. As you get better at identifying and using the techniques taught in this tutorial, you should become more aggressive and confident in tackling the high-numbered problems on the test.

HARD QUESTIONS

On so-called "hard" problems—those with high numbers (approximately the last third of a section)—watch out for obvious answer choices. Some examples include:

- Answer choices that contain numbers from the question
- An answer choice that looks correct on a geometry figure that is *not* drawn to scale
- Answer choices that contain the words: "cannot be determined from the information given" or "none of these"

On a high-numbered problem, be careful before you select one of these obvious answer choices.

HAPPY FACE TOPICS

As in the Writing part of the tutorial, topics that are indicated with the symbol below may be a review for many students. You may choose to move quickly through this material or (for advanced students) skip it altogether and go straight to the lesson problems. If you struggle on any lesson problems, go back and review the relevant material.

STUDENT PRODUCED RESPONSE (SPR) QUESTIONS

These questions ask you to fill in numbers on a grid that looks like this:

Make sure you are familiar with the directions for SPR questions, which are printed at the beginning of each SPR section on the SAT. Take notice of the following important points:

1. While there are boxes for you to write your answers, **only the bubbles that you fill in beneath the boxes are read by the College Board**. Make sure you are accurate when you fill in these bubbles.

2. **No question will have a negative number** (there is no negative sign for you to fill in).

3. **Do not answer with a mixed number** (a number including a whole number <u>and</u> a fraction). For example, the mixed number $3\frac{1}{2}$ must be gridded as 3.5 or $\frac{7}{2}$.

4. Decimal answers that contain more digits than the grid can accommodate must be rounded or truncated, **but you must fill the entire grid** (all four columns). For example, $\frac{2}{3}$ can be written as .666, .667, or 2/3. Less accurate answers such as .66 or .67 will be scored as incorrect.

(!) **Even though the SPR section always starts with question 9, SPR questions start easy and increase in difficulty as you work through the section. So, expect question 9 to be fairly easy. (Since question 8 is the last multiple choice question of the previous section, expect it to be quite difficult.)**

(!) Unlike the other multiple choice questions on the SAT, you do not lose points on missed SPR questions. **Thus, if you have a notion of the correct answer for an SPR question, it is better to guess than leave the question blank.**

2. CALCULATORS ☺

You can and will use a calculator on the SAT. Now that functions and their graphs are part of the test, a graphing calculator is highly recommended.

Many students make careless mistakes because they try to solve difficult computations in their heads. Other students, on the other hand, tend to use calculators for all computations, even the easy ones, costing them valuable seconds on the test. Find a good balance. Don't use your calculator for 2×1, but if you have a tendency to make careless mistakes, *do* use it for 20×100.

Make sure you are comfortable with your calculator. Bring it to all of your tutoring lessons and use it on your homework assignments.

> Your calculator can be used to solve problems involving *fractions*, *radicals*, *scientific notation*, and the π symbol.

If you are not comfortable with any of the above numerical forms, just use your calculator to simplify the problem into a *decimal*. Of course, you will likely have to convert the answer choices to decimals (or fractions) so you can compare them to the answer you found with your calculator. Make sure to stay accurate. Always round decimals to at least four decimal places to the right of the decimal point. For example:

$$\tfrac{1}{3} \neq .3 \rightarrow \tfrac{1}{3} = .3333$$

FRACTIONS AND YOUR CALCULATOR

It will be very helpful to learn how to use the **fraction key** that is found on most calculators. This will allow you to maintain perfect accuracy and check answer choices more quickly (when they are in fraction form). Check your calculator's manual to see how to enter fractions or convert decimals to fractions, or ask a tutor for assistance.

MIXED FRACTIONS

Mixed fractions include a whole number and a fraction, for example:

$$2\frac{3}{4}$$

To enter a mixed fraction into your calculator, think about how you *say* the number:

$$2\frac{3}{4} \equiv \text{“two \textbf{and} three-fourths”}$$

You probably know that the word "and" is used to describe addition ("1 *and* 1 is 2"). So to enter a mixed number into your calculator, use addition:

$$2\frac{3}{4} \rightarrow 2 + \frac{3}{4}$$

ORDER OF OPERATION

Most calculators follow the standard *order of operation* rules. You should be familiar with these rules for tackling more difficult algebra problems. Remember *PEMDAS*: 1. parentheses, 2. exponents, 3. multiplication/division (in order from left to right), and 4. addition/subtraction (in order from left to right).

CALCULATOR LESSON PROBLEMS

Try the following problems using *only* your calculator. The point of these problems is to become comfortable with your calculator. Do not worry about topics such as fractions, scientific notation, and radical simplification. You only need to know how to plug these numbers into your calculator. Answers to all lesson and homework problems start on page 501, which you may want to mark for future reference.

1. $-2^2 =$

2. $(-2)^2 =$

3. $\dfrac{317 + 257}{2} =$

4. $254 - 550 \div 25 =$

5. $2 \times (16 - 3)^2 =$

6. $2\frac{3}{4} + 3\frac{3}{8} =$

7. $\frac{3}{4} \times \frac{2}{3} =$

8. $\frac{3}{4} \div \frac{2}{3} =$
    - (A) $\frac{1}{2}$
    - (B) $\frac{7}{8}$
    - (C) 1
    - (D) $1\frac{1}{8}$
    - (E) $1\frac{3}{8}$

9. $\dfrac{\frac{1}{2} + \frac{2}{3}}{\frac{3}{4} + \frac{4}{5}} =$
    - (A) $^{70}\!/_{93}$
    - (B) $1\frac{1}{2}$
    - (C) $2^{17}\!/_{90}$
    - (D) $2^{16}\!/_{45}$
    - (E) 3

10. $125,000 \times 200,000 =$
    - (A) 25,000
    - (B) 250,000
    - (C) 2.5×10^8
    - (D) 2.5×10^{10}
    - (E) 2.5×10^{12}

Make sure to use a calculator on this problem:

11. $\sqrt{108} + \sqrt{48} =$
    - (A) $\sqrt{13}$
    - (B) $2\sqrt{39}$
    - (C) $\sqrt{156}$
    - (D) $6\sqrt{3}$
    - (E) $10\sqrt{3}$

3. BASIC MATH CONCEPTS

TERMINOLOGY ☺

The following are some commonly misunderstood terms that show up on the SAT:

Integer– positive or negative whole number or zero.

...-3, -2, -1, 0, 1, 2, 3...

Zero – remember, zero is an integer. Zero is also an *even* number, but it is not a *positive* or a *negative* number—think of it as *neutral*.

Factor (or **divisor**) – any of the numbers multiplied together to form a *product*. For example:

$2 \times 3 = 6$
2 and 3 are *factors* (or *divisors*) of the *product* 6.

Multiples – the multiples of a number are simply the products of that number and integers. For example: the multiples of 3 are 3, 6, 9, 12, 15, ...

Prime number – number *greater than one* whose only integer factors are one and itself. For example:

The number 11 is only divisible by 11 and 1; it is therefore a *prime number*.

Remainder – the portion of a number that is not evenly divisible by some other number. You must use long division for remainder problems; calculators do not give remainders.

Absolute value – the positive form of a number. Simply get rid of the negative sign, if there is one. For example:

$\left|-20\right| = 20$

BASIC OPERATIONS ☺

It may be helpful to memorize the rules below. You can use an example to prove and help memorize each rule:

- even + even or even − even = even
- odd + odd or odd − odd = even
- odd + even or odd − even = odd
- even × even = even
- odd × odd = odd
- odd × even = even
- positive × positive or positive ÷ positive = positive
- negative × negative or negative ÷ negative = positive
- positive × negative or positive ÷ negative = negative

ROUNDING ☺

To round, you must be familiar with the names of the *places* of a number. Each place can hold one *digit*, which is an integer from 0 to 9. For example, the number 2,345.06 has a 2 in the *thousands* place, a 3 in the *hundreds* place, a 4 in the *tens* place, a 5 in the *units* (*ones*) place, a 0 in the *tenths* place, and a 6 in the *hundredths* place.

When rounding to a place, look at the digit to the *right* of this place. If it is *5 or more*, round *up*. If it is *4 or less*, keep the number the same.

> **A note about example problems:** If you are working on your own, you will see italicized solutions following example problems. Make sure you understand the solutions—the solutions typically display the correct application of a mathematical technique or method. You do *not* need to solve these example problems on your own. You will be able to practice the techniques on the hundreds of lesson, homework, and practice problems at the end of lessons and chapters.

Round 2,345.06 to the nearest:

(EX) thousands place: *Look to the right of the thousands place. Since 3 < 5, the 2 in the thousands place remains unchanged. The other places become 0s. The answer is **2000**.*

(EX) tens place: *Since the number in the ones place (5) is greater than or equal to 5, round the number in the tens place (4) up. The numbers to the right of the tens place become 0s. The answer is **2,350**.*

(EX) tenths place: *The number in the hundredths place is 6. Since 6 is greater than 5, round the number in the tenths place (the 0) up. The answer is **2,345.1***

FACTOR TABLE

When you are asked to find the *positive integer factors* (sometimes simply called the *positive factors*) of a number, use a *factor table*.

Look for the words *positive integer factors (or divisors)* or *positive factors (or divisors)*

1. Start with 1 in the first column and the original number in the second column of a table.
2. If the original number is even, mentally increase the number in the first column by 1. If the original number is odd, mentally increase the number in the first column by 2 (only odd numbers are divisors of odd numbers).
3. Is the new number a factor of the original number? Hint: you may want to use your calculator. If it is, place it in a new row in column one, and write the quotient (the number displayed on your calculator) in column 2.
4. Repeat steps 2 and 3 until the number in column one exceeds the number in column 2. When done, the numbers in the table will be the positive factors of the original number.

(EX) What are the positive integer factors of 66?

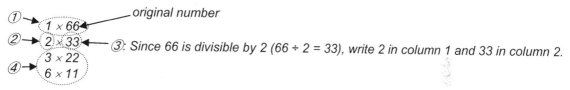

The positive integer factors of 66 are **1**, **2**, **3**, **6**, **11**, **22**, **33**, and **66**.

FACTOR TREE

When you are asked to find the *prime factors* of a number, use a *factor tree*. This is different from a factor table, so make sure you read carefully for the mention of *prime* factors.

Look for the words *prime factors (or prime divisors)*.

1. Write the original number in your work space.
2. Think of a prime number that divides evenly into the original number. Write this prime number and its quotient as *branches* below the original number. Circle or underline the prime number.
3. Repeat step 2 with the quotient branch.
4. When all branches end with prime numbers, those prime numbers are the prime factors of the original number.

(EX) What are the prime factors of 66?

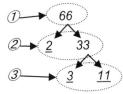

④: *The prime factors of 66 are **2**, **3**, and **11**.*

REMAINDERS

Your calculator won't help you on remainder problems. You must use long division.

To identify these remainder problems, simply look for the word *remainder.*

Make sure you can rewrite a division problem in standard notation as a long division problem, which means using a *divided-into* sign:

$$\frac{2}{3} = 3\overline{)2} \quad \leftarrow (2 \ divided \ by \ 3 \ is \ equal \ to \ 3 \ into \ 2)$$

Notice that the number under the *divided-by line* on the left (the 3) ends up on the outside of the *divided-into sign*, the opposite of what you may visually expect. Make sure not to mix up the numbers.

(EX) $16 \div 5 = $ ***3.2*** *(Use a calculator; no mention of remainders—no need for long division.)*

(EX) What is the remainder when 16 is divided by 5?

$$\frac{16}{5} \quad \rightarrow \quad 5\overline{)\begin{smallmatrix}3\\16\end{smallmatrix}}$$
$$\underline{15}$$
$$\mathbf{1} \leftarrow remainder$$

Rather than asking you to find the *remainder*, difficult remainder problems will *give* the remainder and one of the two original numbers. You must find the other number. Use the following method:

1. Set up a long division problem with a *variable* in place of the unknown number.
2. **Guess 1 as the quotient** (the number above the divided-into sign).
3. Using the rules of long division, create an equation and solve algebraically.

(EX) 16 divided by what number has a remainder of 5?

$$\frac{16}{x} \xrightarrow{①} x\overline{)16} \xleftarrow{1}$$
$$\underline{-x}$$
$$5 \leftarrow remainder \qquad ③:\ 16 - x = 5 \rightarrow x = \mathbf{11}$$

LESSON PROBLEMS

1. Circle all integers:

   203   2.03 π 0   -2 $\frac{2}{3}$ 4.0

2. What are the prime numbers between 1 and 10?

3. What are the positive integer factors of 42?

4. What are the prime factors of 42?

5. What is the remainder when 10 is divided by 3?

6. What is the remainder when 100 is divided by 51?

7. 26 divided by what number has a remainder of 3?

8. What number divided by 26 has a remainder of 3?

9. $|10 - 40| =$

10. If $|x| = 4$, what are all possible values of x?

11. Round 2004 to the nearest tens place:

II
ARITHMETIC

The Arithmetic chapter covers topics and techniques that do not require excessive algebraic or geometric operations. You may have to use some simple algebra, such as solving for a single variable in a simple equation, but more complex algebra will be covered in chapter III.

1. PERCENT PROBLEMS

PERCENT ↔ DECIMAL ☺

You must be able to quickly convert a number in percent form to a number in decimal form, and vice versa. This will always involve moving the decimal point *two places* to the right or to the left. An easy way to see which way to move the decimal point is to use 50%. You probably already know that 50% is equivalent to one half, or .50, so when you are working on a percent problem and can't remember which way to move the decimal point, just write:

$$50\% ↔ .50$$

You can easily see which way to move the decimal point:

50% → .50 for *percent to decimal* - move decimal point two places to the <u>left</u>.

.50 → 50% for *decimal to percent* - move decimal point two places to the <u>right</u>.

When using your calculator on percent problems, remember that the calculator only "understands" *decimals* and will only give answers as *decimals*. You must convert percents to decimals before entering data into your calculator, and remember to convert decimal answers back to percents, if necessary.

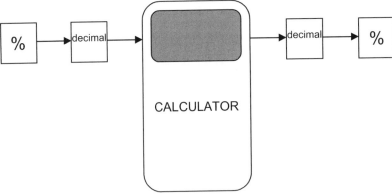

CALCULATOR

Answers to all lesson and homework problems in this chapter start on page 502.

1. 4.25 equals what percent?   4 25%

2. 25% is equivalent to what fraction?   1/4

3. 220% is equivalent to what decimal?   2.20

4. ⁷⁄₈ equals what percent?   .88%

5. .0013 equals what percent?   .13%

A percent problem is easy to identify because it will display a % sign or the word *percent*.

OF/IS PERCENT PROBLEMS ☺

Of/Is problems require you to turn percent word problems into mathematical equations. Use the information in the following table.

word	operation
of ✕ as big as, as old as, as fast as, etc.	AS ✕
is are, was, has, will be, equals, etc.	=
what, what percent what number, how much, etc.	variable (*a, x,* etc.)

Of/Is problems are percent problems that do not involve *change*. In other words, no time passes and no values or variables change in the problem. **These problems are usually identifiable by the words *of* and *is* in the question.** For harder problems where the *of* or the *is* is not written, try creating an Of/Is sentence in your head.

(EX) 20% of 50 = **10**

(EX) 15% of what number is 60? .15 · x = 60 → x = **400**

(EX) 18 is what percent of 20? 18 = x · 20 → x = .9 = **90%**

(EX) Bill is 20. Fred is 3/5 as old as Bill. How old is Fred? B = 20, F = 3/5 × 20 = **12**

Throughout this tutorial, you will notice question numbers that do not follow a logical order. These problems are using numbers from the SAT to represent the level of difficulty for the problem. **For convenience, assume these problems are taken from the 20-question section of the SAT. This means that a problem 1 should be fairly easy and a problem 20 should be quite difficult**, as discussed in the introduction.

1/4 1/4

1. 25% of 25% of 32 is

(A) 1/4

(B) 1/2

(C) 1

(D) 2

(E) 4

2. During a 10%-Off sale at a store, if a shopper buys an item originally priced at $5.50, how much is the item discounted?

(A) $0.50

(B) $0.55

(C) $1.50

(D) $4.95

(E) $5.40

5.50

x .1 = .55

15. 7$\frac{1}{2}$ percent of 8 is equivalent to what percent?

(A) .06%

(B) .6%

(C) 6%

(D) 60%

(E) 600%

.6

20. The volume of a cube with edge of length 1 inch is what percent of the volume of a cube with edge of length 2 inches?

(A) 12$\frac{1}{2}$%

(B) 20%

(C) 25%

(D) 40%

(E) 50%

|

PART-OVER-WHOLE PERCENT PROBLEMS ☺

As the name implies, part over whole percent problems deal with finding a percent *of completeness* by comparing *part* of something to its *whole*.

Like Of/Is problems, part-over-whole percent problems do not involve change (no time passes, and no values or variables change in the problem). **Look for part of something, and look for its whole.**

(EX) If you've traveled 200 miles of a 1000 mile trip, what percent of the trip have you completed?

$$\frac{part}{whole} = \frac{200}{1000} = .20 = \mathbf{20\%}$$

2. If a 12-ounce can of soda currently contains 8 ounces of soda, how full is the can?

    (A) $33^{1}/_{3}\%$

    (B) 50%

    (C) $66^{2}/_{3}\%$

    (D) 75%

    (E) 80%

(30) PERCENT INCREASE/DECREASE

These problems deal with increasing or decreasing a value by a given percent. For a percent increase or "mark-up" problem, *multiply* the original value by 100% *plus* the percent increase to find the final value. For a percent decrease or "discount" problem, *multiply* the original value by 100% *minus* the percent decrease to find the final value.

% Increase: Final value = Original value X (100% + increase%)

% Decrease: Final value = Original value X (100% − decrease%)

The key to these problems is to be able to quickly convert the (100% ± %change) expression into a decimal. For example:

A **20% increase** is equivalent to multiplying by **1.20**. ← (100% + 20% = 120% = 1.20)

A **20% decrease** is equivalent to multiplying by **.80**. ← (100% − 20% = 80% = .80)

If you can find these decimal numbers (called *multipliers*) quickly in your head, these problems should become fairly simple.

Write the *multiplier* for the following percent changes:

1. increased by 25%

2. increased by 70%

3. increased by 7%

4. increased by 100%

5. decreased by 20%

6. decreased by 85%

7. decreased by 60%

8. decreased by 6%

9. decreased by 50%

10. increased by 20%
and then decreased by 20%

Notice that for a *100% increase*, the multiplier is *2*, as you might expect, and for a *50% decrease*, the multiplier is *.5*, again, as you might expect. Also notice that in problem 10 above, you had to tackle the problem in two steps:

$$(100\% + 20\%) \times (100\% - 20\%) = 1.20 \times .80 = .96$$

! NEVER COMBINE PERCENT CHANGES

As you see from number 10 above, you cannot combine percent changes. You might assume that increasing a number by 20% and then decreasing by 20% would result in the original number (a 0% change), but this is incorrect. For example:

Increase the number 10 by 20% and then decrease the resulting number by 20%.

$$10 \times 1.2 = 12 \rightarrow 12 \times .80 = 9.6 \neq 10$$

Similarly, increasing a number by 30% and then decreasing by 10% is *not* the same as increasing by 20%. The math is left to you. Never combine percent changes.

Percent increase/decrease problems involve *change*, which obviously means a value or values in the problem change, sometimes over a period of time. The easiest way to identify these problems is to look for a **given percent change**—either a percent increase or a percent decrease.

(EX) Jeremy increased his test score by 20% from test 1 to test 2. If he scored 80 points on test 1, what was his score on test 2?

$$80(1.20) = \mathbf{96}$$

(EX) A store normally sells a book for $12. How much will the book cost during a "10% off" sale?

$$12(.90) = \textbf{10.80}$$

7. A store marks up all items 10% of their wholesale cost. In dollars, how much would a radio sell for if its wholesale cost is $200?

(A) 20
(B) 180
(C) 190
(D) 210
(E) 220

13. A book sold for $4.80 after a 20% discount was taken off the list price. What was the list price in dollars?

(A) 3.84
(B) 5
(C) 5.76
(D) 6
(E) 6.50

③⓪ DIFFERENCE-OVER-ORIGINAL PERCENT PROBLEMS

In difference-over-original percent problems, you are trying to find the percent that a value or values have changed. These problems compare some new value to an older or *original* value. The *difference* is simply the new number subtracted from the original number.

> As with percent increase/decrease problems, these percent problems involve change, which again means a value or values in the problem change, such as a person's age, a population, or the value of a variable. Usually, there is a passing of time in these problems. The easiest way to identify difference-over-original problems is to see if the question is asking you to find the percent that something has increased or decreased; in other words, **the question is asking you to find a percent change**.

(EX) A school had 1000 students in 1980. It now has 1200 students. What percent did the school's population change since 1980?

$$\frac{difference}{original} = \frac{200}{1000} = \textbf{20\%}$$

14. When Bob started his job, he earned $7 per hour. At the end of 3 years, he earned $28 per hour. By what percent did his hourly rate increase?

(A) 3%

(B) 4%

(C) 25%

(D) 300%

(E) 400%

———

Let's summarize the ways to identify each of the four percent techniques:

Of/Is: Look for the words "of" and "is."
Part-Over-Whole: Look for *part* of something and look for the *whole*.
Percent Increase/Decrease: The question *gives* you a percent change.
Difference-Over-Original: The question *asks you to find* a percent change.

(30) PICK 100

Often, difficult percent problems will involve several percent changes. If no original number is given, it becomes easier to tackle these types of problems by *picking 100* as the original number. Pick 100, and after you've gone through the steps of the problem, compare your final answer to 100. (You can also pick 100 on other types of problems that do not have original numbers given. This will give you a number to work with and a place to start.)

Look for percent problems that have no original number given. Harder problems may have several percent changes.

19. The number of workers at a company increased 30 percent between 1990 and 2000. Employment increased 40 percent between 2000 and 2009. The employment in 2009 was what percent greater than in 1990?

(A) 30%

(B) 35%

(C) 70%

(D) 80%

(E) 82%

30 6. If $300 is deposited into a savings account that pays 4% interest per year, how much money will be in the account after one year?

  (A) $304
  (B) $312
  (C) $340
  (D) $420
  (E) $430

7. If it rained 12 days in November and was clear the other 18 days, what percent of the days did it rain?

  (A) 40%
  (B) 50%
  (C) $66^2/_3\%$
  (D) 75%
  (E) 80%

30 9. John scored 80 points on test 1 and 92 points on test 2. What was the percent increase?

  (A) 8%
  (B) 12%
  (C) 13%
  (D) 15%
  (E) 87%

30 14. At a company, 60 percent of the employees are women. If one-third of the women and one-half of the men drive to work, what percent of the employees do NOT drive to work?

  (A) 20%
  (B) 40%
  (C) 60%
  (D) 75%
  (E) $83^1/_3\%$

30 17. A positive number p is reduced by 25 percent to produce q. If q is increased by 50 percent to produce r, then r is:

  (A) p decreased by 25 percent
  (B) p decreased by 12.5 percent
  (C) p increased by 12.5 percent
  (D) p increased by 25 percent
  (E) p increased by 75 percent

19. Pedro spends $12, which was 15% of his money. How much does he have now?

(A) $10.20

(B) $68.00

(C) $69.80

(D) $80.00

(E) $92.00

(30) 20. A machine takes m hours to close 50 boxes. After the machine is upgraded to a new design, it can close 90 boxes in $.6m$ hours. By what percent did the machine's per-hour production rate increase after the upgrade?

(A) 40%

(B) 80%

(C) 180%

(D) 200%

(E) 300%

2. PROPORTIONS

A *proportion* is two equal *ratios*, or fractions. They may look something like this:

$$\frac{2}{3} = \frac{34}{51}$$

In proportion problems, solve unknown values by cross multiplying: ☺

(EX) $\frac{2}{3} = \frac{62}{x}$ $2 \cdot x = 3 \cdot 62$ → $x = 93$

> Proportion problems have at least one *known*, or complete relationship given between two items. Some examples of *known relationships* are: 12 socks cost 4 dollars, 2 ounces of vanilla are needed to make 3 cakes, or 20 miles per gallon.

The following method should be used for all proportion problems. Some of the steps are very easy, so move quickly:

1. **Identify and underline all known relationships in the problem.** Easier problems will have only one, but harder problems may have two or more. We'll start with a relatively easy example (below), but the second example is more difficult.

2. **Write the *units* of each known relationship as fractions in your workspace.** This step and the next one are relatively easy—move quickly.

3. Write the given numbers of each known relationship to the *right* of these units. **Make sure the units of the given numbers match the units in your proportion.**

4. Somewhere in the question, there will be an extra number that is not part of a known relationship. Observe the units of this number and plug it into the proportion to the right of the known relationship. **Make sure the units match those that you wrote in step 2.**

5. Solve for the unknown value in the proportion by cross multiplying.

(EX) If 5 dozen flowers cost $25, how much do 24 flowers cost?

① known relationship: "5 dozen flowers cost $25" (underline this)

② ③ ④

$\dfrac{\text{dozen flowers}}{\$} \dfrac{5}{25} = \dfrac{2}{x}$ ◄—(24 flowers is 2 dozen flowers)

⑤ → $5 \cdot x = 2 \cdot 25$ → $x = \mathbf{10}$ *dollars*

(EX) Bouquets each contain 24 flowers. If 8 flowers cost $20, how much would it cost to buy 1 bouquet for each of your 8 aunts?

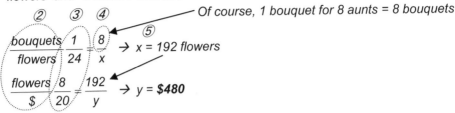

① known relationships (there are two of them): "Bouquets each contain 24 flowers" and "8 flowers cost $20"

Of course, 1 bouquet for 8 aunts = 8 bouquets

② ③ ④

$\dfrac{bouquets}{flowers} \dfrac{1}{24} = \dfrac{8}{x}$ → x = 192 flowers

⑤

$\dfrac{flowers}{\$} \dfrac{8}{20} = \dfrac{192}{y}$ → y = **$480**

LESSON PROBLEMS

4. If Bryan takes 6 minutes to light 15 candles, how many minutes would it take him working at the same rate to light 35 candles?

(A) 8

(B) 9

(C) 10

(D) 12

(E) 14

$\dfrac{6}{15} = \dfrac{x}{35}$

9. A bullet train takes 45 minutes to travel 300 kilometers. If it continues at the same rate, how many hours will it take the train to travel 1600 kilometers?

(A) 3

(B) 4

(C) 5

(D) 6

(E) 8

$\dfrac{45}{300} = \dfrac{x}{1600}$

18. A 7-pound bag of apples costs 10 dollars and 5 pounds of apples are needed to make 2 apple pies. What is the dollar cost of apples needed to make 14 apple pies?

(A) 40

(B) 50

(C) 60

(D) 70

(E) 80

3. If cans of soda sell at the rate of 25 every 4 hours, how many cans of soda will be sold in 20 hours?

    (A) 125

    (B) 100

    (C) 80

    (D) 50

    (E) 5

8. A tree casts a shadow 140 feet long. To determine the height of the tree, Craig stands next to the tree and has someone measure the length of his shadow. If Craig is 6 feet tall and casts a 14-foot shadow, what is the height of the tree?

    (A) 12

    (B) 36

    (C) 60

    (D) 132

    (E) 140

12. Robot A can assemble 30 computer chips per hour and robot B can assemble 39 computer chips per hour. How many more minutes will it take robot A than robot B to assemble 26 computer chips?

    (A) 12

    (B) 15

    (C) 20

    (D) 34

    (E) 52

3. RATIOS

BASIC RATIO PROBLEMS

Basic ratio problems can be recognized by numbers or variables separated by the word *to* or a colon (:), such as 2:3, 2 to 3, *x:y*, or *x* to *y*.

These problems have numbers or variables separated by the word *to* or a colon (:). These ratio signs are equivalent to a *divided-by line*, so they can be rewritten as standard fractions. Use the following method for ratio problems:

1. First, get rid of all ratio signs by rewriting the ratios as fractions.
2. Use your calculator and your knowledge of proportions or algebra to solve.

The following examples illustrate basic ratio techniques:

(EX) What fraction is equivalent to the ratio 3:5 (or 3 to 5)? $\dfrac{3}{5}$

(EX) If the ratio of blue marbles to yellow marbles in a jar is 3:5, and there are 39 blue marbles in the jar, how many yellow marbles are in the jar?

$$\dfrac{blue}{yellow}\; \dfrac{3}{5} = \dfrac{39}{y} \;\rightarrow\; y = \mathbf{65}$$

(EX) What is the *fraction* of blue marbles in the jar described above?

$$\dfrac{part}{whole}\; \dfrac{39}{39 + 65} = \dfrac{3}{8}$$

This problem is similar to a percent problem; just leave the answer in **fraction** *form.*

RATIO SHARE PROBLEMS

Ratio share problems are different from basic ratio problems, even though their identification is similar.

Ratio share problems are also recognized by numbers or variables separated by the word *to* or a colon (:), but **they involve splitting some *whole* value or quantity into different *shares*.** Any problem with a ratio containing more than two terms, for example 2:3:4, is *definitely* a ratio share problem.

The method is straightforward and is best explained using the examples below:

1. Multiply each number in the ratio by a variable, such as x, and set the *sum* of these products equal to the *whole* value that is being divided into shares.

2. Solve for x.

3. Multiply the value of x by the appropriate number in the original ratio to find each share.

(EX) If two friends split $700 dollars in a ratio of 3:4, how much does each friend get?

$$3x + 4x = 700 \;\rightarrow\; x = 100 \;\rightarrow\; \$300{:}\$400$$
$$\quad\quad ① \quad\quad\quad\quad\quad ② \quad\quad\quad\quad ③$$

(EX) If three friends split $700 dollars in a ratio of 3:4:7, how much does each friend get?

$$3x + 4x + 7x = 700 \;\rightarrow\; x = 50 \;\rightarrow\; \$150{:}\$200{:}\$350$$
$$\quad\quad ① \quad\quad\quad\quad\quad\quad ② \quad\quad\quad\quad ③$$

(EX) A high school play is made up entirely of sophomores, juniors, and seniors. If the ratio of sophomores, juniors, and seniors in the play is 1:3:2, respectively, each of the following could be the number of students in the play EXCEPT

(A) 12

(B) 15

(C) 18

(D) 24

(E) 30

Using the technique above, you could write: $x + 3x + 2x =$ total number of students. Then check to see if one of the answer choices gives you a non integer (since numbers of students must be integers).

However, there is a good shortcut for this type of problem: **The total must be a multiple of the sum of the share numbers.**

In this case, the share numbers—1, 3, and 2—add up to 6. Notice that only (B) is not a multiple of 6. Thus, the answer is (B). You can confirm this using the original equation:

$x + 3x + 2x = 15 \;\rightarrow\; 6x = 15 \;\rightarrow\; x = 2.5$, which is not an integer.

LESSON PROBLEMS

4. If the ratio of x to y is 1 to 6, then the ratio of 15x to y is

(A) $\dfrac{5}{18}$

(B) $\dfrac{5}{6}$

(C) $\dfrac{5}{2}$

(D) 3

(E) $\dfrac{15}{2}$

12. Prize money for the top three finishers in a golf tournament is divided up in a ratio of 10:4:1. If the total prize money for the three top golfers is $75,000, how much does the first place golfer receive?

(A) $5,000

(B) $20,000

(C) $50,000

(D) $67,500

(E) $70,000

4. The ratio of n to 9 is equal to the ratio of 33 to 198. What is the value of n?

(A) $\dfrac{2}{3}$

(B) 1

(C) $1\frac{1}{2}$

(D) 3

(E) 54

15. Apple juice, grape juice, and orange juice are mixed by volume in the ratio of 5:4:1, respectively, to produce fruit punch. In order to make 10 gallons of punch, how many gallons of orange juice are needed?

(A) $\dfrac{1}{2}$

(B) 1

(C) 3

(D) 4

(E) 5

16. A basket contains only red and green apples. If there are 20 apples in the basket, which of the following could NOT be the ratio of red to green apples?

(A) $\dfrac{1}{2}$

(B) $\dfrac{1}{3}$

(C) $\dfrac{2}{3}$

(D) $\dfrac{1}{9}$

(E) $\dfrac{3}{2}$

4. AVERAGES, MEDIANS, & MODES

Make flash cards and memorize the following terms if you are not already familiar with them:

FLASH
CARDS

☺ **Average** or **arithmetic mean** – the sum of a set of values divided by the number of values in the set

☺ **Median** – the middle number in a set of increasing values. If the set has an even number of values, average the two middle numbers. **Don't forget the values must be in order before you can find the median.**

☺ **Mode** – the value in a set of numbers that occurs the most frequently

Average problems are easy to identify because you only need to look for the words *average*, *median*, or *mode*. Note: Some *rate* problems also have the word *average*, but these problems use another technique that we will discuss in the next section.

1. What is the median of the following numbers?

    2, 6, 0, 10, -5

2. What is the median and mode of the following numbers?

    2, 6, 0, 10, -5, 10

The table below shows the hourly wages for 11 workers at a small company. Two workers make $9 per hour, two workers make $10 per hour, and so on.

Hourly wage (in $)	# of workers
9	2
10	2
12	1
13	2
14	4

3. What is the average of the 5 wages?

4. What is the median of the 5 wages?

5. What is the average hourly wage of the 11 workers? (hint: write all 11 workers' wages in a list)

6. What is the median hourly wage of the 11 workers?

7. What is the mode of the workers' wages?

12. Spencer measures the noon temperature once a day for a week and records the following values: $62°$, $70°$, $80°$, $72°$, $72°$, $65°$, $x°$. If the median temperature for the seven days is $70°$, then x could be any of the following EXCEPT

    (A) 59

    (B) 66

    (C) 67

    (D) 70

    (E) 73

$ANS \rightarrow A \times N = S$

The *ANS*wer to average problems can usually be found using <u>ANS.</u> This technique will help make harder average problems much easier, but it is also simple enough to use on easier problems. We know that the average (*A*) is the sum (*S*) of a set of <u>values</u> divided by the number (*N*) of values in the set:

$$A = \frac{S}{N}$$

By multiplying both sides by *N*, we can create the simple equation:

$A \times N = S$

Average x Number of items in set = Sum of the items in the set

Use the following technique for *ANS* problems:

1. Write $A \times N = S$ at the top of your workspace and work in the columns below each letter.

2. Read the problem carefully, and plug values into the *ANS* table. Make sure to keep *averages* under the *A* column, *numbers in set* under the *N* column, and *sums* under the *S* column. Remember, the *S* column is for the added sum of the items in the set.

3. Anytime two entries in a row are known, calculate to find the missing entry.

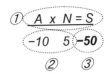 The average of five numbers is −10. What is the sum of these numbers?

$$\textcircled{1}\quad \underline{A \times N = S}$$
$$\underline{-10 \quad 5 \quad -50}$$
$$\textcircled{2} \qquad \textcircled{3}$$

HARDER *ANS* PROBLEMS

On harder *ANS* problems, you will usually have to deal with more than one group of numbers (each group with its own average). This will require you to use multiple rows in the *ANS* table, each group of numbers getting its own row. You will also probably use a *total* row beneath the other rows.

1. Write *ANS* and plug values into the *ANS* table, as described before. Remember, anytime two entries in a row are known, calculate to find the missing entry.

2. If a total row is needed, look for verbal clues to determine whether you should add or subtract the *N* and *S* columns. Whatever operation you perform on one of these columns, you will also perform on the other column. For example, if you add the *N* column, you must also add the *S* column. The entries in the *A* column should never be added or subtracted into the total row. These *A* entries are only used to calculate missing information in their respective rows.

3. **Never find the *average* of values in the *A* column.** In other words, never average averages.

(EX) If the average age of 500 students at school A is 14 and the average age of 300 students at school B is 18, what is the average age of all the students at the two schools?

$$\underline{A \times N = \quad S}$$
$$14 \times 500 = 7000$$
$$18 \times 300 = 5400$$
$$A \quad 800 \quad 12{,}400 \;\to\; A \cdot 800 = 12{,}400 \;\to\; A = \textbf{15.5} \;(\textit{Note: since we were}$$
finding the average of "all" students, we **added** *the N and S columns.*)

LESSON PROBLEMS

5. If the average of x, y, and z is 20 and average of p and q is 25, what is the value of $x + y + z + p + q$?

(A) 9
(B) 22.5
(C) 45
(D) 60
(E) 110

11. An average of 14 people use a park's tennis courts each weekday and an average of 42 people use the courts each weekend day. What is the average daily use of the courts over the entire week?

(A) 20
(B) 22
(C) 25
(D) 26
(E) 27

19. If the average of six numbers is −2 and the average of four of the numbers is 2, what is the average of the other two numbers?

(A) −10
(B) −2
(C) $-\frac{2}{5}$
(D) 0
(E) $\frac{2}{5}$

12. Samara takes a logic test five times and scores 12, 10, x, 20, and 27 points. If the average of her five scores is 18, what is the median of the five scores?

(A) 10
(B) 15
(C) 18
(D) 20
(E) 21

14. A 20-year-old bank gave away an average of 152 toasters a year for the first 15 years of its existence. For the past five years, the bank did not give away any toasters. What was the average number of toasters given away per year over the bank's entire 20 years?

(A) 76
(B) 98
(C) 114
(D) 120
(E) 152

5. RATES, TIMES, & DISTANCES

RTD → R × T = D

You must be familiar with the following equation:

$$R \times T = D$$

$$\text{Rate or speed } (\frac{distance}{time}) \times Time = Distance$$

Rate problems usually deal with some sort of travel over time and distance, such as: driving a car, flying an airplane, etc. However, any problem that deals with accomplishing something (not exclusively travel) over a period of time can be an *RTD* problem. For example, a problem dealing with *pages read per hour* or *machines made per day* could be an *RTD* problem. Note that the *D* column in these examples would be used for whatever is being accomplished over time (*pages read, machines made*).

> *RTD* problems will mention something that is accomplished over a period of *time*, usually travel. Look for key words like *rate, speed, pace,* or *velocity,* or look for any mention of *per time,* such as *per hour* or *per minute.* You will also notice the word *average,* but don't use *ANS* on *RTD* problems.

RTD problems are solved very similarly to *ANS* problems:

1. Write *R* x *T* = *D* at the top of your workspace, and work in the columns below each letter.
2. Read the problem carefully, and plug values into the *RTD* table. Make sure to keep *rates* under the *R* column, *times* under the *T* column, and *distances* (or whatever is being accomplished) under the *D* column.
3. Anytime two entries in a row are known, you can calculate to find the missing entry.
4. Rates are actually *average* speeds, so they follow the same rules as *ANS* problems. If a total row is needed, look for verbal clues to determine whether you should add or subtract the *T* and *D* columns. Whatever operation you perform on one of these columns, you will also perform on the other column. The entries in the *R* column should never be added or subtracted into the total row. These *R* entries are only used to calculate missing information in their respective rows.
5. **Never find the *average* of values in the *R* column.**

(EX) Kyle travels ⅔ of a 6-mile trip by bicycle, and the bicycle portion takes 15 minutes. What is the average speed, in miles per hour, of the bicycle portion of the trip?

*It is helpful to convert units **before** plugging numbers into RTD:*

15 min. → .25 hrs.

① R x T = D   ③

② R   .25   4 → R·.25 = 4 → R = **16** *miles per hour*

LESSON PROBLEMS

8. A car travels 48 miles in 45 minutes. What is the car's average speed in miles per hour?

(A) 52

(B) 56

(C) 60

(D) 64

(E) 68

18. Erica rides a bicycle from her home to her work 24 miles away at an average speed of 12 miles per hour. She returns home along the same route at an average speed of 8 miles per hour. What was Erica's average speed in miles per hour for the entire trip?

(A) 9.2

(B) 9.6

(C) 9.8

(D) 10.0

(E) 10.5

5. A helicopter flies 360 miles in 3 hours. If it continues at this rate, how many hours will it take the helicopter to travel 800 miles?

(A) $2\frac{2}{9}$

(B) $3\frac{2}{3}$

(C) $4\frac{2}{9}$

(D) $5\frac{7}{9}$

(E) $6\frac{2}{3}$

19. Hilary and Vivian begin a 5-mile walk at the same time. When Hilary finishes the walk, Vivian is half a mile behind. If Hilary walked the 5 miles in 75 minutes, what was Vivian's average speed in miles per hour for the portion of the walk that she has completed?

(A) 3.0
(B) 3.2
(C) 3.4
(D) 3.6
(E) 3.8

Number pattern problems deal with sequences, which are lists of numbers. Sometimes the lists are relatively short and sometimes they may be quite long. These problems can take several different forms.

> Number pattern problems will either give you a long list of numbers or give you enough information to create a long list of numbers on your own. You may see the words *sequence* or *pattern*.

SHORT SEQUENCES

Most number pattern problems deal with a short sequence of numbers, usually less than 20. There will usually be instructions on how to find each number in the sequence. Follow the instructions and simply *count* to the term you are looking for. These problems usually don't take as long as you may expect.

1, 1, 2, 4, 8, 16, 32, …

2. In the sequence above, each term after the first is obtained by finding the sum of all terms preceding the given term. If the pattern continues indefinitely, 256 will be which term of the sequence?

(A) 7th
(B) 8th
(C) 9th
(D) 10th
(E) 11th

15. A number is a "perfect cube" if it is the cube of a positive integer. How many positive integers less than or equal to 1,000 are perfect cubes?

(A) 10
(B) 15
(C) 20
(D) 25
(E) 30

LONG SEQUENCES

You must find a repeating pattern in problems that deal with a long sequence. If you have trouble finding a pattern, you may decide to simply count to the term you're looking for, but if the list of numbers is too long, use the following method:

1. Write out enough numbers so you can identify the pattern that is being repeated. You are looking for a group of numbers or *items* that repeats over and over again.

2. Count the number of *items* in the pattern.

3. **If the *term-number* whose value you are being asked to find is divisible by the number of items in the pattern, then the term is equal to the *last item* in the pattern.** For example, if there are *three* items in a pattern, then any term whose term number is divisible by three (such as the 3rd term, 6th term, 9th term, 12th term, etc.) will equal the *third* (or last) item in the pattern.

4. **If the term-number whose value you are being asked to find is *not* divisible by the number of items in the pattern, then find a nearby term-number that *is*, and count up or down to the term you're looking for.**

10, 20, 30, 10, 20, 30, ... ① *The pattern is [10, 20, 30]*

(EX) How many items are in the pattern above? **3** ← *step* ②

In the pattern above, what is the...

3rd term in the pattern? **30** ← *step* ③

6th term in the pattern? **30** ← *step* ③

30th term in the pattern? **30** ← *step* ③

32nd term in the pattern? **20** ← *step* ④

133rd term in the pattern? **10** ← *step* ④ *The 132nd term is 30 (since 132 is divisible by 3); count up one term.*

Some long number pattern problems don't *appear* to have any repetition in the pattern because the actual numbers never repeat, but you may be able to identify some other repetition in the pattern.

(EX) The first two numbers of a sequence are 1 and 3, respectively. The third number is 4, and, in general, every number after the second is the sum of the two numbers immediately preceding it. How many of the first 50 numbers in this sequence are even?

(A) 16
(B) 17
(C) 18
(D) 32
(E) 34

1, 3, 4, 7, 11, 18, 29, 47, 76...
o o e o   o   e   o   o   e   The pattern is [o, o, e]

First, use a proportion for the first 48 numbers (since 48 is divisible by 3):

$$\frac{even\ 1}{total\ 3} = \frac{x}{48} \rightarrow x = 16$$

Now check 49th and 50th: Both not div. by 3, so both are odd. Answer is 16.

(A)

-2, -1, 0, 1, 2, -2, -1, 0, 1, 2, ...

6. In the pattern above, the numbers -2, -1, 0, 1, 2 repeat as shown. What is the 45th term in the pattern?

(A) -2
(B) -1
(C) 0
(D) 1
(E) 2

SPECIAL SEQUENCES

ARITHMETIC SEQUENCES

Arithmetic sequences are formed by taking a starting value and *adding* the same value over and over again. For example:

2, 8, 14, 20, 26, ... The starting value is 2, and the number added each time is 6. (2 + 6 = 8, 8 + 6 = 14, and so on)

We can refer to terms in the sequence using an a_n, where the n represents the nth term in the sequence. In the example above, the a_1 term is the first term in the sequence (2), the a_2 term is the second term in the sequence (8), and so on. The number that is added each time, in this case 6, is called the *difference* and is represented by the variable d. There is no great trick for these problems, so memorize the formula for an arithmetic sequence:

$$\boxed{\begin{array}{l} \textit{FLASH} \\ \textit{CARDS} \end{array}} \quad a_n = a_1 + (n - 1)d$$

If you think you might have trouble memorizing this formula, you could easily reproduce it by observing how the example above works:

1st term:	2 =	2 + 6 × 0 =	2
2nd term:	2 + 6 =	2 + 6 × 1 =	8
3rd term:	2 + 6 + 6 =	2 + 6 × 2 =	14
4th term:	2 + 6 + 6 + 6 =	2 + 6 × 3 =	20

For each term, notice that 6 is multiplied by one less than the term number (hence the $n - 1$ in the equation). For this example, we have $a_n = 2 + 6(n - 1)$ → $a_n = 2 + (n - 1)6$.

Any sequence of numbers that has the same value *added* over and over again is an arithmetic sequence problem.

14. The nth term of a sequence is defined as $2 + (n - 1)2$. The 500th term is how much greater than the 499th term?

    (A) 1
    (B) 2
    (C) 4
    (D) 6
    (E) 8

GEOMETRIC SEQUENCES

Geometric sequences are similar to arithmetic sequences, except they are formed by taking a starting value and *multiplying* the same value over and over again. The following are examples:

2, 8, 32, 128, … The starting value is 2, and the number multiplied each time is 4.
(2 × 4 = 8, 8 × 4 = 32, and so on)

2, 1, $\frac{1}{2}$, $\frac{1}{4}$, … The starting value is 2, and the number multiplied each time is ½.

2, −8, 32, −128, …The starting value is 2, and the number multiplied each time is −4.

The number multiplied each time is represented by the constant *r*. Memorize the formula for a geometric sequence:

FLASH CARDS

$$a_n = a_1 r^{n-1}$$

Notice that if you plug in $a_1 = 2$ and $r = 4$, you would have a formula that could give you every term in the first example sequence above.

$$a_n = 2 \times 4^{n-1}$$
$$a_2 = 2 \times 4^{2-1} = 2 \times 4^1 = 8 \ (n = 2)$$
$$a_3 = 2 \times 4^{3-1} = 2 \times 4^2 = 2 \times 16 = 32 \ (n = 3)$$
and so on...

Any sequence of numbers that has the same value *multiplied* over and over again is a geometric sequence problem.

15. The *n*th term of a sequence is defined as $4 \times (\frac{1}{2})^{n-1}$. What is the average of the 2nd, 3rd, and 4th terms in this sequence?

(A) $\frac{7}{12}$

(B) $\frac{7}{6}$

(C) $\frac{7}{3}$

(D) $\frac{7}{2}$

(E) 2

HW

150, 30, 6 . . .

2. In the sequence above, each term after the first term is $\frac{1}{5}$ of the term preceding it. What is the fifth term of this sequence?

(A) −6

(B) 0

(C) $\frac{6}{25}$

(D) 1

(E) $\frac{6}{5}$

3, 2, 1, 0, 1, 2, 3, 3, 2, 1, 0, 1, 2, 3,...

15. In the pattern above, the numbers 3, 2, 1 ,0 ,1 ,2 ,3 repeat as shown. What is the sum of the 49th and 50th terms in the pattern?

    (A) 0

    (B) 1

    (C) 3

    (D) 5

    (E) 6

18. The first two numbers of a sequence are 1 and 3, respectively, and the third number is 4. Every number after the second is the sum of the two numbers immediately preceding it. How many of the first 1000 numbers in this sequence are odd?

    (A) 333

    (B) 500

    (C) 665

    (D) 666

    (E) 667

19. If the first term in a sequence is 7 and each term after the first is −2 times the term before it, what is the nth term in the sequence?

    (A) $7 \times (-2)^{n-1}$

    (B) $7 \times -2^{n-1}$

    (C) $7 \times (-2)^{n}$

    (D) $7 \times -2(n-1)$

    (E) $7 \times -2n$

7. *GREATEST POSSIBLE VALUE*

Some problems may ask you to find the *greatest possible value* (GPV) of a number or a group of numbers. There are a few different types of these problems.

GREATEST POSSIBLE VALUE OF A NUMBER

> Look for the words *greatest possible value* and a group of numbers with a known (or calculable) sum. You will be asked to find the greatest possible value of one of the numbers.

Use the following method:

1. Create an equation, and label each number with a variable.
2. Read the problem carefully to determine the *least* possible values for all of the numbers except for one of them.
3. Calculate to find the one remaining number. This is the GPV.

(EX) Three different positive integers add up to 100. What is the greatest possible value of one of these numbers?

$$① \; x + y + z = 100$$
$$② \; x = 1, y = 2 \; \text{(these are the two smallest \textbf{different} positive integers)}$$
$$③ \; \rightarrow z = 100 - 1 - 2 = \textbf{97}$$

GPV OF NUMBERS MULTIPLIED TOGETHER

> In these problems, you will probably be given the *sum* of two numbers, and you will be asked to find the greatest possible value of the *product* of these numbers.

The GPV will occur when the values of the two numbers are as close to each other as possible.

(EX) If the sum of two positive integers is 12, what is the greatest possible value of the product of the two integers?

$$x + y = 12$$
$$x = 6, y = 6 \; \text{(6 and 6 are as close as you can get!)}$$
$$\rightarrow 6 \times 6 = \textbf{36}$$

OTHER GPV PROBLEMS

You may have to use logic on other types of GPV problems. For example, if you are asked to find the GPV of $-x$, then you would want to *minimize* the x: the smaller the value of x, the larger the value of $-x$.

(EX) If x is a member of the set $\{-2, 0, 2\}$ and y is a member of the set $\{-3, -1, 1, 3\}$, what is the greatest possible value of $x - y$?

$$\textit{maximize } x \rightarrow x = 2$$
$$\textit{minimize } y \textit{ (since y is negative)} \rightarrow y = -3$$
$$x - y = 2 - (-3) = 2 + 3 = \mathbf{5}$$

Least possible value problems are not common, but if you ever come across one, then all of the above rules should be reversed. Here is a very challenging example:

(EX) If $0 \le x \le y$ and $xy \ge 100$, what is the <u>least</u> possible value of y?

> *Since $xy \ge 100$, the LPV of y will coincide with the GPV of x. (As x gets bigger, y gets smaller).*
>
> *Now, look at the first inequality: $0 \le x \le y$. Since $y \ge x$, and since we're trying to maximize x (and minimize y), the LPV of y will occur when x = y. This is the trick to the problem.*
>
> *Substitute y for x: $xy = y^2 \ge 100 \rightarrow y \ge 10$ (remember, y is positive (see first inequality)).*
>
> $\rightarrow$ *So the LPV of y is $\mathbf{10}$.*

13. The average of two non-negative integers is 20. What is the greatest possible value of one of the numbers?

    (A) 10
    (B) 20
    (C) 40
    (D) 100
    (E) 200

15. The sum of three positive integers is 40. If one of the integers is 11, what is the greatest possible value of the product of the other two integers?

8. EXPONENTS

RULES FOR EXPONENTS ☺

The key to problems involving exponents is to memorize the exponential rules.

These problems involve *exponents* (raised numbers) or *roots* ($\sqrt{}$ s).

MULTIPLYING WHEN BASES ARE THE SAME

Remember, the bases must be the same.

$$a^m \times a^n = a^{m+n}$$ (EX) $p^2 \times p^3 = p^5$

DIVIDING WHEN BASES ARE THE SAME

$$a^m \div a^n = a^{m-n}$$ (EX) $p^3 \div p^2 = p^1 = p$

RAISING POWERS TO POWERS

Don't confuse this rule with the first rule above.

$$(a^m)^n = a^{mn}$$ (EX) $(p^2)^3 = p^6$

DISTRIBUTING EXPONENTS

Don't forget to distribute the outside exponent to *number terms* within the parentheses.

$$(ab)^m = a^m \times b^m$$ (EX) $(2p^2q^3)^2 = 2^2(p^2)^2(q^3)^2 = 4p^4q^6$

NEGATIVE EXPONENTS

$$a^{-m} = \frac{1}{a^m}$$

(EX) $p^2 \div p^3 = p^{-1} = \dfrac{1}{p} \neq -p$

ROOTS AND FRACTIONAL EXPONENTS

Convert all roots to fractional exponents. The rules above also apply to these fractional exponents. Get comfortable plugging these into your calculator.

$$\sqrt{a} = a^{\frac{1}{2}}$$

$$\sqrt[n]{a} = a^{\frac{1}{n}}$$

(EX) $\sqrt[3]{64} = 64^{\frac{1}{3}} = 4$ *(OK to use calculator)*

$$\sqrt[n]{a^m} = a^{\frac{m}{n}}$$

(EX) $\sqrt[3]{p^2} = p^x$, $x = \frac{2}{3}$ *since* $\sqrt[3]{p^2} = p^{\frac{2}{3}}$

COMPARE APPLES TO APPLES

Sometimes, you will be asked to compare the exponents of expressions with different bases, but that's like comparing apples and oranges. For example:

$$2^x = 4^4$$

The trick is to make the bases the same so you can easily compare the exponents (compare apples to apples, as the expression goes):

Since $4 = 2^2$, we can write

$$2^x = (2^2)^4$$

$$2^x = 2^8$$

$$x = 8$$

COMMON MISTAKES

There is no way to simplify the *sum* of terms with different bases or different exponents:

1. $p^2 + p^3 \neq p^5$

2. $(p+q)^2 \neq p^2 + q^2$

3. $\sqrt{p^2 + q^2} \neq p + q$

4. When solving for *squared* variables, take the square root of both sides of the equation. **Expect two different answers:** $p^2 = 4 \rightarrow \sqrt{p^2} = \sqrt{4} \rightarrow p = \pm 2$ ($p \neq 2$ only).

LESSON PROBLEMS

1. $x^2 x^7 =$

2. $\dfrac{x^5}{x^2} =$

3. $(x^4)^5 =$

4. $(5xy)^2 =$

5. If $a^2 = 16$, then $a =$

6. $4^{\frac{3}{2}} =$

(HW)

12. If $(2^t)^t = 2^{20}$ and $t > 0$, what is the value of t?

(A) $\sqrt{10}$

(B) $2\sqrt{5}$

(C) 10

(D) $4\sqrt{5}$

(E) 20

14. $(-2xy^3)^2(3x^3y) =$

(A) $-12x^6y^6$

(B) $-12x^5y^6$

(C) $-6x^5y^7$

(D) $12x^6y^6$

(E) $12x^5y^7$

17. If $9^x = \sqrt[3]{81}$, then what is the value of x?

9. *EXPONENTIAL GROWTH*

Exponential growth problems deal with multiplying a value or population by some constant value several times. Use the following formula for these problems:

$$\text{Final amount} = \text{Original} \times (\textbf{Multiplier})^{\textbf{Number of changes}}$$

FLASH
CARDS

$$\textbf{Number of changes} = \frac{\textbf{Total time}}{\textbf{Frequency of change}}$$

> In exponential growth problems, a value or population changes several times. The value is multiplied by the same constant, called the *multiplier*, each time.

Use the following method:

1. **Identify the *multiplier*.** The multiplier is the same one discussed in the percent increase/decrease section. For example: The multiplier for a *10% increase* is 1.10. The multiplier for *doubling* a value is 2. If the problem involves percent change, you may want to review the percent increase/decrease section to find these multipliers.

2. **Find the *number of changes*.** Remember that the exponent is for the *number of changes*— not necessarily the number of hours, years, etc. that have passed. Use the second equation above to find the number of changes.

3. **Plug the given information into the first formula above.**

4. Solve for the unknown information.

(EX) The population of a colony of penguins doubles every 8 years. At this rate, if a colony of this type starts with 5 penguins, how many penguins will be in the colony after 56 years?

① *Multiplier* = 2   ④

② *Number of changes* = $56 \big/ 8 = 7$ → ③ $F = 5(2)^{56/8} = 5(2)^7 = \textbf{640}$

18. A house increases in value by 10% each year. If the house was purchased for $500,000, how much will the house be worth, in dollars, after 5 years from the date of purchase?

(A) 500,050

(B) 550,000

(C) 732,050

(D) 750,000

(E) 805,255

18. The cells of a certain type of bacteria increase in number by splitting into two every 10 minutes. At this rate, if a colony starts with a single cell, how many <u>hours</u> will elapse before the colony contains 2^{12} cells?

10. PROBLEMS FOR BASIC CONCEPTS AND ARITHMETIC

PRACTICE PROBLEMS

The following assignments are from *The Official SAT Study Guide** by the College Board (2nd Edition). It is very important to look back to the KlassTutoring tutorial and review the techniques while completing these problems. Try to determine which technique applies to each problem and apply the methods taught in the tutorial. Do not time yourself on these problems. These problems are provided to give you an opportunity to practice, and hopefully master, the techniques in this tutorial before you must apply them on real SATs in a timed setting.

In the assignments below, "30" problems are part of the 30-hour program, "40" problems are part of the 40-hour program, **bold** problems may be difficult, and *italicized* problems may be only partially covered by techniques in the KlassTutoring tutorial.

- ☐ Test 1: Sect. 3 (1,3,11,13[30]), Sect. 7 (10,13,15), Sect. 8 (8,13)
- ☐ Test 2: Sect. 2 (2,12,16), Sect. 5 (16[30]), Sect. 8 (1, 16[30])
- ☐ Test 3: Sect. 2 (11,13,15), Sect. 5 (1,9,**16**[30],17), Sect. 8 (4,9,15[30])
- ☐ Test 4: Sect. 3 (6,9[30],13,15), Sect. 6 (6,14[30]), Sect. 9 (3,13[30])

TEST CORRECTIONS

After each practice test is graded and as you complete the chapters in this tutorial, you should correct problems that you skipped or left blank. (The practice tests are found in *The Official SAT Study Guide**.) Go back to the tutorial and review the techniques as you correct the problems. The idea is to: (1) identify techniques that have given you trouble, (2) go back to the tutorial so you can review and strengthen these techniques, and (3) apply these techniques to the specific problems on which you struggled.

- ☐ Test 5: Sect. 2 (2,5), Sect. 4 (9,10,12,15), Sect. 8 (3,12,**13**)
- ☐ Test 6: Sect. 2 (1,7), Sect. 4 (3,9,10)
- ☐ Test 7: Sect. 3 (1,5[30],8,17), Sect. 7 (4,13), Sect. 9 (3,5,6)
- ☐ Test 8: Sect. 3 (1,5,10[30]), Sect. 7 (8,13,19), Sect. 9 (10,15[30])
- ☐ Test 9: Sect. 2 (2,6,9,16[30]), Sect. 5 (1[30]), Sect. 8 (11,16[40])
- ☐ Test 10: Sect. 2 (1,11,13[30],16,18), Sect. 5 (6,7), Sect. 8 (12)

[30] Covered by 30-hour program, [40] Covered by 40-hour program

*SAT is a registered trademark of the College Board, which was not involved in the production of and does not endorse this book.

III
ALGEBRA

This is the most important chapter in the tutorial, not only because algebra is such an important part of the SAT, but also because a number of *tricks* will be taught that will allow supposedly difficult, high-numbered problems to be solved with relative ease. As you will see, these tricks can be used on a wide range of problems, including problems from the other chapters of this tutorial.

1. BASIC ALGEBRA

EQUALITIES ☺

For problems 1-10, solve for a. Answers to all lesson and homework problems in this chapter start on page 508.

1. $3a = -54$

2. $10a - 4 = 6$

3. $4 - 5a = 14$

4. $3a + 6 = 4\frac{1}{2}a$

5. $3a - 4 = 2a + 2$

6. $2(a - 6) = -4$

7. $\frac{2}{3}(9 - a) = \frac{1}{2}a - 8$

8. $\frac{1}{a+2} = \frac{3}{5}$

9. $\frac{1}{2a+2} = \frac{3}{a+11}$

10. $a = b - 2$ and $b = 2a$, solve for a

INEQUALITIES ☺

If you can solve equalities like the ones on the previous page, then solving *inequalities* shouldn't be a problem. Just treat the inequality sign ($<, >, \leq, \geq$) as if it were an equal sign, but you must remember one important rule:

When multiplying or dividing both sides of an inequality by a negative number, the inequality sign changes direction. For example:

$$-2a \geq 14 \;\rightarrow\; \frac{-2a}{-2} \leq \frac{14}{-2} \;\rightarrow\; a \leq -7$$

inequality sign changes direction

Solve for *a*:

1. $4a < 120$

2. $-\frac{1}{2}a + 6 \leq 8$

RADICAL EXPRESSIONS ☺

To solve radical expressions:

1. Isolate the radical expression so it is alone on one side of the equal sign.
2. Square both sides.

EX If $2\sqrt{a} = 12$, then $a =$

$$\sqrt{a} = 6 \;\rightarrow\; a = \mathbf{36}$$

Solve for *a*:

1. $2\sqrt{a} - 5 = 11$

2. $2\sqrt{a - 5} = 8$

ALGEBRA WORD PROBLEMS

We've already looked at the mathematical equivalent of words like *of*, *is*, and *what* in the percent section. In order to turn word problems into mathematical equations, you should be familiar with a number of other important words and their mathematical equivalents.

Word	Operation
product *of* *multiplied* *times*	×
sum of *more than* *older than* *farther than* *greater than* *added*	+
difference *less than* *younger than* *fewer* *subtracted*	−
quotient *per* *for* *divided*	÷
square	x^2
cube	x^3

If necessary, just set up the following problem. Techniques for solving it will be discussed on the following pages:

14. When the square of the product of x and 4 is subtracted from the square of the difference of x and 4, the result is 0. What is one possible value of x?

(A) $-\frac{4}{3}$

(B) $-\frac{3}{4}$

(C) 1

(D) $\frac{3}{4}$

(E) $\frac{4}{3}$

---

2. If $50(4x) = 200$, then $4x =$

    (A) $\dfrac{1}{4}$

    (B) 1

    (C) 2

    (D) 4

    (E) 50

12. Four times a number is four more than the two times the number. What is the number?

    (A) −2

    (B) 0

    (C) 2

    (D) 4

    (E) 8

17. Nick purchased a box that contained red, blue, and yellow straws. There were ⅓ as many red straws as there were blue straws. If ⅓ of the straws were blue and 20 of the straws were yellow, how many straws were in the box?

    (A) 12

    (B) 24

    (C) 36

    (D) 48

    (E) 60

2. THE PICK TRICKS

The two most important techniques in this tutorial are called *Pick Numbers* and *Pick Answers*—collectively these will be called the *Pick Tricks*. These techniques make problems easier, often by eliminating difficult algebra. In addition, the Pick Tricks may allow you to solve a problem that would otherwise require a specific mathematical approach with which you may not be familiar. **Because the Pick Tricks apply to so many different types of problems—particularly high-numbered "difficult" problems—always be prepared to use them.**

You are *not* required to use the Pick Tricks. Most problems that can be solved with Pick Tricks can also be solved using more traditional mathematical approaches. However, learn these techniques. Even the most advanced student gets stuck from time to time. Regardless of how often you choose to use them, the Pick Tricks are tools that can get you out of jams. The next several pages will ensure that you are comfortable using these tools.

PICK NUMBERS

The Pick Numbers technique allows variables (or unknowns) to be replaced with actual numbers that you pick. There are four types of pick numbers problems:

>   Type 1: Variables in the answer choices
>   Type 2: Variables in the question only
>   Type 3: No variables
>   Type 4: Guess and check

PICK NUMBERS TYPE 1:
VARIABLES IN THE ANSWER CHOICES

The first type is the easiest to identify and the most straightforward and systematic to solve. Simply look for problems with **variables in the answer choices**.

Note: When there are equal signs (=) or inequalities (<,>...) in the answer choices, this technique may not work, but you may be able to use other Pick Tricks.

The following is a step-by-step method for solving these types of problems:

1. **Pick numbers for variables found in the answer choices.** The numbers 0 and 1 are usually not good choices. If there is more than one variable, pick *different* numbers for each variable. Write your picked numbers somewhere close to the answer choices—you will have to plug them in later. Draw a *box* around the numbers so they are easy to keep track of.

2. **Answer the question using an appropriate technique.** Remember, the variables should now be read as the numbers you picked in step 1, thereby simplifying the problem. Once you've solved the problem, *circle* or *underline* the answer.

3. **Plug your picked numbers into *each* of the answer choices.** You must plug in the number values that you picked in step 1. Cross out any answer choices that don't match your circled or underlined answer from step 2. **YOU MUST CHECK EVERY ANSWER CHOICE!** If only one answer equals your circled answer from step 2, you're done. Occasionally, more than one answer choice works, and you will have to go back to step 1 and pick new numbers to complete the elimination process. Once an answer choice has been eliminated, you do not have to check it again.

(EX) If a pen costs p cents, how many pens can be purchased for $4.00?

(A) $4p$ ① $\boxed{p = 2}$

(B) $400p$

(C) $p/4$ ② $\dfrac{pen}{cents}\dfrac{1}{2} = \dfrac{x}{400} \;\rightarrow\; x = \underline{200}$

(D) $4/p$ ③ Plug $p = 2$ into the answer choices. Make sure to **check every answer**

(E) $400/p$ **choice,** and **cross off** the incorrect ones. The answer is **(E)**.

9. A store sells y pairs of socks for z dollars. At this price, how many pairs of socks can be purchased for $15?

(A) $15yz$

(B) $15z/y$

(C) $15y/z$

(D) $15/yz$

(E) $15/z$

13. Six people visit Anna's blog every x seconds. At this rate, how many people will visit her blog in y minutes?

(A) $10xy$

(B) $10x/y$

(C) $10y/x$

(D) $360x/y$

(E) $360y/x$

16. If m and n are consecutive even integers and $m > n > 0$, how many integers are greater than $m + n$ and less than $m \times n$?

(A) 1

(B) 2

(C) $m - n$

(D) $n^2 - 3$

(E) $m^2 - n^2$

PICK NUMBERS TYPE 2:
VARIABLES IN THE QUESTION ONLY

> These problems have **variables in the question** and **no variables in the answer choices**. This means the answer choices are actual numbers, or the problem is an SPR.

Picking numbers for some or all of the variables in the question may lead you to the correct answer. You must read the question carefully to avoid picking numbers that break the specific rules of the problem. **You will usually _not_ pick numbers for _every_ variable.** Use the following method:

1. Start with the easiest equation or expression in the problem and pick a number for _one_ of the variables.

2. Solve for as many other variables as possible.

3. If necessary, pick numbers for additional variables (that could not be solved in step 2) until you have enough information to solve the problem.

Remember to read the problem carefully. To avoid picking numbers for too many variables, make sure all of the specific rules for the problem are being followed.

(EX) If $a(b - c) = 6$ and $ab = 12$, what is the value of ac?

(A) −6

(B) 2

(C) 3

(D) 4

(E) 6

Start with the second equation because it is simpler:

① _Pick a = 3_

② $3 \cdot b = 12$ → $b = 4$ → $3(4 - c) = 6$ → $c = 2$

③ $ac = 3 \cdot 2 = 6$ **(E)**

10. If $\frac{a}{b} = \frac{2}{3}$ and $\frac{b}{c} = \frac{2}{5}$, then $\frac{a}{c} =$

(A) $\frac{4}{15}$

(B) $\frac{3}{10}$

(C) $\frac{2}{5}$

(D) $\frac{2}{3}$

(E) $\frac{5}{3}$

12. For the equation $x = 10y$, if y is increased by 10, x will increase by how much?

    (A) 0

    (B) $\frac{1}{10}$

    (C) 10

    (D) 20

    (E) 100

PICK NUMBERS TYPE 3: NO VARIABLES

> These problems are harder to identify because many types of problems do not involve variables. If you are ever stuck on what seems to be a difficult problem with **no variables**, you may be able to use this technique.

The idea is to create an example problem with numbers that you pick. This will give you a place to start and something to work with. The number 100 is sometimes a convenient number to pick, as we've already seen in the percent problems in chapter II.

6. Last week, Bill scored 10 fewer points than Fred in a game, and today, Bill scored 2 more points than Fred. Which of the following must be true about Bill's point total for the two games compared to Fred's?

    (A) Bill scored 1/5 of what Fred scored

    (B) Bill scored 5 times of what Fred scored

    (C) Bill scored 8 points more than Fred

    (D) Bill scored 8 points less than Fred

    (E) Bill scored 12 points less than Fred

11. When the perimeter of a square doubles, then the square's area increases by what percent?

    (A) 50%

    (B) 100%

    (C) 200%

    (D) 300%

    (E) 400%

PICK NUMBERS: GUESS AND CHECK

There are times when the conditions of the problem are too strict to allow you to freely pick numbers. In other words, every time you try to pick a number for a variable, some rule in the problem is broken. For example, if you pick a number and end up with 2 = 3, you know something's wrong. Or perhaps you know the answer is supposed to be an integer and you keep getting fractions. You may have to *guess* numbers and *check* to see if you're getting closer to the correct answer. Use the following general method:

1. Pick a number or numbers for variables, similar to the Pick Numbers (Type 2) technique. You will usually not pick numbers for every variable. This is your *guess*.

2. *Check* to see if your picked number or numbers lead you to the correct answer. **Always keep track of your results.** You need to make sure that you're getting closer to the correct answer when you pick new numbers.

3. Continue picking numbers until you find the correct answer. Be prepared to pick decimals, fractions, or negative numbers. Not all problems on the SAT deal only with positive integers.

> This technique works on many types of difficult, high-numbered problems. Often, they involve one or more difficult equations that you cannot easily solve.

(EX) If $7x + 3y = 29$, where x and y are positive integers, what is the value of $x + y$?

   (A) 3   *The equation suggests that x will be a small integer. (x = 5 is already too*

   (B) 7   *large since 7·5 > 29).*

   (C) 8   *Pick (guess) x = 1: 7 + 3y = 29 → 3y = 22 → y is not an integer*

   (D) 10   *Pick (guess) x = 2: 14 + 3y = 29 → 3y = 15 → y = 5*

   (E) 17   *→ x + y = 2 + 5 = 7* **(B)**

20. If $xy = 91$ and $x + y = 20$, then $x^2y + xy^2 =$

   (A) 111

   (B) 1,820

   (C) 1,919

   (D) 2,000

   (E) 2,091

PICK ANSWERS

The other type of trick is called *Pick Answers*. If the answer choices are actual numbers, picking answers may make the problem easier to solve. This tip is especially useful on harder problems or problems that have you stumped. Essentially, this technique allows you to solve a problem by picking answers and working backwards.

Before picking answers, you must identify the *bare-bones question*. This is the question in its simplest form and describes exactly what the problem is asking. Bare-bones questions are usually very simple, such as: "...what is the value of *x*?" or "...what was the list price of the book?"

These problems generally have numbers as answer choices (no variables). Usually, the bare-bones question is very simple and **involves at most one variable**. If you are ever stuck on a high-numbered problem, consider picking answers.

The method is as follows:

1. **Identify and underline the bare-bones question**, as described above.

2. **Answer this question by picking one of the answer choices.** Since the answers are usually in ascending order, start with answer choice C. This may allow you to eliminate answers more quickly. If there appear to be answer choices that are easier to check than others, check these first.

3. **Look at the rest of the question to see if the answer you picked makes sense.**
   Essentially, you are creating an *if-then* question: *If* the answer to the bare-bones question is, say, C, *then* are the parameters of the problem possible? **Once you find the answer that works, stop—you do *not* have to check all the answers for picking answer problems.**

(EX) If Ed and Lorena divide a deck of 52 cards so that Lorena has 8 fewer cards than Ed, how many cards does Lorena receive?

(A) 18	① *Answer the bare bones question ("How many cards does*
(B) 22	*Lorena receive?") starting with (C):*
(C) 26	② *Pick (C): L = 26*
(D) 30	③ *E = 26 + 8 = 34 → 26 + 34 > 52, so the original number was too big.*
(E) 34	*Eliminate (C), (D), and (E).*
	Pick (B): L = 22 → E = 22 + 8 = 30 → 22 + 30 = 52 ✓ (B)

10. Ryan had *d* dollars when he took Amy on a date. He spent one-fourth of his money on flowers and two-thirds of his <u>remaining</u> money on dinner. If he only spent money for flowers and dinner, and he is left with 35 dollars at the end of the night, what is the value of *d*?

    (A) 70

    (B) 140

    (C) 160

    (D) 180

    (E) 210

16. Joshua is ½ as old as Keith and ¼ as old as Sean. If the average of all three ages is 21, how old is Keith now?

    (A) 3

    (B) 9

    (C) 12

    (D) 18

    (E) 36

⑩ PICK TRICK COMBINATION PROBLEMS

There are several ways you can combine the Pick Tricks. The following examples illustrate a couple of these ways.

> These Pick Trick combination problems tend to be high-numbered problems. The answer choices may have a range of values, but other problems may have simple numbers or variables in the answer choices. Just remember that if you are ever stuck on a problem where you have already used a Pick Trick, you may try using a Pick Trick again.

PICK ANSWERS → PICK NUMBERS

Often these problems have answer choices that cover a range of values.

1. Pick an answer choice.
2. Pick a number that falls in the range of the answer choice.
3. Check that number against the parameters of the problem. The goal is to eliminate four of the answer choices.
4. You should usually check every answer choice.

(EX) If $\dfrac{x-5}{2}$ is an integer, then x must be

(A) a negative integer   (A) → $x = -2$ → $-7 \div 2 = -3.5 \neq integer$
(B) a positive integer   (B) → $x = 2$ → $-3 \div 2 = -1.5 \neq integer$
(C) a multiple of 5   (C) → $x = 15$ → $10 \div 2 = 5 = integer$ ✓
(D) an even integer   (D) → $x = 2$ → $-3 \div 2 = -1.5 \neq integer$
(E) an odd integer   (E) → $x = 3$ → $-2 \div 2 = -1 = integer$ ✓

   Since both (C) and (E) work, keep picking numbers:

   (C) → $x = 10$ → $5 \div 2 = 2.5 \neq integer$, so the answer must be **(E)**

PICK NUMBERS → PICK ANSWERS

As the name implies, with these problems, you will first pick a number and then check the answer choices with your picked number.

(EX) On a roller coaster ride at an amusement park, riders must be greater than 4 feet tall but less than 6½ feet tall. If x represents the allowable height of a rider, in feet, which of the following represents all of the possible values of x?

(A) $|x - 2.5| < 5.25$

(B) $|x - 4| < 6$

(C) $|x - 5.25| < 1.25$

(D) $|x - 5.25| < 2.5$

(E) $|x - 6.5| < 4$

*Pick a number between 4 and 6½ and eliminate answer choices that are **false**:*

*x = 5 → Unfortunately, all answer choices are true, so try picking a number outside of the range and eliminate answer choices that are **true**:*

*x = 3 → (A), (B), (D), and (E) are all true and should be eliminated. The answer is **(C)**.*

Note: The faster approach to this problem is to use the following formula: $|x - \textbf{midpoint}| < \frac{1}{2} \cdot \textbf{(the range)}$

*→ $|x - 5.25| < .5 \times (6.5 - 4)$ → $|x - 5.25| < 1.25$ **(C)***

Try to memorize this formula, but If you ever forget it, you can use the Pick Tricks.

———

PICK TRICK HOMEWORK PROBLEMS

Try to use at least one of the Pick Tricks on all of the following problems. Remember, the goal is to get comfortable with these tools so you can choose to use them on the SAT.

8. If $y \neq 0$, then $\dfrac{4}{6y} + \dfrac{5}{6y} + \dfrac{6}{6y} =$

(A) $\dfrac{5}{6y}$

(B) $\dfrac{3}{2y}$

(C) $\dfrac{5}{2y}$

(D) $\dfrac{15}{2y}$

(E) $\dfrac{15}{y}$

9. If a, b, c, and d are consecutive even integers and $a < b < c < d$, then $a + d$ is how much less than $b + c$?

(A) 0

(B) 1

(C) 2

(D) 4

(E) 8

12. If m and n are positive integers, what is the least value of m for which $\dfrac{2m}{11} = n^2$?

(A) 1

(B) 2

(C) 11

(D) 22

(E) 44

13. At a cost of x dollars for 20 songs, how many songs can be downloaded for y dollars?

(A) $y/20x$

(B) $x/20y$

(C) $20/xy$

(D) $20x/y$

(E) $20y/x$

14. If $3^x = 8$, then $3^{2x} =$

(A) 4

(B) 16

(C) 24

(D) 40

(E) 64

15. When p is divided by 7, the remainder is 1. When q is divided by 7, the remainder is 2. What is the remainder when the product pq is divided by 7?

(A) 1

(B) 2

(C) 3

(D) 5

(E) 7

16. Jody played a video game three times and improved his score by the same percent each time. If he scored 600 points the first time and 864 points the third time, what was the percent change after each game?

(A) 13.2%

(B) 20%

(C) 22%

(D) 26.4%

(E) 44%

17. If a telephone call is billed at a constant rate of x cents per 3 minute interval, a call that costs y dollars can last for how many hours?

(A) $x/20y$

(B) $5y/x$

(C) $5x/y$

(D) $300y/x$

(E) $300x/y$

17. If the ratio of a to b is 5:4 and the ratio of $2b$ to c is 6:7, then the ratio of $a:c$ is

(A) 15/28

(B) 2/3

(C) 5/7

(D) 15/14

(E) 35/24

$$\begin{array}{r} X0 \\ \times\, 2Y \\ \hline \end{array}$$

18. In terms of the digits X and Y, what is the solution to the multiplication problem above?

(A) $2 \cdot X + X \cdot Y$

(B) $X + Y + 2$

(C) $20 \cdot X + 20 + Y$

(D) $200 \cdot X + 2 \cdot X \cdot Y$

(E) $200 \cdot X + 10 \cdot X \cdot Y$

19. A business is owned by 3 men and 1 woman, each of whom has an equal share. If one of the men sells $\frac{1}{3}$ of his share to the woman, and another man keeps $\frac{1}{3}$ of his shares and sells the rest to the woman, what fraction of the business will the woman own?

(A) $\frac{5}{12}$

(B) $\frac{1}{2}$

(C) $\frac{3}{4}$

(D) $\frac{11}{12}$

(E) $1\frac{1}{4}$

19. If $\dfrac{a}{a^2+1} + \dfrac{1}{a^2+1} = \dfrac{5}{b}$ for integers a and b and $a > 1$, what is a possible value of b?

(A) 2

(B) 4

(C) 5

(D) 17

(E) 85

(40) 20. There are 270 questions on a high-school entrance exam. To achieve a maximum scaled score of 100, the school scales the exam so that a student's score equals $\frac{1}{3}C+10$, where C is the number of correct answers. If a student can take the exam twice, how many additional questions must a student answer correctly on the second exam in order to raise her score by 20 points?

(A) 30

(B) 45

(C) 60

(D) 75

(E) 90

(40) 20. If $x \geq 0$, which of the following is the solution set of $\left| x^2 - 10 \right| \leq 6$?

(A) $0 \leq x \leq 2$

(B) $0 \leq x \leq 4$

(C) $1 \leq x \leq 4$

(D) $2 \leq x \leq 4$

(E) $2 \leq x \leq 8$

3. *CONSECUTIVE INTEGERS*

Consecutive integers (for example: −2, −1, 0, 1, 2, 3) can be written algebraically as:

$x, x + 1, x + 2...$

Consecutive *even* or *odd* integers (for example: 2, 4, 6, 8 or 1, 3, 5, 7) can be written algebraically as:

$x, x + 2, x + 4...$

These problems almost always include the words *consecutive integers, consecutive odd integers*, or *consecutive even integers*. Some problems may instead mention that terms are *one more than the preceding term* or *two more than the preceding term*. This is just another way of saying that terms are consecutive.

Usually on the SAT, you will *not* have to express consecutive integers algebraically. The following method is faster. The consecutive integers in these problems are usually given as a *sum*.

1. Divide the sum of the consecutive integers by the *number* of consecutive integers.

2. If there is an *odd* number of integers, this technique will give the actual middle integer. It is worth noting that this number is also the *average* and the *median* of the consecutive integers.

(EX) What is the middle integer of three consecutive even integers if the sum of these integers is 12?

$$① \quad \frac{12}{3} = 4 \quad \rightarrow \quad ② \text{ The number 4 is the middle integer.}$$

$$2, \underline{4}, 6$$

3. If there is an *even* number of integers, the above technique will give a value *exactly in between* the two middle integers. This is also the average and the median of the consecutive integers. Once you know this value, you can easily see what the two middle consecutive integers are.

(EX) What are the two middle numbers of four consecutive integers if the sum of these integers is 26?

$$① \quad \frac{26}{4} = 6.5 \quad \rightarrow \quad ③ \text{ The number 6.5 in exactly in between the two middle integers.}$$

$$5, \underline{6}, \underline{7}, 8$$

4. Once you know the middle integer or integers, count to the term in question.

(EX) What is the largest of 5 consecutive odd integers if the sum of these integers is 75?

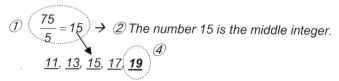

① $\frac{75}{5} = 15$ → ② The number 15 is the middle integer.

④

11, 13, 15, 17, **19**

LESSON PROBLEMS

Note: Number 11, below, is an SPR question (the third question in the SPR section).

11. What is the smaller of 2 consecutive even integers if the sum of these integers is 290?

10. Which of the following is the sum of two consecutive integers?

(A) 90

(B) 91

(C) 92

(D) 94

(E) 100

12. A set of 20 consecutive integers has a sum of 50. If x is a member of this set, and if x is less than the median of the set, what is the greatest possible value of x?

(A) 0

(B) 2

(C) 3

(D) 19

(E) 24

14. The integer 15 is to be expressed as a sum of n consecutive positive integers. Which of the following cannot be a value for n?

(A) 2

(B) 3

(C) 4

(D) 5

(E) None of these

(30) *4. SIMULTANEOUS EQUATIONS*

LINEAR SIMULTANEOUS EQUATIONS ☺

A *linear equation* has the form $ax + by = c$, where a, b, and c are numbers, called *coefficients*.

Coefficient – a number or constant that multiplies a variable (ex.: 2 in the expression $2x$).

When there are two linear equations and two unknowns, the equations can be solved *simultaneously*.

To identify these problems, look for *two* linear equations with *two* unknowns.

Use the following method:

1. Stack the equations (one above the other)—make sure that the variables line up vertically.
2. If necessary, multiply one or both of the equations by a constant (or constants) so that one of the variables has the same coefficient in each equation.
3. Add or subtract the equations to eliminate this variable.
4. Solve for the remaining variable using algebra.
5. Plug this value into one of the original equations to find the other variable.

Solve for x and y:

(EX) $x + 2y = 8$ and $x - 2y = -4$

$$x + 2y = 8$$
$$-(x - 2y = -4)$$
$$4y = 12 \ \rightarrow \ \bm{y = 3}$$
$$\rightarrow x + 2\cdot3 = 8 \ \rightarrow \ \bm{x = 2}$$

2. $100x + y = 25$ and $200x + y = 45$

1. $2x + 2y = 8$ and $3x - 2y = 2$

3. $5x - 5y = -10$ and $2x + 3y = 16$

SIMULTANEOUS EQUATION SHORTCUTS

Often, on SAT simultaneous equation questions, you will *not* have to solve for each variable. Stack the equations, as usual, but pay close attention to what the question is asking for. Usually, simply adding or subtracting the equations is all that is necessary to find the correct answer.

(EX) If $m + n = 3$ and $4m + 2n = -5$, then $\dfrac{5m + 3n}{2} =$

(A) -2

(B) -1

(C) 1

(D) 2

(E) 4

$$m + n = 3$$
$$+(4m + 2n = -5)$$
$$5m + 3n = -2 \rightarrow \frac{5m + 3n}{2} = \frac{-2}{2} = -1 \textbf{ (B)}$$

14. If $4x + y = 6$ and $2x + 3y = 2$, then $x - y =$

(A) $\frac{1}{4}$

(B) $\frac{1}{2}$

(C) 1

(D) 2

(E) $\frac{5}{2}$

(40) OTHER SIMULTANEOUS EQUATIONS

Harder simultaneous equation questions may have *nonlinear equations* or equations with more than two variables. If you notice two equations that can not be easily solved, see if simply adding, subtracting, multiplying, or dividing the equations leads you to the correct answer. This is probably the fastest way to tackle these problems, but don't forget that you may be able to use the Pick Tricks.

> Look for two equations with two (or more) unknowns that are not simple linear equations.

(EX) If $xy = 2$ and $x - y = 3$, then $x^2y - xy^2 =$

(A) 2

(B) 3

(C) 4

(D) 5

(E) 6

*You may try addition, subtraction, or division, but only **multiplication** will get you to the expression in question:*

$(x - y) \cdot (xy) = x^2y - xy^2$

$\quad 3 \ \times \ 2 \ = \ \ 6 \qquad \rightarrow$ *so* $x^2y - xy^2 = 6$ ***(E)***

ⓐ⁰ SIMULTANEOUS EQUATIONS WITH NO SOLUTIONS

Some simultaneous equation problems will ask you to find the value of a coefficient for which the system of equations has no solutions.

> Look for two equations and two unknowns and the words *no solution.*

The following method is the most straightforward way to tackle these problems:

1. Stack the equations, as described before. Make sure the variables line up vertically.
2. Set the ratio of the x coefficients equal to the ratio of the y coefficients.
3. Cross multiply to solve for the unknown.

$$x + 2y = 20$$
$$5x - ky = 40$$

ⒺⓍ For which of the following values of k will the system of equations above have <u>no</u> solutions?

(A) −10

(B) −2

(C) 0

(D) 2

(E) 10

① *The equations are already stacked.*

② $\dfrac{1}{5} = \dfrac{2}{-k}$

③ *Cross multiply to find k: $1 \cdot (-k) = 2 \cdot 5$ → $k = -10$* **(A)**

Note: For the interested student, if you solve the system of equations with $k = -10$, you will get the following impossibility: $0 = -20$. This means the system of equations has no solution.

5. If $2x - y = 12$ and $3x + 6y = 33$, what is the value of $x + y$?

    (A) 9

    (B) 21

    (C) 39

    (D) 40

    (E) 45

16. If x and y are positive numbers and $x^2 + 2y^2 = 21$ and $y^2 - x^2 = 6$, then one possible value of y is

    (A) 3

    (B) 4

    (C) 6

    (D) 8

    (E) 9

(40)

15. If $a + b + c = -30$ and $a + c = 2b$, what is the value of b?

    (A) −30

    (B) −10

    (C) 10

    (D) 30

    (E) It cannot be determined from the information given.

18. If $m^2 = 10x$ and $m^3 = 20x$, where m is a positive integer, what is the value of m?

$$kx + 2y = 10$$

$$x + 5y = 20$$

20. For which of the following values of k will the system of equations above have <u>no</u> solutions?

(A) $-2\frac{1}{2}$

(B) $-\frac{2}{5}$

(C) 0

(D) $\frac{2}{5}$

(E) $2\frac{1}{2}$

20. Pam rode her bike to work in the morning at an average speed of 10 miles per hour. After work, she discovered that she had a flat tire, so she walked home along the same route at an average speed of 2 miles per hour. If Pam spent a total of 3 hours commuting to and from work, what was the total distance in miles that Pam traveled to and from work?

(A) 2

(B) 3

(C) 5

(D) 10

(E) 12

5. DIRECT & INVERSE VARIATION

You must memorize two very simple equations for direct and inverse variation problems.

If two positive numbers are *directly proportional*, then as one number increases (or decreases) the other number also increases (or decreases). To help remember the following equation, notice that <u>d</u>irect variation and <u>d</u>ivision start with the same letter—the equation for direct variation shows that the <u>d</u>ivision of two numbers y/x will always equal a constant number k:

$$\frac{y}{x} = k$$

These problems usually mention the words *directly proportional*, but could also say: *x and y are in direct variation*, *x and y are in proportion*, or *x varies directly as y*.

If two positive numbers are *inversely proportional*, then as one number increases the other number does the opposite—it decreases, or if one number decreases the other number increases. The equation for inverse variation shows that the *product* of two numbers xy will always equal a constant number k:

$$xy = k$$

These problems usually mention the words *inversely proportional*, but could also say *x varies indirectly as y*.

To solve these problems, you will usually be given initial values for x and y.
1. Using the correct equation above with the given values of x and y, solve for k.
2. Once you know the value for k, you can solve for y (for any given value of x) or solve for x (for any given value of y).

(EX) If y is directly proportional to x and $y = -5$ when $x = 5$, what is the value of y when $x = 15$?

Direct variation:

$$① \frac{y}{x} = \frac{-5}{5} = -1 \ (so \ k = -1) \ \rightarrow \ ② \frac{y}{15} = -1 \ \rightarrow \ y = \mathbf{-15}$$

Note: Since x is positive and y is negative, $k < 0$ and y decreases as x increases (the opposite of what you might expect in a direct-proportion problem). As you can see, just make sure to use the correct equation, and you will find the correct answer.

17. If x varies indirectly as y and $x = 20$ when $y = 2$, what is the value of y when $x = -2$?

(A) -40

(B) -20

(C) $-\frac{1}{5}$

(D) 10

(E) 20

18. If x varies directly as y and $x = \frac{1}{2}$ when $y = 4$, what is the value of $\frac{y}{x}$ when $y = 2 \times 10^8$?

(A) 2

(B) 8

(C) 2×10^8

(D) 4×10^8

(E) 8×10^8

③⓪ 6. FACTORING

There are only three types of factoring you need to be familiar with for the SAT:

1. Common factors
2. Factoring quadratics
3. Difference of two squares

COMMON FACTORS ☺

First, some terminology:

Term – a product of numbers and/or variables, such as $4x$ or $\frac{1}{2}x^2$

Expression – one or more terms added or subtracted together, such as $4x + \frac{1}{2}x^2$

If you are solving a difficult equation, always check to see if you can pull a common factor out of every term of an expression. This may sound complicated, but the method is actually fairly straightforward and is best displayed with examples:

Factor the following expressions:

EX) $\frac{1}{2}x^2 + 4x = x(\frac{1}{2}x + 4)$

1. $20q^2 - 40q =$

EX) $12a^3b - 6a^2b^2 = 6a^2b(2a - b)$

2. $2x^2y + 3xy^2 =$

> Look for difficult equations that have common factors in every term (or at least in every term on one side of the equal sign).

SOLVING EQUATIONS BY FACTORING

Factoring will often help you solve an otherwise difficult equation. First, remember that whenever the product of two expressions equals zero, either the first expression equals zero or the second expression equals zero (or they both do). This is called the *zero product theorem*:

If $ab = 0$, then $a = 0$ or $b = 0$

For example, if $x(\frac{1}{2}x + 4) = 0$, then x = 0 or $(\frac{1}{2}x + 4) = 0$.

The solutions would be $x = 0$ or -8.

The following method is useful on many *common factor* problems:

1. For most of these problems, add or subtract terms so that one expression equals zero (all terms on one side of the equal sign).
2. Factor out common factors.
3. Set each new expression equal to zero and solve (as explained by the zero product theorem).

(EX) If $x^2 + 9x = 0$, then what is the <u>sum</u> of the possible values of x?

       ① *The expression already is equal to zero.*

       ② *x(x + 9) = 0*

       ③ *x = 0 or x = −9 → 0 + (−9) = **−9***

12. If $x^2 = 4x$, which of the following is a possible value of $x - 4$?

    (A) −4

    (B) −2

    (C) 2

    (D) 4

    (E) 8

FACTORING QUADRATICS ☺

Quadratics usually take the form $ax^2 + bx + c = 0$, where a, b, and c are numbers. In general, on the SAT, a will equal 1, which is fortunate because it makes solving the quadratic much easier.

If you are uncomfortable factoring quadratics, use the following method:

1. Set the quadratic equal to zero with the *x-squared term* (x^2) first and the *number term* (no x) last.

2. Find two numbers that *multiply* to the number term. If necessary, use a *factor table* to find the pairs of factors (see Basic Mathematical Concepts), but don't forget about negative numbers, as well.

3. The factor pair from step 2 that *adds* to the coefficient of the *x-term* is the correct pair.

4. Write the quadratic in a factored form (see example).

5. Solve for x using the zero product theorem.

(EX) Factor $x^2 - 7x + 10 = 0$ and solve for x.

　　　　① *The equation already equals zero.*

　　　　② *Find the factors of 10 (the number term): 1·10, 2·5, −1·−10, −2·−5*

　　　　③ → *the fourth pair adds to −7 (the x-term coefficient).*

　　　　④ *A quadratic in factored form looks something like this: (x + ?)(x + ?) = 0.*

　　　　　 The factored quadratic is (x − 2)(x − 5) = 0

　　　　⑤ *x = 2 or x = 5*

Factor the following quadratics and solve for x:

1. $x^2 + 5x = -6$

3. $x^2 + 4x = 21$

2. $x^2 - 12x + 12 = -8$

4. $x^2 + 22x - 23 = 0$

DIFFERENCE OF TWO SQUARES ☺

A *square* is just a number or variable (or term) that has been squared. Some examples of squares are: 16 (square of 4), x^2 (square of x), and $36y^4$ (square of $6y^2$). Expressions that are a *difference* (subtraction) of two squares can be factored using the following formula:

$$a^2 - b^2 = (a + b)(a - b)$$

To identify these problems, look for an expression that is a difference of squared items. Note that these squared items can be numbers, variables, terms, or expressions.

(EX) If $(x - 4)^2 - (4x)^2 = 0$, what is the <u>product</u> of the possible values for x?

Note that this is the same equation we found for number 14 in the Algebra Word Problems section. We were able to solve the equation by picking answers, but what if there are no answer choices, as in an SPR question?

The equation is a difference of two squares: $(x - 4)$ and $4x$.

$[(x - 4) + 4x][(x - 4) - 4x] = 0$

→ *By the zero product theorem:* $(x - 4) + 4x = 0$ or $(x - 4) - 4x = 0$

→ $5x - 4 = 0$ → $x = \dfrac{4}{5}$ or $-3x - 4 = 0$ → $x = -\dfrac{4}{3}$

→ $\dfrac{4}{5} \cdot \left(-\dfrac{4}{3}\right) = -\dfrac{16}{15}$

10. If $a^2 - ka + 6 = (a - 3)(a - 2)$, then $k =$

    (A) 1

    (B) 3

    (C) 5

    (D) 6

    (E) 7

11. If $x^3 + x^2 = 0$, which of the following is the <u>sum</u> of the possible values of x?

    (A) −3

    (B) −2

    (C) −1

    (D) 0

    (E) 1

17. If $4a^2 - 25b^2 = 0$, what is the <u>sum</u> of the possible values of a in terms of b?

    (A) $-\frac{5}{2}b$

    (B) $-\frac{2}{5}b$

    (C) 0

    (D) $\frac{2}{5}b$

    (E) $\frac{5}{2}b$

7. QUADRATICS

FOIL ☺

There are three specific quadratic equations you must memorize. The *difference of squares* one was covered in the previous section. All three are easy to derive if you are comfortable using *FOIL* (multiply *First* terms, *Outer* terms, *Inner* terms, and *Last* terms and add these products). For example:

$$(x + y)^2 = (x + y)(x + y) = x^2 + xy + xy + y^2 = x^2 + 2xy + y^2$$

THE THREE QUADRATIC EQUATIONS

FLASH CARDS

1. $(x + y)(x - y) = x^2 - y^2$

2. $(x + y)^2 = x^2 + 2xy + y^2$

3. $(x - y)^2 = x^2 - 2xy + y^2$

To identify these problems, look for any of the elements of the three equations: $(x + y)$, $(x - y)$, $(x + y)^2$, $(x - y)^2$, $x^2 + 2xy + y^2$, $x^2 - 2xy + y^2$, $2xy$, etc.

The method for tackling these problems is as follows:

1. **Identify which of the three quadratic equations above is being tested.** Look for clues; for example, if you see the expressions $(x + y)$ and $(x - y)$, you know that the first equation above is being tested.

2. **Write the appropriate equation as it appears above.** Enter no numbers at this point.

3. **Beneath the equation, write all given numerical values.**

4. You should be able to solve for the variable, term, or expression in question.

(EX) If $m - n = 5$ and $m + n = 7$, then $m^2 - n^2 =$

    (A) 12   ① *Use equation number 1, above.*

    (B) 25   ② $(m - n)(m + n) = m^2 - n^2$ ④

    (C) 35   ③ $(5) \times (7) = m^2 - n^2$ → $m^2 - n^2 = 35$ **(C)**

    (D) 49

    (E) 74

19. If $a + b = 5$ and $2ab = 5$, then $a^2 + b^2 =$

    (A) 0

    (B) 5

    (C) 10

    (D) 20

    (E) 25

1. Use *FOIL* to derive quadratic equation number 3 on the previous page: $(x - y)^2 = x^2 - 2xy + y^2$. Show your work:

16. If $x^2 - y^2 = 20$ and $x - y = 5$, what is the value $x + y$?

17. If $a - b = 4$ and $a^2 + b^2 = 26$, what is the value of ab?

8. *SHORTCUTS*

Obviously, you should always look for shortcuts on SAT math questions, but some harder problems have specific shortcuts that are not obvious. Because there is a wide variety of these types of problems, we will look at just a few examples that will hopefully give you an idea of what to look for.

(EX) The integer m is between 50 and 100. If m is divided by 3, the remainder is 1, and when m is divided by 11, the remainder is 2. What is one possible value of m?

> *Since there are fewer numbers that satisfy the second criteria (divided by 11, remainder is 2), the shortcut is to start with these numbers:*
>
> $m = 57$ ($\div 11 \rightarrow$ *remainder* $= 2$; $\div 3 \rightarrow$ *remainder* $= 0 \neq 1$) ✗
>
> $m = 68$ ($\div 11 \rightarrow$ *remainder* $= 2$; $\div 3 \rightarrow$ *remainder* $= 2 \neq 1$) ✗
>
> $m = \mathbf{79}$ ($\div 11 \rightarrow$ *remainder* $= 2$; $\div 3 \rightarrow$ *remainder* $= 1$) ✓

(EX) What is the least positive integer n for which $18n$ is the cube of an integer?

> $18n = I^3$ ← *since I^3 gets larger faster than $18n$, pick numbers for I:*
>
> $18n = 4^3 \rightarrow n = 3.55...$ *(not an integer)* ✗
>
> $18n = 5^3 \rightarrow n = 6.94...$ *(not an integer)* ✗
>
> $18n = 6^3 \rightarrow n = \mathbf{12}$ ✓
>
> *Note: you would have picked up to 12 numbers if you picked numbers for n.*

18. If the sum of the consecutive integers from −9 to x, inclusive, is 33, what is the value of x?

   (A) 8

   (B) 9

   (C) 10

   (D) 11

   (E) 12

9. ALGEBRA PROBLEMS

PRACTICE PROBLEMS

The following assignments are from *The Official SAT Study Guide** by the College Board (2nd Edition). It is very important to look back to the KlassTutoring tutorial and review the techniques while completing these problems. Try to determine which technique applies to each problem and apply the methods taught in the tutorial. Do not time yourself on these problems. These problems are provided to give you an opportunity to practice, and hopefully master, the techniques in this tutorial before you must apply them on real SATs in a timed setting.

In the assignments below, "30" problems are part of the 30-hour program, "40" problems are part of the 40-hour program, **bold** problems may be difficult, and *italicized* problems may be only partially covered by techniques in the KlassTutoring tutorial.

- ☐ Test 1: Sect. 3 (2,7,14^{30},16,20), Sect. 7 (3,4,8,9,14^{30},**16**), Sect. 8 (5,7,10)
- ☐ Test 2: Sect. 2 (1^{30},6,7,9,14,19), Sect. 5 (1,2,3,4,5^{40},9,12,15,**17**), Sect. 8 (4,6,10,11^{40},**13^{30}** or 13^{40})
- ☐ Test 3: Sect. 2 (1,6,7,9,14^{40}), Sect. 5 (3,**6,8^{30}**,11,14), Sect. 8 (1,5,7,11,12)
- ☐ Test 4: Sect. 3 (1,2,3,8,18,20), Sect. 6 (5^{40},9, 12^{30}), Sect. 9 (1,7,9,12,14,16)

TEST CORRECTIONS

After each practice test is graded and as you complete the chapters in this tutorial, you should correct problems that you skipped or left blank. (The practice tests are found in *The Official SAT Study Guide**.) Go back to the tutorial and review the techniques as you correct the problems. The idea is to: (1) identify techniques that have given you trouble, (2) go back to the tutorial so you can review and strengthen these techniques, and (3) apply these techniques to the specific problems on which you struggled.

- ☐ Test 5: Sect. 2 (1,2,7,8,10,14,16,18^{40},**20**), Sect. 4 (1,4,6,16), Sect. 8 (2,7,9^{40},14)
- ☐ Test 6: Sect. 2 (3,10,13,19), Sect. 4 (1,2,4,**8**,11,**13**,17^{40}), Sect. 8 (1,3,5,9,11,14,16^{30})
- ☐ Test 7: Sect. 3 (2,3,7,9,10,13), Sect. 7 (1,3,6,8,9,10,11,14^{30},15^{40},18^{40},**19**), Sect. 9 (4,7,8,9,10,12)
- ☐ Test 8: Sect. 3 (4,8,9,12^{30},13,15,18), Sect. 7 (2,3,7,10,16), Sect. 9 (1,2,4,6,11)
- ☐ Test 9: Sect. 2 (3,7,10,12,**13**,15,**17**), Sect. 5 (2,6,7,9,12,13,15,17^{30}), Sect. 8 (1,2,6,9,12,**14,16**)
- ☐ Test 10: Sect. 2 (2,6,7,8^{30},9,14), Sect. 5 (1,4,9,12,14,17^{30},20), Sect. 8 (2,4,7,11,13,15,16)

^{30} Covered by 30-hour program, ^{40} Covered by 40-hour program

*SAT is a registered trademark of the College Board, which was not involved in the production of and does not endorse this book.

IV
GEOMETRY

This chapter will cover all relevant geometry topics. Preparing for geometry problems is a matter of familiarizing yourself with the geometry formulas and rules that are found on the SAT and completing practice problems.

1. GEOMETRY INTRODUCTION

REFERENCE INFORMATION

Make sure you are familiar with the information that is found on the front page of each math section on the SAT. Each formula will be discussed in the following sections.

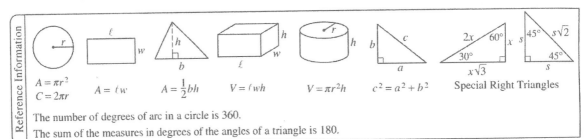

$A = \pi r^2$
$C = 2\pi r$

$A = \ell w$

$A = \frac{1}{2}bh$

$V = \ell wh$

$V = \pi r^2 h$

$c^2 = a^2 + b^2$

Special Right Triangles

The number of degrees of arc in a circle is 360.

The sum of the measures in degrees of the angles of a triangle is 180.

GEOMETRY FIGURES

All drawings on the geometry section are drawn perfectly to scale unless you see the words:

!

<u>Note</u>: Figure not drawn to scale.

These *not drawn to scale* figures are often intentionally misleading, so be careful.

If the drawing does *not* have the note above, then assume that the drawing *is* drawn to scale. The drawings on the SAT are usually very precise. This means that you can make educated guesses based on the drawing. If you are trying to find lengths of elements in the drawing, you can actually create a make-shift ruler with the edge of your answer sheet, scale it to the dimensions of the drawing, and use it to approximate unknown lengths. This approach can be used on the following problem:

(EX) In the figure above, $AB = 5$. If the perimeter of the rectangle is 10 less than twice the square of AB, what is the *area* of the rectangle?

(A) 2

(B) 25

(C) 50

(D) 70

(E) 75

Using the figure above, mark the distance AB on a piece of paper and measure AC. → *AC ≈ 15*

Area = AB·AC ≈ 5·15 = 75 **(E)**

2. AREA, PERIMETER, & CIRCUMFERENCE

Memorize the basic area and circumference formulas found on the front of the test. You should not be spending time looking for these formulas while taking the test.

AREA OF A TRIANGLE ☺

The area of a triangle can be a source of some trouble.

$$A = \frac{1}{2}bh$$

The base, b, can be *any* side of the triangle, not just the lowest and, oftentimes, horizontal side. The height is defined as the *perpendicular distance* from the corner *opposite the base* to the *line containing the base*. The following method will help you find the height of a triangle relative to a given base:

1. **Identify the base.** Note that the base is a *line segment*.
2. **Identify the corner opposite this base.** This is the corner that is *not* an endpoint of the base's line segment.
3. **With your pencil starting on this corner, draw a perpendicular line to the line containing the base.** Sometimes, the height line will intersect the actual base, as in the first example below. Other times, you may have to extend the base's line segment, as shown in the second example below. Note that this does not change the length of the base, which is bound by the endpoints of the triangle.

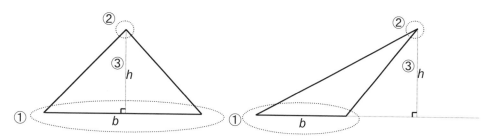

In the drawings below, sketch the height relative to the given base. Answers to all lesson and homework problems in this chapter start on page 514.

1.

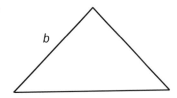

2.

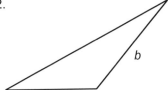

PERIMETER ☺

The *perimeter* of a shape is simply the sum of the measures of each side. The "perimeter" of a circle is called the *circumference*, which is the measure of the distance around a circle along its arc. Try the following problem:

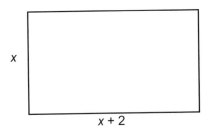

7. If the rectangle above has a perimeter of 20, what is the area of the rectangle?

(A) 16
(B) 24
(C) 36
(D) 40
(E) 49

SHADED REGION PROBLEMS

There are two ways to solve shaded region area problems:

1. **Divide** the shaded region into simpler shapes whose areas you can find, and add up these areas:

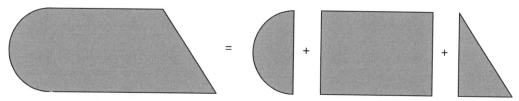

2. **Subtract** the areas of known shapes from the total area of the entire figure so that you're left with the shaded area.

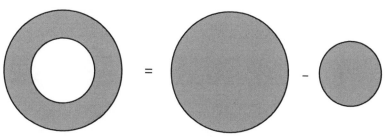

LESSON PROBLEMS

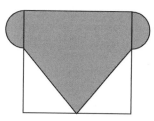

14. The figure above is made up of a square with side of length 8 and two semicircles with diameters of length 3. What is the area of the shaded region?

    (A) $24 + \frac{9}{4}\pi$

    (B) $24 + \frac{9}{2}\pi$

    (C) $44 + \frac{9}{4}\pi$

    (D) $44 + 9\pi$

    (E) $64 + 9\pi$

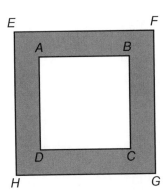

16. Square *ABCD* has side of length 8. The width of the border between squares *ABCD* and *EFGH* is 2. What is the area of the shaded region?

    (A) 36

    (B) 40

    (C) 48

    (D) 80

    (E) 100

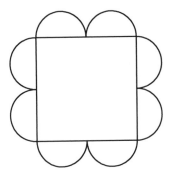

17. The eight equal semicircles above are placed so that they exactly cover the sides of the square. If the perimeter of the square is 32, what is the area of one of the semicircles?

    (A) 2π

    (B) 4π

    (C) 8π

    (D) 16π

    (E) 32π

㉚ REVOLUTION PROBLEMS

These problems have to do with a circle or wheel rolling along a straight line. When a circular wheel rolls *one* revolution without slipping, it will travel a distance equal to the *circumference* $(2\pi r)$ of the circle. This is a *known relationship* that you must memorize. You will use this known relationship as part of a proportion problem:

$$\frac{\text{revolutions}}{\text{distance (units)}} \rightarrow \frac{1}{2\pi r\ \text{(circumference)}} = \frac{\text{total revolutions}}{\text{total distance}}$$

Ⓔ🅧 A wheel with circumference of 10 inches rolls a distance of 40 inches with out slipping. How many revolutions did the wheel make?

$$\frac{\text{revolutions}}{\text{inches}} \frac{1}{10} = \frac{x}{40} \rightarrow x = \textbf{4 } \textit{revolutions}$$

18. A device measures distance by counting the revolutions of a wheel with a diameter of 6 inches. What is the distance, in feet, if the device measures 1000 revolutions?

    (A) 200π

    (B) 400π

    (C) 500π

    (D) 1000π

    (E) 6000π

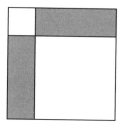

6. In the figure above, the large square is divided into two smaller squares and two rectangles (shaded). If the perimeters of the two smaller squares are 8 and 24, what is the sum of the perimeters of the two shaded rectangles?

    (A) 12

    (B) 16

    (C) 24

    (D) 32

    (E) 36

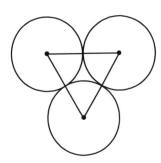

10. The equilateral triangle above is formed by connecting the centers of three tangent circles. If the perimeter of the triangle is 12, what is the sum of the circumferences of the three circles?

  (A) 4π

  (B) 8π

  (C) 12π

  (D) 18π

  (E) 24π

Note: the problem above uses the word "**tangent**," which means *touching at exactly one point.* Notice that each circle above touches each of the other circles at exactly one point. The circles are, thus, *tangent* to one another.

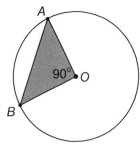

12. In the figure above, O is the center of the circle of diameter 12. What is the area of $\triangle AOB$?

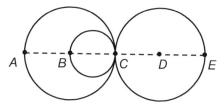

14. In the figure above, points A, B, C, D, and E are equally spaced on line segment AE. If the sum of the areas of the three circles is 18π, what is the radius of the smaller circle?

(A) 1

(B) $\sqrt{2}$

(C) 2

(D) $2\sqrt{2}$

(E) 3

15. The area of circle O is a square inches, and the circumference of circle O is b inches. If $a = b$, what is the radius of the circle?

(A) 1

(B) 2

(C) 3

(D) 4

(E) 5

16. Kevin had a bicycle with 30-inch diameter wheels. He decided to replace the front wheel with a 20-inch diameter wheel. If he traveled 300 feet on the modified bicycle, how many more full revolutions did the front wheel make than the back wheel?

    (A) 19
    (B) 20
    (C) 21
    (D) 22
    (E) 60

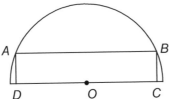

19. In the figure above, *ABCD* is a rectangle inscribed in the semicircle with center *O*. If *AD* = 5 and the semicircle has an area of 84.5π, what is the length of segment *AB*?

    (A) 12
    (B) 13
    (C) 24
    (D) 26
    (E) 28

3. TRIANGLES

In addition to finding the area of a triangle, as discussed in the previous section, there are a number of other topics related to triangles:

TYPES OF TRIANGLES ☺

Isosceles triangles have two equal sides (and two equal angles).

Equilateral triangles have three equal sides (and three equal angles, each measuring 60°).

RIGHT TRIANGLES ☺

PYTHAGOREAN THEOREM

Memorize the *Pythagorean Theorem*. Make sure the *c* side is the *hypotenuse*, which can be identified because it is the longest side, and it is opposite the right angle.

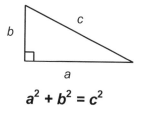

$$a^2 + b^2 = c^2$$

Look for right triangles.

SPECIAL RIGHT TRIANGLES

30-60-90 AND 45-45-90 TRIANGLES

Memorize the relationships for the two special right triangles, the *isosceles-right* (*45°-45°-90°*) and *30°-60°-90°* triangles. These formulas can be found on the front of the SAT, but memorizing them will save valuable time.

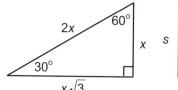

Many students run into difficulty when trying to solve these triangles algebraically. When you know the length of one side, the table below shows how to calculate the length of any other side. Note that the *30-60-90* triangle has a *hypotenuse*, a *short leg*, and a *long leg*, and the *45-45-90* triangle has a *hypotenuse* and two equal *legs*:

30-60-90		45-45-90	
short leg → hypotenuse	× 2	leg → hypotenuse	× $\sqrt{2}$
hypotenuse → short leg	÷ 2	hypotenuse → leg	÷ $\sqrt{2}$
short leg → long leg	× $\sqrt{3}$	leg → leg	× 1
long leg → short leg	÷ $\sqrt{3}$		
long leg ←→ hypotenuse: go through short leg.			

Look for 30-60-90 or 45-45-90 triangles. Remember that all isosceles-right triangles are 45-45-90 triangles. Also realize that you only need to know two of the three angles of the above triangles. For example, if you know that one of the angles of a *right* triangle is 30°, then it is a 30-60-90 triangle. **Never assume a triangle is a special right triangle; you must know the angle measures.**

3-4-5 AND 5-12-13 TRIANGLES

These right triangles with integer sides show up frequently. You can save time if you have them memorized. You might also see multiples of these sides, such as 6-8-10.

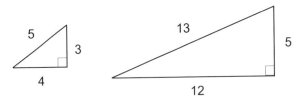

SIMILAR TRIANGLES ☺

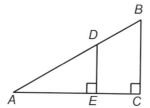

$\triangle ABC$ is similar to $\triangle ADE$

Similar triangles can be identified because they have equal angles. There are two relationships to remember:

1. **The ratio of any two sides of one triangle is equal to that of any two *related* sides of a similar triangle.** For example, in the triangle above:

$$\frac{AB}{AC} = \frac{AD}{AE}$$

1. $\dfrac{DE}{AE} =$

2. **The ratio of *equivalent* sides of similar triangles remains constant.**

$$\frac{AD}{AB} = \frac{AE}{AC} = \frac{DE}{BC} = k \text{ , where } k \text{ is some constant.}$$

> To identify similar triangle problems, look for triangles that have equal angles. Usually, on the SAT, triangles that *appear* similar are indeed similar, but if you can, try to identify angles.

ANGLE-SIDE RELATIONSHIPS

In any triangle, the largest angle is opposite the longest side; the smallest angle is opposite the shortest side; and so on. Similarly, if two angles are equal, then their opposite sides are equal.

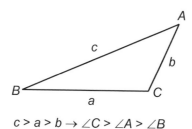

$c > a > b \rightarrow \angle C > \angle A > \angle B$

THIRD SIDE RULE

In any triangle, the sum of the two shortest sides must be greater than the longest side. If a, b, and c are the lengths of sides of a triangle and $a \leq b \leq c$, then:

FLASH
CARDS

$$a + b > c$$

To illustrate the point, imagine sticks of different lengths. In the first example below, where the sum of the two shortest sides is *larger* than the third side, a triangle can obviously be constructed. In the second example, where the sum of the two shortest sides is *smaller* than the third side, the triangle is incomplete. You may want to make a flash card to remember this rule.

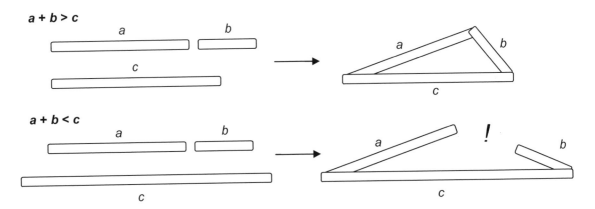

TRIANGLE PROBLEMS WITH NO TRIANGLES

Many geometry problems on the SAT are triangle problems even though there is no triangle given. Remember that drawing a triangle, usually a right triangle, can often help you solve a problem. Question 19 in the previous section is a good example of this. We will see many more of these types of problems.

LESSON PROBLEMS

In the following triangles, find the lengths of all sides. The answers can be expressed as "unsimplified" radicals or as decimals:

1.

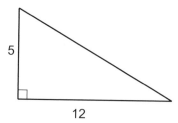

5.

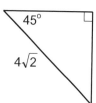

2.

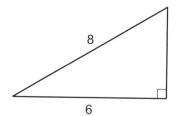

6.

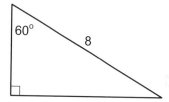

3.

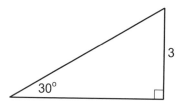

7.

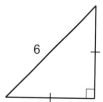

4.

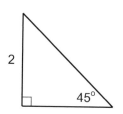

8.

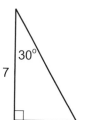

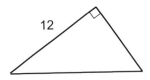

5. If the area of the triangle above is 54, what is the length of the hypotenuse?

   (A) 5
   (B) 13
   (C) 15
   (D) 18
   (E) 21

12. If the area of a square is 50, how long is the longest straight line that can be drawn between any two points of the square?

   (A) 5
   (B) $5\sqrt{2}$
   (C) 10
   (D) 25
   (E) $25\sqrt{2}$

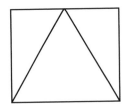

14. If an equilateral triangle with a perimeter of 6 is inscribed in a rectangle, as shown in the figure above, what is the area of the rectangle?

   (A) $\sqrt{3}$
   (B) 3
   (C) $2\sqrt{3}$
   (D) 4
   (E) $3\sqrt{3}$

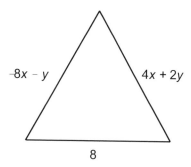

7. Given the equilateral triangle above, what is the value of x?

   (A) -2

   (B) -1

   (C) 0

   (D) 1

   (E) 2

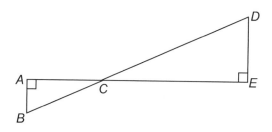

14. In the figure above, AB and DE are each perpendicular to AE. If $AB = 2$, $DE = 4$, and $CD = 10$, what is the length of AE?

   (A) $\sqrt{21}$

   (B) $2\sqrt{21}$

   (C) 5

   (D) $3\sqrt{21}$

   (E) 15

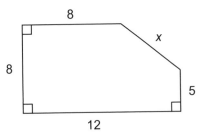

Note: Figure not drawn to scale.

15. What is the <u>perimeter</u> of the figure shown above?

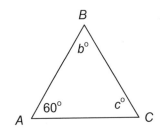

Note: Figure not drawn to scale.

15. In △ABC above, AB > AC. Which of the following must be true?

(A) BC > AB

(B) BC = AB

(C) b = c

(D) c = 70

(E) b < 60

16. A triangle has sides of length 4 and 5. If the third side is an integer, what is the shortest possible length for this side?

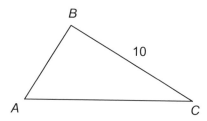

Note: Figure not drawn to scale.

19. In △ABC above, the measure of ∠A is 45° and the measure ∠C is 30°. What is the perimeter of the triangle?

(A) $5 + 5\sqrt{3}$

(B) $10 + 5\sqrt{2} + 5\sqrt{3}$

(C) $15 + 5\sqrt{5}$

(D) $10 + 10\sqrt{3}$

(E) $15 + 5\sqrt{2} + 5\sqrt{3}$

4. ANGLES

This section covers the many angle topics tested on the SAT. Answers are on page 518.

LINE

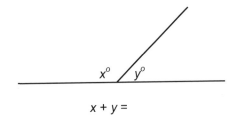

$$x + y =$$

TRIANGLE

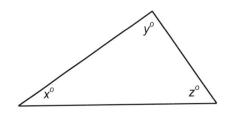

$$x + y + z =$$

CIRCLE

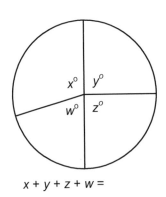

$$x + y + z + w =$$

RIGHT ANGLE

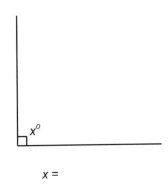

$$x =$$

VERTICAL ANGLES

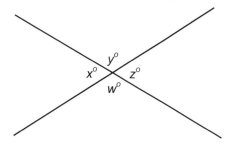

If x = 50°, then:

z =

y =

w =

PARALLEL LINES

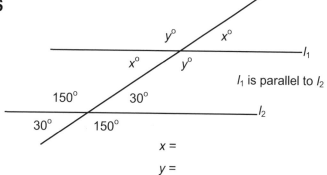

l_1 is parallel to l_2

x =

y =

LINE TANGENT TO A CIRCLE

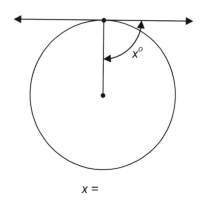

x =

SUM OF INTERIOR ANGLES

There is a simple method for finding the sum of the interior angles for any polygon of four or more sides:

1. Start at one corner of the polygon.
2. From this one corner, draw straight lines to all opposite corners.
3. Count the number of triangles and multiply by 180°.

QUADRILATERAL

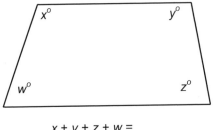

$$x + y + z + w =$$

OTHER POLYGONS

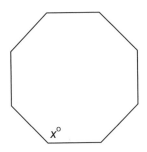

1. What is the sum of the interior angles of the polygon above?

2. If the above polygon is a *regular polygon* (all sides and angles are equal), what is the value of x?

LESSON PROBLEMS

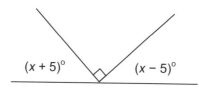

3. In the figure above, what is the value of *x*?

    (A) 0

    (B) 30

    (C) 45

    (D) 60

    (E) 90

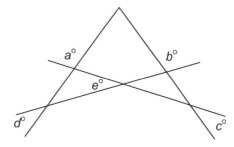

10. In the figure above, what is the value of *a* + *b* + *c* + *d* + 2*e*?

    (A) 90

    (B) 180

    (C) 360

    (D) 450

    (E) 540

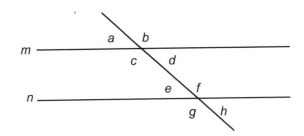

10. If lines *m* and *n* are parallel in the figure above, *a* + *g* must equal which of the following?

    (A) $a + d$

    (B) $3e$

    (C) $b + 2h - d$

    (D) $c + 2e - g$

    (E) $d + 2h + 60$

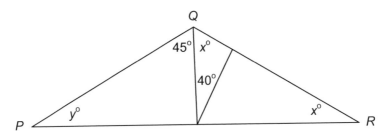

Note: Figure not drawn to scale.

16. In triangle *PQR* above, what is the value of *y* in terms of *x*?

    (A) x

    (B) $2x$

    (C) $85 - 2x$

    (D) $135 - 2x$

    (E) $180 - 2x$

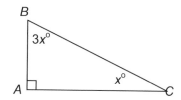

Note: Figure not drawn to scale.

4. In the right triangle above, what is the value of x?

(A) $22\frac{1}{2}$

(B) 30

(C) 45

(D) $67\frac{1}{2}$

(E) 90

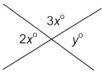

9. In the figure above, what is the value of y?

(A) 36

(B) 45

(C) 60

(D) 72

(E) 80

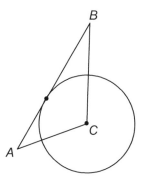

15. In the figure above, segment AB is tangent to circle C and has a length of 12. If circle C has a radius of 4, what is the area of $\triangle ABC$?

(A) 12

(B) 18

(C) 24

(D) 30

(E) 36

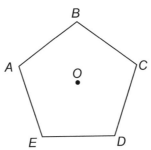

17. Pentagon *ABCDE* above has equal angles and equal sides. If *O* is the center of the pentagon, what is the degree measure of ∠*AOB* (not drawn)?

(A) $45°$

(B) $60°$

(C) $72°$

(D) $108°$

(E) $540°$

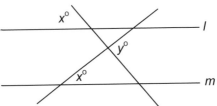

Note: Figure not drawn to scale.

18. In the figure above, lines *l* and *m* are parallel. What is *y* in terms of *x*?

(A) *x*

(B) $\frac{3}{4}x$

(C) $2x$

(D) $180 - x$

(E) $180 - 2x$

5. SECTORS OF CIRCLES

We have already discussed the area and circumference of a circle and how circumference relates to revolution problems. We have also looked at the sum of the degrees in a circle (360°). The last step for circles is to look at *sectors of circles*.

There are three measurements we can use to evaluate the size of a sector:

1. **Angle measure** – this is the measure of $\angle AOB$ in the figure below and is sometimes called the "measure of arc *AB*" or the "central angle" to arc *AB*

2. **Arc length** – this is the actual curved distance from point *A* to point *B* along the circle

3. **Area**

We can write each of these measurements as a *part over whole* ratio, where the *part* is relating to the sector of the circle and the *whole* is relating to the entire circle. The trick to sector problems is to realize that each of these ratios is equal:

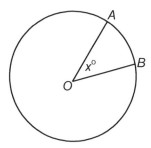

$$\frac{\text{part (sector)}}{\text{whole (circle)}} \rightarrow \frac{x}{360°} = \frac{\text{length of arc } AB}{\text{circumference of circle}} = \frac{\text{area of sector } AOB}{\text{area of circle}}$$

Look for circles with sectors, but don't confuse these problems with circle-graphs (pie-graphs), which also have sectors drawn.

The following method should be used for circle sector problems:

1. **Identify which *two* of the three measurements of the sector are mentioned in the problem.** Remember, the three measurements are *degrees*, *arc length*, and *area*. Usually, only *two* of them will be tested in a problem.

2. **Set up a proportion problem with the two appropriate ratios above, and solve for the missing information.** Keep in mind that if the radius (or diameter) of the circle is given, then you can calculate the circumference or area of the circle.

(EX) In the circle shown above (previous page), if the area of circle O is 240 in^2 and the area of sector AOB is 20 in^2, what is the value of x?

① *The two measurements are* degrees *and* area.

degrees   area

② $\dfrac{\overbrace{x}}{360} = \dfrac{\overbrace{20}}{240}$ → $x = \textbf{30}$

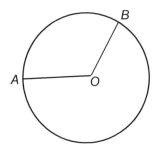

10. If the length of arc AB in the circle above with center O is 5 and angle AOB is 120°, what is the circumference of the circle?

   (A) 10
   (B) 15
   (C) 5π
   (D) 10π
   (E) 100

(HW)

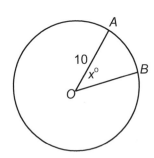

12. In circle O above, $x = 36$. What is the area of sector AOB?

   (A) 2π
   (B) 10
   (C) 20
   (D) 10π
   (E) 100π

6. COORDINATES

The coordinate plane consists of two perpendicular axes called the *x*-axis and the *y*-axis. The *x*-axis is horizontal and the *y*-axis is vertical.

The most common mistake on simple coordinate problems is to confuse the *x* and *y* coordinates of points. **Remember, the *x*-coordinate is always the *first* coordinate of a point, and the *y*-coordinate is always the *second* coordinate of a point.** Identify the coordinates of the following points:

1. *A* =
2. *B* =
3. *C* =
4. *D* =
5. *E* =

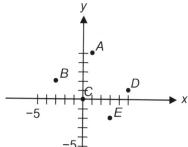

HORIZONTAL AND VERTICAL DISTANCES

The coordinate plane allows you to easily find horizontal and vertical distances between points, just by knowing the points' *x* and *y* coordinates.

1. **To find the *horizontal* distance between two points, find the *positive difference* between the points' *x*-coordinates.** In other words, *subtract* the x-coordinates and take the *absolute value* of the result.

2. **To find the *vertical* distance between two points, find the *positive difference* between the points' *y*-coordinates.** In other words, *subtract* the y-coordinates and take the *absolute value* of the result.

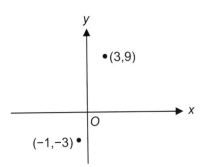

(EX) In the figure above, what is the <u>sum</u> of the horizontal and vertical distances between the two points?

(A) 4

(B) 10

(C) 12

(D) 16

(E) 20

horizontal: $\left|-1-3\right| = 4$

vertical: $\left|-3-9\right| = 12$

→ *4 + 12 = 16* **(D)**

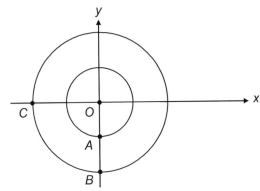

5. In the figure above, both circles are centered at point O and $OA = AB$. If the coordinates of A are $(0,-6)$, what are the coordinates of C?

(A) (−6,0)

(B) (−12,0)

(C) (0,−12)

(D) (0,−6)

(E) (0,12)

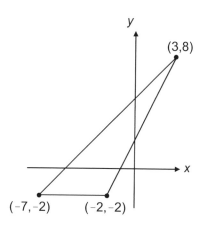

14. What is the area of the triangle in the figure above?

(A) 10

(B) 15

(C) 25

(D) 50

(E) 100

(40) DISTANCE FORMULA

There are few problems on the SAT that require you to find non-horizontal or non-vertical distances between two points; however, if you must find one of these "slanted" distances, you may use the *distance formula*:

The distance between two points with coordinates (x_1, y_1) and (x_2, y_2) is:

$$\boxed{\text{FLASH CARDS}} \quad d = \sqrt{(x_1 - x_2)^2 + (y_1 - y_2)^2}$$

7. LINES

(30) There are many different types of problems that deal specifically with lines. First, let's look at some general definitions.

LINE

A *line* is perfectly straight and extends infinitely in both directions. Line AB can be notated as $\overleftrightarrow{AB}$:

$$A \qquad\qquad B$$

LINE SEGMENT

A *line segment* is a section of a line, having two endpoints. Segment AB can be notated as $\overline{AB}$:

$$A \qquad\qquad B$$

RAY

A *ray* has one endpoint and extends infinitely in one direction. Ray AB can be notated as $\overrightarrow{AB}$:

$$A \qquad\qquad B$$

(30) LINE SEGMENTS

In *line segment* problems, if no distances are given, you can usually pick a number for the distance between two points on the line, allowing you to work with numbers rather than variables.

> Look for line segments with **no distances given**.

(EX) On line segment AB, If point C lies one third of the distance from A to B and point D is the midpoint of AC, what is $\dfrac{DB}{AB}$?

Pick # → 2   2   8

$$A \quad D \quad C \qquad\qquad B$$

$$\frac{DB}{AB} = \frac{10}{12} = \frac{5}{6}$$

5. If point *C* is the midpoint of segment *AB* and point *D* is the midpoint of segment *CB*, which of the following is NOT true?

    (A) $AC - CD = DB$

    (B) $CB < AD$

    (C) $AB - CD = AD$

    (D) $CB < AC$

    (E) $3DB = AD$

(30) NUMBER LINES

In *number line* problems, the lines may have tick marks that are *not* a distance of *1* apart, but the marks will be equally spaced. Number lines almost always increase to the right. To find the distance between two points, find the *positive difference* between them. In other words, *subtract* the endpoints and find the *absolute value* of the result.

Look for lines with numbers at points on the line. These lines may or may not have tick marks.

6. The marks on the number line are equally spaced. What is the distance between points *A* and *B*?

    (A) $\dfrac{1}{5}$

    (B) $\dfrac{4}{5}$

    (C) 1

    (D) $\dfrac{6}{5}$

    (E) 6

SLOPE OF A LINE

Memorize the formula for the slope of a line in a coordinate plane:

$$\boxed{\begin{array}{c} FLASH \\ CARDS \end{array}} \quad m = \frac{y_1 - y_2}{x_1 - x_2} \begin{array}{l} \leftarrow (rise) \\ \leftarrow (run) \end{array}$$

Make sure the difference of the y coordinates (the "rise") is in the *numerator* and the difference of the x coordinates (the "run") is in the *denominator*. The order of the points does not matter as long as the order in the numerator is the same as that in the denominator.

SOME IMPORTANT CHARACTERISTICS OF SLOPE

- Lines with a *positive* slope angle up to the right, and lines with a *negative* slope angle up to the left:

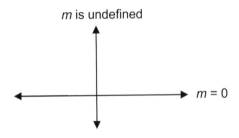

- Vertical lines have an *undefined* slope, and horizontal lines have a slope of *zero*:

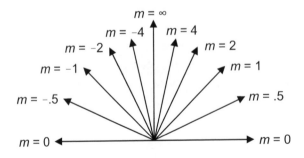

- The greater the absolute value of the slope, the steeper the line:

USING SLOPE TO FIND UNKNOWN COORDINATES

These problems will ask you to solve for an unknown *coordinate* of a point on a line. If there are two missing coordinates, you should pick a number for one of the coordinates, and then follow the method below.

Use the method below on the following lesson problem:

1. **Find the slope of the line.** Remember, if the line appears to go through the origin, then point (0,0) can be used as one of the points on the line.

2. **Use the equation for slope with one of the known points and the point with the missing coordinate.** Set the equation equal to the slope found in step 1.

3. **Use algebra to find the missing coordinate.**

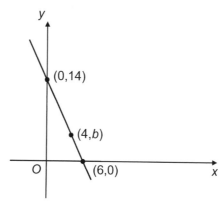

10. In the figure above, the three points lie on the same line. What is the value of *b*?

    (A) 3¾

    (B) 4

    (C) 4¼

    (D) 4⅓

    (E) 4⅔

(30) SLOPE OF PARALLEL AND PERPENDICULAR LINES

For the following examples, the slope of line *a* is m_a, and the slope of line *b* is m_b.

When two lines are parallel, their slopes are *equal*:

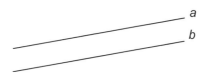

Line *a* is parallel to line *b*.

$$m_a = m_b$$

When two lines are perpendicular, use the following formula:

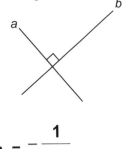

$$m_a = -\frac{1}{m_b}$$

EQUATION OF A LINE

THE SLOPE-INTERCEPT EQUATION

The most common equation of a line found on the SAT is called the *slope-intercept* equation. This equation is convenient because, at a glance, it gives you the *slope* of the line and the place where the line crosses the *y-axis* of the coordinate plane (called the *y-intercept*).

FLASH CARDS

$$y = mx + b$$

Slope-intercept equation of a line

In the equation above, *m* is the slope, *b* is the *y*-intercept, and *x* and *y* are the variables. The variables *x* and *y* are the coordinates of points on the line—for example, if you know an *x* coordinate of a point, you could use the equation to find the *y* coordinate.

CONVERTING OTHER LINE EQUATIONS INTO THE SLOPE-INTERCEPT FORM

If the equation for a line is not in the slope-intercept form, use basic number operations to rearrange the equation so that *y* is alone on the left side of the equal sign.

(EX) What is the *y*-intercept of the line defined by the equation $(y + 2) = 2(x - 1)$?

The line is not in slope-intercept form. Basic number operations allow you to remove the parentheses from the x side of the equation and isolate the y:

$y + 2 = 2x - 2$ → $y = 2x - 2 - 2$ → $y = 2x - 4$ → *y-intercept* = **−4**

FINDING THE SLOPE-INTERCEPT EQUATION

When you are given the *y*-intercept and the slope of a line, finding the slope-intercept equation is straightforward. Just plug values for *m* and *b* into the slope-intercept equation above.

You can also find the slope-intercept equation when you are given:

1. A point on the line and the slope of the line

OR

2. Two points on the line

Use the following method:

1. Identify or calculate the slope of the line (*m*).

2. Plug the *x* and *y* values of a given point and the slope (*m*) from step 1 into the slope-intercept equation.

3. Solve for *b*.

4. Rewrite the equation with *x* and *y* as variables: $y = mx + b$.

(EX) What is the slope-intercept equation of the line that goes through the point (2,0) and has a slope of 3?

① *The slope is given as 3. The slope-intercept equation is: $y = 3x + b$.*

② *Plug $x = 2$ and $y = 0$ into the equation: $y = 3x + b$ → $0 = 3 \cdot 2 + b$*

③ *$b = -6$*

④ *$y = 3x - 6$*

THE LINE $y = x$

This line shows up frequently. The slope of the line is 1 and the *y*-intercept is 0. The equation ($y = x$) makes clear that for each point on the line, the *x*-coordinate equals the *y*-coordinate (for example: (1,1), (−20,−20), etc.). Note that the line makes a 45° angle with the *x*-axis (assuming the *x* and *y* scales are the same, as they usually are).

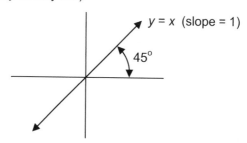

WHERE'S THE *x*? WHERE'S THE *y*?

Equations that involve only the *x* variable are vertical lines. Equations that involve only the *y* variable are horizontal lines. Write the equations for the following lines:

(EX) Line *A*: *x* = -6

1. Line *B*:
2. Line *C*:
3. Line *D*:
4. Line *E*:

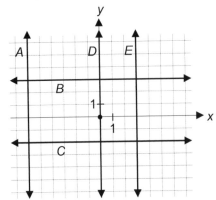

(40) MIDPOINT OF A LINE

You may have to find the *midpoint* of a line. The formula is straightforward. The *x* coordinate of the midpoint is the average of the *x* coordinates of the line's endpoints. Similarly, the *y* coordinate of the midpoint is the average of the *y* coordinates of the line's endpoints:

FLASH CARDS

$$M = (\frac{x_1 + x_2}{2}, \frac{y_1 + y_2}{2})$$

(30) GENERAL LINE PROBLEMS

In *general line problems*, draw your lines carefully and consider all possible scenarios; some may not be obvious. Watch out for traps on the higher-numbered problems.

14. Points *P*, *Q*, and *R* lie on a line *l*, and points *R*, *S*, and *T* lie on a different line *m* that is perpendicular to line *l*. How many lines can be drawn that contain exactly two of the five points?

(A) 1
(B) 2
(C) 3
(D) 4
(E) 5

THIRD SIDE RULE, REVISITED

Recall from the triangle section that in any triangle the sum of any two sides must be greater than the third side ($a + b > c$). This assumes that the desired shape is a triangle. When trying to find allowable distances between three points, a straight line is also acceptable, as shown in the drawing below. This changes the inequality to: $a + b \geq c$

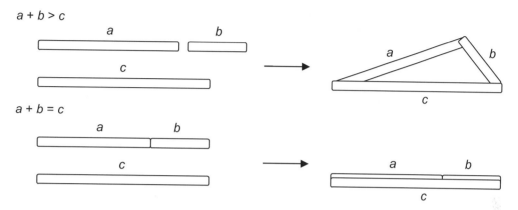

Look for problems asking you to find acceptable distances between **three points in a plane**.

Use the following method when you are trying to find acceptable distances between three points in a plane. You may choose to draw a triangle—don't worry about drawing the triangle to scale:

1. Identify the two shortest distances between the points.
2. Make sure the sum of these two distances is *greater than or equal to* the longest distance.

19. Points *A*, *B*, and *C* lie in a plane. If the distance between *A* and *B* is 4 and the distance between *B* and *C* is 2, which of the following could NOT be a distance between *A* and *C*?

    (A) 2
    (B) 4
    (C) 5
    (D) 6
    (E) 7

10. The point (2,*m*) lies on the line with equation $y - 3 = 2(x - 4)$. What is the value of *m*?

(30) 11. On a number line, if point *A* has coordinate −5 and point *B* has coordinate 3, what is the coordinate of the point that is 3/4 of the way from *A* to *B*?

   (A) −1

   (B) 0

   (C) 1

   (D) 3

   (E) 6

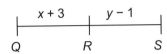

(30) 12. If *R* is the midpoint of segment *QS*, then *x* =

   (A) $y - 4$

   (B) $y - 3$

   (C) $y - 2$

   (D) $y - 1$

   (E) y

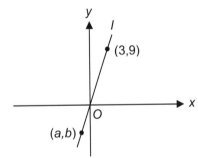

13. In the figure above, line *l* passes through the origin. What is the value of $\dfrac{b}{a}$?

   (A) −3

   (B) $-\frac{1}{3}$

   (C) $\frac{1}{3}$

   (D) $\frac{2}{3}$

   (E) 3

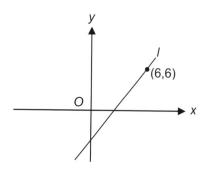

Note: Figure not drawn to scale.

18. In the figure above, if line *l* has a slope of $\frac{3}{2}$, what is the *y*-intercept of *l*?

(A) −1

(B) $-\frac{3}{2}$

(C) −2

(D) −3

(E) −6

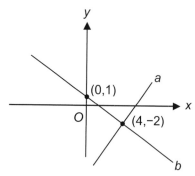

(30) 19. In the figure above, line *b* is perpendicular to line *a*. What is an equation of line *a*?

(A) $y = -\frac{3}{4}x + 1$

(B) $y = \frac{3}{4}x - \frac{10}{3}$

(C) $y = -\frac{3}{4}x - \frac{22}{3}$

(D) $y = \frac{4}{3}x - \frac{10}{3}$

(E) $y = \frac{4}{3}x - \frac{22}{3}$

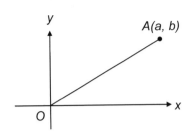

20. If *OA* has length 2*b*, what is the slope of the segment?

(A) $\frac{1}{2}$

(B) $\frac{\sqrt{3}}{3}$

(C) 1

(D) $\sqrt{3}$

(E) cannot be determined from the information given

�30 8. *SOLIDS*

Solids are shapes that occupy three dimensions, such as cubes, cylinders, or rectangular boxes. Most solids problems are *volume* problems that deal with rectangular solids or cubes. Though less common, some problems will require you to know the formula for the volume of a cylinder, which can be found on the front of the SAT.

Volume – the amount of space occupied by a solid or a substance

Surface area – the sum of the areas of all the faces of a solid

RECTANGULAR SOLIDS

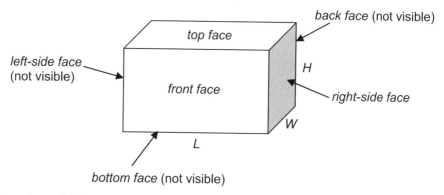

Use the *rectangular solid* above and answer the following questions in terms of *L*, *W*, and *H*. Answers are on page 522.

1. Volume =

2. Area of *front face* =

3. What face has the same area as the *front face*?

4. Area of *top face* =

5. What face has the same area as the *top face*?

6. Area of *right-side face* =

7. What face has the same area as the *right-side face*?

8. What is the *surface area* of the rectangular solid?

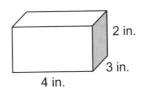

Use the rectangular solid above to answer the following questions:

1. What is the area of the front face?

2. What is the area of the top face?

3. What is the area of the right-side face?

4. What is the total surface area of the box?

5. What is the volume of the box?

CUBES

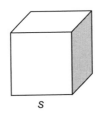

1. What is the area of *one face* of the cube with edge of length *s* above?

2. What is the surface area of the cube, in terms of *s*? (Hint: consider the number of faces.)

3. What is the volume of the cube, in terms of *s*?

SURFACE AREA → VOLUME

It is important to be able to find the *volume* of a cube when the *surface area* is given. Consider a

cube with a surface area of 600 in^2:

1. What is the area of one face?

2. What is the length of an edge?

3. What is the volume of the cube?

The above example illustrates the following method for finding the volume of a cube when the
surface area is given:

1. *Divide* the surface area by 6 to find the area of one face.

2. Take the *square root* of this area to find the length of a side.

3. *Cube* this length to find the volume of the cube.

VOLUME FITTING AND AREA FITTING PROBLEMS

Some volume problems will ask you to find the number of small solids (usually cubes) that can *fit* into a larger solid. These problems closely follow the method you would use for an *area fitting* problem.

Area fitting problems will ask how many shapes can fit into a larger shape. Volume fitting problems will ask how many solids can fit into a larger solid.

The method for area and volume fitting problems is straightforward:

1. For area fitting problems, find the *areas* of the large shape and the small shape. For volume fitting problems, find the *volumes* of the large solid and the small solid.

2. Divide the large area or volume by the small area or volume.

Number of *small areas* that will fit into the *larger area* = $\dfrac{\text{Large Area}}{\text{Small Area}}$

Number of *small volumes* that will fit into the *larger volume* = $\dfrac{\text{Large Volume}}{\text{Small Volume}}$

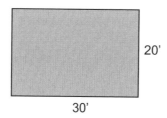

30'

20'

(EX) How many 2' by 2' square tiles are needed to cover the 20' by 30' floor shown above?

$$\frac{20 \cdot 30}{2 \cdot 2} = \textbf{\textit{150 tiles}}$$

16. A cylindrical cup has a radius of 2 inches and a height of 6 inches. A cylindrical water jug has a radius of 10 inches and a height of 12 inches. If the jug is full of water, how many cups of water can be filled before the jug is empty?

⓬ DIAGONALS OF RECTANGULAR SOLIDS

A *diagonal* is a segment that connects a pair of opposite vertices. The formula is below.

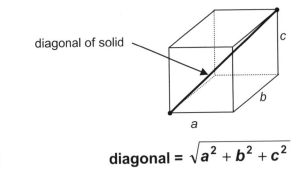

diagonal of solid

$$\text{diagonal} = \sqrt{a^2 + b^2 + c^2}$$

FLASH
CARDS

Note that a cube is just a rectangular solid where $a = b = c$. The formula is the same.

⓬ SOLIDS IN SOLIDS

These problems, where one solid is *inscribed* in another solid, are more common on the SAT Math Subject Test, but they may show up on the SAT Reasoning Test. When one solid is inscribed in another solid, the outer solid is as small as possible while completely containing the inner solid. **The trick is to determine which dimension is shared between the two shapes.** The following are some examples:

- **When a cube is inscribed in a sphere, the *diameter* of the sphere equals the length of a *diagonal* of the cube:**

- When a sphere is inscribed in a cube, the *diameter* of the sphere equals the *length of a side* of the cube:

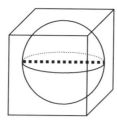

- When a sphere is inscribed in a cylinder, the *diameters* of the two solids equal:

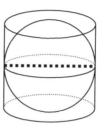

There are other possible solid-in-solid problems. Just remember to look for a dimension that is *shared* between the two shapes.

(EX) A cylinder with a radius of 2 and height of 3 is inscribed in a sphere. What is the diameter of the sphere?

(A) $\sqrt{13}$

(B) 4

(C) 5

(D) 6

(E) 7

The diameter of the sphere will equal the diagonal of the cylinder, which is the hypotenuse of a right triangle with legs of length 3 and 4. So the length of the diameter is 5. **(C)**

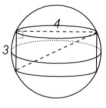

5. Elisa has two boxes, each with lengths 10 inches, widths 8 inches, and heights 6 inches. If she wants to ship these boxes in a third, larger box with length 20 inches, width 10 inches, and height 8 inches, how much additional space, in cubic inches, will be left in the larger box?

(A) 600

(B) 640

(C) 680

(D) 720

(E) 1120

7. A rectangular water tank 4 ft wide, 8 ft long, and 10 ft high is filled to 20% of capacity. How many additional cubic feet of water must be added to the tank so that it is 30% full?

  (A) 32
  (B) 64
  (C) 96
  (D) 160
  (E) 256

19. Soap cubes, each with a total surface area of 54 square centimeters, are stacked in a cube box. If the box has a volume of 729 cubic centimeters, what is the maximum number of soap cubes that can fit in the box?

  (A) 13
  (B) 27
  (C) 100
  (D) 192
  (E) 8304

(40) 20. A cube with side of length 2 inches is inscribed in a sphere. What is the length of the diameter, in inches, of the sphere?

  (A) $\sqrt{3}$ (approx. 0.33)
  (B) 2
  (C) $2\sqrt{3}$ (approx. 3.46)
  (D) 4
  (E) 6

9. TABLES AND GRAPHS

! Tables and graphs can have many different forms. **Always carefully study and understand the table or graph before trying to answer the question. Most mistakes on table and graph problems are a result of careless reading. Also, pay close attention to the problem numbers; watch out for traps on the high-numbered questions.**

NET INCOME FOR COMPANY X, 1995-2000

11. According to the graph above, Company X showed the greatest change in net income between which two consecutive years?

    (A) 1995 and 1996

    (B) 1996 and 1997

    (C) 1997 and 1998

    (D) 1998 and 1999

    (E) 1999 and 2000

STREET CLEANING IN CITY A	
Number of Streets	Cleaning Time per Street
7	20 minutes
8	40 minutes
10	80 minutes
15	100 minutes

18. How many <u>hours</u> will it take to clean all 40 streets in City A listed in the table above?

INCOME FOR STADIUM *A* IN 1999

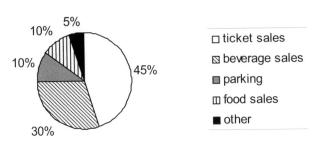

6. The circle graph above represents all income for a sports stadium in 1999. If the stadium made $15,000 in beverage sales, what was the total dollar income of the stadium in 1999?

    (A) 19,500

    (B) 45,000

    (C) 50,000

    (D) 55,000

    (E) 60,000

9. Chris lives 6 miles from school. On a particular day, he walked for 2 miles, stopped for 5 minutes to talk with some friends, and then ran the rest of the way to school. Which of the following graphs could correctly represent his journey to school on this day?

(A)

(B)
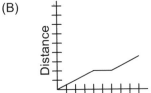

(C)
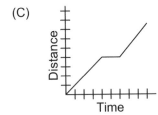

(D)
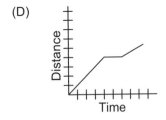

(E)
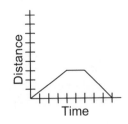

VOLTS ELECTRIC CAR COMPANY'S
SALES FOR 2011

	All-electric	Hybrid	Total
Compact	a	b	
Family		c	
Total			d

15. Volts Electric Car Company manufactures only compact and family cars, both of which are available as either all-electric or hybrid. On the basis of the information in the table above, how many family, all-electric cars will the company produce in 2011?

(A) $a + b - c$

(B) $d - (a + b)$

(C) $d - (a - b - c)$

(D) $d + (a - b - c)$

(E) $d - a - b - c$

10. GEOMETRY PROBLEMS

PRACTICE PROBLEMS

The following assignments are from *The Official SAT Study Guide** by the College Board (2nd Edition). It is very important to look back to the KlassTutoring tutorial and review the techniques while completing these problems. Try to determine which technique applies to each problem and apply the methods taught in the tutorial. Do not time yourself on these problems. These problems are provided to give you an opportunity to practice, and hopefully master, the techniques in this tutorial before you must apply them on real SATs in a timed setting.

In the assignments below, "30" problems are part of the 30-hour program, "40" problems are part of the 40-hour program, **bold** problems may be difficult, and *italicized* problems may be only partially covered by techniques in the KlassTutoring tutorial.

- [ ] Test 1: Sect. 3 (4,6,8,9^{30},10,12,15^{40},17,**19**), Sect. 7 (1,2,5,6^{30},7,12^{30},17), Sect. 8 (1,2,4,6,11^{30},12^{30},15^{30})
- [ ] Test 2: Sect. 2 (3,4,8,10,11,18^{40},20^{30}), Sect. 5 (6,10,11^{30},13,18), Sect. 8 (2,5,7,12,14,15)
- [ ] Test 3: Sect. 2 (4,5,8^{30},**17**,18^{30},20), Sect. 5 (2,5,7,10,12,13,**15**), Sect. 8 (3,6,8,10^{30},16^{40})
- [ ] Test 4: Sect. 3 (11,12,14,16^{40},19), Sect. 6 (2,3,8,10^{30},11,13,15, 17), Sect. 9 (2,4,6,8,**15**^{30})

TEST CORRECTIONS

After each practice test is graded and as you complete the chapters in this tutorial, you should correct problems that you skipped or left blank. (The practice tests are found in *The Official SAT Study Guide**.) Go back to the tutorial and review the techniques as you correct the problems. The idea is to: (1) identify techniques that have given you trouble, (2) go back to the tutorial so you can review and strengthen these techniques, and (3) apply these techniques to the specific problems on which you struggled.

- [ ] Test 5: Sect. 2 (6^{30},9,11^{30},15,19), Sect. 4 (2,3,5,7,11,14,17^{30},18^{40}), Sect. 8 (4,5,8,10^{30},16^{30})
- [ ] Test 6: Sect. 2 (2^{30},4,5,6^{30},8,12^{30},14,16,18), Sect. 4 (5,7,12,15,16), Sect. 8 (6,7,12,15)
- [ ] Test 7: Sect. 3 (4,6^{40},11,14,16), Sect. 7 (5,7,12,16,17), Sect. 9 (2,13,**15**)
- [ ] Test 8: Sect. 3 (2,3,6,7,11^{30},14,16), Sect. 7 (4,5,6,12,14,15^{30},**20**), Sect. 9 (3,7,8^{30},9,12,**16**)
- [ ] Test 9: Sect. 2 (4,5,8^{30},14^{30}), Sect. 5 (3^{30},5^{30},8,11,16,18,20), Sect. 8 (3,5,7,10,13)
- [ ] Test 10: Sect. 2 (3,4,5,10,12,15,17), Sect. 5 (2,3,5,11,13,15,18), Sect. 8 (5,6^{30},8,10^{30},14)

^{30} Covered by 30-hour program, ^{40} Covered by 40-hour program

*SAT is a registered trademark of the College Board, which was not involved in the production of and does not endorse this book.

V
FUNCTIONS

This chapter will cover all relevant topics related to functions. On the SAT, function problems tend to be high-numbered (potentially difficult) questions.

1. SYMBOL PROBLEMS

Symbol problems use unfamiliar symbols to represent some mathematical operation or expression. These problems are usually not as difficult as they look—they tend to be easier than the problem number indicates, so be confident and aggressive.

EXPRESSION SYMBOL PROBLEMS

Recall the terminology from the *factoring* section in chapter III: A *term* is a product of numbers and/or variables, such as $4x$ or $\frac{1}{2}x^2$. An *expression* is one or more terms added or subtracted together, such as $4x + \frac{1}{2}x^2$.

Expression symbol problems use a symbol to represent a mathematical *expression*.

> Look for problems with unfamiliar symbols that are defined as a mathematical **expression**.

Use the following method:

1. **The first step is to make sure you completely understand the symbol's definition.** The symbol will always be *clearly defined* somewhere in the question. The definition will tell you what to do with one or more variables.

2. **Rewrite the problem *without* the symbol by following the rules of the symbol's definition.** The definition tells you where to put the question's numbers or variables in a mathematical expression.

3. Use basic math to answer the question.

For all numbers p and q, where $p \neq q$, $p \diamondsuit q = \dfrac{p \times q}{p - q}$.

(EX) $3 \diamondsuit 2 =$ $\rightarrow \dfrac{3 \cdot 2}{3 - 2} = 6$

(EX) $2 \diamondsuit 3 =$ $\rightarrow \dfrac{2 \cdot 3}{2 - 3} = -6$

(EX) $q \diamondsuit p =$ $\rightarrow \dfrac{q \times p}{q - p}$

(EX) $(x - y) \diamondsuit (x + y) =$ $\rightarrow \dfrac{(x - y) \cdot (x + y)}{(x - y) - (x + y)}$

(EX) $\bigcirc \diamondsuit \square =$ $\rightarrow \dfrac{\bigcirc \cdot \square}{\bigcirc - \square}$

(EX) If $2 \diamondsuit b = -4$, what is the value of b?

$\dfrac{2b}{2 - b} = -4$

$\rightarrow 2b = -8 + 4b$

$\rightarrow -2b = -8$

$\rightarrow b = 4$

MULTI-QUESTION PROBLEMS

The following problem is an example of a *multi-question* problem because there are two or more questions relating to the same definition. On these types of problems, **regardless of the number, the first one will be easy, but the last one will be hard**. Watch out for these problems on the SAT.

Questions 13-14 refer to the following definition. Answers to all lesson and homework problems in this chapter start on page 523.

For all numbers a and b, where $p \neq q$, $p \diamondsuit q = \dfrac{p \times q}{p - q}$.

13. $(6 \diamondsuit 4) - (8 \diamondsuit 6) =$

    (A) -24

    (B) -12

    (C) -4

    (D) 12

    (E) 24

TRUE-FALSE PROBLEMS

The next question is an example of a *true-false* problem. Always work on one *Roman numeral* (I, II, or III) at a time. As soon as you are able to eliminate a Roman numeral or determine that it is definitely true, eliminate answer choices accordingly. **Sometimes, you will be able to eliminate enough answer choices to avoid checking all of the Roman numerals.**

Remember that the following question relates to the symbol defined above:

14. If $p \neq 0$ and $q \neq 0$, which of the following is (are) necessarily true?

    I. $p \diamondsuit q = q \diamondsuit p$

    II. $\left(\dfrac{1}{p} \diamondsuit \dfrac{1}{q}\right)^{-1} = q - p$

    III. $(-p) \diamondsuit (-q) = -(p \diamondsuit q)$

    (A) I only

    (B) II only

    (C) I and II only

    (D) II and III only

    (E) I, II, and III

NON-EXPRESSION SYMBOL PROBLEMS

These problems can generally *not* be solved using a simple mathematical expression. Non-expression problems usually ask you to perform some mathematical operation on a number.

Look for problems with unfamiliar symbols that are *not* defined as a mathematical expression.

The method is similar to that of expression symbol problems:

1. **The first step is to make sure you completely understand the symbol's definition.** The symbol will always be *clearly defined* somewhere in the question. The definition will tell you what to do with usually *one* variable.

2. **Replace the variable in the symbol's definition with the number or variable in the question.**

3. The definition tells you what to do with the number or variable in question. Use your math skills to answer the question.

(EX) Let $\underline{x}$ be defined as the largest prime number that is a factor of *x*. What is the value of $\underline{10} \times \underline{16}$?

② *"Let $\underline{10}$ be defined as the largest prime number that is a factor of 10".*

③ *The prime factors of 10 are 5 and 2 (review finding prime factors in Basic Math Concepts if necessary).* → $\underline{10} = 5$

Repeat the above process for 16:

② *"Let $\underline{16}$ be defined as the largest prime number that is a factor of 16".*

③ *The prime factors of 16 are 2, 2, 2, and 2.* → $\underline{16} = 2$

$\underline{10} \times \underline{16} = 5 \times 2 = \textbf{10}$

SYMBOLS IN THE ANSWER CHOICES

Some symbol problems are made more difficult by including the symbol in the answer choices. In these problems, make sure you apply the symbol to the numbers in the answer choices.

12. Let ♦n be defined for any positive integer n as the number obtained by adding the digits of n. For example, ♦5 = 5, ♦25 = 7, and ♦550 = 10. What is the value of ♦25 + ♦50?

(A) ♦5

(B) ♦7

(C) ♦12

(D) ♦66

(E) 75

WORD SYMBOL PROBLEMS

These problems use a *word* as a symbol. The word will be clearly defined somewhere in the problem. As with other symbol problems, the problem may appear more difficult at first than it actually is.

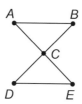

14. Segments AB, AE, BD, and DE intersect at the labeled points as shown in the figure above. Two points are defined as "independent" if they do not lie on the same segment in the figure. Of the labeled points in the figure, how many pairs of independent points are there?

(A) None

(B) One

(C) Two

(D) Three

(E) Four

———

6. For all integers n, where $n \neq -1$, let $n\heartsuit = \dfrac{n-1}{n+1}$. What is the value of $(-3)\heartsuit$?

    (A) -2

    (B) -1

    (C) 0

    (D) 1

    (E) 2

16. For all numbers where $a \neq -1$, let $a\uparrow = \dfrac{a}{a+1}$. If $a \neq 1$ and $a \neq 2$, then $(a-2)\uparrow \times (1-a)\uparrow =$

    (A) 1

    (B) $\dfrac{1}{a+1}$

    (C) $\dfrac{a+1}{a-2}$

    (D) $\dfrac{a-1}{2}$

    (E) $-a^2 + 3a - 2$

17. Let $\Uparrow$ be defined by $a\Uparrow b = a^b$. If $x = 2\Uparrow p$, $y = 2\Uparrow q$, and $p + q = 5$, what is the value of xy?

    (A) 7

    (B) 10

    (C) 25

    (D) 32

    (E) 128

19. For all positive integers x and y, let $x \, \Re \, y$ be defined as the whole number remainder when x is divided by y. If $15 \, \Re \, y = 5$, what is the value of y?

2. FUNCTION BASICS

In standard math, instead of using strange looking symbols to describe mathematical operations, as in the previous section, a standard *function notation* is used. This notation is comprised of a letter (often *f*) and parentheses containing a variable, number, or expression. The letter is the "name" of the function. Whatever is inside the parentheses is the *input* of the function. It may be helpful to think of a function as a *rule* that tells you how to find an *output* for any given input. For example:

$$f(x) = 2x + 3$$

The function above is called "the function *f*." The variable inside the parentheses, *x*, represents the input. The rule for this function is: "multiply the input by 2 and then add 3." Several examples are below.

Look for the function notation, such as $f(x)$, $g(a)$, $P(2)$, etc. When functions are represented graphically, they may only contain the letter of the function without the parentheses (*f, g, P,* etc). Not surprisingly, the word "function" will also help you identify these problems.

Use $f(x) = 2x + 3$ for the following examples:

EX $f(2) = 2 \cdot 2 + 3 = \mathbf{7}$

EX $f(\frac{a-3}{2}) = 2(\frac{a-3}{2}) + 3 = a - 3 + 3 = \mathbf{a}$

EX $f(2 + 3) = f(5) = \mathbf{13}$

EX $f(g(x)) = \mathbf{2[g(x)] + 3}$

EX $f(a) = \mathbf{2a + 3}$

EX If $f(x) = -1$, what is the value of *x*?
$2x + 3 = -1 \ \rightarrow \ \mathbf{x = -2}$

Use the following general method for function problems:

1. **Identify the function rule.** It will usually be represented as an equation (as above), but functions can also be represented by graphs or tables. In all cases, the function will give you a rule that will allow you to find outputs for given inputs.
2. **Find a new expression or equation that contains the function found in step 1.**
3. **Write the problem without the function notation by following the rule of the function.** This is similar to the method for symbol problems—the trick is to get rid of the symbol (or function).
4. Use basic math or algebra to answer the question.

(EX) Let the function g be defined by $g(x) = x + 3$. If $g(m) = 2m$, what is the value of m?

① The function rule is $g(x) = x + 3$

② The "new" equation is $g(m) = 2m$. Notice that this equation contains the function, g.

③ Using the function rule, $g(m) = m + 3$. We now have: $m + 3 = 2m$.

④ Use algebra to solve for m: $3 = 2m - m$ → $m = \mathbf{3}$

Questions 16-17 refer to the following functions f and g.

$f(n) = n^2$

$g(n) = n^2 - n$

16. $f(6) - f(-6) =$

(A) −6

(B) 0

(C) 6

(D) 36

(E) 46

17. Which of the following is equivalent to $g(m + 1)$?

(A) $f(m) + 1$

(B) $f(m) + 3$

(C) $f(m) + m$

(D) $g(m) + 1$

(E) $g(m) + m$

14. Let the function f be defined by $f(x) = \left| x^2 - 6 \right|$. When $f(x) = 5$, what is one possible value of $x - 6$?

    (A) −25

    (B) −7

    (C) −6

    (D) 0

    (E) 6

19. Let the function g be defined by $g(x) = x + 4$. If $\frac{1}{2}g(\sqrt{a}) = 4$, what is the value of a?

    (A) 4

    (B) 6

    (C) 16

    (D) 36

    (E) 64

x	$g(x)$	$h(x)$
0	3	4
1	1	3
2	2	2
3	0	1

20. According to the table above, if $a = g(3)$, what is the value of $h(a)$?

    (A) 0

    (B) 1

    (C) 2

    (D) 3

    (E) 4

3. GRAPHS OF FUNCTIONS

The function $f(x)$ can be represented graphically on a coordinate plane. When graphing a function, the x-axis represents the values of x (the inputs of the function) and the y-axis represents the values of $f(x)$ (the outputs of the function). There are several characteristics of these graphs that you should be comfortable with, and they will be taught using the following graph of $f(x)$:

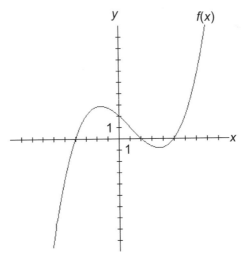

The following examples are based on the graph of $f(x)$ above:

(EX) $f(-2) \approx$ **3**

(EX) $f(1) \approx$ **1**

(EX) If $x < 0$ and $f(x) = 2$, then $x \approx$ **-3**

(EX) For what values of x is $f(x) = 0$? **$x = -4, 2, 5$**

(EX) If $x = 0$, then $f(x) =$ **2**

(EX) What are the values of x for which $f(x)$ is positive? **$-4 < x < 2$ and $x > 5$**

(EX) What are the values of x for which $f(x)$ is negative? **$x < -4$ and $2 < x < 5$**

(EX) What are the approximate values of x for which $f(x)$ is increasing? **$x < -2$ and $x > 3.5$**

(EX) What are the approximate values of x for which $f(x)$ is decreasing? **$-2 < x < 3.5$**

GRAPHING CALCULATOR

If you have a graphing calculator, make sure you are comfortable using its graphing features. If you don't have a graphing calculator, don't worry—no problems on the SAT *require* you to graph functions. When the specific function is not given, as in the example graph above, your calculator's graphing features will generally *not* help you.

AXIS INTERCEPTS

You can find the x and y intercepts of a function using algebra.

1. To find the *y*-intercept, let *x* = 0. Solve for *y*.
2. To find the *x*-intercept, let *y* = 0. Solve for *x*.

16. What is the *y*-intercept of the quadratic function *f* given by $f(x) = ax^2 + bx + c$ where *a*, *b*, and *c* are different positive integers?

   (A) *a*

   (B) a/c

   (C) *b*

   (D) b/c

   (E) *c*

(40) SYMMETRY

When a function is symmetrical across an axis or a line, it appears to have a mirror image reflected across that axis or line. The quadratic function is a common function that is symmetrical across some vertical line. In the figure below, the line of symmetry is *x* = 2.

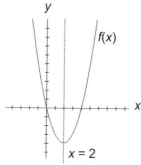

(EX) The figure above shows a quadratic function *f*. The vertex of *f* is (2,–4). If two points (not shown) on *f* are (–2,12) and (*a*,12) and *a* > 0, what is the value for *a*?

> The function f is symmetrical across the line x = 2. Since the y-coordinates of the two points are the same, the two points will have the same horizontal distance from the line of symmetry. The first point is 4 horizontal units from the line, so a must be 2 + 4 = **6**.

㊵ ADVANCED TECHNIQUES FOR GRAPHS OF FUNCTIONS

The following examples illustrate some advanced techniques for using graphs to find missing information.

> To identify these advanced problems, look for graphs and points on graphs where the problem is asking you to solve for an **unknown variable**. The variable may be a **constant in the equation of the graph** or an **unknown coordinate of a point on the graph**.

FUNCTION KNOWN, POINT UNKNOWN

If the equation of a function is known, it can be used to find an unknown coordinate of a point on the graph of that function:

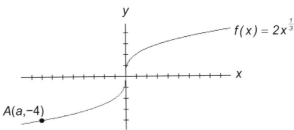

㊊ If point A lies on the graph of $f(x)$ above, what is the value of a?

Plug point A into the function equation and solve for a:

$$-4 = 2a^{\frac{1}{3}} \;\rightarrow\; -2 = a^{\frac{1}{3}} \;\rightarrow\; (-2)^3 = (a^{\frac{1}{3}})^3 \;\rightarrow\; \boldsymbol{a = -8}$$

POINT KNOWN, FUNCTION UNKNOWN

If the equation of a function contains an unknown value, it can be found by using a known point on the graph of the function:

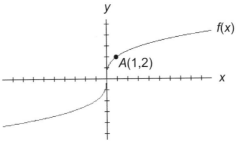

㊊ If $f(x) = ax^{\frac{1}{3}}$ and point A lies on the graph of $f(x)$ above, what is the value of a?

Plug point A into the function equation and solve for a:

$$2 = a \cdot 1^{\frac{1}{3}} \;\rightarrow\; \boldsymbol{a = 2}$$

INTERSECTING GRAPHS

Harder problems may have two graphs that intersect:

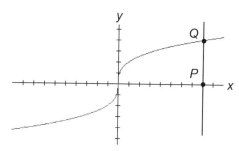

(EX) The figure above shows the graph of $y = ax^{\frac{1}{3}}$ and the line $x = 8$. If $\overline{PQ} = 4$, what is the value of a?

First, find a point on the graph:

$Q = (8, 4)$

Now plug point Q into the function equation and solve for a:

$4 = a \cdot 8^{\frac{1}{3}}$ → $4 = a \cdot 2$ → $\boldsymbol{a = 2}$

_____

(HW)

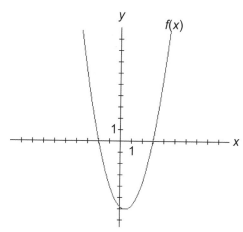

15. Based on the graph of the function f above, what are the values of x for which $f(x)$ is negative?

(A) $-6 < x < 0$

(B) $-\frac{7}{2} \le x < -2$

(C) $-\frac{7}{2} \le x < -2$ or $3 < x \le \frac{9}{2}$

(D) $-2 < x < 3$

(E) $-2 < x < 0$

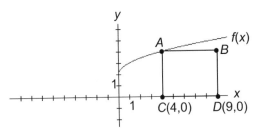

(40) 16. In the figure above, ABCD is a rectangle, and point A lies on the graph of f(x). If $f(x) = \sqrt{x} + 2$, what is the area of ABCD?

    (A) 10

    (B) 18

    (C) $6\sqrt{10}$

    (D) 20

    (E) $10\sqrt{6}$

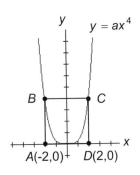

(40) 18. In the figure above, ABCD is a square centered on the y-axis. If points B and C lie on the graph $y = ax^4$ where a is a constant, what is the value of a?

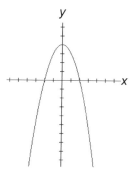

19. The graph of $f(x)$ is shown above. Which of the following is the graph of $|f(x)|$?

(A)

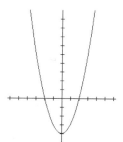

(B)

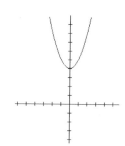

(C)

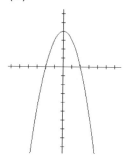

(D)

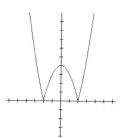

(E)

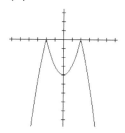

DOMAIN

The *domain* of a function $f(x)$ is the set of *inputs* that may be put into a function without violating any laws of math. In other words, the domain is all allowable values of x.

> These function problems will mention the word *domain* in the question, or they will ask for the values of x for which $f(x)$ is a real number.

There are two rules used for finding the domain of a function:

1. **The denominator of a fraction can not equal zero.**

2. **It is impossible to take the square root (or any *even* root) of a negative number.**

The following rules are used to find the domain of a function:

1. **If there is a variable in the denominator of a fraction, set the entire denominator *not-equal* ($\neq$) to zero.** Solve for the variable. Any values of the variable that make the denominator zero are *not* part of the function's domain.

   (EX) What is the domain of $f(x) = \dfrac{25}{x-25}$? $\quad x - 25 \neq 0 \;\rightarrow\; \boldsymbol{x \neq 25}$

2. **If there is a variable under an even root ($\sqrt{}, \sqrt[4]{}, \sqrt[6]{}$, etc.), set the entire expression under the root *greater than or equal* ($\geq$) to zero.** Solve for the variable. These values are the domain of the function.

   (EX) What is the domain of $f(x) = \sqrt{x-25}$? $\quad x - 25 \geq 0 \;\rightarrow\; \boldsymbol{x \geq 25}$

3. **If there is a variable under an even root that is in the denominator of a fraction, set the entire expression under the root *greater than* (>) zero.** Solve for the variable. These values are the domain of the function.

   (EX) What is the domain of $f(x) = \dfrac{25}{\sqrt{x-25}}$? $\quad x - 25 > 0 \;\rightarrow\; \boldsymbol{x > 25}$

$$f(x) = \dfrac{5}{\sqrt{x+4}}$$

20. For the function f, defined above, what are the values of x for which $f(x)$ is a real number?

   (A) $x = -4$

   (B) $x = 0$

   (C) $x \geq -4$

   (D) $x \geq 0$

   (E) $x > -4$

RANGE

The *range* of a function $f(x)$ is the set of values that can be *produced* by the function. In other words, the range is all possible values of $f(x)$, the *outputs* of the function. These outputs are the y values on the xy-coordinate plane. Range questions are not very common on the SAT, and the method for finding range is not as straight forward as that of domain. You should, however, be able to recognize the range of a function by looking at the function's graph. Don't forget, you may use your graphing calculator if the function is given.

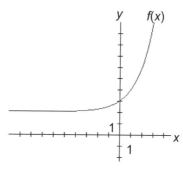

(EX) What is the range of the function f shown above?

   (A) All real numbers   *The graph clearly appears greater than $y = 2$:*

   (B) $f(x) \geq 0$ $f(x) > 2$ *(C)*

   (C) $f(x) > 2$

   (D) $f(x) \geq 3$

   (E) $f(x) < 3$

$$f(x) = (x+2)^{\frac{1}{4}}$$

20. What is the domain of the function f, defined above?

   (A) All real numbers

   (B) $x \geq -2$

   (C) $x \geq 0$

   (D) $x \geq \frac{1}{4}$

   (E) $x \geq 2$

5. TRANSFORMATIONS

Some questions may ask you to identify the effects of a *transformation* on the graph of a function. Transformations either *move* or *reflect* the graph of a function. A function can be *moved* up, down, to the right, or to the left. As mentioned in a previous section, *reflecting* a function creates a mirror image of the function across a line (called the *line of reflection*). For example, triangle *ABC* is reflected across line *l* below:

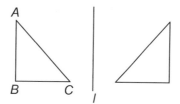

TRANSFORMATION RULES

- **$f(x) + a$ → moves graph UP *a* units**
- **$f(x) - a$ → moves graph DOWN *a* units**
- **$f(x + a)$ → moves graph to the LEFT *a* units**
- **$f(x - a)$ → moves graph to the RIGHT *a* units**
- **$-f(x)$ → reflects graph across *x*-axis**
- **$f(-x)$ → reflects graph across *y*-axis**
- **$af(x)$, where $a > 1$ → STRETCHES the graph vertically**
- **$af(x)$, where $0 < a < 1$ → CONTRACTS the graph vertically**
- **$f(ax)$, where $a > 1$ → CONTRACTS the graph horizontally**
- **$f(ax)$, where $0 < a < 1$ → STRETCHES the graph horizontally**

Instead of memorizing the rules above, you may choose to test the rules during the test using a standard function (such as $f(x) = \sqrt{x}$) and your graphing calculator. First, you must be familiar with the graph of $f(x) = \sqrt{x}$:

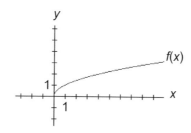

Use your calculator to check any of the rules above. Pick a small number for *a* if one is not given. For example, to check the transformation g(x + 3) for some function g, check the graph

$f(x+3) = \sqrt{x+3}$ on your calculator:

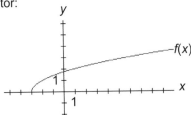

Since f(x) moved to the left 3 spaces, the graph of function g will also move to the left 3 spaces. Note: *Horizontal* stretches and contractions are easier to see if you use a function such as $f(x) = x^2$.

These questions involve the *movement* or *reflection* of a graph of a function.

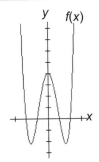

17. The graph of f(x) is shown above. Which of the following could be the graph of −f(x−1)?

(A)

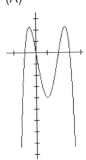

(B)

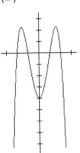

(C)

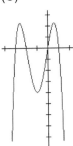

(D)

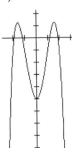

(E)

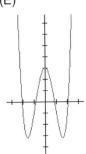

14. In the *xy*-plane, the equation of line *l* is $y = -3x - 4$. If line *m* is the reflection of line *l* in the *y*-axis, what is the equation of line *m*?

    (A) $y = -3x + 4$

    (B) $y = 3x + 4$

    (C) $y = 3x - 4$

    (D) $y = \frac{3}{4}x - 4$

    (E) $y = \frac{3}{4}x + 4$

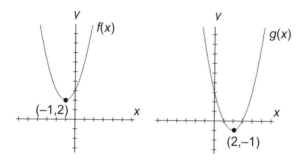

20. The figures above show the graphs of *f* and *g*. The function *f* is defined by $f(x) = x^2 + 2x + 3$. The function *g* is defined by $g(x) = f(x + h) + k$, where *h* and *k* are constants. What is the value of $h - k$?

    (A) −6

    (B) −3

    (C) 0

    (D) 3

    (E) 6

³⁰ 6. *FUNCTIONS AS MODELS*

Functions are often used to *model* real life situations. **These problems may look difficult, but they can be solved using the techniques from the previous pages.**

$$p(t) = vt$$

(EX) The position of a rolling bowling ball on a bowling alley is given by the function p, above, where v is the initial velocity of the ball, in feet per second, t is time, in seconds, and p is the distance, in feet, from the start of the alley where the ball is thrown. If a bowling alley is 63 feet long and a bowling ball is rolled at an initial velocity of 10½ feet per second, how long, in seconds, will it take for the bowling ball to reach the pins?

(A) 5

(B) 6

(C) 7

(D) 8

(E) 9

$v = 10.5$ → $p(t) = 10.5 \cdot t$

Let T be the time it takes the bowling ball to travel 63 feet.

$p(T) = 10.5 \cdot T = 63$ → $T = 6$ seconds **(B)**

16. Dennis deposited $1000 into a savings account that paid 2% interest per year. The amount of money in the account n years from the original deposit is given by the function M, where

$$M(n) = 1000\left(\tfrac{51}{50}\right)^n.$$

Approximately how much money will be in the account, in dollars, after 10 years?

(A) 1002

(B) 1200

(C) 1219

(D) 1220

(E) 10,200

17. If the profit, in dollars, of a small company is given by the function P, where $P(x) = 100\sqrt{x}$, and x is the number of products sold, how many products must the company sell to make a profit of $10,000?

(A) 100

(B) 1000

(C) 1×10^4

(D) 1×10^6

(E) 1×10^8

7. FUNCTION PROBLEMS

PRACTICE PROBLEMS

The following assignments are from *The Official SAT Study Guide** by the College Board (2nd Edition). It is very important to look back to the KlassTutoring tutorial and review the techniques while completing these problems. Try to determine which technique applies to each problem and apply the methods taught in the tutorial. Do not time yourself on these problems. These problems are provided to give you an opportunity to practice, and hopefully master, the techniques in this tutorial before you must apply them on real SATs in a timed setting.

In the assignments below, "30" problems are part of the 30-hour program, "40" problems are part of the 40-hour program, **bold** problems may be difficult, and *italicized* problems may be only partially covered by techniques in the KlassTutoring tutorial.

- ☐ Test 1: Sect. 3 (18), Sect. 7 (18), Sect. 8 (3,9,16^{30})
- ☐ Test 2: Sect. 2 (15,17), Sect. 5 (7^{40},14), Sect. 8 (3,9^{40})
- ☐ Test 3: Sect. 2 (10^{30},16,**19**), Sect. 5 (18^{40}), Sect. 8 (2,14^{40})
- ☐ Test 4: Sect. 3 (10,17), Sect. 6 (1,4^{30},16^{30}), Sect. 9 (5,**11**)

TEST CORRECTIONS

After each practice test is graded and as you complete the chapters in this tutorial, you should correct problems that you skipped or left blank. (The practice tests are found in *The Official SAT Study Guide**.) Go back to the tutorial and review the techniques as you correct the problems. The idea is to: (1) identify techniques that have given you trouble, (2) go back to the tutorial so you can review and strengthen these techniques, and (3) apply these techniques to the specific problems on which you struggled.

- ☐ Test 5: Sect. 2 (4,13^{30},17^{40}), Sect. 4 (8,13), Sect. 8 (6,11,15)
- ☐ Test 6: Sect. 2 (9,17^{40},**20**), Sect. 4 (6,18^{40}), Sect. 8 (8^{30},13)
- ☐ Test 7: Sect. 3 (12^{40},**18^{30}**), Sect. 7 (2^{40},20^{40}), Sect. 9 (11^{40},**14**,16)
- ☐ Test 8: Sect. 3 (17), Sect. 7 (9,11,17^{30}), Sect. 9 (13,14)
- ☐ Test 9: Sect. 2 (11,18), Sect. 5 (14,19), Sect. 8 (8^{40})
- ☐ Test 10: Sect. 5 (10,16,19), Sect. 8 (9)

^{30} Covered by 30-hour program, ^{40} Covered by 40-hour program

*SAT is a registered trademark of the College Board, which was not involved in the production of and does not endorse this book.

VI

PROBABILITY, ETC.

This chapter covers *probability* and related topics, including *permutations* and *combinations*. *Sets* and *group* problems are also introduced. Many of these topics are advanced, not only because they are relatively difficult, but also because there are not many of these types of problems on the SAT.

1. PROBABILITY

BASIC PROBABILITY

Probability (P) – a way of describing the mathematical likelihood of a particular event occurring. It is usually written as a fraction and is always a number between 0 and 1 ($0 \leq P \leq 1$). Memorize the following equation:

$$\text{Probability} = \frac{\text{Outcomes giving a desired result}}{\text{Total possible outcomes}}$$

Probability problems will include one of the following words: *probability, likelihood, chance,* or *odds*.

(EX) If a fair die is rolled one time, what is the probability of rolling a 6? $\frac{1}{6}$

(EX) If a fair die is rolled one time, what is the probability of rolling an even number? $\frac{1}{2}$

(EX) If a fair die is rolled one time, what is the probability of rolling a prime number? $\frac{1}{2}$ *(2, 3, and 5)*

Some probability problems will require you to find the total number of possible outcomes (the denominator of the probability equation). For harder problems, you may have to use techniques taught on the following pages. On easier problems, however, you may use the following technique:

1. Choose a *first event*, and hold it constant.
2. Count the possible ways that the other events can occur with that first event.
3. Multiply this number by the number of possible first events.

This technique is best explained with an example:

(EX) When a coin is tossed three successive times, there are several possible outcomes, for example: *head-head-tails* (*heads* for the first flip, *heads* for the second flip, and *tails* for the third flip). How many total possible outcomes exist?

       ① *Let the first event be heads (H).*

       ② *The other two events can be HH, TT, HT, or TH.*

       → *So, there are **4** ways these other events can occur.*

       ③ *There are **2** possible first events (H or T).* → *4 × 2 = 8, so there are **8 possible outcomes**.*

(EX) For the example above, what is the probability of getting <u>exactly</u> two tails?

HTT, THT, TTH → $\frac{3}{8}$

(EX) What is the probability of getting <u>at least</u> two tails?

above + TTT → $\frac{4}{8} = \frac{1}{2}$

(EX) What is the probability of getting two heads on the first two flips?

HHT, HHH → $\frac{2}{8} = \frac{1}{4}$

(40) PROBABILITY OF MULTIPLE EVENTS

These problems will ask you to find the probability of multiple events occurring together when the probability of each individual event can be found.

The following method can be used to find the probability of multiple events:

1. Find the probability of each event. **Important: Make sure to consider how the occurrence of one event may affect the probability of another event.**

2. ***Multiply*** the probabilities. This is the probability of multiple events occurring together.

(EX) If the probability of winning a game of bingo is $\frac{1}{25}$, what is the probability of winning two games of bingo in a row?

(A) $\frac{1}{625}$

(B) $\frac{1}{125}$

(C) $\frac{1}{50}$

(D) $\frac{1}{25}$

(E) $\frac{2}{25}$

① *The probability of each event is given as* $\dfrac{1}{25}$

② $\dfrac{1}{25} \cdot \dfrac{1}{25} = \dfrac{1}{625}$ ***(A)***

*Notice that the events are **independent**. The probability of winning the second game is the same as the probability of winning the first game.*

Answers to all lesson and homework problems in this chapter start on page 525.

6. A box contains 30 marbles. If the chance of drawing a red marble from the bag is ⅔, how many marbles in the bag are <u>not</u> red?

(A) 5

(B) 10

(C) 15

(D) 20

(E) 25

17. A kitchen drawer is filled with forks, spoons, and knives. The probability that a spoon is selected at random is $\frac{1}{2}$, and the probability that a knife is selected at random is $\frac{1}{6}$. If all of the forks are removed from the drawer, what is the probability of selecting a knife at random?

(A) $\frac{1}{6}$

(B) $\frac{1}{4}$

(C) $\frac{1}{3}$

(D) $\frac{1}{2}$

(E) $\frac{3}{4}$

18. A committee must select three students from the group of Matt, Ben, Kim, and Jasmine. If the students are selected at random, what is the probability that Matt and Ben will both be selected?

(A) $\frac{1}{4}$

(B) $\frac{1}{3}$

(C) $\frac{1}{2}$

(D) $\frac{2}{3}$

(E) $\frac{3}{4}$

19. The target above is made up of three circles with the same center. The radius of the small circle is one-third of the radius of the middle circle and one-fifth of the radius of the large circle. If an archer hits the target, what is the probability that he hits the shaded region?

(A) $\frac{1}{25}$

(B) $\frac{17}{35}$

(C) $\frac{3}{5}$

(D) $\frac{17}{25}$

(E) $\frac{26}{35}$

40 20. A bag contains exactly 7 blue marbles. If there are 21 marbles in the bag, what is the probability that the first three marbles drawn at random will be blue if the marbles are not replaced after they are drawn?

(A) $\frac{1}{3}$

(B) $\frac{1}{9}$

(C) $\frac{1}{27}$

(D) $\frac{1}{38}$

(E) $\frac{1}{46}$

2. COUNTING, PERMUTATIONS, AND COMBINATIONS

The following techniques will allow you to solve problems that may be too difficult to solve using the techniques in the previous section.

PRINCIPLE OF COUNTING

In math books, this topic is usually called the *fundamental principle of counting*. It allows you to figure out how many different ways multiple **independent** events can occur together. When events are *independent*, the occurrence of one event has no effect on the occurrence of another event.

> Counting problems will have **multiple events that are independent of each other**, as described above. The problems will ask you to find the number of ways that these events can occur together.

FUNDAMENTAL PRINCIPLE OF COUNTING

When one event can happen in m ways and a second event can happen in n ways, the total ways in which the two events can happen is $m \times n$.

(EX) Mike has 5 dress shirts and 3 ties. How many different shirt-tie combinations are possible?

$$5 \times 3 = 15$$

PERMUTATIONS

A *permutation* is an arrangement of items **in a definite order**. Some examples of situations where the order of the items matters include:

- A phone number (555-1234 is different from 555-4321—same numbers, different order)
- A code or password (think about the importance of the order of your inputs when you type in a password)
- A word ("TAR" is different from "RAT")

Permutation problems ask for the number of possible arrangements of items or events in a *definite order*.

The following method should be used for permutation problems:

1. Draw underlines representing each position you have to fill.
2. From left to right, write the number of items available for each position. **It is important to remember that items put into previous positions may not be available for a new position.**
3. Multiply the numbers together to find the number of possible permutations.

(EX) How many 4-letter arrangements can be made from the letters in the word MATH? (Assume each letter can only be used once.)

① First draw four underlines for the 4 positions to fill: _ _ _ _

② There are 4 letters available for the first position, 3 for the second, and so on:

$\underline{4}\ \underline{3}\ \underline{2}\ \underline{1}$

③ Multiply the numbers: $\underline{4}\cdot\underline{3}\cdot\underline{2}\cdot\underline{1}$ = **24**

(EX) How many 4-letter arrangements can be made from the letters in the word NUMBER? (Assume each letter can only be used once.)

$$\underset{①}{\_\ \_\ \_\ \_} \rightarrow \underset{②}{\underline{6}\ \underline{5}\ \underline{4}\ \underline{3}} \rightarrow \underset{③}{\underline{6}\cdot\underline{5}\cdot\underline{4}\cdot\underline{3}} = \textbf{360}$$

15. How many different ways may 6 books be arranged on a book shelf?

   (A) 36
   (B) 120
   (C) 720
   (D) 7,776
   (E) 46,656

COMBINATIONS

Combinations are different from permutations because order does *not* matter. Some examples of situations where the order of the items does *not* matter include:

- The members of a team (typically, the *order* of the players makes no difference)
- The members of a group (as above, the important thing is *who* is in the group, not the order of the members)
- Items found in or on something (for example, think about different combinations of pens in a drawer—the order of the pens does not matter)

> Combination problems ask for the number of possible arrangements of items or events where **order does not matter**.

The method is similar to that of permutation problems, with one extra step, which uses a mathematical operation called *factorial*. This operation involves finding the product of a series of integers counting from a specified number down to 1. Factorials are represented with an exclamation point (!). For example:

$$\text{“six factorial”} = 6! = 6 \times 5 \times 4 \times 3 \times 2 \times 1 = 720$$

The method for combinations problems:

1. Draw underlines representing each position you have to fill.
2. From left to right, write the number of items available for each position. **It is important to remember that items put into previous positions may not be available for a new position.**
3. Multiply the numbers together to find the number of possible permutations.
4. Divide this number by the *factorial of the number of positions to be filled*. This will give you the number of combinations of the items.

(EX) How many 4-person teams can be made from a roster of 10 players?

(A) 24

(B) 210

(C) 417

(D) 1,260

(E) 5,040

$$\underline{}\,\underline{}\,\underline{}\,\underline{} \rightarrow \underline{10}\,\underline{9}\,\underline{8}\,\underline{7} \rightarrow 10\cdot9\cdot8\cdot7 = 5040$$
① ② ③

④ $\dfrac{5040}{4!} = \dfrac{5040}{24} = 210$ **(B)**

19. A pizza parlor offers 8 possible toppings for its pizzas. If a pizza must have three different toppings, how many different kinds of pizza can be made?

    (A) 6

    (B) 21

    (C) 56

    (D) 336

    (E) 512

USING PERMUTATIONS AND COMBINATIONS WITH THE PRINCIPLE OF COUNTING

These problems deal with finding permutations or combinations when there is **more than one independent group of items**.

Use the following method:

1. Find the number of permutations and/or combinations for each independent group.

2. Using the principle of counting, multiply the values you calculated in step 1.

(EX) A security code has 4 digits. If the first 2 digits must be letters from the set {A, B, C, D, E, G, H}, and the second two digits must each be a <u>different</u> positive even integer less than 10, how many 4-digit codes are possible?

    ① *Find the number of outcomes for each group separately:*

    First 2 digits: $\underline{7} \cdot \underline{7} = 49$ (Note: letters may be repeated)

    Second 2 digits: $\underline{4} \cdot \underline{3} = 12$

    ② *Principle of Counting: $49 \times 12 = $ **588***

———————

10. Employees at a small company are given a two-digit ID code, *AB*, where *A* represents the first digit and *B* represents the second digit. If $1 \le A \le 6$ and $1 \le B \le 6$, how many different ID codes are possible?

    (A) 12

    (B) 15

    (C) 18

    (D) 30

    (E) 36

13. How many ways can a family of 5 be arranged in a 5-seat car if the father drives the car?

    (A) 1

    (B) 5

    (C) 12

    (D) 24

    (E) 120

20. Four newspaper reporters are each to be assigned one of four assignments. Two of the assignments are in Mexico, one is in Canada, and one is in England. If Amy and Ryan are two of the four reporters, what is the probability that they will both be assigned the jobs in Mexico?

    (A) $\frac{1}{16}$

    (B) $\frac{1}{12}$

    (C) $\frac{1}{6}$

    (D) $\frac{1}{4}$

    (E) $\frac{1}{2}$

20. There are 4 juniors and 5 seniors on a debate team. If the teacher must choose 2 juniors and 3 seniors to compete, how many ways may this 5-person team be assembled?

    (A) 6

    (B) 12

    (C) 60

    (D) 126

    (E) 720

3. SETS AND GROUPS

SETS

A *set* is a collection of items. These items are called *elements* or *members* of the set. A set is usually represented by brackets, for example:

set *A* = {1, 3, 4, 5, 7, 8, 9}
set *B* = {2, 4, 6, 8, 10}

You may be asked to find the *intersection* or the *union* of two or more sets. It may be helpful to look at sets as circles and the members of the sets as numbers inside the circles. These are called Venn diagrams.

Intersection – the common elements of the sets. The intersection of sets *A* and *B* above is {4, 8} since 4 and 8 are common members of both sets:

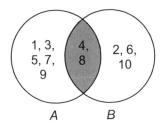

Union – consists of the elements that are in either set *or* in both sets (in other words—all the elements). The union of sets *A* and *B* above is {1, 2, 3, 4, 5, 6, 7, 8, 9, 10} since these numbers are in either set (1, 2, 3, 5, 6, 7, 9, and 10) or in both sets (4 and 8):

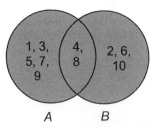

Look for problems with the word *set,* or look for elements surrounded by brackets.

set M = {all prime numbers less than 10}

set N = {all odd numbers less than 10}

7. Sets M and N are shown above. How many numbers in set M are also in set N?

    (A) 1

    (B) 2

    (C) 3

    (D) 4

    (E) 5

(40) GROUPS

These problems are not very common, but if one does show up, use the following formula:

FLASH CARDS   **Total = Members of Group 1 + Members of Group 2 + Neither − Both**

It might help to visualize group problems using a Venn diagram. Notice that when you add Group 1 and Group 2, the "Both" region is counted twice. This is why "Both" is subtracted in the formula above:

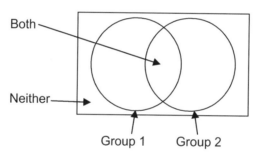

(EX) If at a school of 200 students, 75 students take Spanish and 25 students take Latin. 10 of the students who take Latin also take Spanish, how many students are not taking Spanish or Latin?

$$200 = 75 + 25 + Neither - 10$$

$$\rightarrow Neither = \mathbf{110}$$

18. At a school of 90 students, all of the students take Spanish, Latin, or both. If 75 students take Spanish and 25 students take Latin, how many students take Spanish or Latin but <u>not</u> both?

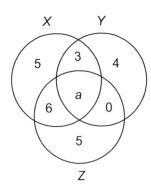

12. The figure above is a Venn diagram for sets X, Y, and Z. The number in each region indicates how many elements are in that region. If there are 20 elements common to sets X and Y, what is the value of a?

    (A) 2

    (B) 5

    (C) 11

    (D) 17

    (E) 20

(40) 13. At a car repair shop, 10 of the cars have mechanical problems and 16 of the cars have electrical problems. If there are 20 cars at the shop, and all of the cars have either mechanical problems, electrical problems, or both, how many cars have both mechanical and electrical problems?

    (A) 6

    (B) 8

    (C) 16

    (D) 20

    (E) 26

(40) 19. Of the 120 international students at a camp, 90 spoke Spanish and 40 spoke French. What is the least possible number of campers that could speak both Spanish and French?

    (A) 0

    (B) 10

    (C) 40

    (D) 50

    (E) 80

4. PROBABILITY, ETC. PROBLEMS

PRACTICE PROBLEMS

The following assignments are from *The Official SAT Study Guide** by the College Board (2nd Edition). It is very important to look back to the KlassTutoring tutorial and review the techniques while completing these problems. Try to determine which technique applies to each problem and apply the methods taught in the tutorial. Do not time yourself on these problems. These problems are provided to give you an opportunity to practice, and hopefully master, the techniques in this tutorial before you must apply them on real SATs in a timed setting.

In the assignments below, "30" problems are part of the 30-hour program, "40" problems are part of the 40-hour program, **bold** problems may be difficult, and *italicized* problems may be only partially covered by techniques in the KlassTutoring tutorial.

- ☐ Test 1: Sect. 3 (5), Sect. 7 (11), Sect. 8 (14^{40})
- ☐ Test 2: Sect. 2 (13), Sect. 5 (8^{40}), Sect. 8 (**8**)
- ☐ Test 3: Sect. 2 (2,12)
- ☐ Test 4: Sect. 3 (7), Sect. 6 (**18^{40}**)

TEST CORRECTIONS

After each practice test is graded and as you complete the chapters in this tutorial, you should correct problems that you skipped or left blank. (The practice tests are found in *The Official SAT Study Guide**.) Go back to the tutorial and review the techniques as you correct the problems. The idea is to: (1) identify techniques that have given you trouble, (2) go back to the tutorial so you can review and strengthen these techniques, and (3) apply these techniques to the specific problems on which you struggled.

- ☐ Test 5: Sect. 2 (3^{40},12), Sect. 8 (1)
- ☐ Test 6: Sect. 8 (2^{40},10)
- ☐ Test 7: Sect. 3 (15^{40}), Sect. 9 (1)
- ☐ Test 8: Sect. 9 (5)
- ☐ Test 9: Sect. 2 (1), Sect. 5 (4^{40}), Sect. 8 (4)
- ☐ Test 10: Sect. 5 (8), Sect. 8 (1^{40},3)

³⁰ Covered by 30-hour program, ⁴⁰ Covered by 40-hour program

*SAT is a registered trademark of the College Board, which was not involved in the production of and does not endorse this book.

5. OTHER PROBLEMS

PRACTICE PROBLEMS

The following assignments are from *The Official SAT Study Guide** by the College Board (2nd Edition). It is very important to look back to the KlassTutoring tutorial and review the techniques while completing these problems. Try to determine which technique applies to each problem and apply the methods taught in the tutorial. Do not time yourself on these problems. These problems are provided to give you an opportunity to practice, and hopefully master, the techniques in this tutorial before you must apply them on real SATs in a timed setting.

In the assignments below, "30" problems are part of the 30-hour program, "40" problems are part of the 40-hour program, **bold** problems may be difficult, and *italicized* problems may be only partially covered by techniques in the KlassTutoring tutorial.

- ☐ Test 1: None
- ☐ Test 2: Sect. 2 (5)
- ☐ Test 3: Sect. 2 (3), Sect. 5 (4), Sect. 8 (13)
- ☐ Test 4: Sect. 3 (4,5), Sect. 6 (**7**), Sect. 9 (10)

TEST CORRECTIONS

After each practice test is graded and as you complete the chapters in this tutorial, you should correct problems that you skipped or left blank. (The practice tests are found in *The Official SAT Study Guide**.) Go back to the tutorial and review the techniques as you correct the problems. The idea is to: (1) identify techniques that have given you trouble, (2) go back to the tutorial so you can review and strengthen these techniques, and (3) apply these techniques to the specific problems on which you struggled.

- ☐ Test 5: None
- ☐ Test 6: Sect. 2 (11,15), Sect. 8 (4)
- ☐ Test 7: None
- ☐ Test 8: Sect. 7 (1,**18**)
- ☐ Test 9: Sect. 5 (10), Sect. 8 (**15**)
- ☐ Test 10: None

[30] Covered by 30-hour program, [40] Covered by 40-hour program

*SAT is a registered trademark of the College Board, which was not involved in the production of and does not endorse this book.

VII
MATH ANSWERS

The following answers are to all lesson and homework problems in the previous chapters.

I. MATH INTRODUCTION AND BASIC CONCEPTS
2. CALCULATORS
1. *-4*
2. *4*
3. *287*
4. *232*
5. *338*
6. *6.125* (see the lesson on how to enter mixed fractions into your calculator)
7. *.5*
8. *(D)*
9. *(A)*
10. *(D)*
11. $\sqrt{108} + \sqrt{48}$ = 17.3205... Check the answers. You will see that $10\sqrt{3}$ = 17.3205... *(E)*

3. BASIC MATH CONCEPTS
1. *203, 0, -2, 4.*
2. *2, 3, 5, 7*
3. *1, 2, 3, 6, 7, 14, 21, and 42*
4. *2, 3, and 7*

5. $\dfrac{10}{3}$ → $3\overline{)10}$
   $\underline{-9}$
   $\;\mathbf{1}$ ← remainder

6. $\dfrac{100}{51}$ → $51\overline{)100}$
   $\underline{-\;51}$
   $\;\mathbf{49}$ ← remainder

7. $\dfrac{26}{x}$ → $x\overline{)26}$
   $\underline{-x}$
   $\;3$ ← remainder $26 - x = 3$ → $x = \mathbf{23}$

8. $\dfrac{x}{26}$ → $26\overline{)x}$
   $\underline{-26}$
   $\;3$ ← remainder $x - 26 = 3$ → $x = \mathbf{29}$

9. $|-30| = \mathbf{30}$
10. $x = \mathbf{4}$ or $\mathbf{-4}$
11. *2000*

II. ARITHMETIC
1. PERCENT PROBLEMS
PERCENT ↔ DECIMAL:
1. *425%*
2. *¼*
3. *2.20*
4. *87.5%*
5. *.13%*

OF/IS PERCENT PROBLEMS:

1. $.25 \times .25 \times 32 = 2$ **(D)**
2. 10% of 5.50 is $\rightarrow .10 \times 5.50 = .55$ **(B)**
15. $.075 \times 8 = .6 = 60\%$ **(D)**
20. volume of a cube $= (length\ of\ edge)^3$ ← this will be covered in the Geometry chapter
   1^3 "is what percent of" 2^3
   $1^3 = x \cdot 2^3 \rightarrow 1 = x \cdot 8 \rightarrow x = 12.5\%$ **(A)**

PART OVER WHOLE PERCENT PROBLEMS:

2. $\frac{8}{12} = .666... = 66\frac{2}{3}\%$ **(C)**

PERCENT INCREASE/DECREASE:

1. **1.25**
2. **1.70**
3. **1.07**
4. **2.00**
5. **.80**
6. **.15**
7. **.40**
8. **.94**
9. **.50**
10. $(1.20)(.80) = $ **.96** (The multiplier is not 1.0)
7. $200(1.10) = 220$ **(E)**
13. $x \cdot (.80) = 4.80 \rightarrow x = 6$ **(D)**

original   final

DIFFERENCE-OVER-ORIGINAL PERCENT PROBLEMS:

14. $\frac{28 - 7}{7} = \frac{21}{7} = 3$ **(D)**

PICK 100:

19. Pick 100 for employment in 1990:

$100(1.30) = 130 \rightarrow 130(1.40) = 182 \rightarrow \frac{diff.}{orig.} \frac{182 - 100}{100} = \frac{82}{100} = 82\%$ **(E)**

30% increase   40% increase

PERCENT HW:

6. The multiplier for a 4% increase is 1.04 (100% + 4% = 104% = 1.04).
   $300(1.04) = 312$ **(B)**
7. $\frac{part}{whole} \frac{12}{30} = .4 = 40\%$ **(A)**
9. $\frac{diff.}{orig.} \frac{92 - 80}{80} = \frac{12}{80} = 15\%$ **(D)**
14. Pick 100 for the number of employees:
   60 women $\rightarrow \frac{1}{3} \cdot 60 = 20$ women drive to work
   40 men $\rightarrow \frac{1}{2} \cdot 40 = 20$ men drive to work
   $100 - 40 = 60$ employees do **not** drive to work $\rightarrow \frac{60}{100} = 60\%$ **(C)**

17. The multiplier for a 25% decrease is .75. The multiplier for a 50% increase is 1.50.
Pick 100 for p: 100(.75) = 75 → 75(1.50) = 112.50

$$\frac{diff.}{orig.} = \frac{112.5 - 100}{100} = .125 = 12.5\% \text{ (increase)} \quad \textbf{(C)}$$

19. 12 "was" 15% "of" x → 12 = .15 · x → x = 80 (so he **had** $80)
80 − 12 = 68 **(B)**

20. This is a difficult problem. First find the rates by dividing machines by hours:

$$\text{rate before upgrade} = \frac{50}{m}, \text{ rate after upgrade} = \frac{90}{.6m} = \frac{150}{m}$$

$$\frac{diff.}{orig.} = \frac{\frac{150}{m} - \frac{50}{m}}{\frac{50}{m}} = \frac{\frac{150-50}{m}}{\frac{50}{m}} = \frac{\frac{100}{m}}{\frac{50}{m}} \rightarrow \text{ multiply top and bottom by } m:$$

$$\frac{m \cdot \frac{100}{m}}{m \cdot \frac{50}{m}} = \frac{100}{50} = 2 = 200\% \quad \textbf{(D)}$$

If the algebra above is too difficult, the easiest approach to this problem is to pick a number for m and use a technique called RTD. Make a note to come back to this problem after you cover pick numbers (type 2) in the Algebra chapter. The solution is below:

m = 10 ← plug into the first row of RTD below as T.

R x T = D (boxes)
10   50 → R = 50 ÷ 10 = 5
6   90 → R = 90 ÷ 6 = 15

$$\frac{diff.}{orig.} = \frac{15 - 5}{5} = 2 = 200\% \quad \textbf{(D)}$$

2. PROPORTIONS

4. known relationship: "6 minutes to light 15 candles"

$$\frac{minutes}{candles} \frac{6}{15} = \frac{x}{35} \rightarrow x = 14 \text{ minutes} \quad \textbf{(E)}$$

9. known relationship: "45 minutes to travel 300 kilometers"

$$\frac{min.}{km} \frac{45}{300} = \frac{x}{1600} \rightarrow x = 240 \text{ minutes} \rightarrow \frac{240}{60} = 4 \text{ hours} \quad \textbf{(B)}$$

18. known relationships (there are two): "7-pound bag of apples cost 10 dollars" and "5 pounds of apples are needed to make 2 apple pies"
Note: complete the second proportion before the first one.

$$\frac{pounds}{dollars} \frac{7}{10} = \frac{35}{y} \rightarrow y = 50 \text{ dollars} \quad \textbf{(B)}$$

$$\frac{pounds}{pies} \frac{5}{2} = \frac{x}{14} \rightarrow x = 35 \text{ pounds}$$

PROPORTIONS HW:

3. $\dfrac{cans}{hours} \dfrac{25}{4} = \dfrac{x}{20} \rightarrow x = 125 \text{ cans} \quad \textbf{(A)}$

8. $\dfrac{object(ft.)}{shadow(ft.)} \dfrac{6}{14} = \dfrac{x}{140} \rightarrow x = 60 \quad \textbf{(C)}$

12. There are two known relationships: "30 chips per hour" and "39 chips per hour," so we need two proportions.

A: $\dfrac{chips}{hour} \dfrac{30}{1} = \dfrac{26}{a}$ → $a = .8666...hours$ → $.8666... \times 60 = 52$ minutes

B: $\dfrac{chips}{hour} \dfrac{39}{1} = \dfrac{26}{b}$ → $b = .6666...hours$ → $.6666... \times 60 = 40$ minutes

→ $52 - 40 = 12$ minutes **(A)**

3. RATIOS

4. First, rewrite the ratios above as fractions.

$\dfrac{x}{y} = \dfrac{1}{6}, \ \dfrac{15x}{y} = ?$

Rewrite $\dfrac{15x}{y}$ as $15 \cdot \dfrac{x}{y}$. Now, substitute $\dfrac{1}{6}$ for $\dfrac{x}{y}$:

$15 \cdot \dfrac{x}{y} = 15 \cdot \dfrac{1}{6} = \dfrac{15}{6} = \dfrac{5}{2}$ **(C)**

12. $10x + 4x + 1x = 75,000$ → $15x = 75,000$ → $x = 5,000$
$10x = 10 \cdot 5,000 = 50,000$ **(C)**

RATIOS HW:

4. $\dfrac{n}{9} = \dfrac{33}{198}$ → $n = 1.5$ **(C)**

15. $5x + 4x + x = 10$ → $10x = 10$ → $x = 1$ **(B)**

16. Use the shortcut described in the last example of the lesson: The total must be a multiple of the sum of the share numbers. The share numbers of (A)—1 and 2—add to 3. Since 20 is not a multiple of 3, **(A)** cannot be the ratio of red to green apples.
To confirm, you may set up the equation:

$x + 2x = 20$ → $3x = 20$ → $x = \dfrac{20}{3}$, which is not an integer.

Notice that for all of the other answer choices, 20 is a multiple of the sum of the share numbers.

4. AVERAGES, MEDIANS, & MODES

1. $-5, 0, 2, 6, 10$ → median = **2**
2. $-5, 0, 2, 6, 10, 10$ → median = $\dfrac{2+6}{2}$ = **4**, mode = **10**

3. $\dfrac{9 + 10 + 12 + 13 + 14}{5}$ = **11.60**

4. **12**

5. $\dfrac{9 + 9 + 10 + 10 + 12 + 13 + 13 + 14 + 14 + 14 + 14}{11} = 12$

6. **13**
7. **14**
12. Put the known values in order: 62, 65, 70, 72, 72, 80
Since 70 is the median, it must be the fourth (middle) number in the final list. So x must be less than or equal to 70. The answer is **(E)**.

ANS:

5. <u>$A \times N = S$</u>
   20   3   60 ← 60 is the sum of x, y, and z
   <u>25   2   50</u> ← 50 is the sum of p and q
            110 **(E)**

11. $\underline{A \times N = S}$
    14   5   70   ← *There are 5 weekdays in a week*
    42   2   84   ← *There are 2 weekend days in a week*
    A   7   154   → A = 22 **(B)**
         "entire week"

19. $\underline{A \times N = S}$
    −2   6   −12
    2   4   8   *(Note: 6 − 4 = 2, so we* **subtract** *the*
    A   2   −20   *values in the S column as well.)*
         "other **two** *numbers"*
    → A = −10 **(A)**

ANS HW:

12. $\underline{A \times N = S}$
    18   5   90   → 12 + 10 + x + 20 + 27 = 90   → x = 21
    Make sure to put the scores in increasing order:
         10, 12, 20, 21, 27
           median **(D)**

14. $\underline{A \times N = S}$
    152   15   2280
    0   5   0
    A   20   2280   → A = 114 **(C)**
         "20 years"

5. RATES, TIMES, & DISTANCES

8. *It may be helpful to convert units* **before** *plugging numbers into RTD:* 45 min. → .75 hrs.
   $\underline{R \times T = D}$
   R   .75   48   → R = 64 **(D)**

18. $\underline{R \times T = D}$ *(Note: Distance is the same for both rows.)*
    12   2   24
    8   3   24
    R   5   48   → R = 9.6 mph **(B)**

RTD HW:

5. $\underline{R \times T = D}$ *(Note: Rate is the same for both rows.)*
   120   3   360   ← 360 ÷ 3 = 120
   120   x   800   → x = 6.6666... hours **(E)**

19. $\underline{R \times T = D}$ *(Note: Time is the same for both rows.)*
    H: 1.25   5
    V: x   1.25   4.5   → x = 3.6 miles per hour **(D)**

6. NUMBER PATTERNS

2. 1, 1, 2, 4, 8, 16, 32, 64, 128, **256 (D)**

15. *You may think that this problem will take forever—1,000 is a big number. Luckily, cubed numbers get big quickly.* $1^3 = 1$, $2^3 = 8$, $3^3 = 27$ *(see? we're already up to 27). You might skip ahead:* $9^3 = 729$, $10^3 = 1,000$. *We're done. There are 10 perfect cubes less than or equal to 1,000* **(A)**. *As you can see, there really isn't a trick to these types of problems, but they are generally not as difficult as they look.*

6. *45 is divisible by 5, so the 45th term is the last term in the pattern (2).* **(E)**

14. $2 + (n − 1)2$ *the difference between any two terms is 2.* **(B)**
    You could also simply plug 500 and 499 into the equation and subtract, but this takes considerably longer.

15. 2nd term $= 4 \times (½)^{2-1} = 4 \times ½ = 2$

3rd term $= 2 \times ½ = 1$ (since each term is ½ times the previous term)

4th term $= 1 \times ½ = ½$ *(You could use the equation to find the 3rd and 4th terms, but this takes longer.)*

Average of 2, 1, and ½ is $1.1666... = \frac{7}{6}$ *(or convert answer choices to decimals)* **(B)**

NUMBER PATTERNS HW:

2. 150, 30, 6, $\frac{6}{5}$, $\frac{6}{25}$ **(C)**

15. *There are 7 items in the pattern.*

49 is divisible by 7, so the 49th term is 3 (the last item in the pattern).

The 50th term is the next term (also 3).

→ 3 + 3 = 6 **(E)**

18. *1, 3, 4, 7, 11, 18...*

$[o\ o\ e]\ o\ o\ e...$ $\dfrac{odd}{all} \dfrac{2}{3} = \dfrac{x}{999}$ → $x = 666$

Check the 1000th term: Since 1000 is not divisible by 3, it is odd.

666 + 1 = 667 **(E)**

19. *Use the equation for a geometric sequence.* **(A)**

7. GREATEST POSSIBLE VALUE

HW:

13. *Use ANS (if necessary) to determine the sum of the two integers (x and y):*

$\underline{A\ \times\ N = S}$

20   2   40   → $x + y = 40$

$x = 0$ (smallest non-negative integer) → $y = 40 - 0 = 40$ **(C)**

Note: On GPV multiple-choice problems, the correct answer will almost never be the largest answer choice. Similarly, on LPV problems, the answer will almost never be the smallest answer choice.

15. $11 + x + y = 40$ → $x + y = 29$ → $x = 14$, $y = 15$ → $x \cdot y = $ **210**

8. EXPONENTS

1. x^9

2. x^3

3. x^{20}

4. $25x^2y^2$

5. $a = \pm 4$

6. **8** *(use calculator)*

EXPONENTS HW:

12. $2^{t^2} = 2^{20}$ → $t^2 = 20$ → $t = \sqrt{20} = 2\sqrt{5}$ (t > 0) **(B)**

(You could use your calculator to convert $\sqrt{20}$ into a decimal; don't forget the answer choices.)

14. *Start with the first part of the expression:*

$(-2xy^3)^2 = (-2)^2 x^2 y^{3 \cdot 2} = 4x^2y^6$

Next, combine like terms:

$(4x^2y^6)(3x^3y) = 4 \cdot 3 \cdot x^2 \cdot x^3 \cdot y^6 \cdot y = 12x^5y^7$ **(E)**

17. *Compare apples to apples:*

$(3^2)^x = (3^4)^{\frac{1}{3}}$ → $3^{2x} = 3^{\frac{4}{3}}$ → $2x = \frac{4}{3}$ → $x = \frac{2}{3}$

OR $9^x = (9^2)^{\frac{1}{3}} = 9^{\frac{2}{3}}$ → $x = \frac{2}{3}$

9. EXPONENTIAL GROWTH

18. $500{,}000(1.10)^5 = 805{,}255$ **(E)**

EXPONENTIAL GROWTH HW:

18. $2^{12} = 1(2)^x$ $\rightarrow$ $x = 12$

$12 = \dfrac{\text{total time}}{10 \text{ minutes}}$ $\rightarrow$ total time = 120 minutes = **2 hrs**

III. ALGEBRA

1. BASIC ALGEBRA

EQUALITIES:

1. $a = \mathbf{-18}$
2. $a = \mathbf{1}$
3. $a = \mathbf{-2}$
4. $a = \mathbf{4}$
5. $a = \mathbf{6}$
6. $a - 6 = -2$ $\rightarrow$ $a = \mathbf{4}$
7. $6 - \tfrac{2}{3}a = \tfrac{1}{2}a - 8$ $\rightarrow$ $14 = \tfrac{7}{6}a$ $\rightarrow$ $a = \mathbf{12}$
8. *(cross multiply)* $3a + 6 = 5$ $\rightarrow$ $3a = -1$ $\rightarrow$ $a = \mathbf{\tfrac{1}{3}}$
9. *(cross multiply)* $a + 11 = 6a + 6$ $\rightarrow$ $5 = 5a$ $\rightarrow$ $a = \mathbf{1}$
10. *(use substitution)* $a = 2a - 2$ $\rightarrow$ $-a = -2$ $\rightarrow$ $a = \mathbf{2}$

INEQUALITIES:

1. $\mathbf{a < 30}$
2. $-\tfrac{1}{2}a \le 2$ $\rightarrow$ $\mathbf{a \ge -4}$

RADICAL EXPRESSIONS:

1. $2\sqrt{a} = 16$ $\rightarrow$ $\sqrt{a} = 8$ $\rightarrow$ $a = \mathbf{64}$
2. $\sqrt{a-5} = 4$ $\rightarrow$ $a - 5 = 16$ $\rightarrow$ $a = \mathbf{21}$

ALGEBRA WORD PROBLEMS:

14. $(x - 4)^2 - (4x)^2 = 0$

*The most important part of this problem is to get the equation above. If you have trouble solving this equation, come back to it after you learn the Pick Answers technique in the next section. You could also solve it by factoring (difference of squares)—see section 6 in the Algebra chapter. The answer is **(A)**.*

BASIC ALGEBRA HW:

2. *The shortcut to this problem is to <u>not</u> multiply 50 and 4x. Instead, divide both sides by 50:*

$50(4x) = 200$ $\rightarrow$ $\dfrac{\cancel{50}(4x)}{\cancel{50}} = \dfrac{200}{50}$ $\rightarrow$ $4x = 4$ **(D)** *Note: the question is asking for 4x, not x.*

12. $4x = 2x + 4$ $\leftarrow$ *Note the position of the word "is" in the sentence. This helps you figure out where to put the equal sign.* $4x - 2x = \cancel{2x} - \cancel{2x} + 4$ $\rightarrow$ $2x = 4$ $\rightarrow$ $x = 2$ **(C)**

17. *Tackle this difficult problem one step at a time.*

First, label your variables. Let r = number of red straws, b = number of blue straws, y = number of yellow straws, and t = total number of straws = r + b + y.

*Now look at the words: "⅓ as many red straws as there were blue straws." There is no "is," so it's hard to know where to put the equal sign. Let's restate the phrase as: "number of red straws **is** ⅓ of the number of blue straws." Now we can write: r = ⅓ · b*

"⅓ of the straws were blue" → b = ⅓ · t

"20 of the straws were yellow" → y = 20

Finally, put it all together. Your goal is to get one equation in terms of t (which is what you're looking for):

$$t = r + b + y = \frac{1}{3}b + \frac{1}{3}t + 20 = \frac{1}{3}\left(\frac{1}{3}t\right) + \frac{1}{3}t + 20 = \frac{4}{9}t + 20 \;\rightarrow\; t - \frac{4}{9}t = 20 \;\rightarrow\; \frac{5}{9}t = 20$$

$$\rightarrow\; t = 36 \;\textbf{(C)}$$

This is another question where you could Pick Answers. If the algebra is too difficult, you might come back to it after you learn the Pick Answers technique in the next section.

2. THE PICK TRICKS

PICK NUMBERS TYPE 1:

9. $\boxed{y = 2,\, z = 5}$ → $\dfrac{socks}{dollars} \dfrac{2}{5} = \dfrac{x}{15}$ → $x = \underline{6}$ → **(C)** *Remember, **check every answer choice**.*

13. $\boxed{x = 30,\, y = 2}$ → $\dfrac{people}{seconds} \dfrac{6}{30} = \dfrac{x}{120}$ *(120 seconds = 2 minutes)* → $b = \underline{24}$ → **(E)**

   *Remember, **check every answer choice**. Note: the numbers used above are convenient, but any numbers will work. Remember to plug in the numbers that you picked in step 1.*

16. $\boxed{m = 4,\, n = 2}$ → *Greater than 4 + 2 = 6 and less than 4·2 = 8* → *1 integer (7)*
   Only (B), (C), and (E) can be eliminated, so pick new numbers:
   $\boxed{m = 6,\, n = 4}$ → *Since there is obviously more than 1 integer greater than 10 and less than 24, eliminate (A). The answer must be **(D)**.*
   *Remember, **check every answer choice**.*

PICK NUMBERS TYPE 2:

10. *Pick a = 2* → $\dfrac{2}{b} = \dfrac{2}{3}$ → *b = 3* → $\dfrac{3}{c} = \dfrac{2}{5}$ → $c = \dfrac{15}{2}$ → $\dfrac{a}{c} = \dfrac{4}{15}$ **(A)**

   As always, if you are uncomfortable with fractions, you can convert them into decimals (including answer choices) using a calculator.

12. *Pick y = 2* → *x = 10·2 = 20* → *Increase y by 10: y = 2 + 10 = 12* → *x = 10·12 = 120, so x increased by 100* ← *(120 − 20).* **(E)**

PICK NUMBERS TYPE 3:

6. *Pick any numbers that satisfy the constraints above:*
   Game 1: Bill = 10, Fred = 20
   Game 2: Bill = 10, Fred = 8
   Combined: Bill = 20, Fred = 28 **(D)**

11. *Original square: Pick side = 2, so perimeter = 8 and area = 4.*
   Final square: Perimeter doubles: 8 × 2 = 16 → *side = 16 ÷ 4 = 4* → *area = 4 × 4 = 16*
   $\dfrac{difference}{original} \dfrac{16 - 4}{4} = \dfrac{12}{4} = 3 = 300\%$ **(D)**

PICK NUMBERS: GUESS AND CHECK:

20. Start with the second equation, which may be easier than the first:
    Pick (guess) $x = 10$ and $y = 10$ → (now look at 2nd equation) $xy = 100 \neq 91$ ✗
    Pick (guess) $x = 11$ and $y = 9$ → $xy = 99 \neq 91$ ✗ (but we're getting closer!)
    Pick (guess) $x = 13$ and $y = 7$ → $xy = 91$ ✓
    → $x^2y + xy^2 = 13^2 \cdot 7 + 13 \cdot 7^2 = 1,820$ **(B)**
    Note: a shortcut to this problem will be taught in the Simultaneous Equation section.

PICK ANSWERS:

10. Bare bones question: "what is the value of d?"
    Pick (C): $d = 160$ → $¼ \times 160 = 40$ → $160 - 40 = 120$ left after flowers → $⅔ \times 120 = 80$ →
    $120 - 80 = 40$ left after dinner → $40 > 35$, so eliminate (C), (D), and (E).
    Pick (B): $d = 140$ → $¼ \times 140 = 35$ → $140 - 35 = 105$ left after flowers → $⅔ \times 105 = 70$ →
    $105 - 70 = 35$ left after dinner. ✓ **(B)**

16. Bare bones question: "how old is Keith now?"
    Pick (C): $K = 12$ (note: "as old as" means multiplication - see Of/Is technique)
    → $J = ½ \cdot 12 = 6$ → $6 = ¼ \cdot S$ → $S = 24$
    → Average $= 14 < 21$, so eliminate (C), (B), and (A)
    Pick (D): $K = 18$ → $J = 9$ → $S = 36$ → Average $= 21$ ✓ **(D)**

PICK TRICKS HW:

8. Pick Numbers (type 1): $\boxed{y = 2}$ → $\dfrac{4}{12} + \dfrac{5}{12} + \dfrac{6}{12} = \dfrac{15}{12} = \dfrac{5}{4}$ → **(C)**

   Remember, **check every answer choice**.

9. Pick Numbers (type 2): Pick $a = 2$ → $b = 4$, $c = 6$, $d = 8$ → $a + d = 10$, $b + c = 10$
   → $10 - 10 = 0$ **(A)**

12. Pick Answers: Since you are looking for the **least** value of m, start with (A):
    (A): $m = 1$ → $\dfrac{2}{11} = n^2$ (n is not an integer) ✗
    (B): $m = 2$ → $\dfrac{4}{11} = n^2$ (n is not an integer) ✗
    (C): $m = 11$ → $\dfrac{22}{11} = 2 = n^2$ (n is not an integer) ✗
    (D): $m = 22$ → $\dfrac{44}{11} = 4 = n^2$ → $n = 2$ ✓ **(D)**

13. Pick Numbers (type 1): $\boxed{x = 2, y = 3}$ → $\dfrac{songs}{dollars} \dfrac{20}{2} = \dfrac{songs}{3}$ → $songs = \underline{30}$ → **(E)**

    Remember, **check every answer choice**.

14. Pick Numbers (guess and check):
    $x = 2$ → $3^2 = 9 > 8$ (but close)
    $x = 1.8$ → $3^{1.8} = 7.225... < 8$ (so pick a number between 1.8 and 2)
    $x = 1.9$ → $3^{1.9} = 8.064... \approx 8$ (close enough)
    → $3^{2x} = 3^{(2 \cdot 1.9)} = 65.022... \approx 64$ **(E)**
    Note: $8.064 > 8$, so it's not surprising that $65.022 > 64$.

15. Pick Numbers (type 2): $p = 8$, $q = 9$ (Of course, these numbers must satisfy the conditions of the problem.)

    $\begin{array}{r} 10 \\ 7{\overline{\smash{)}72}} \\ \underline{70} \\ 2 \end{array}$ ← remainder **(B)**

16. *Pick Answers:*
   Note: a 22% increase is equivalent to multiplying by 1.22 (review Percent Increase/Decrease)
   Pick (C): 600 × 1.22 = 732 → 732 × 1.22 = 893 > 864 (eliminate (D) and (E))
   *Pick (B): 600 × 1.20 = 720 → 720 × 1.20 = 864 ✓ **(B)***

17. *Pick Numbers (type 1):* $\boxed{x = 25, y = 2}$ → $\dfrac{cents}{minutes}\dfrac{25}{3} = \dfrac{200}{m}$ → *m = 24 minutes = .4 hours →*

   (B) *Remember,* **check every answer choice.**

17. *Pick Numbers (type 2): Pick a = 5 →* $\dfrac{5}{b} = \dfrac{5}{4}$ *→ b = 4 →* $\dfrac{2 \cdot 4}{c} = \dfrac{6}{7}$ *→ c =* $28\big/3$

   → $a\big/c = 15\big/28$ *(A)*

18. *Pick Numbers (type 1):* $\boxed{X = 2, Y = 3}$ → *20 × 23 = 460 → **(E)***

19. *Pick Numbers (type 3): Pick 60 for each person ← any number divisible by 3 is convenient.*
   Total = 60 × 4 = 240
   Woman = 60 + 20 + 40 = 120
   $\dfrac{120}{240} = \dfrac{1}{2}$ *(B)*

19. *Pick Numbers (guess and check):*

   First, simplify the equation: $\dfrac{a}{a^2 + 1} + \dfrac{1}{a^2 + 1} = \dfrac{a+1}{a^2 + 1} = \dfrac{5}{b}$

   Now, guess and check for a (remember, a > 1):

   a = 2 → $\dfrac{3}{5} = \dfrac{5}{b}$ *→ b is not an integer ✗*

   a = 3 → $\dfrac{4}{10} = \dfrac{5}{b}$ *→ b is not an integer ✗*

   a = 4 → $\dfrac{5}{17} = \dfrac{5}{b}$ *→ b = 17 ✓ **(D)***

   Note: You could also pick answers, but the math is more difficult.

20. *Pick Numbers → Pick Answers:*
   Pick initial number for C: C = 30 → score = ⅓·30 +10 = 20
   Answer the bare bones questions starting with (C):
   *(C): C = 30 + 60 = 90 → score = ⅓·90 +10 = 40 = 20 + 20 ✓ **(C)***

   initial C   *initial score*

20. *Pick Answers → Pick Numbers: Look at answer choices first, and pick a number that will eliminate at least two of them:*
   x = 0 → $|0 - 10|$ *is not ≤ 6, so eliminate (A) and (B).*
   x = 1 → $|1 - 10|$ *is not ≤ 6, so eliminate (C).*
   x = 5 → $|25 - 10|$ *is not ≤ 6, so eliminate (E). Answer is **(D)**.*

3. CONSECUTIVE INTEGERS

11. $\dfrac{290}{2} = 145$

   144, 146

10. *(A):* $\dfrac{90}{2} = 45$

   44, 46 *(not consecutive integers)*

   (B): $\dfrac{91}{2} = 45.5$

   45, 46 *(consecutive integers ✓) **(B)***

CONSECUTIVE INTEGERS HW:

12. $\dfrac{50}{20} = 2.5$

... 2, 3,... (2.5 is the median of the numbers, so 2 is the greatest possible value of x) **(B)**

14. (A): $n = 2 \rightarrow \dfrac{15}{2} = 7.5 \rightarrow$ 7.5 falls between 2 consecutive integers (7 and 8) ✓

(B): $n = 3 \rightarrow \dfrac{15}{3} = 5 \rightarrow$ 5 is the middle of 3 consecutive integers (4, **5**, and 6) ✓

(C): $n = 4 \rightarrow \dfrac{15}{4} = 3.75 \rightarrow$ 3.75 does <u>not</u> fall exactly between two integers. ✗

The answer must be **(C)**.

4. SIMULTANEOUS EQUATIONS

LINEAR SIMULTANEOUS EQUATIONS:

1. $2x + 2y = 8$
   $\underline{+(3x - 2y = 2)}$
   $5x = 10 \rightarrow \boldsymbol{x = 2} \rightarrow 2 \cdot 2 + 2y = 8 \rightarrow \boldsymbol{y = 2}$

2. $100x + y = 25$
   $\underline{-(200x + y = 45)}$
   $-100x = -20 \rightarrow \boldsymbol{x = {}^1\!/_5} \rightarrow 100 \cdot {}^1\!/_5 + y = 25 \rightarrow \boldsymbol{y = 5}$

3. $(5x - 5y = -10) \times 2 \rightarrow 10x - 10y = -20$
   $(2x + 3y = 16) \times 5 \rightarrow \underline{-(10x + 15y = 80)}$
   $ -25y = -100 \rightarrow \boldsymbol{y = 4} \rightarrow 5x - 5 \cdot 4 = -10 \rightarrow \boldsymbol{x = 2}$

SIMULTANEOUS EQUATION SHORTCUTS:

14. $4x + y = 6$
   $\underline{-(2x + 3y = 2)}$
   $ 2x - 2y = 4 \rightarrow \dfrac{2x - 2y}{2} = \dfrac{4}{2} \rightarrow x - y = 2$ **(D)**

SIMULTANEOUS EQUATIONS HW:

5. $2x - y = 12$
   $\underline{+(3x + 6y = 33)}$
   $ 5x + 5y = 45 \rightarrow \dfrac{5x + 5y}{5} = \dfrac{45}{5} \rightarrow x + y = 9$ **(A)**

16. $x^2 + 2y^2 = 21$
   $\underline{+(-x^2 + y^2 = 6)}$
   $ 3y^2 = 27 \rightarrow y^2 = 9 \rightarrow y = \pm 3$ **(A)**

15. Remember, (E) is probably not the correct answer. Review "hard problems" in the Math Introduction.
   Stack equations with variables lined up:
   $a + b + c = -30$
   $\underline{-(a - 2b + c = 0)} \rightarrow$ **subtract** equations to eliminate a and c:
   $3b = -30 \rightarrow b = -10$ **(B)**
   Note: Substitution is probably the easiest way to tackle this problem. Replace a + c in the first equation with 2b and solve for b. If you don't see this trick, then using the simultaneous equation method above will get you out of the jam.
   You could also Pick Answers → Pick Numbers.

18. **Divide:** $\dfrac{m^3}{m^2} = \dfrac{20x}{10x} \rightarrow \boldsymbol{m = 2}$

20. Set the ratio of the x coefficients equal to the ratio of the y coefficients.

$\frac{k}{1} = \frac{2}{5}$ → Cross multiply to solve for k: $k = \frac{2}{5}$ **(D)**

20. The first step to this problem is to use RTD to find the equations.
Let's call x the time to work, y the time to home, and d the distance each way.

<u>R × T = D</u>   (Note: Distance is the same for both rows.)
10 x   d
<u>2   y   d</u>
         3

Using the information above, we can write three equations: $10 \cdot x = d$, $2 \cdot y = d$, and $x + y = 3$
Use substitution to combine (1) and (2): $10x = 2y$ → $10x - 2y = 0$
Finally solve for x using simultaneous equations:

$10x - 2y = 0$ → $10x - 2y = 0$
$x + y = 3$ → ×2 → <u>+(2x + 2y = 6)</u>
                    $12x \quad = 6$ → $x = .5$ → $d = 5$ → $2d = 10$ **(D)**

Note: The above approach displays the simultaneous equation technique, but the faster and easier approach is to pick answers.

5. DIRECT & INVERSE VARIATION

17. Inverse variation: $xy = 20 \cdot 2 = 40$ (so k = 40) → $-2 \cdot y = 40$ → $y = -20$ **(B)**

DIRECT & INVERSE VARIATION HW:

18. Direct variation:

$\frac{y}{x} = \frac{4}{1/2} = 8$ (so k = 8) → by definition, y/x always equals 8 **(B)**

You could always plug in 2×10^8, but this takes much longer:

$\frac{2 \times 10^8}{x} = 8$ → $x = 2.5 \times 10^7$ → $\frac{y}{x} = \frac{2 \times 10^8}{2.5 \times 10^7} = 8$ ✓

6. FACTORING

1. $20q(q - 2)$
2. $xy(2x + 3y)$
12. $x^2 - 4x = 0$ → $x(x - 4) = 0$ → $x = 0$ or $x = 4$ → $x - 4 = 0 - 4 = -4$ **(A)** Note: 4 − 4 = 0 is not an available answer choice.

FACTORING QUADRATICS:

1. $x^2 + 5x + 6 = 0$ → $(x + 2)(x + 3) = 0$ → x = **−2 or −3**
2. $x^2 - 12x + 20 = 0$ → $(x - 10)(x - 2) = 0$ → x = **10 or 2**
3. $x^2 + 4x - 21 = 0$ → $(x + 7)(x - 3) = 0$ → x = **−7 or 3**
4. $(x + 23)(x - 1) = 0$ → x = **−23 or 1**

FACTORING HW:

10. −k must equal the sum of the two numbers in the factored form (see step 3 in Factoring Quadratics): $-k = (-3) + (-2)$ → $k = 5$ **(C)**
Alternate solution:
Use FOIL to expand the right side of the equation: $(a - 3)(a - 2) = a^2 - 5a + 6$
Compare this to the left side of the original equation: $a^2 - ka + 6 = a^2 - 5a + 6$
Notice that the coefficients in front of the a^2 terms are equal (both 1) and the number terms are equal (both 6). Similarly, the coefficients in front of the a terms must also equal. So:
$-k = -5$ → $k = 5$
(continued)

This is a good general rule to keep in mind when you compare polynomials (multi-termed expressions).

If the techniques above are confusing, you could: (1) Pick Answers and factor the resulting quadratics until you find the one that equals the right side of the equation, or (2) Pick Numbers for a and solve for k.

11. $x^2(x + 1) = 0$ → $x = 0$ or -1 → $0 + (-1) = -1$ **(C)**

17. Pick Numbers (type 1: variables in the answer choices):

$\boxed{b = 2}$ → $4a^2 - 100 = 0$ → Difference of squares: $(2a - 10)(2a + 10) = 0$

→ $a = 5$ or -5 → $5 + (-5) = \underline{0}$ → **(C)** Remember, **check every answer choice**.

You could also solve $4a^2 - 100 = 0$ using exponential rules. Just don't forget that when you solve for a squared variable, you will get a positive and a negative answer: $4a^2 = 100$ → $a^2 = 25$ → $a = 5$ or -5 → $5 + (-5) = \underline{0}$ → **(C)**

7. QUADRATICS

19. Equation 2: $(a + b)^2 = a^2 + 2ab + b^2$ (remember: write the equation first)

$(5)^2 = a^2 + 5 + b^2$ → $25 = a^2 + b^2 + 5$ → $a^2 + b^2 = 25 - 5 = 20$ **(D)**

QUADRATICS HW:

1. $(x - y)^2 = (x - y)\cdot(x - y) = x\cdot x + x\cdot(-y) + (-y)\cdot x + (-y)\cdot(-y) = x^2 - xy - xy + y^2 = x^2 - 2xy + y^2$

16. Equation 1: $(x - y)(x + y) = x^2 - y^2$

$(5) \cdot (x + y) = (20)$ → $x + y = 20 \div 5 = \mathbf{4}$

17. Equation 3: $(a - b)^2 = a^2 - 2ab + b^2$

$(4)^2 \cdot = a^2 + b^2 - 2ab$

$(4)^2 \cdot = (26) -2ab$ → $-2ab = 16 - 26 = -10$ → $ab = \mathbf{5}$

8. SHORTCUTS

HW:

18. This shortcut is worth memorizing:

$\underbrace{-9 + -8 + -7 + ... + 7 + 8 + 9}_{= 0} + \underbrace{10 + 11 + 12}_{= 33}$

Since the first 19 numbers (−9 to 9) add up to 0, start adding at 10.

→ $10 + 11 + 12 = 33$, so $x = 12$ **(E)**

IV. GEOMETRY

2. AREA, PERIMETER, & CIRCUMFERENCE

1 & 2. The first triangle appears to be a right triangle, so the height is the length of a leg adjacent to the base, as shown below. On the second triangle, the base must be extended.

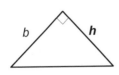
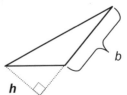

PERIMETER:

7. $(x) + (x + 2) + (x) + (x + 2) = 20$ → $4x + 4 = 20$ → $4x = 16$ → $x = 4$

→ Area = $(4)\cdot(4 + 2) = 4\cdot6 = 24$ **(B)**

You could pick numbers for x (guess and check), but this could take a while.

SHADED REGION PROBLEMS:

14. *Divide the shaded region within the square into a triangle and a rectangle (see figure). The triangle has a height of 5 and a base of 8* → *Area = 20*

The rectangle area = 8 × 3 = 24.

The area of one semicircle is $\frac{1}{2}\pi r^2 = \frac{1}{2}\pi(\frac{3}{2})^2 = \frac{9}{8}\pi$

The total area is: 20 + 24 + $\frac{9}{8}\pi$ + $\frac{9}{8}\pi$ = 44 + $\frac{9}{4}\pi$ **(C)**

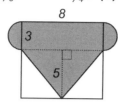

Shortcut: If you find the area of the two semicircles first and recognize that this area is the second part of each answer choice, you can eliminate (B), (D), and (E). The area of the square is 64, and the shaded part of the square is clearly more than half of the total area, so 24 is too small. The answer must be (C).

16. *AB = 8, EF = 8 + 2 + 2 = 12* → *area of EFGH = 12^2 = 144* → *area of ABCD = 8^2 = 64* → *144 − 64 = 80* **(D)** *Note: you could also "divide the shaded region."*

17. *length of square side = 8* → *diameter of semicircle = 4* → *radius of semicircle = 2*

→ *area = $\frac{\pi r^2}{2} = \frac{\pi 2^2}{2} = \frac{4\pi}{2} = 2\pi$* **(A)**

REVOLUTION PROBLEMS:

18. *circumference (in feet) = .5π* → $\frac{revolutions}{feet}$ $\frac{1}{.5\pi} = \frac{1000}{x}$ → *x = 500π* **(C)**

AREA, PERIMETER, & CIRCUMFERENCE HW:

6. *Perimeter of one shaded region = 2 + 2 + 6 + 6 = 16* → *16 + 16 = 32* **(D)**

10. *side of triangle = 12 ÷ 3 = 4* → *radius of one circle = $\frac{4}{2}$ = 2* → *circumference of one circle =* $2\pi r = 2·2·\pi = 4\pi$ → *(4π)·3 = 12π* **(C)**

12. $\frac{1}{2}bh = \frac{1}{2}6·6 = $ **18**

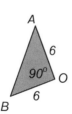

14. *Pick Answers:*
   Bare bones question: "what is the radius of the smaller circle?"
   Pick (C): r of small = 2 → *BC = CD = r of large = 4*
      → *Total area of three circles= 4π + 16π + 16π = 36π > 18π* ✗
      → *Eliminate (C), (D), and (E).*
   Pick (A) (easier than (B)): r of small = 1 → *r of large = 2*
      → *Total area = π + 4π + 4π = 9π < 18π* ✗
      → *Eliminate (A). The answer must be* **(B)**. *Check if there is time.*

15. $a = \pi r^2$ and $b = 2\pi r$

Since $a = b$, $\pi r^2 = 2\pi r$ → divide both sides by πr: $\dfrac{\cancel{\pi} r^{\cancel{2}}}{\cancel{\pi r}} = \dfrac{2\cancel{\pi r}}{\cancel{\pi r}}$ → $r = 2$ **(B)**

You could also pick answers.

16. 30-inch wheel: $\dfrac{\text{revolutions}}{\text{inches}} \dfrac{1}{30\pi} = \dfrac{x}{300 \cdot 12}$ → $x \approx 38.2$ → 38 full revolutions

20-inch wheel: $\dfrac{\text{revolutions}}{\text{inches}} \dfrac{1}{20\pi} = \dfrac{x}{300 \cdot 12}$ → $x \approx 57.3$ → 57 full revolutions

→ $57 - 38 = 19$ revolutions **(A)**

19. There are three ways that you could solve this problem:
   (1) First, find the diameter of the circle:

   Area of semicircle $= \dfrac{1}{2}\pi r^2 = 84.5\pi$ → solve for r: $r^2 = 169$ → $r = 13$ → diameter $= 26$.

   Now look at segment AB. Since the drawing is drawn to scale, the length of AB appears to be a little less than the diameter of the circle. If you look at the answer choices, (D) and (E) can be eliminated because they are not less than 26 (the diameter). The answer is clearly **(C)**.
   (2) If you have trouble finding the radius (and diameter) of the circle, you could measure the drawing, as described in the Geometry Introduction. Use the drawing to mark a distance of 5 on a piece of paper and use this as a ruler to estimate the distance of AB.
   (3) You will learn about the Pythagorean Theorem in the triangle section. Once you find the radius of the circle, create a right triangle and use the Pythagorean Theorem to find half the distance of AB (see the drawing below): $5^2 + b^2 = 13^2$ → $b = 12$ → $2 \cdot 12 = 24$ **(C)**.

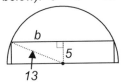

3. TRIANGLES

1. $\dfrac{DE}{AE} = \dfrac{BC}{AC}$

TRIANGLE LESSON PROBLEMS:
1. **hypotenuse = 13**
2. **short leg $= \sqrt{28} = 2\sqrt{7} \approx 5.29...$**
3. **hypotenuse = 6, long leg $= 3\sqrt{3} \approx 5.20...$**
4. **leg = 2, hypotenuse $= 2\sqrt{2} \approx 2.83...$**
5. **legs = 4**
6. **short leg = 4, long leg $= 4\sqrt{3} \approx 6.93...$**
7. **legs $= \dfrac{6}{\sqrt{2}} = 3\sqrt{2} \approx 4.24...$**
8. **short leg $= \dfrac{7}{\sqrt{3}} = \dfrac{7}{3}\sqrt{3} \approx 4.04...$, hypotenuse $= 2 \times \dfrac{7}{\sqrt{3}} = \dfrac{14}{\sqrt{3}} = \dfrac{14}{3}\sqrt{3} \approx 8.08...$**

---

5. The two legs of a right triangle can be used as the base and height since they are perpendicular to each other.
   $\frac{1}{2} \cdot 12 \cdot b = 54$ → $b = 9$ → $9^2 + 12^2 = c^2$ → $c = 15$ **(C)**

12. $x \cdot x = x^2 = 50$ → $x = \sqrt{50} = 5\sqrt{2}$ (or use calc.) → $x^2 + x^2 = c^2$ → $50 + 50 = 100 = c^2$
→ $c = 10$ **(C)**

   You might also notice that the triangle is a 45-45-90, so $c = x \cdot \sqrt{2} = 5\sqrt{2}\sqrt{2} = 5 \cdot 2 = 10$ **(C)**

14. The length of each side of the triangle is 2. Notice the 30-60-90 triangle (see figure). The sides of the rectangle are: $\sqrt{3}$ and 2. → Area of rectangle = $\sqrt{3} \cdot 2 = 2\sqrt{3}$ **(C)**

   As always, if you are uncomfortable with radicals, use a calculator to convert radicals into decimals (answer choices too).

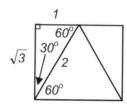

TRIANGLES HW:

7. The triangle is equilateral, so $-8x - y = 8$ and $4x + 2y = 8$. Since we are solving for x, let's eliminate y using simultaneous equations. First, multiply the first equation by 2:
   $2 \times (-8x - y = 8) = -16x - 2y = 16$
   $-16x - 2y = 16$
   $+ (4x + 2y = 8)$
   $\overline{-12x\quad = 24}$ → $x = -2$ **(A)** Note: you could also pick answers.

14. $4^2 + CE^2 = 10^2$ → $CE = \sqrt{84}$

   $\triangle ABC$ is similar to $\triangle CDE$

   $\dfrac{AB}{AC} = \dfrac{DE}{CE}$ → $\dfrac{2}{AC} = \dfrac{4}{\sqrt{84}}$ → $AC = \dfrac{\sqrt{84}}{2}$ → $AC + CE = \dfrac{\sqrt{84}}{2} + \sqrt{84} \approx 13.75$ → check

   answer choices with calc. **(D)**

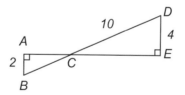

15. $3^2 + 4^2 = x^2$ → $x = 5$ → $12 + 5 + 5 + 8 + 8 = \mathbf{38}$

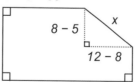

15. Since AB > AC, $c > b$ → Pick Numbers: $c = 61$ → $b = 59$ **(E)**
    Note: since $c > a > b$ → AB > BC > AC

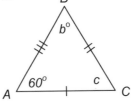

16. $c + 4$ must be > 5 → *Pick Number (guess and check) if necessary:*
    $c = 1$ ✗
    $c = 2$ ✓

19. This is a potentially difficult problem and a great test of the special right triangles.
    Draw a perpendicular line from B to segment AC. This creates a 45-45-90 triangle and a 30-60-90 triangle. See the figure. The answer is **(E)**. If you are not comfortable with radicals, work with decimals.
    Note: △ABC is *not* a 30-60-90 triangle.

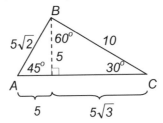

4. ANGLES

LINE: $x + y = $ **180**
TRIANGLE: $x + y + z = $ **180**
CIRCLE: $x + y + z + w = $ **360**
RIGHT ANGLE: $x = $ **90**
VERTICAL ANGLES: $z = $ **50**, $y = $ **130**, $w = $ **130**
PARALLEL LINES: $x = $ **30**, $y = $ **150**
LINE TANGENT TO A CIRCLE: $x = $ **90**

SUM OF INTERIOR ANGLES:
QUADRILATERAL: $x + y + z + w = 2 \cdot 180 = $ **360**

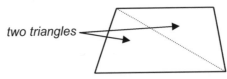

two triangles

OTHER POLYGONS:
1. $6 \cdot 180 = $ **1080°**
2. There are 8 congruent angles → $1080 \div 8 = $ **135**

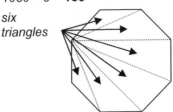

six
triangles

ANGLES LESSON PROBLEMS:

3. $(x + 5) + 90 + (x − 5) = 180$ → $2x + 90 = 180$ → $2x = 90$ → $x = 45$ **(C)**
    Note: you could also pick answers.

10. *Use vertical angles to show that the angles above make up the angles of two triangles.*
    → $2 \cdot 180 = 360$ **(C)**
    You could also pick numbers (type 2) for a, b, and c (or any three angles)—then solve for the other two.

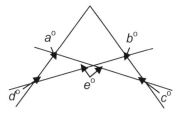

10. *Use the figure to pick numbers (type 1); write the numbers directly on the figure so they are easy to keep track of.* $\boxed{a = d = e = h = 40}$ → $b = c = f = g = 140$ → $a + g = \underline{180}$ → **(C)**
    *Remember, **check every answer choice**.*

16. *Pick Numbers (type 1):*

    $\boxed{x = 30}$ → *The fastest approach is to look at the large triangle (ΔPQR)—look at angles P, Q,*

    and R. Notice that $y + (x + 45) + x = 180$ → $y + (30 + 45) + 30 = 180$

    → $y + 75 + 30 = 180$ → $y = \underline{75}$ → **(D)**

    To find y (after picking a number for x), you could also start at angle Q (x + 45°) and solve for all angles as you work your way around the triangle clockwise.

ANGLES HW:

4. $3x + x = 90$ → $x = 22½$ **(A)** *Note: you could also pick answers.*
9. $5x = 180$ (straight line) → $x = 36$ → $y = 2x$ (vertical angles) → $y = 2 \cdot 36 = 72$ **(D)** *Note: you could also pick answers.*
15. *Since AB is tangent to the circle, it is perpendicular to the radius drawn from the point of tangent to the center of the circle. The area* = $½ \cdot 12 \cdot 4 = 24$ **(C)**

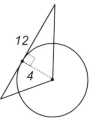

17. *Since there are five "central angles" (∠AOB is one of them), you can divide 360° by five:*
    $360° ÷ 5 = 72°$ **(C)** *Another approach: sum of interior ∠s* = $3 \cdot 180° = 540°$ → *Each interior* ∠ = $108°$ → ∠BAO = ∠ABO = $108° ÷ 2 = 54°$ → ∠AOB = $180° − 54° \cdot 2 = 180° − 108° = 72°$ *(see drawing)*

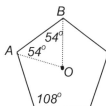

18. *Pick Numbers (type 1):*

$\boxed{x = 40}$ → $y = \underline{80}$ → **(C)** *Remember,* ***check every answer choice****.*

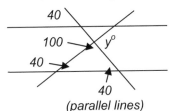

(parallel lines)

5. SECTORS OF CIRCLES

10.
$$\frac{\overbrace{120}^{degrees}}{360} = \frac{\overbrace{5}^{arc\ length}}{circumference} \to c = 15 \ \textbf{(B)}$$

SECTORS OF CIRCLES HW:

12.
$$\frac{\overbrace{36}^{degrees}}{360} = \frac{\overbrace{area\ of\ AOB}^{area}}{\pi 10^2} \to area\ of\ AOB = 10\pi \ \textbf{(D)}$$

6. COORDINATES

1. $A = (1,5)$
2. $B = (-3,2)$
3. $C = (0,0)$
4. $D = (5,1)$
5. $E = (3,-2)$

5. $OA = 6$ → $AB = 6$ → $OB = OC = 12$ → *The coordinates of point C are* $(-12,0)$ **(B)**

14. *The base of the triangle is:* $\left|-7-(-2)\right| = \left|-5\right| = 5$

The height of the triangle is: $\left|8-(-2)\right| = \left|10\right| = 10$

$\frac{1}{2}bh = \frac{1}{2} \cdot 5 \cdot 10 = 25$ **(C)**

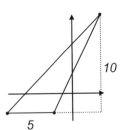

7. LINES

LINE SEGMENTS:

5. *Only* **(D)** *is NOT true when the answer choices are checked:* $CB = 4$, $AC = 4$, → $CB \not< AC$

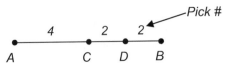

NUMBER LINES:

6. *Point A is at* $-\frac{7}{5}$*, Point B is at* $-\frac{1}{5}$*.* → $\left|-\frac{7}{5} - \left(-\frac{1}{5}\right)\right| = \frac{6}{5}$ **(D)**

You could also calculate the "unit distance" (the distance between tick marks) and multiply this by the number of units between A and B: $\frac{1}{5} \times 6 = \frac{6}{5}$

SLOPE OF A LINE:

10. $m = \dfrac{14 - 0}{0 - 6} = -\dfrac{7}{3}$ → $\dfrac{b - 0}{4 - 6} = -\dfrac{7}{3}$ → $b = -\dfrac{7}{3} \cdot -2 = \dfrac{14}{3} = 4\dfrac{2}{3}$ **(E)**

WHERE'S THE *x*? WHERE'S THE *y*?

1. Line B: **y = 3**
2. Line C: **y = –2**
3. Line D: **x = 0**
4. Line E: **x = 3**

GENERAL LINE PROBLEMS:

14. Notice that R lies on both lines. Remember, a line extends infinitely in both directions. **(D)**

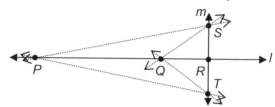

19. It may be helpful to draw a triangle to see the distances; the triangle does not have to be drawn to scale. The correct answer is **(E)**, since the sum of the two shortest sides is < the longest side.

   (A) 2 → 2 + 2 ≥ 4 ✓
   (B) 4 → 2 + 4 ≥ 4 ✓
   (C) 5 → 2 + 4 ≥ 5 ✓
   (D) 6 → 2 + 4 ≥ 6 ✓
   (E) 7 → 2 + 4 < 7 ✗

Plug in Picked Answers here

LINES HW:

10. Note: m is **not** the slope in this problem. Plug 2 in for x and m in for y: $m - 3 = 2(2 - 4)$
   → **m = –1**

11. $|-5 - 3| = 8$ → $\frac{3}{4} \cdot 8 = 6$ → $-5 + 6 = 1$ **(C)**

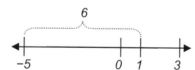

12. Pick Numbers (type 1):
   $\boxed{y = 4}$ → $x + 3 = 4 - 1$ → $x = \underline{0}$ → **(A)** Remember, **check every answer choice**.
   You could also solve algebraically by solving for x in the equation: $x + 3 = y - 1$.

13. $m = \dfrac{9 - 0}{3 - 0} = 3$ (The line goes through the origin (0,0).)

   Pick Number (type 2) for a: $a = -1$ → $\dfrac{b - 0}{-1 - 0} = 3$ → $b = -3$ → $\dfrac{b}{a} = 3$ **(E)**

18. $y = \frac{3}{2}x + b$ → $6 = \frac{3}{2} \cdot 6 + b$ → $b = -3$ **(D)**

19. $m_b = \dfrac{-2 - 1}{4 - 0} = -\dfrac{3}{4}$ → $m_a = -\dfrac{1}{-\frac{3}{4}} = \dfrac{4}{3}$

   Line a: $y = \frac{4}{3}x + b$ → (plug in the known point) $-2 = \frac{4}{3} \cdot 4 + b$ → $b = \frac{-22}{3}$
   → $y = \frac{4}{3}x - \frac{22}{3}$ **(E)**

20. *Create a triangle, as shown. Then pick a number (type 2) for b:*

$b = 2$ → *You now have 2 sides.* → *Use Pythagorean's Theorem:* $2^2 + a^2 = (2 \cdot 2)^2$

$$→ \quad a = \sqrt{12} \quad → \quad m = \frac{2}{\sqrt{12}} ≈ .577...$$

Use your calculator to check the answer choices. The answer is (B).

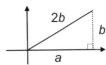

If interested, here is the simplification of the radical: $m = \dfrac{2}{\sqrt{12}} = \dfrac{2}{2\sqrt{3}} = \dfrac{1}{\sqrt{3}} \cdot \dfrac{\sqrt{3}}{\sqrt{3}} = \dfrac{\sqrt{3}}{3}$

Alternate solution: You might notice that the hypotenuse is twice the short leg—this is a 30-60-90 triangle: $a = \sqrt{3} \cdot b$ → *slope* $= \sqrt{3}/3$

8. SOLIDS
RECTANGULAR SOLIDS:
1. **L·W·H**
2. **L·H**
3. **back**
4. **L·W**
5. **bottom**
6. **W·H**
7. **left-side**
8. $L \cdot H \times 2 + L \cdot W \times 2 + W \cdot H \times 2 =$ **2·L·H + 2·L·W + 2·W·H**

1. **8**
2. **12**
3. **6**
4. **52**
5. **24**

CUBES:
1. $s \cdot s = \mathbf{s^2}$
2. $\mathbf{6 \cdot s^2}$
3. $\mathbf{s^3}$

SURFACE AREA → VOLUME:
1. $600 ÷ 6 = \mathbf{100}$
2. $\sqrt{100} = \mathbf{10}$
3. $10^3 = \mathbf{1000}$

VOLUME FITTING AND AREA FITTING PROBLEMS:
16. *Volume of jug* $= \pi r^2 h = \pi \cdot 10^2 \cdot 12 = 1200\pi \ in^2$; *Volume of cup* $= \pi \cdot 2^2 \cdot 6 = 24\pi \ in^2$

$$\frac{1200\pi}{24\pi} = \mathbf{50} \ cups \ of \ water$$

SOLIDS HW:
5. *Each small box: 10 × 8 × 6 = 480 cubic inches*
   Large box: 20 × 10 × 8 = 1600 cubic inches
   → *1600 – (2 × 480) = 1600 – 960 = 640 cubic inches (B)*

7. Volume of tank = 4·8·10 = 320
    320 × 20% = 64
    320 × 30% = 96
    → 64 + x = 96 → x = 96 − 64 = 32 **(A)**
    You could also simply find 10% of the volume since this is the percent of the volume that you're adding: 320 × 10% = 32

19. Soap cubes: Area of face = $\dfrac{54}{6}$ = 9 → Length of side = $\sqrt{9}$ = 3 → Volume = 3^3 = 27

    $\dfrac{\text{volume of box}}{\text{volume of soap cube}} = \dfrac{729}{27} = 27$ **(B)**

20. The diagonal, d, of the cube will equal the diameter of the sphere.

    $d = \sqrt{a^2 + b^2 + c^2} = \sqrt{4 + 4 + 4} = \sqrt{12} = 2\sqrt{3}$ **(C)**

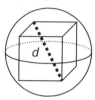

9. TABLES AND GRAPHS

11. The greatest change occurs between 1996 and 1997 (−$3 million). **(B)**

18. Note: this is a "difficult" problem (18 out of 18). The Cleaning Time is "per street."

    7·20 + 8·40 + 10·80 + 15·100 = 2760 minutes → $\dfrac{2760}{60}$ = **46 hours**

TABLES AND GRAPHS HW:

6. $\dfrac{\text{part}}{\text{whole}} \dfrac{15,000}{\text{whole}}$ = .30 → whole = 50,000 (total income) **(C)**

    *Or, you could use the Of/Is technique: 15,000 is 30% of what? → 15,000 = .30·x
    → x = 50,000 (total income)*

9. It is important to recognize that the faster Chris walks (or runs), the steeper the graph (more distance is covered in less time). If Chris stops, the graph is a horizontal line (time continues but the distance remains the same). The correct answer is **(A)**.

15. Familiarize yourself with these types of tables. **Any time two entries in a row or column are known, you can find the missing item.**
    First, notice that the total number of compact cars sold is a + b.
    Since the total number of all cars is d, the total number of family cars can be found:
    Family + Compact = Total → Family + (a + b) = d → Family = d − (a + b) = d − a − b
    Now, you can find the number of family, all electric cars:
    Family, all-electric + c = d − a − b → Family, all-electric = d − a − b − c **(E)**
    Note: The answer choices are tricky; you might want to pick numbers (type 1) at the beginning of the problem to avoid any algebraic mistakes.

V. FUNCTIONS
1. SYMBOL PROBLEMS

13. $\left(\dfrac{6·4}{6−4}\right) − \left(\dfrac{8·6}{8−6}\right) = \dfrac{24}{2} − \dfrac{48}{2} = 12 − 24 = −12$ **(B)**

14. As we learned earlier, this should be a difficult question because it is the last of a multi-question problem.

Pick Numbers: $\boxed{p = 3, q = 2}$

I: $6 \neq -6$ ✗ (Eliminate (A), (C), and (E).)

Since II is in both remaining answer choices, it must be true! So we only need to check III:

$(-p) \diamond (-q) = (-3) \diamond (-2) = -6$, $-(p \diamond q) = -(3 \diamond 2) = -6$, ✓

→ Both II. and III. are true. **(D)**

Note: a full-proof (but more difficult) method would be to simplify the expressions of each Roman numeral and solve algebraically.

12. $\blacklozenge 25 = 2 + 5 = 7$, $\blacklozenge 50 = 5 + 0 = 5$ → $\blacklozenge 25 + \blacklozenge 50 = 7 + 5 = 12$ **(D)** Note: $\blacklozenge 66 = 12$

14. Points A and D are "independent," and points B and E are "independent." → Two pairs **(C)**

SYMBOL PROBLEMS HW:

6. $(-3) \heartsuit = \dfrac{-3-1}{-3+1} = \dfrac{-4}{-2} = 2$ **(E)**

16. Pick Numbers (type 1):

$\boxed{a = 3}$ → $(3 - 2)\uparrow = (1)\uparrow = \frac{1}{2}$, $(1 - 3)\uparrow = (-2)\uparrow = \frac{-2}{-1} = 2$ → $\frac{1}{2} \times 2 = \underline{1}$ → Eliminate (B), (C), and (E). Since both (A) and (D) work, pick a new number:

$\boxed{a = 4}$ → $(4 - 2)\uparrow = (2)\uparrow = \frac{2}{3}$, $(1 - 4)\uparrow = (-3)\uparrow = \frac{-3}{-2} = \frac{3}{2}$ → $\frac{2}{3} \times \frac{3}{2} = \underline{1}$ → Eliminate (D).

Only **(A)** works.

17. $x = 2^p$, $y = 2^q$

Pick Numbers (type 2): $p = 3$ → $q = 5 - 3 = 2$ (or use knowledge of exponents)

$xy = 2^3 \cdot 2^2 = 8 \cdot 4 = 32$ **(D)**

19. As discussed in the Basic Concepts chapter, rewrite the fraction as long division and guess 1 as the quotient:

$$\frac{15}{y} \rightarrow y)\overline{\underset{\underline{-y}}{\overset{1}{15}}} \rightarrow 15 - y = 5 \rightarrow y = 10$$

5 ← remainder

2. FUNCTION BASICS

16. $f(6) = 36$, $f(-6) = 36$ → $36 - 36 = 0$ **(B)**

17. Pick Numbers (type 1):

$\boxed{m = 2}$ → $g(2 + 1) = g(3) = \underline{6}$ → Eliminate (A), (B), (D), and (E). The answer is **(C)**. You could also use algebra to solve this problem. Simplify $g(m + 1)$ and check the answer choices.

FUNCTION BASICS HW:

14. Pick Answers: Note the bare bones question: "what is one possible value of **x − 6**?"

Start at (C). Remember to stop when you find the correct answer.

(A)

(B) $x - 6 = -7 \rightarrow x = -1 \rightarrow f(-1) = 5$ ✓

~~(C)~~ $x - 6 = -6 \rightarrow x = 0 \rightarrow f(0) \neq 5$ ✗

~~(D)~~ $x - 6 = 0 \rightarrow x = 6 \rightarrow f(6) \neq 5$ ✗

~~(E)~~ $x - 6 = 6 \rightarrow x = 12 \rightarrow f(12) \neq 5$ ✗

If you are comfortable solving equations with absolute values, the algebraic approach is faster:

$\left| x^2 - 6 \right| = 5$ → $x^2 - 6 = 5$ or -5 → $x^2 = 11$ or 1 → $x = \pm\sqrt{11}$ or $x = \pm 1$

→ When $x = -1$, $x - 6 = -7$ **(B)**

19. $g(\sqrt{a}) = 8$ → $\sqrt{a} + 4 = 8$ → $\sqrt{a} = 4$ → $a = 16$ **(C)**

20. $g(3) = 0 = a$ → $h(a) = h(0) = 4$ **(E)**

3. GRAPHS OF FUNCTIONS

16. Plug x = 0 into the equation to find the y-intercept: $f(0) = a \cdot 0 + b \cdot 0 + c = c$ **(E)**

HW:

15. **(D)**

16. We do not know the length of $\overline{AC}$, but we can find the y-coordinate of point A since it lies on the graph of the function. We know the x-coordinate is 4. Plug x = 4 into the function equation:
$f(4) = \sqrt{4} + 2 = 4 \rightarrow \overline{AC} = 4 \rightarrow Area = base \times height = 5 \times 4 = 20$ **(D)**

18. Since ABCD is a square, you can find point C (or B):
$C = (2,4) \rightarrow$ Plug point C into the function equation: $4 = a \cdot 2^4 \rightarrow 4 = a \cdot 16 \rightarrow a = \frac{1}{4}$
Note that function problems such as this one often have high numbers, but they are not necessarily difficult to solve.

19. Since we are dealing with absolute value, all positive values of f(x) remain positive and all negative values become positive (reflect across the x-axis). The answer is **(D)**.

4. DOMAIN AND RANGE

20. Rule 3: $x + 4 > 0 \rightarrow x > -4$ **(E)**

DOMAIN AND RANGE HW:

20. $x + 2 \geq 0 \rightarrow x \geq -2$ **(B)**

5. TRANSFORMATIONS

17. Reflect the graph across the x-axis and move it one unit to the right. **(A)**

TRANSFORMATIONS HW:

14. Since you are reflecting across the y-axis, change the x in the equation to −x:
$y = -3(-x) - 4 \rightarrow y = 3x - 4$ **(C)**

20. The graphs moves 3 units to the right, so h = −3. The graph moves 3 units down, so k = −3.
$h - k = -3 - (-3) = -3 + 3 = 0$ **(C)**

6. FUNCTIONS AS MODELS

16. $M(10) = 1000\left(\frac{51}{50}\right)^{10} \approx 1219$ **(C)**

FUNCTIONS AS MODELS HW:

17. $10{,}000 = 100\sqrt{x} \rightarrow 100 = \sqrt{x} \rightarrow x = 100^2 = 1 \times 10^4$ **(C)**

VI. PROBABILITY
1. PROBABILITY
HW:

6. Use the equation for probability: $\frac{2}{3} = \frac{red}{30} \rightarrow red = 20 \rightarrow 30 - 20 = 10$ **(B)**

17. This problem is much easier if you pick a number for the total number of eating utensils, preferably one divisible by 2 and 6: Total utensils = 60

$\rightarrow \frac{1}{2} = \frac{spoons}{60} \rightarrow$ spoons = 30

$\rightarrow \frac{1}{6} = \frac{knives}{60} \rightarrow$ knives = 10

So there must be 20 forks (60 − 30 − 10). Remove the forks. There are 10 knives and 40 total remaining utensils: $\frac{knives}{total} = \frac{10}{40} = \frac{1}{4}$ **(B)**

18. *There is no trick to this problem. Just write down the possible three-person groups and count the ones that have both Matt and Ben. It may be helpful to first write down all the groups that include **one** selected member, such as Matt:*

   (1) **Matt Ben** Kim, (2) **Matt Ben** Jasmine, (3) **Matt** Kim Jasmine

   The only team that can be made without Matt is: (4) Ben Kim Jasmine.

   → *So there are **4** total possible teams. Of these, **2** have both Matt and Ben:*

   → *Probability* $= \dfrac{2}{4} = \dfrac{1}{2}$ **(C)**

19. *Pick Number (type 3):*

   Pick: Radius of small circle = 2 → *Radius of medium circle = 3·2 = 6* → *Radius of large circle = 5·2 = 10*

   Shaded area $= \pi(10)^2 - \pi(6)^2 + \pi(2)^2 = 68\pi$

   Total area $= \pi(10)^2 = 100\pi$

   → *Probability* $= \dfrac{68\pi}{100\pi} = \dfrac{17}{25}$ **(D)**

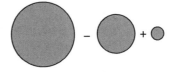

20. $P_1 = \frac{7}{21} = \frac{1}{3}$

   → *(6 blue marbles left; 20 total marbles left)* → $P_2 = \frac{6}{20} = \frac{3}{10}$

   → *(5 blue marbles left; 19 total marbles left)* → $P_3 = \frac{5}{19}$

   Probability $= \frac{1}{3} \times \frac{3}{10} \times \frac{5}{19} = \frac{1}{38}$ **(D)**

   *Notice that the events in this problem are **dependent**. The probability of event 2 is dependent on the outcome of event 1, and similarly the probability of event 3 is dependent on the outcomes of the previous events.*

2. COUNTING, PERMUTATIONS, AND COMBINATIONS

PERMUTATIONS:

15. $\underline{6} \cdot \underline{5} \cdot \underline{4} \cdot \underline{3} \cdot \underline{2} \cdot \underline{1} = 720$ **(C)**

COMBINATIONS:

19. $\underline{8} \cdot \underline{7} \cdot \underline{6} = 336$ → $\dfrac{336}{3!} = \dfrac{336}{6} = 56$ **(C)**

COUNTING, PERMUTATIONS, AND COMBINATIONS HW:

10. $\underline{6} \cdot \underline{6} = 36$ **(E)**

13. *Let the first position be for the father:*

   $\underline{1} \cdot \underline{4} \cdot \underline{3} \cdot \underline{2} \cdot \underline{1} = 24$ **(D)**

   ↖ father

20. *Since this is a probability problem, first find the total possible outcomes:*

   Think of each underline (position) as a country (Mexico1, Mexico2, Canada, and England). Once a reporter has been assigned a position, he or she is no longer available for other positions: $\underline{4} \cdot \underline{3} \cdot \underline{2} \cdot \underline{1} = 24$ *total possible outcomes.*

   Now find the number of desired outcomes. There are two reporters for the first position (Amy and Ryan), one for the second (Amy or Ryan - whomever wasn't selected for the first position), two remaining for the third position, and one for the last position:

   $\underline{2} \cdot \underline{1} \cdot \underline{2} \cdot \underline{1} = 4$ → *Probability* $= \dfrac{4}{24} = \dfrac{1}{6}$ **(C)**

   Mexico1 Mexico2 Canada England

20. Both groups are combinations (since order doesn't matter):

Juniors: $\underline{4\cdot3} = 12$ → $\dfrac{12}{2!} = 6$, Seniors: $\underline{5\cdot4\cdot3} = 60$ → $\dfrac{60}{3!} = 10$

→ Principle of Counting: $6 \times 10 = 60$ **(C)**

3. SETS AND GROUPS

SETS:

7. set M = {2, **3, 5, 7**}, set N = {...1, **3, 5, 7**, 9} → Three numbers are in both sets {3, 5, 7}. **(C)**

GROUPS:

18. Since all of the students take Spanish, Latin, or both, "Neither" = 0.
    Use the formula to find "Both:"
    90 = 75 + 25 − Both → Both = 10
    10 students take both Spanish and Latin. Thus, 90 − 10 = **80** students take only one of the classes.

SETS AND GROUPS HW:

12. The number of elements common to sets X and Y is the same as the intersection of X and Y, which includes the region with 3 elements and the region with a elements:
    3 + a = 20 → a = 17 **(D)**
13. Total = Group 1 + Group 2 + Neither − Both → 20 = 10 + 16 − Both (Neither = 0)
    → 20 − 26 = −Both → Both = 6 **(A)**
19. This is a tricky problem. First, use the equation for groups. Then pick answers.
    Total = Group 1 + Group 2 + Neither − Both
       120 = 90 + 40 + N − B → −10 = N − B
    Now, pick answers. It makes sense to start with (A) since we're looking for the least possible value of B:
    (A): B = 0 → N = −10 ✗ (N must be ≥ 0 since it represents a number of students)
    (B): B = 10 → N = 0 ✓ So, at least 10 students speak Spanish <u>and</u> French.